To Bobby-D,
Christmas '00
Here's to tradition!
A book for every
Occasion. Hope this
is of some use and
entertainment value.
With Love,
Kate

Brave Films Wild Nights

Brave Films Wild Nights

25 YEARS *of* FESTIVAL FEVER

BRIAN
D. JOHNSON

Random House Canada

On the front lawn a sheet
tacked across a horizontal branch.
A projector starts a parade…

from "Claude Glass"
by Michael Ondaatje

 Published in 2000 by Random House Canada, a division of Random House of Canada Limited.

Random House Canada and colophon are trademarks.

Special thanks to the generous sponsors of the Toronto International Film Festival's 25th Anniversary activities: AGF Funds Inc., Bloomberg News, Minacs Worldwide Inc., Sun Life Financial Services of Canada Inc. and Telefilm Canada. The festival's 25th Anniversary events have been financially assisted by the Ontario Cultural Attractions Fund of the Government of Ontario through the Ministry of Citizenship, Culture and Recreation.

Canadian Cataloguing in Publication Data

Johnson, Brian D., 1949–

Brave films, wild nights : 25 years of festival fever

ISBN 0-679-31035-5

1. Toronto International Film Festival — History. I. Title.

PN19934.4.J63 2000 791.43′079′713541 C99-933056-X

Pages 328-329 constitute an extension of this copyright page.

Cover and interior design by Jenny Armour

Photo-editing: Jenny Armour

Printed and bound in Canada

10 9 8 7 6 5 4 3 2 1

Contents

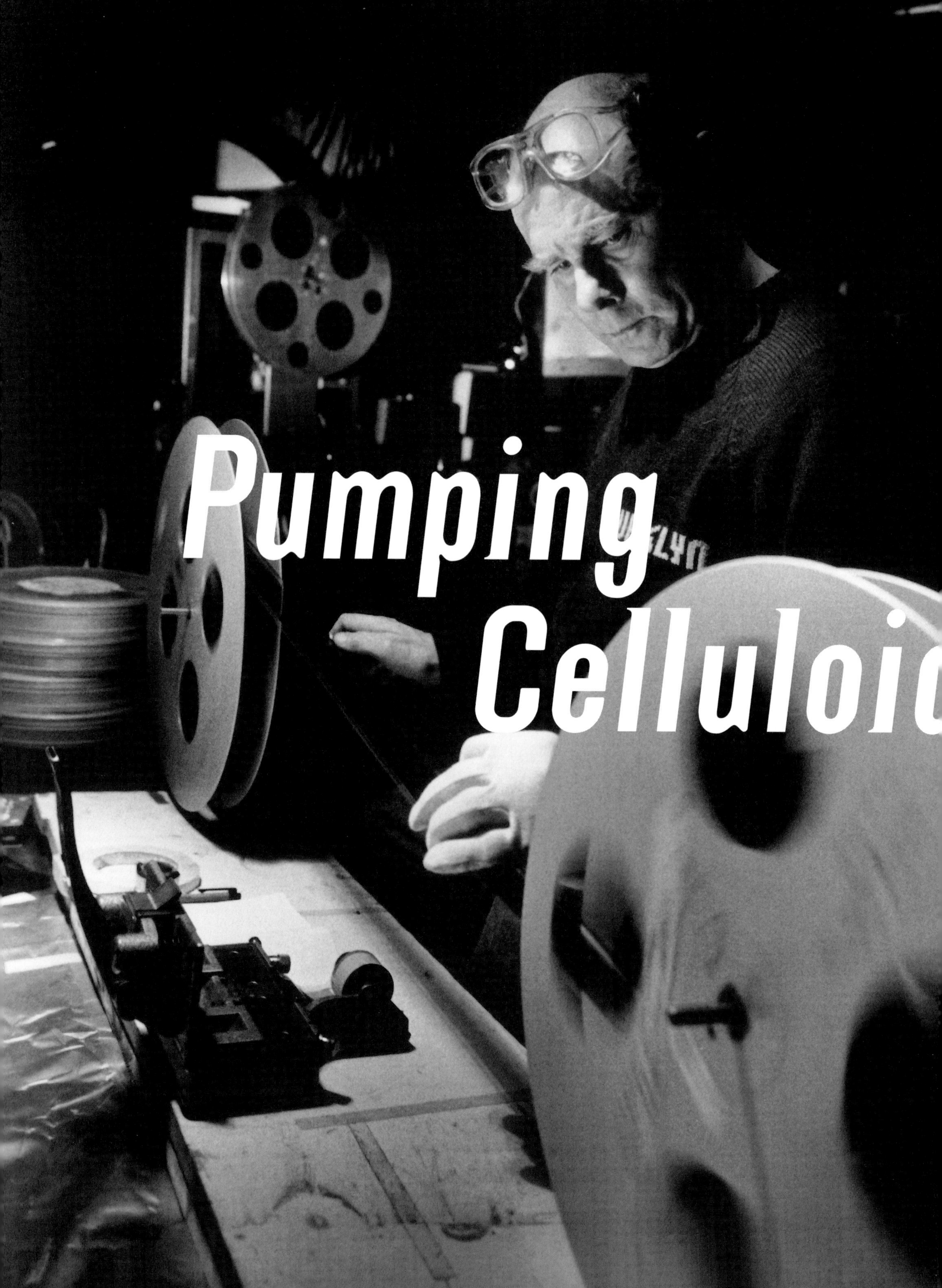

Pumping Celluloi

An Introduction

EFORE I MADE MY LIVING WRITING ABOUT MOVIES, DROVE THEM. FOR THREE YEARS IN THE EARLY '80s I WORKED

a film driver at what was then known as the Festival of Festivals. It as my job to deliver all the movies to all the theatres. Twice a day for n days, I filled a truck with cans of celluloid. It was the best job I've er had.

FESTIVAL VETERAN MARTIN HEATH

PHOTO: PETER BREGG/MACLEAN'S

The work was menial, but I was treated like a god. The whole show was sitting in the back of my van, and whenever I delivered a film, the theatre manager would act as if I'd performed a miracle just by showing up on time and not losing the print en route. I'd pull the van up in front of the theatre with the hazard lights flashing and sling film cans past the queued-up crowds. The cans were heavy but nicely balanced, like free weights. Working the festival was like spending a week at the gym, pumping celluloid. I remember hauling the three-hour director's cut of *The Leopard* up a fire escape to the

projection booth at the old New Yorker on Yonge Street. In some cinemas, to get to the booth you had to walk up the aisle through the house, usually while a film was playing. Driving from movie to movie, I spliced myself in and out of the festival, catching frames at random—a television screen turning to taffy in *Videodrome*, a man's eye impaled by a steel rod in *The Fourth Man*. The days blurred into a montage of arbitrary jump cuts, and each day dissolved into a party.

In retrospect, what I experienced was a fast-forward version of what the festival is to anyone immersed in it. The festival takes place in dreamtime. It becomes its own universe, a centrifuge of filmgoers on urgent missions of discovery. It's a shared experience, but strangely private. No one's festival is the same. You bombard yourself with images morning to night until the movies swim together. Running on no sleep, you occasionally find yourself dropping off in the dark, surfing a REM state between subtitles. And as you navigate the programming maze, it's like gambling, or pinball. There are slumps and streaks.

Before becoming a film critic, I was also a film-critic driver. One afternoon I picked up Roger Ebert and Gene Siskel to deliver them to a rehearsal for one of the festival tributes they hosted. At the time, I had no idea who these two guys were, but they seemed pretty ticked off with each other. Much later, I got to know Ebert, and over lunch in Cannes, a year after Siskel's death, he told me that he eventually made a deal with his partner—that before any public appearance they would make a point of never talking to each other. When I was driving Siskel and Ebert in my van, I had no idea I would become a critic myself. At the time I was a freelance writer working the festival as a lark. But then there were a lot of people at the festival in those early years who ended up in unlikely places.

In the late '70s, future director Peter Mettler worked as a festival limo driver, chauffeuring Jeanne Moreau and Peter O'Toole. As a reviewer for a student newspaper in 1981, Atom Egoyan was thrilled just to get press accreditation. Since then he has brought eight features to the festival, more than any other Canadian filmmaker. In 1989, an aspiring screenwriter and actor named Don McKellar worked as a stressed-out theatre manager, ushering Richard Gere and Matt Dillon to the stage at festival premieres. A decade later, he co-wrote and starred in the opening-night gala *The Red Violin*, and kicked off Perspective Canada with his directorial debut, *Last Night*.

When Bill Marshall and crew created the festival to strengthen the profile of the Canadian film industry, the notion that the staff would take over the industry was probably not what he had in mind. But to some extent, that's what happened. As festival employees, Seaton McLean and Michael MacMillan scrambled to control an angry mob at the oversold premiere of Robert Lantos's *In Praise of Older Women* in 1978. Now, after buying out Lantos, they are running Alliance Atlantis, the largest film and TV empire in the country. As the festival's production manager in the late seventies, Bill House squired festival guests such as Robbie Robertson around town in his white MGB. He later became a senior executive at Telefilm Canada, and currently works for Seaton McLean as vice-president of motion-picture production at Alliance Atlantis. Former festival director Wayne Clarkson, who went on to launch the Ontario Film Development Corporation, now presides over the Canadian Film Centre, the country's finishing school for filmmakers. His former managing director, Anne Mackenzie, is a project evaluator at Telefilm. Anna Stratton and Ilana Frank once ran the festival guest office; both have become successful producers—Stratton had a festival hit in 1995 with John Greyson's Genie Award–winning *Lilies*. Linda Muir, who sold tickets at the festival box office, is a Genie-winning costume designer. Playwright John Allen once relished his role as a bouncer at oversold galas, telling angry gold patrons that there was no room left for them in the theatre. Two decades later, he satirized the same class of people in his hit play, *One-Eyed Kings*. David Gilmour began his literary career twenty years ago when he got a job editing the festival programme book. He has since published four novels and, at last report, was writing a screenplay of the Carol Shields novel *Larry's Party* for Alliance Atlantis.

The festival has become one of the world's busiest crossroads of international cinema—a party, a showcase and a market. No event has played a more strategic role in introducing filmmakers to North America. Toronto is often the first place they meet a civilian audience in the flesh, not just the industry crowd of Cannes or Sundance. In preparing this book, I interviewed more than fifty filmmakers, and time and again they kept coming back to the uncanny enthusiasm of the Toronto audience, ardent filmgoers who would line up on a Monday morning to take a chance on some obscure offering from Iran or Taiwan.

The story of the festival is, in the early years, about the characters who created it, the hosts. And they *were* characters—from co-founder Bill Marshall, who had a taste for Cuban cigars, Chivas Regal and fleeting marriages with flamboyant women, to programmer David Overbey, who picked up Filipino films and Filipino boys with the same discerning eye. Each of the festival directors imprinted the event with a personal signature—Marshall, the Impresario, who created something out of nothing; Wayne Clarkson, the Populist, who went to war with the Ontario Censor Board; Helga Stephenson, the Publicist, who charmed filmmakers from Havana to Helsinki; and Piers Handling, the Cinephile CEO, who trains for Cannes each year by hiking in the Himalayas.

But at any good party, eventually the guests take over. Once the festival is established, the story belongs to the filmmakers. It is a story of films being discovered—from *Diva* to *Roger and Me*—and of filmmakers discovering each other in the crowd: Quentin Tarantino courting Mira Sorvino as they take in a movie from Hong Kong, David Cronenberg meeting producer Jeremy Thomas and hatching plans to make *Naked Lunch* and *Crash*, John Sayles checking out a samurai slasher flick at Midnight Madness.

The story of the festival is also the story of Toronto, media city. This is the place where Marshall McLuhan shrink-wrapped the global village. Multicultural and polymorphous, Toronto is the chameleon that lives to adapt. It has no romance of its own but it dreams of growing up to become the universal server—the medium as the metropolis. Toronto is the city that likes to take measure of the world. It cultivates a talent for observation and commentary, producing comedians, animators and anchormen in disproportionate numbers. It's a place that likes to watch: a movie town. Even in the early seventies, long before it had become a film production capital, Toronto was movie mad, with the highest per-capita film-going audience on the continent. And when Bill Marshall, Henk van der Kolk and Dusty Cohl set out to create the Festival of Festivals in 1976, it had already hosted one of the most ambitious film festivals ever mounted in North America.

In 1973, a group of women organized the Women and Film International Festival (WFIF), a ten-day extravaganza of 182 films by and about women. It was staged in Toronto and then toured eighteen cities across the country in an abbreviated version. The seeds of the Toronto International Film Festival can be found in that event. Anne Mackenzie, a WFIF coordinator, went on to become the Toronto festival's first managing director. One of the WFIF programmers, Linda Beath, became the festival's first programme manager, and another, Kay Armatage, has been a key member of its programming team since 1982. Finally, the only person who has worked with the Toronto festival for every single one of its twenty-five years—an eccentric Englishman named Martin Heath—cut his teeth with Women and Film.

In the late sixties, Heath ran an alternative theatre in London called the Electric Cinema Club with Deanne Taylor, a Canadian multimedia artist who later co-founded Toronto's VideoCabaret as one of the performing Hummer Sisters. In 1972, Heath came to Toronto with Taylor to make a rock 'n' roll documentary, *The Son of Tutti Frutti*, which showed for thirteen weeks every Friday night at the Roxy Theatre. He elected to stay in Canada, and moved into Rochdale, the high-rise hippie co-op. When Taylor and her friends organized WFIF in 1973, he offered to help out with "revising" film—putting it on reels and repairing any damage. "I worked in a concrete bunker behind the screen at the St. Lawrence Centre," he recalls. "Part of my contract was that they would deliver dinner to me every night. They ordered in steaks from Barberian's. They would joke about throwing a piece of meat into my dungeon."

Not much has changed with Martin Heath. In his twenty-five years at the Toronto festival, he has watched it grow from a state of bohemian chaos to a smoothly run corporation, but his job remains essentially the same. With his crew he spends each festival at his workbench preparing film for projection. Wearing white gloves, he checks for damage, feeling for nicks and tears. Each year miles of celluloid pass through his hands. He works out of his house, where during the rest of the year he runs a unique operation called Cinecycle: he repairs bicycles by day and projects films by night from his private collection of two hundred prints, which may or may not include the odd festival entry that went astray. In a corporate festival, Heath remains the die-hard rebel. Once he showed up at a party for a French film dressed in the diplomatic bag that the film had been shipped in. And in the censorship fracas over *In Praise of Older Women*, Heath is still the only one who knows the true story behind the clandestine switching of the uncensored print.

Since then, Toronto has become a less shockable place, and the festival can take some of the credit. It has helped push the city through a cosmopolitan coming of age. For a decade, the festival was on the front lines in the battle against censorship, until the Ontario Censor Board finally granted it special dispensation. And back when Toronto bars closed at one o'clock, friends of the festival stretched last call by opening illegal booze cans. Now the bars close at two and during the festival some stay open until four. Toronto has always had a hard time having fun. Those reckless nights of keeping visiting filmmakers properly entertained has taught us about the beauty of mixing business and pleasure. Now each September, the city dons the festival like a well-worn leather jacket.

Also threaded through these twenty-five years is the story of independent film. While the festival has grown from a cozy sideshow to an industrial carnival, so has the movement of independent film, to the point that its independence is often no more than a posture. This book, published to celebrate a silver anniversary, chronicles a success story. But it also asks the question: what happens to art when it enters the mainstream? Specifically, can independent cinema survive success? And how can a globalized festival keep its edge?

Born from a marriage between the counterculture and the Chivas set, the Toronto festival is still trying to reconcile the experimental with the exponential, the unknown auteur with the Hollywood superstar. Perhaps an impossible challenge. We all agree the festival is not as much fun as it used to be. But that's true of most things. Although it has grown far beyond the community that created it, the festival remains a friendly corporation run by people who care about film. Trying to offer something for everyone, it has become a grand *cirque du cinema*—an attempt to balance the showing of art with the art of show business. And it all began with a band of renegade high rollers who ran off to join the circus on the French Riviera, then tried to bring it all back home.

The Godfath

THERE ARE VARIOUS CREATION MYTHS *ABOUT HOW THE FESTIVAL CAME TO BE. BUT they all contain some version of the Ballad of Bill and Dusty, a tale of two men who threw Canadian caution to the wind, born promoters with a glint of the Wild West in their eyes and a touch of Klondike fever in their veins. Bill Marshall was the Impresario, the man who made it happen; Dusty Cohl was the Accomplice.*

ers
MICHAEL JACKSON
MICHAEL JACKSON

They did not meet until 1975, but their backgrounds have odd parallels. Both were from working-class families headed by proudly proletarian fathers who dreamed of organizing something grand. Not a festival, but a revolution. Marshall was born in Glasgow, the son of a Scots Communist who built railway wagons by day and worked as a doorman at the left-wing Citizens' Theatre by night. Cohl was born and raised in Toronto, the son of a Jewish Communist who worked as a house painter and union organizer, and ended up an insurance agent. His mother sold bed linen at Eaton's.

As teenagers, Bill and Dusty both rejected their parents' left-wing orthodoxy. For Bill, who immigrated to Toronto with his family at fifteen, the turning point came when he became infatuated with the fictional worlds of *The Great Gatsby* and *The Diamond as Big as the Ritz*. "My father thought I was on my way to becoming a perfect socialist until I started reading F. Scott Fitzgerald," says Marshall. "He thought Fitzgerald was a decadent, swinish, upper-class writer." Bill grew up to become his father's worst nightmare, a Gatsbyesque buccaneer who knew how to dress, how to drink and how to throw magnificent parties—but tended to sabotage his own success. Cohl, meanwhile, honed his social skills at Camp Nyvold, a Jewish Communist camp outside Toronto where he spent every summer from the age of five. He became a counsellor, the sports director, and by the age of seventeen, he says, "I was practically running the place. But I was booted out. Expelled. I suppose I'd betrayed the movement in some fashion. They even had one of those show trials to get rid of me." As the final insult to Karl Marx, Cohl became a real-estate lawyer.

e Toronto festival was born in Cannes, on the Carlton terrace, here people buy each other ridiculously expensive rounds of Pimms yale and do business while pretending not to

The legend of how Cohl stumbled on the notion of creating a film festival in Toronto may be as apocryphal as the Haida tale of the raven plucking mankind from a clam shell. But like any good creation myth, it has stuck. As the story goes, Cohl was visiting Europe for the first time in 1960. While driving along the French Riviera with his wife, Joan, he pulled into Cannes—without realizing there was a film festival going on—and grabbed a parking space in front of the fabled Carlton Hotel just as a car was pulling out. Finding a parking space in front of the Carlton at the height of the Cannes International Film Festival is a fluke of almost supernatural proportions, but that is how Cohl says he first landed in the terrace bar of the hotel. "Right away," he recalls, "I saw and felt the pulse of the action. I was like a kid falling into Disneyland."

Cohl and his wife did not return to the Cannes festival until 1968, but for the next two decades they were regulars. With his black cowboy hat, black beard and permanent grin, Dusty became a fixture on the Carlton terrace. He schmoozed, he bought drinks, he met stars. And he charmed the pants off a coterie of influential American critics, from Rex Reed to the not-yet-famous Roger Ebert, who would become a close friend. Ebert remembers meeting Cohl for the first time: "He had the cowboy hat, the cigar, and

M LEFT, JO ANNE LEWIS, LEAN'S CORRESPONDENT MILLER, MARSHALL AND KA VAN DER KOLK IN CANNES

he was wearing a Dudley Do-Right T-shirt. He and Joan had set up a table on the Carlton terrace underneath a big umbrella. I never did figure out exactly how he knew who I was." And in a place where everyone was selling something, no one could ever really figure out what this glad-handing eccentric from Canada was flogging with such gusto, aside from his own outsized personality. "The thing about Dusty," says Ebert, "is that as long as I've known him, you're never quite sure what his agenda is. He doesn't pitch. He seems to work by a process of attraction rather than promotion. Dusty has never really wanted anything from me. Although he was involved in production for a while, he wasn't actually in the business. He was just a friend."

Cohl claims he was the first to imagine a Toronto film festival. And the media friendships he forged in Cannes would become crucial to its success. But Marshall was the impresario who had the vision, and the nerve, to get it off the ground. He also had the motive: Marshall wanted to be a big-shot movie producer and he needed a place where he could play the part. "Bill made it happen," says Helga Stephenson—who was briefly married to Marshall (from 1982–84) as his third wife and, less briefly, married to the festival (1987–93) as its fourth executive director. "I'm not sure that there would have been a festival without him. He had the brains to see it, the guts to try it and the balls to push it. But Bill is not of the brotherhood. His motivations were not to have more Truffaut movies flowing through the system. He wanted to find a platform for his films. He wanted the Canadian industry to grow because he wanted to be part of it."

"I'm not sure there would have been a festival without him. He had t the guts to try it and the balls to push it. But Bill is not of the brothe tions were not to have more Truffaut movies flowing through the sys

Bill Marshall was a player. In high school, he made money in debating contests. During his two-year fling with higher education at the University of Toronto, he'd skip literature classes to play poker and bridge, using his winnings to pay his tuition. At nineteen, he dropped out to join the promotion department at Procter and Gamble, where he hooked up with Gil Taylor. Together they formed a public relations company that hatched one outlandish scheme after another. They put on a hootenanny at Maple Leaf Gardens that flopped. They sank money into a psychedelic nightclub in Jamaica that flopped. They produced a Toronto play called *Futz*, which landed them in court on an obscenity charge after opening night (they were acquitted). And they made a flick called *Flick*, which flopped in Canada but, retitled *Dr. Frankenstein on Campus* in the United States, did some business at drive-ins.

Marshall was also involved in politics, which he treated as a safer, more lucrative form of show business. Forming the Film Consortium of Canada with Henk van der Kolk, a Dutch-born architect turned producer, he churned out industrial and promotional films for the Ontario government. And in the early seventies he masterminded David Crombie's first Toronto mayoralty campaign, securing his victory with a barrage of high-priced TV commercials. Marshall became Crombie's executive assistant, but he soon got bored with life at City Hall. The impresario needed someone new to impress.

"I guess I wanted to go back into the real world of movies as opposed to the make-believe world of politics," he says. "And I was trying to figure out how you can make a living in this industry. What would be good things to have? What do they have in America? And what do they have in the *counter*-American film cultures? They have film festivals." But Marshall met with "huge resistance and lethargy" when he first broached the idea. "People said, 'you couldn't have one here,' or 'you shouldn't have one here' or 'no one will like it.' I tried to point out that it would be worthwhile doing a major festival in a major movie-going city. Just pump up all the bits and pieces—the good audience, the multicultural audience, what it would do for the people in the business, how it would show the rest of the world this was a good place to make movies. All of which came true—not right away, but it did come true."

Dusty Cohl first met Marshall in a Yorkville restaurant back in 1973 to discuss *Pinocchio's Birthday Party*, a children's movie that Cohl was helping to develop. Just who first raised the idea of starting a film festival remains a contentious issue. Cohl says, "It was definitely my idea." Marshall remembers it this way: "Dusty said, 'What are you going to do when you quit City Hall?' I said, 'I think I'll start a world film festival.' He said, 'You're kidding. I've always believed that we should have one here. I've been trying to talk people into it for years and you sound like the guy who is nutty enough to do it. I'm behind you 100 per cent. I'll go out and find some support.'"

ains to see it,
d. His motiva-

Bill and Dusty visited film festivals in Los Angeles, Atlanta and Berlin. Then, in 1975, Cohl introduced Marshall to Cannes. They rented a suite at the Carlton and set up camp in the bar on the terrace, where the parade of luminaries who breezed by ranged from Donald Sutherland to O.J. Simpson. Cannes is the kind of place where people buy each other outrageously expensive rounds of Pimms Royale, cocktails with shrubbery, and do business while pretending not to. Marshall, who tended to work out of the Club 22 bar at the Windsor Arms Hotel in Toronto, felt right at home. Cannes was the Big Time, and if Toronto was going to have a film festival, Marshall wanted it to be Big Time too, right from the word go. But he would need some help from Hollywood. And he knew exactly who to call.

David Leigh MacLeod was a charismatic young man from Toronto with a remarkable pedigree. Like Marshall, he was a backroom boy whose worlds straddled politics and show business. His father, Alex MacLeod, was the last Communist elected to the Ontario legislature, a brilliant political mind who was later hired by Conservative premier Leslie Frost to draft the Ontario Human Rights Code. Following his father into politics, David MacLeod campaigned for the Conservatives and later worked for education minister Bill Davis. He hired Marshall and van der Kolk to produce three documentaries for the education ministry in the late sixties. "He was very happy about them and was putting us up for work," says Marshall, who later worked with MacLeod on Davis's 1971 election campaign for Ontario premier. "I'd known David MacLeod for years. He was

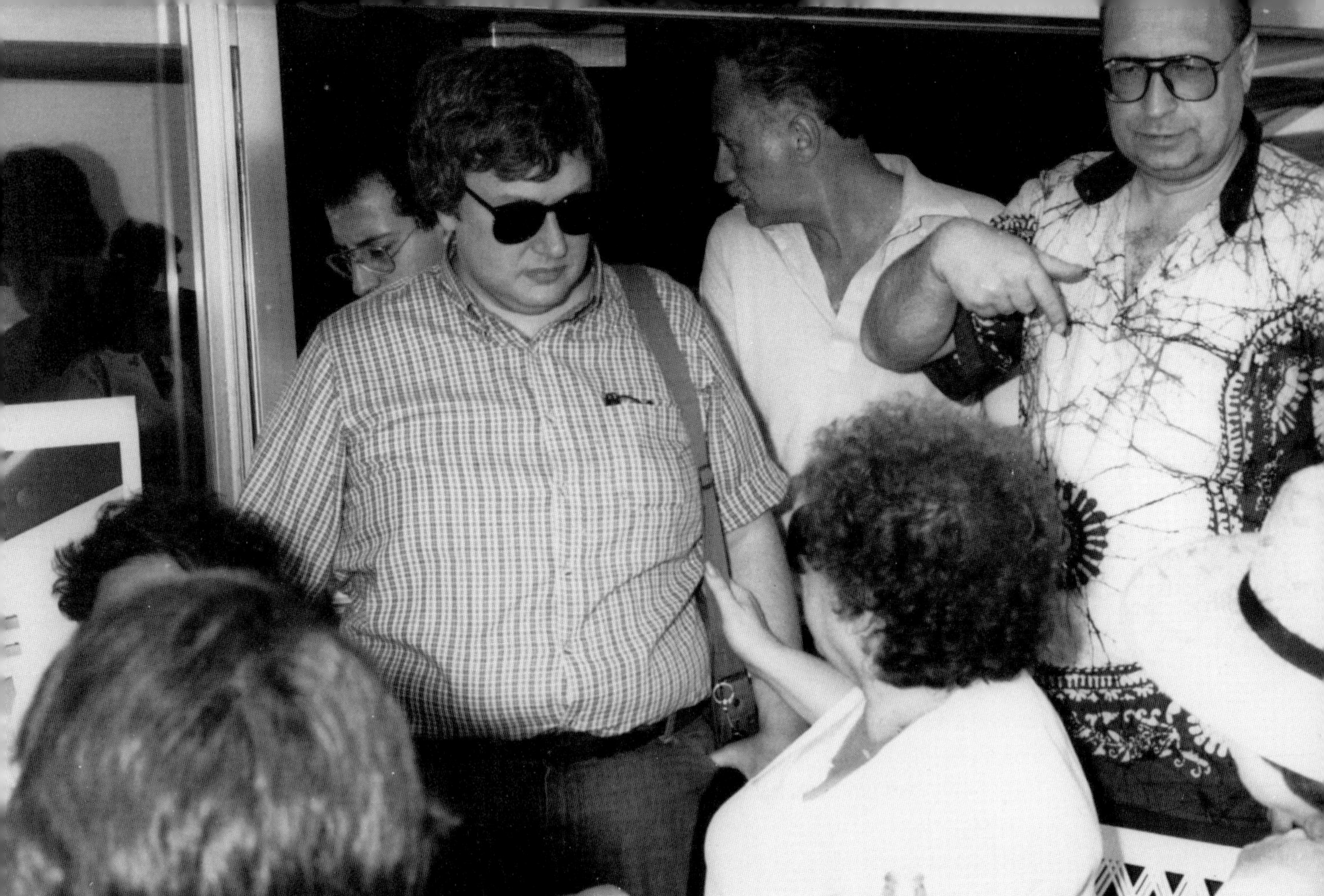

PHOTO: L. MIRKINE

ROGER EBERT AND PIERRE RISSIENT IN CANNES WITH RENÉE FURST (TALKING TO EBERT), 1982

charming and as bright as all get out." He was also Warren Beatty's first cousin. MacLeod, in fact, would end up producing several movies with Beatty, including *Reds* and *Ishtar*. "When I told him about the film festival," Marshall recalls, "he said, 'Well, I can deliver a whole chunk of Hollywood.'"

Plans for that inaugural festival were set during a tennis game at Warren Beatty's house on Mulholland Drive in Los Angeles. Marshall and Cohl were in town, trying to recruit support, and MacLeod had invited them up to his cousin's house. Beatty was not home, but MacLeod gave them a tour, and they played some tennis on the actor's court, which offered a spectacular view of the city sprawled below. "MacLeod was a very good tennis player and I was a very bad tennis player," Marshall recalls. They discussed what scale of festival they should be trying to pull off. Dusty and Bill did not see eye to eye. "Bill wanted to go with a full-blown international film festival," says Cohl. "And I said there was no way we could put all the elements together the first year. How were we going to get the glitter and the stars? But David MacLeod was our man in Hollywood, the man who was close to Warren and close to Jack Nicholson and Julie Christie. He assured us that getting the stars would be no problem, and so the decision was made to go ahead."

Marshall and Cohl made the kickoff announcement that spring in Cannes. The festival would take place in October. It would be international, non-competitive, and rather than vying with other major festivals for films, it would pay tribute to them by culling the best of their programs. Marshall was especially worried about being able to show films destined for the prestigious New York Film Festival. So he came up with the shrewd tactic of "honouring" the other festivals with a series of gala parties each night, and, remarkably, "they all kind of went along with it," says Marshall. "I said to the New York Film Festival, 'You don't mind if I have European movies before you, do you? Because one of our nights is going to be saluting the New York Film Festival.' They said, 'No, no, that's fine.'"

Henk van der Kolk, who stayed out of the spotlight, is the unsung hero among the founders of the Toronto festival. He was in charge of the money. "We didn't go into this festival expecting to put our own butts on the line," he says. "But we were constantly on the verge of going broke. Bill and I both had personal credit cards as well as the corporate cards, and between us we ran up debts of about $40,000 in a very short time. We lost the cards. I had an apartment at the Harbour Castle Hotel. I got Robert Campeau to give the festival half of the friggin' hotel for nothing." As future director Helga Stephenson explains, "Bill's job was to talk it up. But Henk ran it. His job was to make it run in whatever fashion he could, with little or no money. And for a long time, the art of keeping the festival alive—a mantle that was handed over to Anne Mackenzie—was the art of keeping the creditors at bay, keeping them loyal to the festival and willing to wait."

As Marshall and van der Kolk hustled sponsors, and governments, they eventually raised a budget of $275,000 in cash and $225,000 in goods and services. But it was an uphill battle. On the civic level, Mayor Crombie couldn't be seen to be shilling for his former campaign manager. The province did not come on board until after the first festival was over. And on the federal level, Marshall met resistance from the Secretary of State's Festivals Bureau, which opposed creating one in Toronto. "It was only the pushing of John Roberts [then Secretary of State] and Jim Coutts [then principal secretary to Prime Minister Pierre Trudeau] that got us anything," says Marshall. "They both liked movies so they thought it was a terrific idea." Marshall also landed in a turf war with the local custodians of Canadian film. "There was a huge donnybrook with all the entrenched interests," he recalls, namely the Canadian Motion Picture Distributors Association, the Canadian Film Awards and the Ontario Film Institute. OFI director Gerald Pratley had been running the Stratford International Film Festival for five years. Staged each September on a shoestring budget, it was a one-week event, piggybacked onto the theatre festival in Stratford, Ontario. But, dating back to 1956, it was one of Canada's original film festivals. And it attracted such diverse guests as Martin Ritt, Charlton Heston and Roger Corman, who presented their movies and took part in freewheeling afternoon seminars.

In the spring of 1976, over lunch in Cannes, Marshall offered Pratley a programming job at the upcoming Toronto festival. Pratley turned him down, only to see his own festival cancelled for lack of public funding as soon as he got home. "Pratley's festival was nice," allows Marshall, "but I always thought it was a kind of add-on to the Stratford Festival. It wasn't created for its own reasons." Pratley is now sanguine about the whole experience, but at the time, recalls van der Kolk, "he hated our idea. He was a good guy, far more dedicated than we were about film, and here come these two upstarts. We were not film buffs; we were film producers. We started this thing because we thought the only way to be producers in Canada was—rather than breathlessly running around the world trying to catch up to everyone else—we would play host." Like gamblers taking bets on a tax-shelter movie, Bill and Henk built their non-profit corporation out of thin air, while Dusty pitched it to anyone who would listen. "Financially, Dusty never had his ass on the line," says van der Kolk, "but that doesn't diminish his contribution. The festival was basically Dusty's dream."

MARSHALL AND HENK VAN DER KOLK IN CANNES, 1976

Meanwhile, on the strength of his MacLeod connection, Marshall promised that Nicholson, Christie, Martin Scorsese and *Chinatown* screenwriter Robert Towne would appear at a festival series of "craft conferences." Claudia Cardinale was also expected. But in the end none of them would show. All sorts of conflicting claims raged through the press. Marshall reported that he'd sent a bunch of airline tickets to MacLeod, who said he had no idea what happened to them. Nicholson and Christie ended up going to the San Francisco Film Festival instead. And Nicholson's agent said he had never even heard of the Toronto festival.

Although the stars failed to materialize, they unwittingly served to publicize the event. Their names and pictures were splashed through the newspapers—first when Marshall announced them and then, at the very last minute, when they somehow failed to appear. There are those who suggest that none of the stars were actually confirmed in the first place, and that Marshall had indulged in some judicious hyperbole about them coming just to get the first festival off the ground. "Bill had a wonderful talent for making stuff up," says former festival managing director Anne Mackenzie, referring to Marshall's knack for attracting publicity. It's a compliment that Marshall refuses to accept. He insists that "MacLeod told me he'd talked to Warren about it and that Warren and Jack would come. They particularly wanted to meet Margaret Trudeau. This was the year she was having the excitement with the Rolling Stones at the El Mocambo."

In fact, MacLeod confirmed to a reporter at the time that he did, indeed, make the arrangements with the stars and that he had no idea why there was so much confusion. In the end, perhaps the worst thing Marshall could be accused of is ill-timed prophecy, for the stars *eventually* showed—Scorsese, Nicholson, Beatty and Christie all visited the festival in the early eighties. As for the shadowy figure at the heart of the intrigue, he is no longer around to explain himself. David MacLeod, as it turned out, harboured more secrets than anyone suspected. In 1986, just two years after helping to organize the Toronto festival's tribute to Warren Beatty, he was arrested in Times Square and later convicted of having sex with three runaway boys. He was granted two years probation, but the next year he was arrested again. New York City police alleged that MacLeod trolled housing projects in Brooklyn and the Bronx and lured boys aged twelve to sixteen to a New Jersey motel, where he paid them for sex. In 1989, charged with thirty-four counts of criminal solicitation and endangering the welfare of children, MacLeod fled a

PHOTO: YANKA VAN DER KOLK

ill's job was to talk it up, but Henk ran it. His job was to make it rur whatever fashion he could. And for a long time, the art of keepinc e festival alive was the art of keeping the creditors at bay"

Brooklyn courthouse and became a fugitive. The Hollywood producer—indicted *in absentia* by a federal grand jury for taking six boys across state lines to have sex—disappeared for nine years. Then, on December 6, 1998, he was found dead at the age of fifty-four on a street in Montreal. In his hand was a can of lighter fluid, which police alleged he had used to poison himself.

But there was no hint of a double life in the charming young man who played tennis with Marshall and Cohl that day at Beatty's house. "I never saw anything off about him," says Cohl. "He was a real pleasant guy with a seemingly with-it sense of humour. I was completely shocked when the story around his death came up. I had no inkling of that at all." Long before meeting MacLeod, "I was a real fan of his dad," Cohl adds. "He was unquestionably the best speaker in the provincial house." In the late 1940s, while at law school at the University of Toronto, Cohl could often be found in the common room playing bridge. "And whenever we got word that Alex MacLeod was speaking—or the other Communist member, Joe Salzberg—we would quit our card game and go over to Queen's Park to watch. MacLeod was magnificent."

Bill and Dusty both grew up surrounded by politicians, not stars, and they played by the rules of politics, a different code than show business. In Hollywood, promises are passed around like Monopoly money, worthless until a deal is inked. But in politics, if someone promises to deliver names to your party, you expect them to show up. Marshall and Cohl had been raised under an old-fashioned system of loyalty and cronyism, and Cohl worked it like a veteran ward-heeler.

In Cannes with Marshall in 1976, he held court on the Carlton terrace, building support for the festival on an endless bar tab. "We were making friends, trying to get access to pictures, trying to get people to think about the Festival of Festivals," says Cohl. After Cannes, he and Joan rented a room at the ultra-luxurious Hôtel du Cap down the coast in Antibes. Waiting for them was a bouquet of flowers from a bureaucrat at the Canadian Film Development Corporation—"she'd been having a bit of a rough ride so we'd taken her out to dinner," Cohl explains. A chain reaction set in. As a gag, all his friends started sending flowers. "So I go down to the lobby," says Cohl, "and this little guy beside me says, 'Do you know this Mrs. Joan Cohl they keep delivering the flowers to?' And this guy introduces himself as Joseph E. Levine. He's there selling *A Bridge Too Far*. Then he says, 'You'll have to excuse me. I have to join Sophia.'

"'Sophia Loren?'
"'Do you think I'm going to meet some other Sophia?'"

So Dusty meets Sophia Loren, hobnobs with Joseph E. Levine. The next morning he shows up for breakfast feeling like a million bucks. "I walk into the room but I can't make eye contact. I do a quick read, and I realize that it's because they know I'm nobody. I sit down and suddenly the room starts stirring. Joseph E. Levine has come in. They're all greeting him. He's quite perfunctory with them. Then he turns to Joan and me at our table and says, 'Would you mind if I sat down and had coffee with you?' He sits down and from there on everybody who comes and says hello to Joseph E. Levine is talking to us before they get a chance to do anything else. And *he* is pitching them on the Toronto film festival."

But Dusty's most crucial allies in Cannes were the media. Roger Ebert remembers how he courted them: "He knew that the way to get the festival on the map was to have it covered by the press, and he seemed to have a gift for meeting all of the journalists. I mean, here was an attorney from Toronto with no apparent connection to the film business and suddenly he's at the centre of this group of critics. There weren't a lot of critics from America in Cannes in those days, but he knew all of them—Charles Champlin, Rex Reed, Kathleen Carroll, Richard Corliss, Andrew Sarris, Molly Haskell and myself." Cohl managed to get a number of U.S. critics to attend the inaugural festival—Champlin (*The Los Angeles Times*), Carroll (*The New York Daily News*) and William Woolf (*Cue Magazine*).

The major American studios, however, boycotted the event, holding back half a dozen movies that had been lined up, notably sneak previews for the opening and closing galas. Director Hal Ashby (*Shampoo*) had offered *Bound for Glory*, his Woody Guthrie biopic, for opening night, but the studio overrode him. Hollywood executives argued that Canada was part of their domestic market, and they had a policy against contributing movies to domestic festivals. Being snubbed by Hollywood, however, was not such a bad thing. It allowed Marshall to launch the festival in a righteous blaze of cultural nationalism, igniting the first of endless festival debates through the years about how the Canadian film industry might break the stranglehold of American distributors. On the eve of the opening, Marshall ranted in the local press about Hollywood treating Toronto like Toledo, and sucking $60 million to $70 million in film rentals out of the country each year while doing nothing for local production. Picking up the ball, Charles Champlin dealt the studios a stinging rebuke on their home turf: "At a time when Hollywood needs all the friends it can get," he wrote in *The Los Angeles Times*, "some minions of the majors have been giving a grand demonstration of how to lose friends and alienate potential customers."

The studio movies, and their stars, would come soon enough. They would help seduce the media, attract sponsors and stir public excitement. Down the road, in fact, the festival would draw criticism for upsetting its ecosystem with too much star power. But the guts of any festival is its programming, and Toronto's programming has always been its strength. From its inception, the festival took a pluralistic approach. Unlike directors of other major festivals—Cannes, Berlin, Venice—Marshall had neither the desire nor the qualifications to set himself up as a programming czar. Instead, he hired specialists, cinephiles with daring tastes that he didn't necessarily share.

In other words, he gave the inmates the keys to the asylum. And in that first year, they set in place a program of remarkable depth, one that still stands up as the festival's basic template. Call it the *auteur* theory of programming. The serious side was there right from the start with a cutting-edge survey of New German Cinema by Britain's Jan Dawson. She also authored a book to go with it—the first English-language study of Wim Wenders, and the first in a string of books published by the festival. Barbara Martineau's Womanscene, an uncompromising battery of films by women, foreshadowed the feminist programming of Kay Armatage. Young Cinema, by Tony Watts, nurtured an appetite for discovery. All-night marathons of movies from directors Roger Corman and Sergio Leone provided the germ of Midnight Madness. The festival's scope was immediately evident, with fare that ranged from the Siberian steppes to the suburbs of Brazil. There were also documentaries, shorts, silent movies, films about filmmaking—and the mandatory menu of Canadian cinema. A total of 127 features spread over 152 screenings in six days. Then there were the parties. The festival would become famous for its parties.

WILT CHAMBERLAIN AND ELLIOTT GOULD AT THE CLOSING GALA AT CITY HALL, 1977

PHOTO: CHRIS HOLLAND

THE FIRST FESTIVAL WAS SURROUNDED BY WATER. *THE ONTARIO PLACE CINESPHERE, a pod that sits on stilts in Lake Ontario, is a far cry from the French Riviera, but for veterans of Cannes it must have been comforting to have had yachts on the horizon. An*

US

JEANNE MOREAU, 1976

PHOTO: COURTESY OF SHELLEY COHL/ANGEL WELLS

overflow crowd packed the eight-hundred-seat theatre for the opening-night gala, *Cousin, cousine*, which had been shuffled from another spot in the schedule at the last minute after *Bound for Glory* fell through. French director Jean-Charles Tacchella's charming comedy about marital infidelity was warmly received. The American theme of the party afterwards—set up for a Hollywood premiere, with hot dogs, Schlitz beer, soul food, apple pie, pinball and a Dixieland band—was a little incongruous. The irony of launching the festival with a soiree honouring the Los Angeles International Film Exposition after being snubbed by Los Angeles somehow seemed all too Canadian.

*'Talent is the desire to lose oneself and to show oneself. It is th
)ower to draw attention with the face you have, the body you have.
s to dream in front of people who are watching you"*

But the mood was festive, the food and drink generous. "In Toronto," Bill Marshall told a reporter, "we plan to put the word festive back in festival. Most of the international festivals have become diplomatic exchanges instead of what they are supposed to be, which is a chance to get together and celebrate films." Borrowing an idea from Caravan, Toronto's annual multicultural fiesta, the organizers staged lavish parties honouring a different film festival each night: Taormina, Cannes, Berlin, Moscow and Edinburgh. Every party had a free, fully stocked bar of donated liquor. And there was a homespun touch to the hospitality: for the Moscow tribute, after a 70-mm screening of *Dersu Uzala*, Akira Kurosawa's majestic epic about a peasant hunter guiding a Russian soldier through the wilds of Siberia, party-goers feasted on a buffet of homemade food cooked by a team of women from Toronto's Ukrainian community.

The first festival attracted seven thousand people a day and was deemed a success. The one star who did grace the event in its first year was none other than Jeanne Moreau, who sailed into town with her directorial debut, *Lumière*. Moreau seemed to enchant everyone she met. She told George Anthony of *The Toronto Sun* about her dreams, her therapy and the hazards of acting: "If you're going to go deep, deep, deep as an actress, you must go *fearlessly*." The film, which she also wrote, plays as an autobiographical reverie about what it means to be an actress. It contains a buoyant satire of the male filmmaking world, with playful swipes at "phallocrat" auteurs and a send-up of a predatory Hollywood producer, played by Keith Carradine. But *Lumière* is never reductively feminist. Full of loving allusions to cinema, it skims the surface of the New Wave with a jump-cutting wit. This is the actress reflecting the worlds of Truffaut, Godard, Malle and Buñuel from the inside out—Moreau exploring the undirected self. *Lumière* is about a quartet of actresses, four refractions of Jeanne Moreau. She played the oldest version. Playing the youngest was an actress from Quebec named Francine Racette; there is a mesmerizing scene of her character being interviewed in her home by an officious female journalist.

"What is talent?" asks the interviewer. "Talent," replies the actress, "is the desire to lose oneself and to show oneself. It is the power to draw attention. It's the power to attract attention with the face you have, the body you have. It's to dream in front of people who are watching you—to carry them away, to connect them. You can't have any other thought than that."

Mercurial and pensive, like a young Moreau, Racette herself displayed a radiant talent in *Lumière*. Now, she looks back on the shoot with Moreau as a magical time. "But I had a big argument with her," she says. "She wanted my character to say, 'I think about acting twenty-four hours a day.' I said to Jeanne, 'Don't be ridiculous. Don't ask me to say that when you are an actress you have to think about it twenty-four hours a day.' And she said, 'Francine, I've been doing it for many, many years. You are playing me, and at that age you *have* to think about it twenty-four hours a day. So say the line.' I said, 'Okay Jeanne, I'll say the line, but I have to tell you I am not going to think about acting for twenty-four hours a day. And I'm going to change jobs.' She laughed and said, 'Okay.' But it had a very strong impact on me coming from someone I loved and respected so much." Racette had met her husband, Donald Sutherland, two years earlier. And with her on the set of *Lumière* in France was Roeg, the first of their three children. "I was very excited by being a mother," she recalls. "Jeanne is an incredible actress and I wanted to be as good as she was—but to think about acting twenty-four hours a day? If the price to pay was that high, I couldn't do it." Racette, in fact, retired from acting to devote herself to her family.

Considering how cinema has been defined by the male gaze, films by women had a dramatic presence at the first festival. You could walk out of *Duelle*—Jacques Rivette's densely plotted intrigue about goddesses lurking in a noir netherworld—and find astringent relief in minimal-action movies by France's Marguerite Duras and Belgium's Chantal Akerman. Filmed without synchronized dialogue, Duras's *India Song* is a story

NOT A PRETTY PICTURE

of love and death in Calcutta, a humid symphony of poetic images, disembodied voices and haunting music. Akerman's *Jeanne Dielman, 23 Quai du Commerce, 1080 Bruxelles* unfolds as three days in the life of a stay-at-home mother who keeps her apartment compulsively clean and repeats a fugue-like ritual of meticulous routines, which include servicing a paying lover each afternoon at five. In sifting through press clippings from 1976, I was startled to come across the byline of my own wife, Marni Jackson, who reviewed the Womanscene program in *The Toronto Star*. Sixteen years before writing *The Mother Zone*, Marni wrote about *Jeanne Dielman*'s heroine with alarming empathy: "Her days consist of minutiae, fastidiously attended to. Time and space are a prison for her, and the movie makes this fact physical. There is scarcely any dialogue, and no interaction—the whole movie is a solid wall of combustible repression."

Cutting closer to home than the European avant-garde, the female director who attracted the most attention at the festival that year was Martha Coolidge. In *Not a Pretty Picture*, her first feature, Coolidge relives her own rape as a sixteen-year-old girl in 1962, when she was on her way to a weekend party in New York City with a group of friends. Overlaying drama and documentary, the film documents a date rape long before the term existed. Michele Manenti, the actress who plays the director's character in the movie, was a rape victim herself. The film re-enacts the rape scene by showing the actors improvising it in rehearsal; as the tension escalates, the camera turns to Coolidge watching in silent horror, her hand clasped over her mouth.

There was a spirit of resistance in American documentaries at the festival.

BRIAN LINEHAN AND DINO DE LAURENTIIS, 1976

Having just completed King Kong, *De Laurentiis was gloating over the fact that, instead of hiring a $3-million star, he had built one: "I control* everything*"*

Underground—by Emile de Antonio, Haskell Wexler, Vincent Hanlon and Mary Lampson—consisted of clandestine interviews with five members of the fugitive Weather Underground. More remarkable than the film, however, was the battle to keep it out of the clutches of the FBI, a campaign that rallied a Who's Who of Hollywood, from Warren Beatty to Elia Kazan. *The Hollywood Ten*, a damning exposé of the McCarthy-era blacklist, showed Kazan in a less flattering light, as a rat who destroyed his friends' careers by naming them to the House Un-American Activities Committee.

By the late seventies, the New Wave, the New Left and the upheavals of the sixties were history, but aftershocks were reverberating through independent film. There, the counterculture had found a niche. The new cinema was a movement, and nowhere was it more audacious than in Germany, a fact that was driven home by the festival's Jan Dawson as she introduced Canadian audiences to names like Wenders, Fassbinder and Herzog. What they have in common, she said at the time, "is a stubbornly idiosyncratic integrity and a flamboyant independence from the ideology of mass production." Dawson held up the German cinema as a model "that should be of extreme interest to Canadians aspiring to making movies. The Canadian set-up has not encouraged the emergence of the *auteur*. The German set-up has not only encouraged it but brought it about." Because the German system of grants forced filmmakers to set up their own production companies, she explained, "[they] are their own producers, and to put it in

LEFT, VAN DER KOLK, RICHARD BENNER AND MARSHALL AT THE MANHATTAN OPENING OF OUTRAGEOUS!_, 1977_

OUTRAGEC

n the tax shelter era of Canadian embarrassments, Outrageous! *was t xception that proved the rule. Making a star of a drag queen seemed ınlikely mission for a bunch of cigar-and-scotch impresarios from Toron But the film became a minor sensation*

PHOTO: YANKA VAN DER KOLK

Marxist terms, they own the means of production. However, they still face the problem that they don't control the means of distribution."

Hardly the kind of language Bill Marshall would have used to diagnose the Canadian film industry. But the festival had a split personality from the start, one that could accommodate both the dialectics of a Jan Dawson and the megalomania of a Dino De Laurentiis. Then the world's most powerful independent producer, De Laurentiis was the one Hollywood titan to show up in Toronto that year, and he inaugurated a tradition of discussing the business of film at the festival. Having just completed *King Kong*, he was gloating over the fact that, instead of hiring a $3-million star, he had built one. The Neapolitan godfather held court at a press luncheon, where he dispensed wisdom between stoking a fat cigar and fielding calls in Italian on a white phone he had brought to his table. "I control everything . . . *everything*," he said, stressing that *auteurs* were meant to be interfered with, and no one was exempt, except Fellini and Bergman. Not Robert Altman? "Especially not Altman! He's the worst one to leave alone," said De Laurentiis, who had just produced Altman's bomb, *Buffalo Bill and the Indians*.

De Laurentiis also had some advice for Canadians. At the festival producers' conference he urged them to change the law so that Canadian movies would not require any Canadian talent. But even under the existing law, those investing in films with just token

Canadian talent could get a 100-per-cent tax write-off. This was the tax-shelter era (1975–79), in which all manner of "Canadian" movies were made for dubious reasons. Among the Canadian curiosities in the first festival were *The Little Girl Who Lives Down the Lane*, starring thirteen-year-old Jodie Foster as a child living alone in a cottage with a Gothic secret in the basement, and Rex Bromfield's *Love at First Sight*, a comedy starring Dan Aykroyd as a blind ex-barber. Don Owen's *Partners*, meanwhile, provided a weak glimmer of personal cinema—and sparked the festival's first censorship controversy when the Ontario Censor Board demanded a ninety-second cut to a sex scene between Hollis McLaren and Michael Margotta. The producer eventually withdrew the film from the festival rather than cut it.

The first festival was a considerable accomplishment. But the local press was not automatically supportive in the early years, which still irritates the festival's founding fathers. *The Globe and Mail*'s Robert Martin snidely dismissed the event (although Jay Scott took over the coverage the next year and became a loyal supporter). *Toronto Star* movie critic Clyde Gilmour, who felt gorging on movies was a barbaric idea, made a point of taking his vacation during the festival. "He would phone the organizers months in advance to get the schedule," recalls *Star* entertainment columnist Sid Adilman. "They were thrilled he was so interested. But he did it so he could plan his vacation." Adilman, meanwhile, says that in his early years of covering the festival, he was constantly battling with his editors, who deemed it "elitist and snobby." *Star* publisher Beland Honderich considered the Festival of Festivals a confusing name, and to the consternation of everyone involved, insisted that the paper call it the Toronto Festival of Film Festivals. The notable exception to the sour press was *The Toronto Sun*, which has been an enthusiastic sponsor from Year One. Its entertainment editor at the time, George Anthony, served as an unabashed cheerleader. Many of his columns read like pure publicity. "Once we adopted the festival as a cause at the paper," Anthony concedes, "I was certainly doing more than reporting on it. I was trying to make things happen so there would be something to write about." In fact, Bill Marshall and Dusty Cohl cultivated Anthony so effectively that he became part of the organization (and later served on the festival's board of directors). "They had George Anthony in their pocket," says Adilman. "I thought it was wrong."

Adilman has always scorned junket journalism, stressing that his newspaper does not allow staff to take free rides (although it does print articles by freelance junketeers). These days, the junket circuit is a meat market, with studios flying interviewers to New York or L.A. and force-feeding them five or six movies in a single weekend. But in the late seventies, junkets afforded a luxurious access to Hollywood. Journalists would jet in first-class, be met at the airport, and spend a weekend at a luxury hotel to cover just one movie. Back then, Anthony and his friend Brian Linehan of Citytv were among the junket elite, with a privileged access to studio executives that would prove invaluable to the festival. "Like a good trooper I was always working for September, asking about production schedules and release dates—doing reconnaissance for the festival," says Linehan. "And George had tremendous clout. George was crucial."

After the first festival, the organizers flew Anthony to Cannes and put him up in an apartment rented for the programmers. And as a member of Cohl's "Accomplice Committee," he tapped into his Hollywood connections to wrangle stars. He also secured a number of films for the festival, notably *Bobby Deerfield* and *Joseph Andrews*. From the beginning, he made it clear that he was less an observer than a player, and has since left journalism altogether to become a powerful TV executive at the CBC; Bill Marshall's ex-wife Jo Anne Lewis works as his assistant.

Perhaps Marshall and Cohl were ahead of their time. Like the Hollywood publicity machine—which has come to dominate entertainment coverage with junkets that are now orchestrated like military campaigns—they understood that the best way to guarantee positive press was to orchestrate it and, if necessary, pay for it. The festival provided plane tickets and hotel rooms for most of the international journalists who came the first year. "And we shmoozed the life out of them," says Marshall. "We treated them like *they* were the stars." The investment certainly paid off with Charles Champlin of *The Los Angeles Times*. Aside from reprimanding Hollywood for snubbing the festival, he rhapsodized about the event itself: "It is a participatory and not just a spectator festival, with ethnic dances and generous flowings of wine after the major night screenings. At the principal center of the festival, the vast and enchanting recreation center called Ontario Place on the shores of the harbor, the conversation about the movies is young, eager and non-stop. Hollywood should have been here. It's a chance blown."

September 1977. Year Two. Suddenly the festival had a rival just down the road. In Montreal, Serge Losique had created the Montreal World Film Festival and seemed

THE LITTLE GIRL WHO LIVES DOWN THE LANE

JE, TU, IL, ELLE

determined to outflank Toronto at every turn, competing for films, sponsors and government grants. Initially Ottawa offered a typical federal compromise—let Montreal and Toronto host festivals on alternate years—an idea that infuriated Marshall. Then Ottawa offered to treat the festivals as equals, initiating a rivalry that would provoke recriminations on both sides for years to come. But according to Martin Connell, the first chairman of the Festival of Festivals board of directors, the competition "was a very powerful and constructive stimulus, a burr under the saddle that really got people going."

Losique proved a tenacious rival. He opened his festival with no less a star than Ingrid Bergman. Toronto, ironically, countered by opening with a Quebec movie, Jean Beaudin's *J.A. Martin photographe*, which had brought Monique Mercure the best actress prize in Cannes for her incandescent performance as a pioneer wife who goes on the road with her photographer husband. Toronto also mounted a program of forty-three Quebec features, the largest retrospective of Quebec cinema ever shown outside the province. While the Montreal festival paid tribute to eighty-one-year-old Howard Hawks just months before his death, Toronto honoured eighty-year-old Frank Capra. But the one area where Toronto could not compete was in resisting censorship. No one batted an eye when Montreal showed Nagisa Oshima's hard-core masterpiece *In the Realm of the Senses*. In Toronto, however, the Ontario Censor Board demanded that 1,000 feet be cut from Chantal Akerman's *Je, tu, il, elle*. The festival instead elected not to show the film, part of a program selected by French director Agnès Varda.

What the press really wanted, more than stories about censor movies they'd never heard of, was stories about movie stars. In 19 they got their wish. It was George Anthony who persuaded Dona Sutherland and Peter O'Toole to come; after they performed yeom service he had Birks forge them gold pins in the shape of Life Savers

PHOTO: FRANK LENNON/TORONTO STAR SYNDICATE

Twenty years later, I took a look at *Je, tu, il, elle* on video. The footage that the censors found so offensive is the closing scene, a serenely playful improvisation on a bed. It is a thirteen-minute sequence consisting of just three shots. Two women with long dark hair, one of them Akerman, are naked on white sheets. They push and pull, wrestling and rolling around the bed as if they can't get enough of each other one moment and it's all too much the next. You can't "see" much, just two look-alike bodies all mixed up, a tangle of limbs and hair. The only sound is the soft friction of the sheets, and an odd humming barely audible from one of the women. The camera doesn't move. The point being that film sex, like real sex, is best left uncut, which is perhaps why the censors felt it necessary to cut all 1,000 feet. There were no genitals to be neatly excised, no obvious edit points. Just bodies moving in Warholian real time, leaving the censors confounded by the idea of two women making love for an eternity.

What the Toronto press really wanted, more than stories about censored movies that they'd never heard of, was stories about movie stars. In 1977, they got their wish. The stars who showed up were an eclectic crew: Peter O'Toole, Donald Sutherland, Elliott Gould, Peter Ustinov, Susannah York, Eli Wallach, Liza Minnelli, Anne Murray, Henry "the Fonz" Winkler and Wilt "the Stilt" Chamberlain. It was George Anthony who had called up Sutherland and Peter O'Toole and persuaded them to come; after they had performed yeoman service, as a token of gratitude he had Birks forge gold pins in the shape of Life Savers. Custom jewelry would become part of the festival's patronage formula: each year, a newly designed gold star would be created for the organization's high-powered friends.

In 1977, the festival also hosted its first Variety Club lunch, which would become an annual shmooze for visiting celebrities. Anthony placed Peter O'Toole beside Liza Minnelli after O'Toole told him the story of how they'd met backstage during one of her mother's shows. O'Toole had sneaked into Judy Garland's dressing room and hidden in a trunk to surprise her. When Liza walked in instead of Judy, she got the shock of her life to see this strange man pop out like a jack-in-the-box.

LIZA MINNELLI AND PETER O'TOOLE, 1977

O'Toole made himself at home in Toronto, demanding only that he be supplied with soft drugs. He insisted on Pakistani hashish, according to Linehan, who struck up a lasting friendship with the actor after interviewing him. "It had to be Pakistani," Linehan recalls. "Have you ever smelled Pakistani hashish in a small room? You wonder who didn't flush. It's beyond pungent. But it made him happy." O'Toole gamely performed his celebrity duties. He took part in a festival acting workshop, where Montreal director Robin Spry stunned the room by delivering a perversely backhanded compliment. Spry told O'Toole that the actor's performance in *Lawrence of Arabia* had influenced his own directing style, that he had seen the film countless times. Then, turning to the audience, Spry said, "I keep hoping that he will overwhelm me again, and he hasn't." Here is how Jay Scott recorded the awkward moment: "Silence. Ugly silence. The room inhales, holds its breath . . . 'I think,' says Peter O'Toole softly, with a slight smile, eyes at half-mast, 'that you've been whelmed enough.' (A raucous exhalation. Whew. That's over. Applause.)"

In these early years, the stars were by no means aloof from the festival. After being moved to tears by *Voskhozhdeniye* (*Ascent*), Russian director Larisa Shepitko's sacramental drama about Soviet partisans being martyred at the hands of the Nazis, Donald Sutherland and his wife, Francine Racette, were keen to meet the director. Dusty Cohl arranged a rendezvous. Shepitko, a striking woman with flame-red hair, spoke no

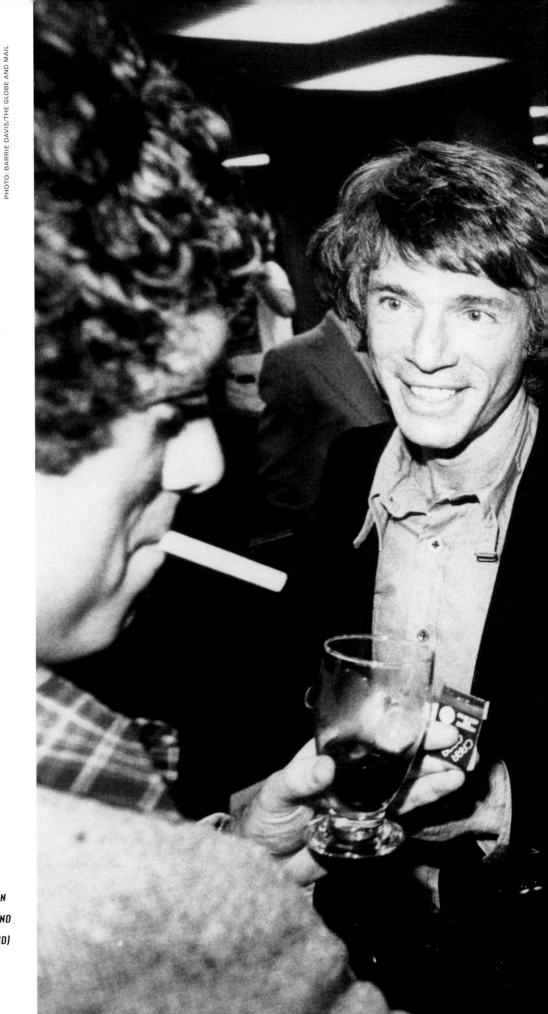

PHOTO: BARRIE DAVIS/THE GLOBE AND MAIL

ELLIOTT GOULD, STEPHEN YOUNG, CELINE LOMEZ, DONALD SUTHERLAND, AND PRODUCER DARYL DUKE (TALKING TO SUTHERLAND)

English; Sutherland and his wife spoke no Russian. At a loss to express his appreciation, Sutherland took off his digital watch and presented it to the director. Shepitko took a jade ring off her hand and placed it on his wife's finger. "Francine just loved her," recalls Sutherland. "She had a very positive relationship with her." In fact, Shepitko and Racette stayed in close touch, writing to each other. Then after two years, the letters from Russia abruptly stopped. One day, about the same time, the jade ring, which Racette still wore, broke in her hand. "It just kind of exploded," she says. "I had a friend with me who was psychic, and she said, 'Oh my God, something has happened to the person who gave it to you.'" Later Racette learned that Shepitko, who was forty-nine, had died in a car crash.

Oddly enough, the biggest star at the '77 festival was Henry Winkler, a huge TV personality trying to kick-start a film career. Then there was Wilt Chamberlain, who was just, well, huge. The seven-foot-plus basketball legend stumbled across the festival quite by accident. "I'm in the office at the Harbour Castle," says Dusty Cohl, "and the biggest guy I've ever seen in my life is walking by. I introduce myself and tell him about the festival and the hospitality suite as quickly as I can. He was in town for something totally else, but he became an ambassador for the festival." That year Chamberlain became a fixture at festival parties. It was easy to spot him: he wore a jacket that rode halfway up his back emblazoned with the logo "Outrageous!"

In the tax-shelter era of Canadian embarrassments, *Outrageous!* was the plucky little movie that proved the exception to the rule. Directed by Richard Benner—and produced by festival founders Bill Marshall and Henk van der Kolk for just $167,000—it is a sweet Cinderella story of a Toronto female impersonator (Craig Russell) and his schizophrenic flatmate (Hollis McLaren). Making a star of a drag queen seemed an unlikely mission for a bunch of cigar-and-Scotch impresarios from Toronto. But the film became a minor sensation. Taking *Outrageous!* to the Cannes market in the summer of 1977, the producers unleashed a back-slapping, drink-buying blitz of publicity from their encampment on the Carlton terrace. Cohl, who led the campaign, says, "I'll never forget when Pauline Kael, who was always a heroine of mine, came up to me at the Carlton and said, 'I've heard about this film of yours, *Outrageous!* I wonder if you could arrange for me to see it.'"

Without even showing in the official selection, the film created a buzz on the Croisette. Marshall, van der Kolk and Cohl handed out red *Outrageous!* windbreakers, which became coveted items during an unusually rainy festival. And there was even some glamour to this trio of gregarious Canadians. Marshall and van der Kolk both ended up marrying fashion models. Henk's wife, Yanka, a stunning green-eyed blonde, and Marshall's bride-to-be, Jo Anne Lewis, a sultry brunette, could have passed for movie stars. They both looked like they *belonged* in Cannes. Henk's marriage to Yanka has lasted three decades, while Bill's 1979 marriage to Jo Anne, the second of four wives, lasted less than a year.

On the Carlton terrace, where business and pleasure were happily married, Dusty and Joan Cohl worked as another power couple. They were part of the American cocktail circle that formed around *New York Daily News* critic Kathleen Carroll's flamboyant partner, a maverick distributor named Billy "Silver Dollar" Baxter—so named because he would show up in Cannes each year with a bag of a thousand American silver dollars. The coins made for cheap tips, and waiters loved them. In *Two Weeks in the Midday Sun: A Cannes Notebook*, Roger Ebert writes: "Dusty and Joan were to daytimes on the Carlton terrace what Silver Dollar Baxter was to nighttimes in the Majestic bar. Indeed, like the royalty of neighboring principalities, they one year exchanged signing privileges at the two bars—and then each immediately raced to the other's bar to sign all the tabs he could."

PHOTO: SHELLEY COHL

HENRY WINKLER, 1977

Baxter would end up buying the U.S. rights to *Outrageous!* And despite rave reviews in New York, the distribution deal was so badly botched that the film never really found an American audience. It did well in Canada, though, after a triumphant screening at the Toronto festival. The *Outrageous!* gala was a "joyous, super-charged affair . . . that tied the loose strands of the festival into a spirit that lasted for the rest of the week," wrote Bruce Kirkland in *The Toronto Star*. Finally, an English-Canadian movie that was *fun*. But the actors were reluctant stars. "Craig Russell was not in good shape," recalls Anthony, alluding to Russell's paralyzing fondness for drugs and alcohol. "And Hollis McLaren was terror-stricken by crowds. So I asked Peter O'Toole to be her escort. He walked up to her and took her by the arm. Her jaw just dropped."

However, the real North American premiere of *Outrageous!* took place six weeks earlier at Filmexpo, a small festival run by the Canadian Film Institute at the National Arts Centre in Ottawa. Marshall didn't expect much. "I thought, well, civil servants, they are not going to get this, but they just kept standing and cheering and clapping," he says. "I think that was about the warmest reception the picture got—Ottawa." Marshall's host that night was one S. Wayne Clarkson, who was making quite a mark for himself. Two years earlier he had snagged the world premiere of *The Rocky Horror Picture Show* for his tiny festival in the nation's capital. And he had organized the Frank Capra tribute in Ottawa before it went to Toronto. Clarkson, in fact, made such an impression that Marshall later hired him to take over his job. Clarkson now shrugs it off: "It wasn't complicated. You met people at the airport, took them to the hotel. You had a welcoming basket of their favourite beverages in the room, in this case Chivas and Armagnac . . . A few months later, they called and said, 'Would you be interested in running the Toronto festival?' Henk's attitude was 'let's get out of the festival business,' because the first year it had a big impact and lost a lot of money. The second year it had less of an impact and lost more money. Henk is saying to Bill, 'You're constantly distracted by this film festival. Let's get someone to run it.'"

Clarkson had the credentials. He wrote his master's thesis at University College,

"It wasn't complicated. You met people at the airport, took them to a welcoming basket of their favourite beverages in the room, in this Armagnac. A few months later they called and said, 'Would you be ning the Toronto festival?'"

PHOTO: GAIL HARVEY

London's Slade School of Fine Arts, on American B-movie maker Samuel Fuller; taught film at Carleton University; was director of Ottawa's National Film Theatre, then deputy director of the Canadian Film Institute. He also looked right for the role: the gold earring, the close-cropped beard, the Frye cowboy boots. Jay Scott, who wrote often and adoringly about Clarkson (never failing to mention the Frye boots), put it this way: "If God had published an encyclopedia of dream candidates for dream jobs, a picture of S. Wayne Clarkson might have appeared next to the entry of Film Festival Director."

MARSHALL, WAYNE CLARKSON, DAVID PETERSON AND DAVID CROMBIE

But when Clarkson took the position, he had no idea what he was getting into. He remembers showing up for work at the festival office, in a suite at the Harbour Castle Hilton, and thinking, "This is awesome. You pick up the phone and order room service for lunch. You go for a swim in the pool. This is Toronto, the big city. . . . Then I get a call from the hotel manager, who wants to see me. 'Mr. Clarkson, do you realize you have a debt with this hotel of $44,000?' And that was just the start."

The festival was a quarter million dollars in the red. It couldn't afford to pay anyone. Clarkson's first job was to find the money for his own salary. He had to bluff the bank for a home-renovation loan to meet the mortgage payments on his new house. "I knew zip about finances," he said, "but fundraising just became part of the job." Later that year Clarkson proudly announced that the next festival would shift its headquarters from the Harbour Castle to the Plaza II Hotel. "Well," he says, now laughing at his naïveté. "If you're the Harbour Castle Hilton and these guys owe you $44,000 and they just announced a deal at the Plaza II, what are you going to do? You're going to put a big steel bar across the door of their offices so they can't get in. And what's in there? All their files. So we sat down and worked out a payment plan. One of dozens. If you ever get hit by a collection agency, call me."

When Clarkson took over the festival, its only other full-time employee was Anne Mackenzie. She had worked there from Day One and did everything from tracking down prints to diverting creditors. "She was invaluable," says Clarkson. "If you wanted something done, Annie was the one who got it done. Today, if I wanted twenty-four elephants to be in front of the Canadian Film Centre in twenty-four hours, Annie is the person I'd get to do it." Clarkson and Mackenzie became a team that would run the festival for seven years. "We were really a duo," he says, "yin and yang every step of the way. It was not her nature to be front and centre, but she took on the mechanics of the festival. She made sure the trains ran on time, and everybody reported to Annie."

otel. You had e, Chivas and rested in run-

While she worked behind the scenes, Clarkson was the festival's public face, and one of his first goals was to make the event more accessible, more democratic. He doubled the number of galas. He created an affordable, all-inclusive pass. And all the screenings would take place within walking distance of the Bloor-Yorkville area. If Marshall was the promoter, Clarkson was the populist who set in motion what would be a lasting love affair between the city and the festival. But like many a love affair, it had a rocky start . . . the proverbial dark and stormy night.

In Praise of

3

Bolder Cinema

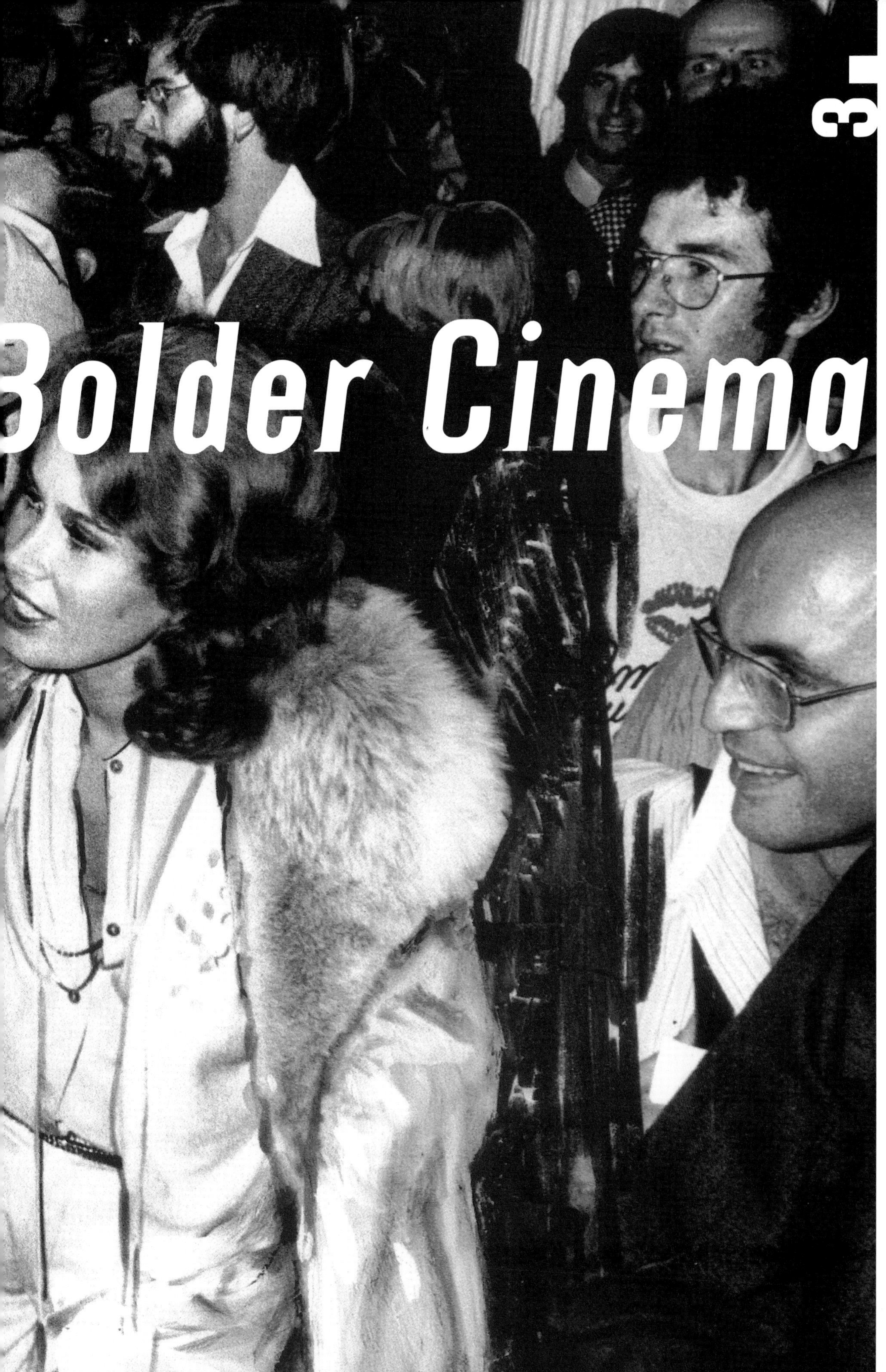

PHOTO: KEITH BEATY/TORONTO STAR SYNDICATE

'T TOOK A NEAR-RIOT TO PUT THE FESTIVAL ON THE MA

'HE OCCASION WAS A SENSATIONAL PREMIERE OF A MEDIOC

Canadian movie. September 14, 1978 was a night of pouring rain, furio crowds and clandestine intrigue. It was also a night of precedents. It w

the first time the festival had opened with a Canadian film. *In Praise of Older Women* was the first major feature produced by mogul-in-training Robert Lantos, the movie that jump-started his career. It was also the first of many movies in the next two decades that would give mild-mannered Canadians a reputation for being unusually fixated on sex. And its chaotic premiere—with hundreds of angry ticket holders mobbed outside in driving rain, clamouring to get into an oversold theatre—set the tone for a festival where getting into movies would become a contact sport.

All thanks to the Ontario Censor Board.

Eight days before the premiere, the board's Donald Sims demanded that two minutes be cut from the film or it could not be screened. Robert Lantos and Bill Marshall swore that the festival would present it uncut. The showdown was set. And in the week that followed, controversy raged through the media, not just in Toronto, but across the country. The board's timing was impeccable; Sims could not have done a better job if Lantos had put him on the payroll as a publicist.

The movie was close to the producer's heart. Based on the semi-autobiographical novel

PREVIOUS PAGES: KIT CARSON AND KAREN BLACK, 1978

by Hungarian-born writer Stephen Vizinczey, *In Praise of Older Women* is about a young man's sexual initiation at the hands of seven women, in Budapest then Montreal. Like Vizinczey, Lantos is a Hungarian who emigrated after the 1956 uprising, flirted with an academic career in Montreal, and displayed a vigorous appetite for amorous adventure. He cut his teeth in Cannes selling rights to the New York Erotic Film Festival. And he had a hand in producing *L'ange et la femme* (the steamy Quebec film in which Gilles Carle cast his young wife, Carole Laure, opposite the putatively gay Lewis Furey only to watch Furey steal Laure away after having unsimulated sex with her on camera). But *In Praise of Older Women*, which Lantos co-produced with RSL Productions partner Stephen Roth, was the first movie that Lantos put together from scratch.

Costing $1 million, it was a pasteurized erotic romp, richly photographed but lacking the wit of the novel. A bland Tom Berenger, fresh from a TV soap opera, made his big screen debut as Andras Vajda, the story's Hungarian hero (although audiences first glimpsed him as the guy who kills Diane Keaton in *Looking for Mr. Goodbar*, which was released earlier). The twenty-seven-year-old actor played love scenes with a formidable lineup of women: Karen Black, Susan Strasberg, Alexandra Stewart, Helen Shaver, Louise Marleau, Alberta Watson and Marilyn Lightstone. The film's devotion to older women seemed disingenuous, however, considering that most of them could have been his contemporaries.

IN PRAISE OF OLDER WOMEN

The movie, which unfolds as a succession of trysts, is lush with nudity, yet somehow the censor board managed to find one particular bit naughtier than the rest—a scene of Lightstone simulating sex with Berenger behind a couch. They were not fully visible, and she was wearing a bra and panties. What was there about it that inflamed the censors? Was it because she was on top? Who knows. Censors don't have to explain themselves. Anyway, as the controversy escalated, the board backtracked, asking that just thirty-eight seconds be cut, which Lantos agreed to do for the film's commercial release. But he insisted the film show uncut at the festival.

Finally, a Canadian movie that Canadians were dying to see.

The Elgin theatre had sixteen hundred seats. The festival issued two thousand invitations, following the usual logic that not everyone will show up. What someone failed to notice was that each of the invitations admitted two people. In other words, four thousand tickets were issued for sixteen hundred seats. "It was a massive blunder," says Clarkson, who had just taken over the job of festival director. "I was petrified. I'd just moved to Toronto. I had a family. My son, Wyeth, was six. I didn't want to fail. And I certainly didn't want to fail on the public stage." As opening night approached, Clarkson had two things working in his favour, a torrential rainstorm and a transit strike that had knocked out subway, bus and streetcar service. He hoped a lot of people would just stay home. Fat chance. "In 1978 the good people of Toronto wanted to see a dirty movie and those fuckers turned up," says Clarkson. "It was the wildest opening night in the history of the festival. People come into the theatre, all the seats are taken, they're backing up in the aisles, it's pissing with rain outside. So how do you get them to leave? They've all got invitations."

By showtime, there were more than four hundred wet, angry ticket-holders outside the theatre, pushing against the glass doors and screaming to get in. "The Elgin staff were panicking," recalls John Allen, who had been summoned to the Elgin to help out. "The glass was almost buckling under the crush of bodies. So Bill House and I went out and physically pushed the crowd back, yelling at them to back off. People were swinging their umbrellas, throwing punches, calling us assholes." Allen, who would become the chief enforcer at oversold galas, had found his calling. "For a twenty-one-year-old kid," he says, "it was heaven. I was pushing around gold patrons dressed to the nines."

Inside, a couple of young festival ushers named Seaton McLean and Michael MacMillan leaned against the glass doors, struggling to hold the fort. Clarkson, who knew them from a film class he'd taught at Carleton, had hired them to work the theatres for $300 each. "It seemed like a lot of money at the time," recalls McLean, who had just started up Atlantis with MacMillan. It's hard to believe that twenty years later their company would buy out Robert Lantos—the man whose movie was creating all the havoc that

Lantos came to understand better than anyone how to play the cult
set the mandate of Canadian film and television with a mix of pres
that would lead some to dryly refer to him as the Great Helmsman

night—to create Alliance Atlantis Communications, Canada's largest production company. But at the Elgin theatre in 1978, McLean and MacMillan didn't feel in control of anything. So they went looking for those in charge. "We couldn't find Wayne or Bill anywhere," says McLean. He finally found Clarkson up the street in Mr. Submarine with John Barrington, a film driver, and programmer Linda Beath, who was offering to open the New Yorker theatre, which she managed, for the overflow crowd. "Wayne was just sitting there, scared shitless," McLean recalls. "I said, 'Wayne, you've got to come back to the Elgin, there are hundreds of people banging on the doors.'"

Here the story becomes a bit like *Rashomon*. Clarkson has no memory of Mr. Submarine. Nor does John Barrington—what he remembers is standing outside the theatre in the rain with a pair of film cans in his hands and being asked to wait. He knew there were two prints of *In Praise of Older Women*, one censored and one uncut. He had no idea which one he was carrying. "I have this image," he says, "of standing there in the rain, looking through the glass doors and seeing Wayne arguing with the fire marshall. And Wayne looked like death. His face was absolutely ashen."

Wayne Clarkson's first festival was turning into his worst nightmare. He pleaded with the fire marshall not to shut down the theatre or he'd have a riot on his hands. The festival's corporate infrastructure was collapsing right in front of him. "It was ugly," says

KAREN BLACK AND
ROBERT LANTOS, 1978

PHOTO: ESMOND CHOUEKE/MACLEAN'S

nstitutions. He
tion and savvy

Clarkson. "Sid Oland, president of Labatt's [the festival's biggest sponsor], had to fight to get in. Gold patrons who had paid $1,000 were being turned away with their noses pressed against the glass in the pouring rain."

And they were all looking for Bill Marshall, the man who had hit them up for the money—and who had given himself the figurehead role of director general after hiring Clarkson. "There were a lot of pulsing veins in foreheads," Marshall recalls, "a lot of do-you-know-who-I-ams. Unfortunately, we did know who they were and didn't want to talk to them about it."

Maureen O'Donnell, the festival's new publicity director, was in a panic. "I'd never been so terrified in all my life," she recalls. "I'd come from the CBC, and then they throw me into the lion's den with Robert Lantos. I don't know if I've ever felt professionally more out of control." She was standing next to George Anthony inside the doors of the Elgin. "George, I don't know what to do," she said. "Take off your star," he suggested, pointing to the gold-patron brooch that she, along with many of the festival's senior staff, was proudly wearing.

"Bill House and I went out and physically pushed the cro back. People were swinging their umbrellas, throwing punch For a twenty-one-year-old kid, it was heaven. Pushing arou gold patrons dressed to the nines"

Outside, Helga Stephenson, then a publicist working with O'Donnell, displayed the take-charge attitude that she would parlay into the job of festival director nine years later in 1987. She rounded up a dozen gold patrons on the sidewalk, bought them cocktails at the Silver Rail, then herded them up to an overflow screening at the New Yorker. Meanwhile limos rolled up to the Elgin with members of the Canadian Film Awards jury. They were supposed to be judging the film, but they couldn't get in. George Anthony whisked them off to a Chinese restaurant, then on to the New Yorker.

At the Elgin the movie started forty-five minutes late. The audience had to wait for Robert Lantos, director George Kaczender and their stars—who were making a grand entrance in a wet procession of five horse-drawn carriages. This was Lantos's idea. Ever since witnessing the limousine motorcades at red-carpet premieres in Cannes, he had dreamed of his own premiere full of pomp and ceremony. The festival's production manager, Bill House, balked at first when this ebullient arriviste from Montreal requested a caravan of calèches. But as producer of Toronto's innovative Theatre Second Floor—which was as legendary for its parties as for its plays—House liked nothing better than staging a memorable event. Arranging horse-drawn transportation for Lantos marked the beginning of a serendipitous relationship. And before becoming an executive at Alliance Atlantis (the house that Lantos built), as Toronto director of Telefilm Canada, House would be involved in a decade of decisions to fund Lantos productions. Lantos would become the country's most powerful producer. This is not to imply that Lantos got favoured treatment. It's just that in building Alliance he came to understand better than anyone how to play the cultural institutions, from the festival to the funding agencies. He set the mandate of Canadian film and television with a mix of presumption and savvy that would lead some in the industry to dryly refer to him as the Great Helmsman. The Long March to moguldom began with the premiere of *In Praise of Older Women*.

Lantos remembers it as "a night of euphoria." Because it was his first opening, he says, "I've always felt I've had some kind of umbilical cord to the festival. It was an enchanted night for me, riding in the calèche down Yonge Street in the rain, getting to the theatre, seeing the lineup. And what a lineup." Inside the theatre, he had no place to sit. People had torn down the rope cordoning off the reserved seats. There were some two hundred people camped in the aisles.

BILL HOUSE AT THE FESTIVAL'S YORKVILLE OFFICE

Clarkson, dishevelled and soaked with sweat, stood up in front of the audience, which included his parents, and tried to reason with the crowd. He had no microphone. Shouting at the top of his lungs, he implored those without seats to leave, begging them to go up the street to the New Yorker theatre, where the film would show forty-five minutes later. He was met with catcalls and shouts of "fraud" and "shame." He even promised refunds, "whether it's $40 or $50—just leave, please!" Hardly anyone moved, and it was decided to go on with the show. Lantos took the stage with Karen Black, her co-stars and Secretary of State John Roberts, who whipped cheers from the audience with a rousing attack on censorship. "We don't really believe that censors have the right to tell people what they should or should not see," declared the federal minister, safely taking a stand on an issue over which his government had no jurisdiction.

As he spoke, an Ontario Censor Board official was in the projection booth, checking to see that the board's orders were being complied with. Sure enough, as the projectionist loaded the first reel, it was wrapped with the official censor band—a strip of canvas printed with the legislative seal, which was also embossed on the head of the film. But what the projectionist didn't know was that two prints of the film had been delivered to the theatre. "Wayne and I must have changed our minds three times about which print we were going to show," says Marshall. "We finally made our decision and we swore an oath that we would never tell anyone which one we ran. It was a three-martini oath." They now admit they showed the uncut print. But they say the only person who knows the secret of how they deked out the censor board is Martin Heath, the festival's "technical factotum." After two decades, he figures it's now safe to tell the story and put the mystery to rest.

Heath's job of "revising" films usually meant checking for damage and preparing them for projection. But with *In Praise of Older Women*, he was called upon to perform a more radical act of revision. He won't talk about it over the phone. But over lunch at his favourite vegetarian café, with the conspiratorial glint of the alchemist in his eye, he remembers receiving the order from Anne Mackenzie who was in charge of print traffic.

PHOTO: CHRIS HOLLAND

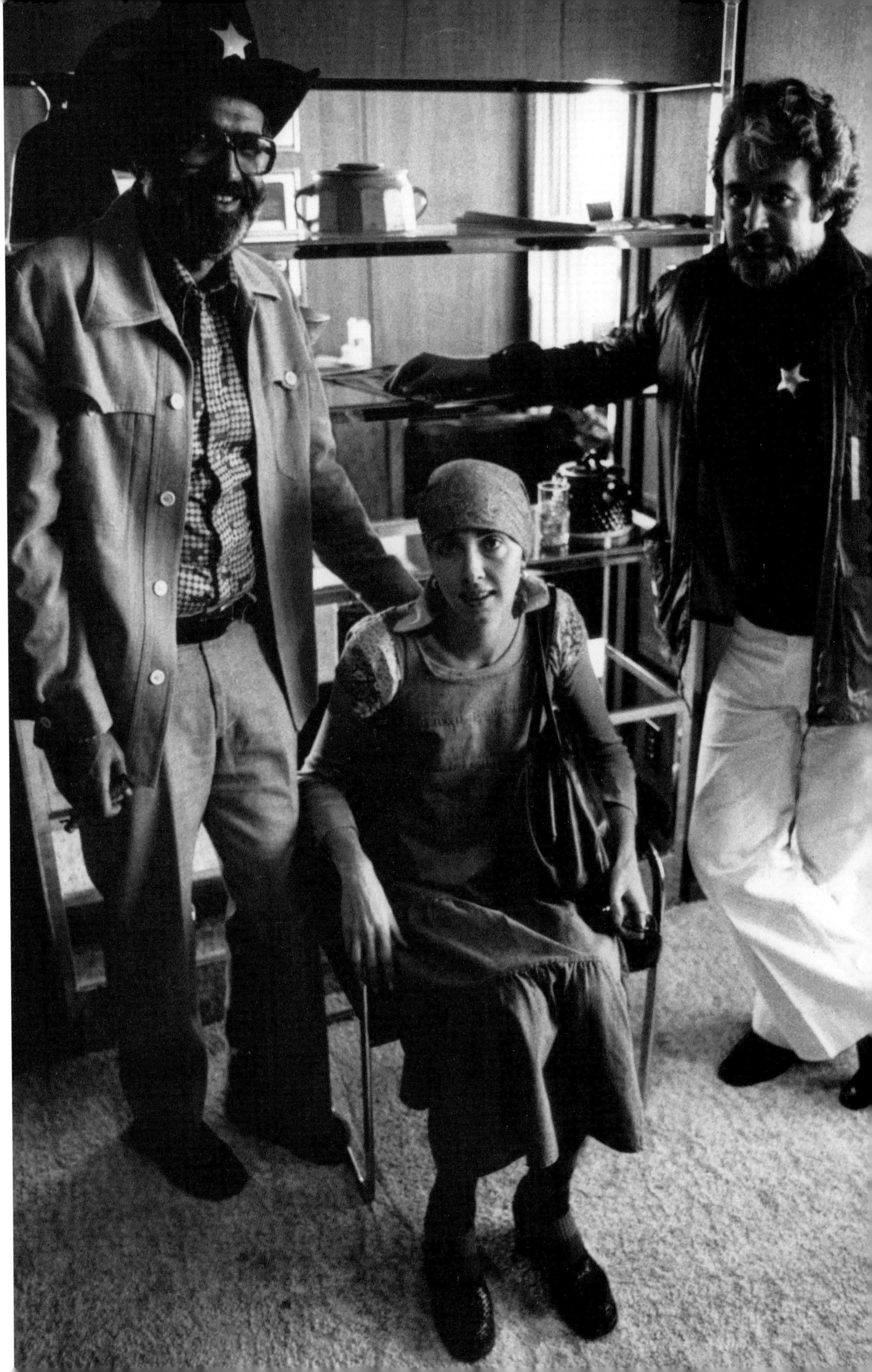

COHL, LINDA BEATH AND MARSHALL, 1977

"Anne Mackenzie said to me, 'Martin, can't you do something?' So I did something. There were two prints and I just switched the reels. The censor's cut was in reel four. I swapped the last half of the two prints. The censored footage just showed a couch jiggling with a sexual rhythm. You couldn't see much. But we were quite worried." With good reason. Anyone tampering with a censored print could face five years in jail and a $5,000 fine.

Both prints were delivered to the theatre. While the uncut print was shown at the premiere, the censored print sat in the lobby, camouflaged in a pair of cans labelled *Wild Strawberries*. Seaton McLean was given the job of "bicycling" the film up to the New Yorker, i.e. transporting it reel by reel as it was projected. "I had a taxi sitting out front of the Elgin," he says. "I would run up the balcony to the booth, wait for the reel to rewind, run down to the cab. We'd drive up Yonge Street, around the back alley to the New Yorker. I'd run up the fire escape with the reel, hand it to the projectionist, back down the fire escape, take the cab back to the Elgin, then go back up to the projection booth for the next reel." He made the round trip four times.

haos at theatres sparked hostility in the press, which Marshall inflamec having the temerity to suggest that "the festival was not oversold was over-attended," and that rude ushers were preferable to the arge policemen" used in Cannes

Meanwhile, as soon as the movie was underway at the Elgin, Marshall and Clarkson retreated next door to the Joe Bird tavern, which was connected to the theatre by passageway. Midway through their first drink, someone walked in to tell them the police wanted to see them in the manager's office. Clarkson quietly panicked. It's all over, he thought. The censor official must have discovered that they're showing the uncut print and reported it to the cops. He asked someone to get the censored print ready to take up to the booth, the one labelled *Wild Strawberries*. His mind was racing as he figured out what to tell the police—"fine, we'll switch the print, and you can send us to jail, but don't interrupt the screening."

Clarkson walked into the manager's office with Marshall and let him do the talking. "Because Bill had been the mayor's assistant," he explains, "and he wasn't intimidated by the police. He walked straight up to the officer and said, 'How do you do, Corporal? My name's Bill Marshall. What seems to be the problem?' The cop says, 'There's a complaint. You have people sitting in the aisles, and if you don't straighten it up, there's a fire hazard.' Well, the look on my face—I just thought, 'Hallelujah and praise the Lord.' Then we pointed out that if we stopped the film, there could be a riot. So we said, 'Please don't make us stop the film. We'll get them out quietly and promise never to do it again.' Or words to that effect. And out he went."

The night ended in a massive party at City Hall. Karen Black showed up late. "Her fake fingernails fell off," recalls Peter Mettler, her limo driver. "We had to go driving around

PHOTO: NANCY ACKERMAN

Yonge Street looking for fingernail glue. Finally we found some at this seedy drugstore beside Sam the Record Man. She was in a really frumpy mood, but when we got to City Hall, there was this transformation. She just became the starlet. I was behind her and she lifted her fur and let it fall to the floor for me to pick up." The party, like the movie, was a crush. With the crowd spilling into Nathan Phillips Square, there was a sense that the festival was taking over the city. (The next day there were complaints about party-goers urinating in the City Hall tribute to the war dead.)

The festival had arrived. For the first time, it felt uncontainable. Clarkson had wanted to give Toronto a popular, non-elitist festival and he had succeeded all too well. That year he had created the I Want It All Pass, a $50 card ($40 for students) that offered entry to any film at any time, plus the opening-night gala and party. "People thought the pass was a guarantee," says Clarkson. "The caveat that Toronto was not used to—because they hadn't been to Cannes—is that we didn't guarantee you could see the film unless you got there early. That's what I failed to grasp. We oversold the theatres and we oversold the passes. And what happened on opening night in 1978 happened again and again. It was horrible. I think Ted Kotcheff's mother got turned away in a wheelchair at the premiere of her own son's movie, *Who is Killing the Great Chefs of Europe?* To this day, the festival's foundation is, in many ways, its biggest conundrum—this terrific public support."

Chaos at theatres sparked hostility in the press, which Marshall inflamed by having the temerity to suggest that "the festival was not oversold, it was over-attended," and that rude ushers were preferable to the "large policemen" used in Cannes. Jay Scott lashed back in *The Globe and Mail*: "To state that a festival which had been advertised as egalitarian, democratic and most of all 'accessible' was superior to Cannes because 'large policemen' did not cart patrons away from screenings for which they had tickets was to display a stunning lack of sensitivity. If there is anything the Festival of Festivals should avoid becoming, it is the Cannes film festival." But Scott went on to praise the organizers for extending the festival with an extra three days of screenings at no extra cost. He also hailed Wayne Clarkson as "a programming genius."

"PARTY" BARB HERSHENHORN, HELEN SHAVER AND DESIGNER ROGER EDWARDS

Writing with eloquence and authority, Scott was quickly establishing himself as Canada's preeminent film writer. Taking an almost proprietary interest in the festival, he became its most ruthless critic and most ardent fan. He wrote about it as if it mattered, documenting its growth with a sense of history. At the end of the 1978 festival, he wrote about "the heartbreak and ecstasy" that heralded a coming of age. "In its third year," he declared, "the Festival of Festivals became one of the biggest and best in the world. It may have hurt, but you know things will never be the same again."

Neither would Robert Lantos.

Despite negative reviews, *In Praise of Older Women* sold around the world and in Canada alone grossed $2 million, double its budget. But aside from launching Lantos as a

player—and introducing Helen Shaver and Alberta Watson—it was not a great milestone for Canadian cinema. It was still a tax-shelter product with a bland American star. The same year, the festival unveiled a variety of dubious offerings by Canadian directors. Martyn Burke hatched *Power Play*, a shabby political thriller starring Peter O'Toole and David Hemmings. R. Martin Walters showed up with *Marie Ann*, only to have its star, Andrée Pelletier, who plays Louis Riel's grandmother, denounce him for turning it into "a Walt Disney film." Les Rose and Richard Gabourie dealt a losing hand of manic depressive realism in *Three Card Monte*. And Ted Kotcheff dished up *Who is Killing the Great Chefs of Europe?*—a half-baked Hollywood confection pairing George Segal and

Jacqueline Bissett that even Kotcheff had trouble getting excited about. Conceding that it was a movie of "limited intentions," Kotcheff discussed the prospect of making films in his native land as a bleak alternative: "After the first flash of success—*Goin' Down the Road*, *Wedding in White*—the Canadian industry has degenerated into making a lot of American B-films."

Our movies did look pretty dismal next to the boldly independent fare showing up from other countries, notably Australia, which was the focus of a sold-out 1978 retrospective featuring work by Fred Schepisi and Bruce Beresford. Schepisi's *The Chant of Jimmie Blacksmith* polarized audiences with the harrowing story of a half-breed Aborigine caught between two cultures who takes murderous vengeance on white women—a far cry from *Marie Ann*'s Disneyfied take on the Métis. Beresford explored another aspect of colonial Australia in *The Getting of Wisdom*, the tale of a defiant teenage girl from the outback who foments rebellion and finds maturity at a snobbish Victorian boarding school. From England, Alan Parker shocked audiences with *Midnight Express*, the visceral tale of an American drug smuggler trapped in a Turkish dungeon. And American director Claudia Weill charmed them with *Girlfriends*, a flight of feminist whimsy starring Melanie Mayron as a photographer with a skittish sense of self-esteem. *Girlfriends* could have been called *In Praise of Smarter Women*; festival audiences voted it most popular film.

The Chant of Jimmie Blacksmith, *Midnight Express*, *Girlfriends*—these were radically different movies, but they bore the conviction of young, fiercely independent directors. And they were all about something. By contrast, Canadian cinema seemed compromised and eager to please, fixated on creating stars and recycling genres. The comparison to Australia would be invoked again and again—here is a country on a similar scale making better movies. Of course, separated from America by more than 6,000 kilometres of water, Australian filmmakers enjoyed an exotic isolation. But in describing their situation in 1978, Schepisi could have been talking about filmmakers in Canada: "It's not going to be possible to cover our costs in Australia any more," he told *The Globe and Mail*'s Katherine Gilday. "We're going to have to make films dealing with our own subjects; in our own voice and with our own people—and somehow sell them on the international market." He questioned the reliance on period settings and rural subjects. "We're an urban society. We fall in love, we have cars that fall apart. We should be making films about what we're doing in the cities. When a country's unsure of its identity it turns to the historical topics first, I guess, in a search for its roots. We're only now about to really come to terms with contemporary subjects."

Schepisi served on the jury of the Canadian Film Awards, which were part of the festival that year. The jury included Robbie Robertson, who had just performed his rock 'n' roll swan song with The Band in Martin Scorsese's *The Last Waltz*. And Robertson gave fes-

"Wayne and I must have changed our minds thre times about which print we were going to show. W finally made our decision and swore an oath that w would never tell anyone which one we ran. It was three-martini oath"

tival organizers their first rude taste of dealing with a major star. Upon arriving, he asked the hotel to block phone calls, then told the press, "I'm here for a serious purpose, to see the nominees, and I don't want to get distracted." Shortly after Robertson had checked into the penthouse suite that the festival had rented for him at the Plaza II, Bill Marshall got a call from the manager telling him that Robertson had ordered up a case of Dom Perignon, the hotel's entire supply. "We were quite prepared to have a reasonable attack on the festival's budget by each of the stars," says Marshall, "but this seemed to be coming a bit fast, ordering the whole stock within an hour of arrival."

Marshall and Clarkson went up to Robertson's suite to investigate and found a full-blown party raging in the middle of the afternoon. Ronnie Hawkins was there, along with a colourful array of local talent. "The room was filled with women," says Clarkson. "It was a true rock 'n' roll fornicatorium." Marshall went up to Robertson and said, "You can have all the champagne you want, but you'll have to pay for it." Then, as Marshall recalls, "I said, 'Robbie, do you realize that at six o'clock tonight and two o'clock tomorrow, you have to go and see these films?' He said 'yes' but not in a really sincere way." In

PHOTO: GAIL HARVEY

fact, Bill House, who organized the Canadian Film Awards that year with Marshall, says, "I wonder if Robbie saw a single movie. He hardly left his hotel room."

But there were occasional sightings. Robertson had a fling with Susan Anspach, who was shooting a movie called *Running* in Toronto with Michael Douglas. The three of them showed up for a festival party at the home of United States consul John Diggins, along with Jackie Burroughs and two hundred other guests. In a dispatch to *Paris Metro*, festival programmer David Overbey wrote: "Robertson insisted he remain incognito: one public appearance, no interviews, and as little contact with audiences and festival staff as possible. As one lady in the press office put it: 'What the hell does he think we invited him for, his cinematic knowledge?' The final straw came when one of the young film students working as chauffeur rebelled. 'Screw him! He wanted me to wait in the car until one in the morning to drive him from 80 Bloor Street to the hotel. I just went home instead.' The hotel is located at 90 Bloor Street."

Robertson's jury gave the prize for best Canadian film to *The Silent Partner*, a caper movie starring Elliott Gould, Christopher Plummer and Susannah York. Oddly enough, it was the only nominee not seen by festival audiences. Catherine O'Hara and John Candy hosted the awards. Marshall McLuhan was among the guests at the party after the show. Robertson had already skipped town.

The most memorable story from the '78 festival, one that has become part of the organization's folklore, involves the infamous briefcase of cocaine. A former festival staffer

THE CHANT OF JIMMIE BLACKSMITH

PETER USTINOV THROTTLING ROBERT RAMSAY

remembers sitting alone one afternoon in the hospitality suite when a local rock personality walked in and inquired as to the whereabouts of a certain celebrity guest. "He had a briefcase with him," recalls the staffer. "I'm not sure why he felt he needed to show it to me—bragging rights, I guess—but he popped open this attaché case, just flashed it open for a second, and it was full of cocaine. Then he went up to the star's suite with it." *In Praise of Older Women* may have introduced Toronto to festival fever, the mad desire to see movies, but while a popular audience was being incubated in the heat of gala premieres, 1978 marked another rite of passage for those backstage: it ushered in the festival's golden age of sex, drugs and rock 'n' roll.

Divine

THE FESTIVAL HAS ALWAYS EMBRACED AT LEAST TW

DIFFERENT CULTURES. IT HAS THE DEVOTEES OF GLITZ WHO LI for the lavish parties, the gala screenings, and the hope of meeting movie star in the flesh. Then there are those who would not be caug dead at a gala, cinephiles who go pearl-diving for brilliant obscuriti that may never be seen outside a festival. The two cultures overlap. Th

BETTE MIDLER, 1980

Madness

PHOTO: ©EVA EVERYTHING 1980

IRA WOHL, DIRECTOR OF BEST BOY, 1979

share a bacchanalian impulse, the urge to push the festival into the night, and a common desire to always be in the right place at the right time. The best movie, the best party, the best conversation. But they share something else, a collective sense of anticipation. Everyone is waiting for the one discovery that will galvanize the festival, the film that comes out of nowhere and sends a universal thrill through the crowd.

That is what happened in 1979 with an unheralded documentary called *Best Boy*. It is an extraordinary coming-of-age story about a fifty-two-year-old "boy" named Philly Wohl, who has the mind of a five-year-old. His cousin, New York director Ira Wohl, spent three years putting his life on film at a time when Philly was forced to become more independent because his aging parents could no longer take care of him. The film spans a universe of emotion, from the delight of seeing Philly backstage at *Fiddler on the Roof*, singing "If I Were a Rich Man" with Zero Mostel, to the pathos of Philly crooning "As Time Goes By" while the camera rests on his dying father. Selected by programmer John Katz, *Best Boy* arrived at the festival without a word of hype. It played three times and received three standing ovations. Critics wrote unanimous raves, and to no one's surprise, it won the People's Choice Award. Then it went on to win the Oscar for best documentary. For the first time, there was a feeling that the festival had made a small, worthy piece of cinematic history. "Up until *Best Boy*, people went out of their way to avoid documentaries," says Katz. "That film broke the ice."

The festival was bigger than ever in 1979, drawing over one hundred thousand people to 150 films. And the annual Trade Forum was launched, corralling the festival's annual debates over the Canadian film industry into an organized event. But 1979 was not a banner year. The festival opened and closed with disappointing movies that boasted token Canadian involvement. The opener was Claude Lelouch's *A nous deux*, a Canada-France co-production starring Catherine Deneuve, and the closer was Norman Jewison's legal satire *...And Justice For All*, with Al Pacino. Donald Sutherland showed up to launch a forgettable caper flick, *A Man, a Woman and a Bank*. Malcolm McDowell checked in for the premiere of *Time After Time*, a Hollywood yarn about H.G. Wells chasing Jack the Ripper through time. Roger Ebert put together a Buried Treasures program that ranged from Martin Scorsese's *Who's That Knocking at My Door?* to Russ Meyer's *Faster, Pussycat! Kill! Kill!* to Fassbinder's *The Marriage of Maria Braun*, which provided a jolt of substance.

THE BAY BOY

On the celebrity front, however, the '79 festival offered a tangle of intrigue that sent gossip columnists into bold-face overdrive. A sample scenario: Six Million Dollar Man Lee Majors, on the rebound from Farrah Fawcett, squires ballerina Karen Kain to a festival soiree (saying, "It's quite a responsibility going out with Canada's national treasure, but then I was married to America's") while Farrah's new fiancé, Ryan O'Neill, comes to Toronto to visit his daughter, Tatum O'Neill, who's playing jail bait to Richard Burton in *Circle of Two*, produced by Bill Marshall, who intervenes to prevent a drunken punch-up at a party between Ryan and Richard. . . .

hen you ask filmmakers to dredge through their memories of the early ys at the festival, they talk about the hospitality suite with the same r of nostalgic affection that comes over people when they talk about odstock or the Summer of Love

Toronto journalists felt they had died and gone to heaven—literally, when they found themselves mingling with celebrities *in* Heaven, a basement disco that hosted festival parties. A dizzy Bruce Blackadar tried to sum up his confusion in *The Toronto Star*: "When the last disco number had been played, the last joint smoked, the last deal signed, there was this, finally, to say about the Festival of Festivals. It has sent Toronto into the big-time ozone of showbiz. . . . The whole week was a moveable feast. It was disorganized, well-run, boring, crazily exciting, endless, finished too soon, choked with gossip, smoothly discreet, a massive drunk, a cool business-like procedure, devoted to the art of films, devoted to the art of money. It was anything you were looking for; it was anything you made it." Blackadar was actually filling in for *Toronto Star* movie critic Ron Base, who was so close to the action that he'd stopped reporting on it altogether. Base was fed up with his editors complaining about festival coverage. "They kept saying it's elitist and snobby," recalls *Star* columnist Sid Adilman. "And Ron was so furious about this attitude, he went out on a bender with Lee Majors and just disappeared for a couple of days."

ART GARFUNKEL AND THERESA RUSSELL, 1980

At the festival, there was no shortage of opportunities to leave the outside world behind. The parties ranged from Heaven's basement to the summit of the CN Tower, but at the end of the night all roads led to the hospitality suite, a hotel room with a free bar that was open to filmmakers, distributors, media, staff and anyone who could talk their way past the door. The rules were: anything goes and everything is off the record. It was soon dubbed the hostility suite. One year, Roger Ebert was booked into the room next door. As a party raged until four in the morning, he finally complained to front desk. "They phoned and told us to keep it down," recalls *The Toronto Star*'s Rob Salem, who was among the revellers along with his colleague Rita Zekas. "Three phone calls later, fifteen people lined up on the adjoining wall and pounded it with their fists for about five minutes. Ebert, to his credit, did not complain again. But he changed his room the next day."

The festival has since grown much too large to have a single suite where everyone who presumes to be anyone can converge at the end of the night. And people miss the intimacy. All over the world, when you ask filmmakers to dredge through their memories of the early days at the Festival of Festivals, they talk about the hospitality suite with the same blur of nostalgic affection conjured up by Woodstock or the Summer of Love. But this was not the sixties, it was the eighties. The coke years.

There are all kinds of stories, stories of stars in the bathroom doing blow or getting blow jobs or both. John Allen, who would end the night as a bouncer at the hospitality suite after working as a bouncer at the galas, has more stories than it is safe to tell. Maybe some are apocryphal, maybe not. He remembers Johnny, "this big black guy who served as the one-man entourage for a visiting star." Johnny was in the hospitality suite "whacking back this amyl nitrate in one hand and this big brandy glass full of cocaine in the other." Demonstrating how the star preferred to do drugs, recalls Allen, "he put his nose in the glass and came up with his face covered in coke."

Then there was the sex. These were the twilight years of casual sex, just before AIDS cast its long shadow. And for John Allen, being part of the festival inner circle was akin to being on the road with an outrageously popular rock band. When he was managing the Elgin theatre, he says he used to have sex in the back row, just under the projection booth. Later he found a way of getting upstairs into the bower-like Winter Garden theatre, which had been abandoned for decades. "Nobody had been in there since just after the war," he says, "and there had been a fire. So the whole Winter Garden was covered in this white foam from the fire extinguishers. All the fake trees and fake foliage, and this 1909 projector in the back, were all covered with this white snow. It was the perfect place to (a) do coke and (b) have sex. I remember doing the coke off the railing of this beautiful wood-panelled balcony and then having sex standing up in the projection booth. That girl was a volunteer working with the festival. Later she married a guy with money who became a patron. Years later we'd meet at the festival and laugh about it—our little knee-trembler."

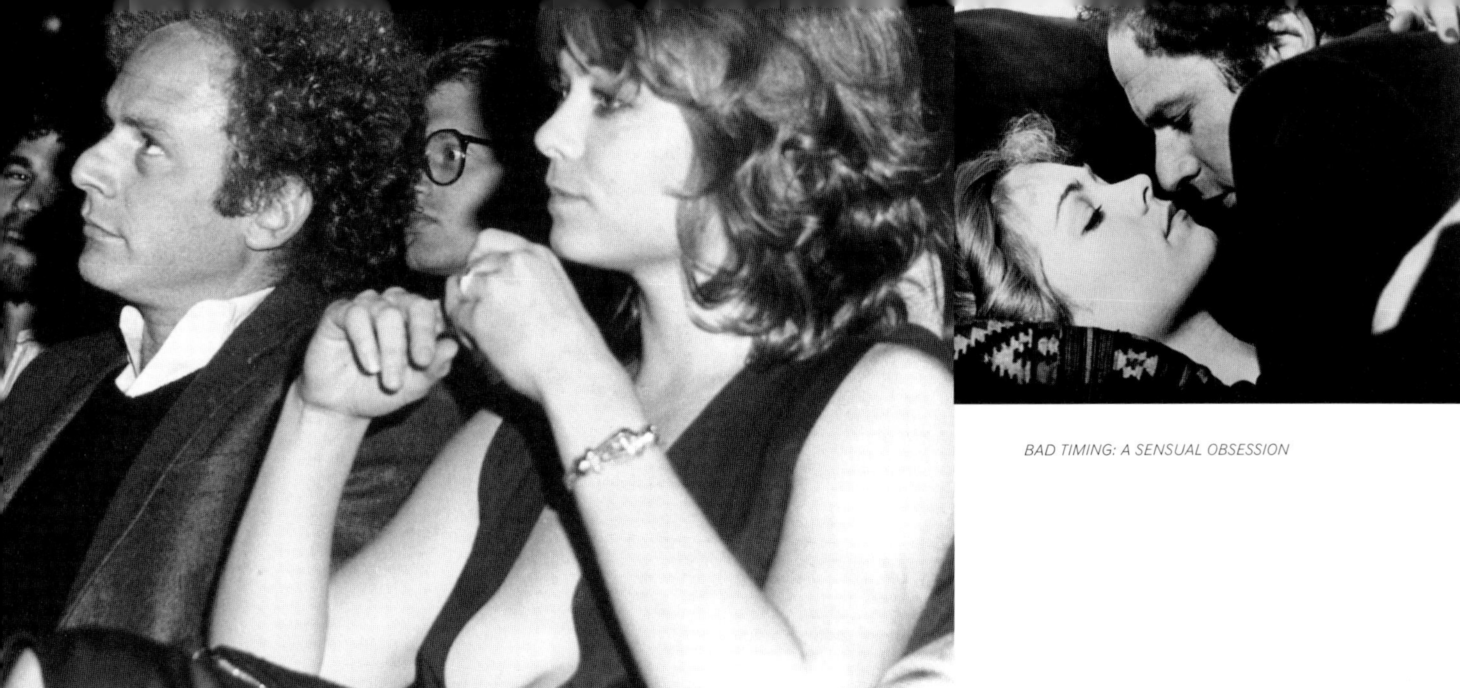

BAD TIMING: A SENSUAL OBSESSION

heresa comes up to me and says, 'Why don't we slip out?' So we slip t, and have sex against the wall of the stairwell. I remember thinking, sh this was on camera. Nobody's going to believe me"

Theresa Russell and Art Garfunkel were at the festival with director Nicolas Roeg for the 1980 premiere of *Bad Timing: A Sensual Obsession*. The movie is a romantic intrigue, but not of the comic variety. Garfunkel plays a research psychiatrist in Vienna, a coldly rational soul who becomes involved with an impulsive vixen played by Russell. The story begins with her attempted suicide and jockeys between flashbacks of their volatile love affair and an interrogation of the psychiatrist conducted by a hard-headed cop (Harvey Keitel). Graphically intercutting images of Russell in surgery with Russell having sex, *Bad Timing* unfolds like an autopsy of erotomania.

During their visit to the festival, Roeg and Russell were a couple, although he was about twice her age. A festival employee who prefers to remain anonymous—we'll call him Sean—remembers meeting them both while test-screening the movie at the Elgin. During the premiere, they had drinks at the restaurant next door. "Nick would get up and go next door to the theatre to see how the film was doing," recalls Sean. "And Theresa and I had this thing. There was instant heat. I said, 'I've never fucked a movie star before.' And she laughed. I knew I was in. Later that night at the hospitality suite, I was getting smashed. Nicky had gone to bed. And Theresa comes up to me and says, 'Why don't we slip out?' So we slip out, go down the stairwell, and have sex against the wall of the stairwell. I remember thinking, I wish this was on camera. Nobody's going to believe me."

Six Million Dollar Man Lee Majors, on the rebound from Farrah Faw Kain to a festival soiree: "It's quite a responsibility going out with treasure, but then I was married to America's"

PHOTO: SYLVIA TRAIN/THE TORONTO SUN

At the end of the festival, at the awards brunch, Russell was presented with a festival jacket. "If you don't mind," she said, "I'd like to give it to someone here who has been very good to me." And she handed Sean the jacket. "I couldn't believe it," he says. "It was such a moment of incredible largesse. I have the jacket at home, still." In *Bad Timing*, curiously, there is a sex scene in a stairway, in which Milena (Russell) angrily rips off her clothes and throws herself at Alex (Garfunkel) in the middle of a fight. Could Sean's memory possibly be a transference from the film? No, he insists, he never had a chance to see the whole film—he was too distracted by its star.

Bad Timing is one of Roeg's most disturbing works, along with *Performance* and *Don't Look Now*, and certainly the darkest film ever to win the People's Choice Award at the Toronto festival. The plot's intrigue is resolved with a scene of Alex ravishing the unconscious, overdosed Milena after carefully cutting through her underclothes with a penknife. With that sound of slow tearing cloth, Garfunkel's image of choirboy innocence, the sweet tenor singing "The Sounds of Silence," seemed lost forever. Roeg, who had messed with Mick Jagger in *Performance*, and outed David Bowie's inner alien in *The Man Who Fell to Earth*, had held a mirror up to another pop star and watched it shatter.

Looking back on the festival at the dawn of the eighties, anyone investigating the death of rock 'n' roll might conclude that it had found a vampirish afterlife in the movies. In 1979, The Who played a reunion concert in Cannes to mark the premiere of *Quadrophenia*, a mods-and-rockers drama based on the album. Bill House actually tried to hire the band to stage a repeat performance at the Toronto festival, but The Who's manager told him, "They don't need the money." When a deal to show *Quadrophenia* as a Toronto gala fell through at the last minute, it was replaced by the concert documentary *Rust Never Sleeps*, in which Neil Young drags rock 'n' roll kicking and screaming into middle age with that song about Johnny Rotten. By 1980 there seemed to be an exodus of pop stars to film. Blondie's Deborah Harry made her screen debut as a bored, unblonded housewife in Mark Reichert's *Union City*. And Bette Midler played queen of the new vaudeville in her concert film, *Divine Madness*.

CHRIS MAKEPEACE AND MAJORS TÊTE-À-TÊTE WITH KAIN, 1979

squires Karen
da's national

The festival also presented nine rock/pop movies in a program called New Music, which could have been more accurately titled Epitaphs for a Doomed Generation. The offerings ranged from *AC/DC: Let There Be Rock*, which captured the stage antics of AC/DC singer Bon Scott shortly before he died of alcohol poisoning, to *D.O.A.*, a chronicle of the Sex Pistols' U.S. tour showing the soon-to-be-late Sid Vicious nodding out on smack in mid-interview. The Sex Pistols resurfaced in Julien Temple's *The Great Rock 'n' Roll Swindle*, a reckless documentary that credits Malcolm McLaren with inventing the band and turning punk into an iconic, self-annihilating commodity (a claim that Johnny Rotten would challenge two decades down the road in Temple's second documentary on the band, *The Filth and the Fury*). Highlights include outtakes from an aborted Russ Meyer film, *Who Killed Bambi?*, which show Sid Vicious getting out of bed, shaking his Nazi cod-piece in a full-length mirror and digging a broken bottle into his chest as he sings an early-morning ditty about "being rude." The Ontario Censor Board took exception—not to that, but to a four-second shot of a man's bare butt engaged in what might have been intercourse. *The Great Rock 'n' Roll Swindle* was one of the most controversial films ever programmed at the festival: the audience expressed its approval by ripping up seats in the theatre.

DIVINE MADNESS

The demise of the counterculture received calmer treatment in a first feature by a twenty-nine-year-old American unknown named John Sayles. *The Return of the Secaucus Seven*, an embryonic *Big Chill*, is about a weekend reunion of seven aging sixties radicals coping with the compromises of adult life. Sayles, who made the film for just $60,000, was taken aback by its enthusiastic response. "I wrote the script in a week and a half and looked on it as an exercise," he said during his visit to the festival. "It was never meant for commercial release—I made it as an audition piece." Apparently, he got the job.

PHOTO: BARRIE GRAY/THE TORONTO SUN

By 1980, the festival had come into its own as a three-ring circus, an event that could pay homage to James Coburn, Jean-Luc Godard and Bette Midler with equal sincerity.

Coburn was ubiquitous. His ferocious grin lit up the opening-night party for *Loving Couples*—he played a surgeon married to Shirley MacLaine who sleeps with his wife's lover (Susan Sarandon). The next night he was back at it, riding a grey Rolls Royce to the premiere of *Mr. Patman*—he played a male nurse in a psychiatric ward who sleeps with a colleague (Kate Nelligan). Coburn, who had churned out five movies in eighteen months, shrugged off questions about the quality of the work ("I'm a hooker like everyone else") while coolly observing that *Mr. Patman* had "lost a lot of its charm and character" since he saw the first script.

An earnest drama about a man patrolling the border of sanity and losing his grip, *Mr. Patman* is a *One Flew Over the Cuckoo's Nest* that never takes flight. Although it is not such a bad film, this Bill Marshall production reflects everything that was wrong with English-Canadian cinema at the end of the tax-shelter era (1975–79). Directed by British veteran John Guillermin (*King Kong*, *Death on the Nile*), it is a producer's mish-mash of available talents that seem oddly out of their element. (James Coburn as a sensitive nurse?) The mood is bittersweet depression, and the story floats in a kind of netherworld, without an author's voice or a sense of location. The same kind of aimlessness afflicts Robin Spry's *Suzanne*, a fifties piece starring Jennifer Dale as a pregnant rape victim caught between her French and English roots. Its co-producer Robert Lantos, who had such a euphoric time launching *In Praise of Older Women* two years earlier, got a rude shock when the festival audience greeted his second feature with boos and derisive laughter. Jay Scott added insult to injury, writing, "*Suzanne* is supposed to be about a young woman growing up with the benefits of two cultures; it's a movie hatched without the benefit of any."

Filmmakers from French Quebec, however, continued to offer strong, personal films. Francis Mankiewicz's intimate masterpiece, *Les bons débarras*, introduced Charlotte Laurier as a thirteen-year-old gamine locked in a battle of wills with her mother in a Laurentian village. And Micheline Lanctôt made an impressive directing debut with *L'Homme à tout faire* (*The Handyman*), an adroit romance starring Andrée Pelletier.

Coburn was u
The next nigh
He'd churnec
quality—"I'm

It seemed that, while Quebec was busy making films, English Canada was busy making deals, and its producers were growing weary of trying to defend the results. At the Trade Forum's ritual inquiry into the health of Canadian cinema, author Mordecai Richler and producer Bill Marshall—who shared few cultural values aside from a fondness for Scotch—waded into a verbal slugfest. Richler accused Marshall of making "home movies" for an industry rife with "unbelievably bad taste and larded with greed." Marshall retaliated by accusing Richler of mining an exhausted literary vein while living off the screen rights to unproduced scripts of his novels. "Mordecai Richler," he sniffed.

ous. His ferocious grin lit up the opening-night party for Loving Couples
vas back at it, riding a grey Rolls Royce to the premiere of Mr. Patman.
five movies in eighteen months, and shrugged off questions abou
oker like everyone else”

“I buy his book every time he writes it.”

For some, the biggest star to attend the festival in 1980 was not Bette Midler, but Jean-Luc Godard. Oblivious to the skirmishes of Canada’s cultural industries, this short, balding icon of the French New Wave talked about the pointlessness of artistic integrity if it

PHOTO: BRIAN WILLER/MACLEAN'S

JEAN-LUC GODARD

didn't pay the rent. Godard showed up for a massive retrospective of his work—as well as films that influenced him and films influenced by him. Wayne Clarkson came up with the idea and hired his Ottawa friend Peter Harcourt, who taught film at Carleton University, to curate it. Harcourt assembled a kaleidoscopic programme of forty-four features, including twenty-three by Godard. (Acquiring the prints was a logistical nightmare, and a number of them never arrived.) Harcourt also composed the most erudite introduction ever published in the programme book, a three-thousand-word essay about paradox and allusion in Godard that jived through myriad references, including Mozart, Stravinsky, Baudelaire, Picasso, Sartre, Brecht, Bergman, Bresson, T.S. Eliot, Sam Fuller, Arthur Koestler, Bob Fosse and Busby Berkeley.

To lure Godard from Switzerland, Harcourt had to undergo a tortuous series of negotiations, which ended with Godard demanding a cash payment of a thousand American dollars. Harcourt finally consented with great reluctance—"What really got my Canadian goat is that he wanted it in U.S. currency." On the day of the director's arrival, Harcourt declined the offer of a limousine and set off with a friend in his rusted Volkswagen to pick up Godard at the airport. "I saw this tired guy, bent over, waiting for me with his bags," he recalls. Godard was only forty-nine, but he had been ill and did not look well. Trying to protect him from the press, Harcourt took the filmmaker with some friends to a small French restaurant in the Annex. Everyone ordered in French, except Godard, who ordered in English. Roger Ebert had managed to join the group, and, notepad in hand, he kept waiting for an appropriate moment for an interview, while

JACK LEMMON MAKING CONTACT WHILE GINO EMPRY LOOKS ON

Harcourt did his best to thwart him. Finally Ebert managed to ask a question, one concerning the 360-degree tracking shot towards the end of *Weekend*, in which the camera circles one way, then the other, then back again. Harcourt recalls the encounter in his memoir, *A Canadian Journey, Conversations with Time*: "'I love that moment,' Roger cooed. 'It always gives me great pleasure. But why did you do it? Why did you move the camera back again?' 'Perhaps dhat ees why I dheed eet,' Jean-Luc replied, 'to geeve a leetle pleazuh to peeple in Chicago.'"

That night, after a screening of *Breathless*, Harcourt introduced Godard to the cheering audience as "the man who changed the language of film." The director seemed startled by the enthusiastic reception. "If I am well known," he mused, "it amazes me because I've done nothing but commercial failures." A weary sphinx, Godard fielded questions with statements such as "I'm not an airport but an airplane—I'm interested in movement." Of course, there were Big Questions. One audience member went so far as to ask, "Why do we die?" Harcourt stepped in to set the record straight: "This isn't God," he said, "It's Godard."

It was left to Bette Midler to play God. And she rose to the task. On closing night, hundreds of fans mobbed the University Theatre to get a glimpse of the Divine Miss M. Midler arrived fashionably late, sending the crowd into a frenzy as she sashayed past the blaze of cameras. Inside the theatre, the audience applauded every turn of her screen performance as if they were watching it live onstage. In *Divine Madness*, Midler comes across as a rock 'n' roll Mae West, splitting the difference between James Brown and Janis Joplin. She had paid her dues playing New York's Continental baths, a dame repatriating the role of drag queen, and here she was high-stepping into the mainstream and giving Hollywood a big wet kiss on the mouth.

e festival had come into its own as a three-ring circus, one that coul
y homage to James Coburn, Jean-Luc Godard and Bette Midler wit
ual sincerity

In time, Midler would become part of the firmament, another pop diva singing sentimental ballads and mugging her way through romantic comedies. But at the dawn of the eighties, she was busy setting the world on fire with a combustible mix of irony and excess, which would become the decade's most celebrated values. If Jean-Luc Godard was the inscrutable artist—the pioneer of deconstruction deconstructing his own celebrity—Bette Midler was celebrity incarnate, a mock movie star who had wrapped herself in self-reflection as if it were so much gold lamé. Somewhere between them, between high art and high camp, the festival would seek a balance. And in David Overbey, it found a burlesque provocateur who blithely embodied both.

Divas

AT A FESTIVAL THAT HAS SEEN MORE THAN ITS SHARE O
ICONOCLASTS, NONE WAS MORE MEMORABLY OUTRAGEOUS THA
David Overbey. He was a walking contradiction. A gay intellectu
from Arkansas. A PhD in 19th-century literature who worshipp
Maria Montez of the camp classic Cobra Woman. *A big, bald man*
blue denim and high-heeled cowboy boots who believed that Be
Davis had occupied his body after her death. To those who knew hi
the claim did not seem far-fetched. The resemblance, says his frier

DAVID OVERBEY AND HENRI BÉHAR IN CANNES

WHO'S
MOVING
PICTURES?

programmer David McIntosh, was "uncanny, from the dangerous, accusing cigarette and the look of bemused disdain to the sharpest and wittiest of put-downs—there were those who called him Bette David."

He was a tall man with oyster eyes that rolled between affection and contempt behind thick glasses. He chain-smoked Gitanes, drank like a fish, and counted his coke dealer among his intimates. He was a festival gypsy with no fixed address for much of his life, and no money to speak of, but who possessed a network of contacts and kindred spirits from Manila to Paris that kept him on a permanent world tour. And as programmer with the Toronto festival for two decades, he left an indelible signature.

David Overbey was born in Detroit, raised in Arkansas, wrote a doctorate on Dickens—then taught literature and film at the Chico campus of the University of California, where he was an anti-war, pro-gay activist. He edited a well-received book on Italian cinema, *Springtime in Italy: A Reader on Neo-Realism*. He was also a huge fan of Fritz Lang (*Metropolis*), and after inviting the director to visit the university they became lasting friends. In the early 1970s, Overbey followed a lover to Paris, although he always claimed it was an allergy to Ronald Reagan that drove him from California. In Paris, Lang introduced David O. to directors Claude Chabrol and François Truffaut, and to Henri Langlois and Lotte Eisner of the Cinémathèque Française. The expatriate Overbey launched a new career by going to parties. He became a journalist at the English-language paper *Passion*—owned by Roots partners Michael Budman and Don Green—working first as a gossip columnist, then a film critic.

"*Passion* was both opinionated and irreverent," says French journalist Henri Béhar. "No doubt David helped set the tone, for he was both, championing unknown films or smashing undeserving icons with the élan of a true pamphleteer." Béhar remembers meeting him at a press screening in Paris. "David cut an impressive figure. Almost like a drawing, if not a cartoon. The thick glasses, the bald pate, shiny and tan, and the hair sticking up at the back of his neck. Years later, when we did some television together, my cameraman took one look at him and decided to film him like 'a mischievous Buddha.'" That, adds Béhar, is "as good a definition of David as any, I guess."

Wayne Clarkson first met Overbey in 1975 at the Cannes festival when Overbey tried to pick him up at a press conference. Clarkson was there scouting for Filmexpo, the Canadian Film Institute's festival in Ottawa. They agreed to go to dinner, and "naive as I was," says Clarkson, "I ended up back in his room, ostensibly for David to pick up a jacket or something." Overbey made a pass, "and I think it became apparent to both of us that it wasn't going to work out. We went on to dinner and have been friends ever since." Their Cannes was far removed from the world of high rollers on the Carlton terrace frequented by Bill and Dusty. Clarkson stayed at the Hôtel de Rose, which charged forty-four francs a night for bed and breakfast. A struggling young director named David Cronenberg was in the room next to him. "In those first years," says Clarkson, "I never went near the beach. You saw at least five movies a day. David introduced me to a lot of

Quebec critics. And we all met every day for lunch in the same place, some cheap little dive by the train station—David Overbey and I and a coterie of the French press."

Clarkson hired Overbey to help out with Filmexpo, then recommended him to Linda Beath, who hired him to create a European programme for the Toronto festival in 1977. It included a dozen films, ranging from Rainer Werner Fassbinder's *Chinese Roulette* to Chabrol's *Alice ou la dernière fugue*. Overbey's preface in the programme book reads like a manifesto, damning Hollywood movies, questioning generalizations such as "New Wave" and "film noir"—and quoting a sweeping definition of the artist by Joseph Conrad, as someone who speaks to "the subtle but invincible conviction of solidarity that knits together the loneliness of innumerable hearts to the solidarity in dreams, in joy, in sorrow, in aspirations, in illusions, in hope, in fear, which binds men to each other, which binds together all humanity—the dead to the living and the living to the unborn."

It was, to say the least, a defiant set of criteria for selecting films. Overbey had singular tastes, which were not always popular, but his love for the unorthodox kept the festival on the cutting edge of world cinema. And he found both an ally and a friend in Jay Scott. In 1978, when Overbey brought German actress Ingrid Caven to Toronto for a programme of films by Swiss director Daniel Schmid, Scott reacted as if the festival had finally imported a star worth getting excited about, a goddess of the avant-garde. "On stage, echoes of Garbo; on screen echoes of Dietrich," he rhapsodized about Caven, before going on to describe the tangle of relationships behind Schmid's "crowning, controversial masterpiece," *Shadows of Angels*, in which the gay director cast Caven as a whore while Fassbinder, the actress's ex-husband, played her bisexual pimp and Fassbinder's Argentine boyfriend, set designer Raul Edoardo Gimenez, played one of her johns. "In North America, people would find the fact that you are all friends a bit strange," Scott suggested to Caven during one of Overbey's late-night soirees at Bemelman's restaurant. "Well," she mused, puffing on a long cigarette holder, "in Europe they find us strange, too. It's normal that they find us strange."

Overbey's Critic's Choice programme became the festival's mainstay of non-commercial cinema. In 1980, the size of the programme was doubled, prompting Scott to write: "At 18 movies strong, it more than anything else determines the tenor of the festival—conceived as an alternative to the 'gala' presentations, it is now twice as large as the thing to which it was meant to provide an alternative." Overbey refused to play to the crowd. Although his screenings were well attended, he said he would programme a film even if just seventy-five people wanted to see it. When English-subtitled prints were unavailable, Overbey offered *Jaguar*, from the Philippines, and Cuba's *The Strange Case of Rachel K* in their original languages of Tagalog and Spanish. "Come and watch the pictures," he said. "If you can't figure out what's going on, you ought to give up going to movies."

Most major festivals select films through an official government organization. "But David always went his own way," says Clarkson. "He'd often pass on the major film that the agency representatives were flogging." In the case of Lino Brocka's *Jaguar*, a raw look at life in the slums of Manila, Overbey programmed it in Toronto after Philippine first lady Imelda Marcos managed to suppress it everywhere else in the world aside from Cannes. When the unsubtitled print of the movie promised in 1980 never arrived, he showed it the following year.

JAGUAR

Overbey would become instrumental in introducing Asian cinema to North America. He championed the Philippine cinema of Brocka and Mike De Leon before most of the world had heard of it. Brocka's class-conscious melodramas, where sex and politics crudely rubbed up against each other, appealed to Overbey's outlaw esthetic. He also had an abiding passion for Hong Kong cinema long before it was fashionable. He introduced the operatic martial art of John Woo to festival audiences with *A Better Tomorrow* (1986). He celebrated the kinetic reveries of Wong Kar-wai (*Fallen Angels, Chungking Express*). And he discovered Sylvia Chang, the Hong Kong actress/writer/director who became the exception to the rule in an industry run by men.

PHOTO: MICHAEL LIBBY

LINO BROCKA, 1987

Hong Kong–born Wayne Wang has visited the festival with eight films, including *Slam Dance*, *Joy Luck Club*, *Blue in the Face* and *Anywhere but Here*. But even before coming to Toronto he knew Overbey from his home town. "He made a very big impression on me," says Wang. "He was such a character. We talked about looking for opium. He knew more about Hong Kong than I did in terms of the nooks and crannies. I grew up in the areas he talked about and didn't know things that he knew. David had such an open, adventurous spirit about finding things in Hong Kong. He was willing to go into the dark corners and have a good time. And he saw something in those John Woo films. Maybe I was too close to that culture. I thought, they're so over the top, but the sense of artificiality and going beyond it—the campiness—was part of David Overbey as well." Wang remembers having late-night discussions about Shu-sun Chiu, the director who inspired Woo. "He made all those sword-fighting movies, the one where the guy is slashed across the stomach and he fights on, with his guts spilling out, for another fifteen minutes. He was well known to be gay and he had all these pretty young men in his movies. David was really into that."

Overbey's love of camp reached its apotheosis with Lothar Lambert, a taboo-busting Berliner who dashed off kinky, disposable features with budgets ranging from $2,000 to $20,000 and titles such as *Fucking City* and *Dirty Daughters*. With his nipple-tweaking trash art, Lambert brought a slice of Berlin decadence to Toronto, where he was fêted with his own retrospective in 1982. But Overbey's idiosyncratic tastes had as many detractors as fans. Among them was James Quandt. Years before he became the esteemed head of the festival's Cinematheque Ontario, when he was freelancing for the *Saskatoon StarPhoenix*, Quandt reviewed the 1981 festival: "Some of the programming was simply perverse: the abysmal quality of several films in David Overbey's Critic's Choice series was matched only by the hype which accompanied them. By the end of the festival, the audiences who were seduced by Overbey's hype, and who sat through a number of catastrophes, were out for his blood."

the case of Lino Brocka's Jaguar*, Overbey programmed it in Toront*
ter Philippine first lady Imelda Marcos managed to suppress i
erywhere else in the world aside from Cannes

That year, however, Overbey could take credit for one of the festival's most triumphant discoveries. *Diva* is a stylish crime story of a Parisian postman and a black American opera singer. This striking first feature by Jean-Jacques Beineix, a young French director, had sunk without a trace at the box office in France. But Overbey saw the film in Paris, adored it and wanted to bring it to Toronto. Serge Silberman, who controlled international sales, refused. In fact, he sent Beineix a letter forbidding him to show the film in any North American festival. It was deemed not good enough to be on the list of French movies available for the international circuit. But that only strengthened Overbey's resolve. He promised to steal the print if he had to.

Twenty years later, Beineix sits in his office in Paris and recalls the bizarre course of events that set his career in motion. "David Overbey did something extraordinary," he says, speaking in French, and choosing his words with the surgical precision that Parisians bring to language and food. "David was a very persuasive individual and he

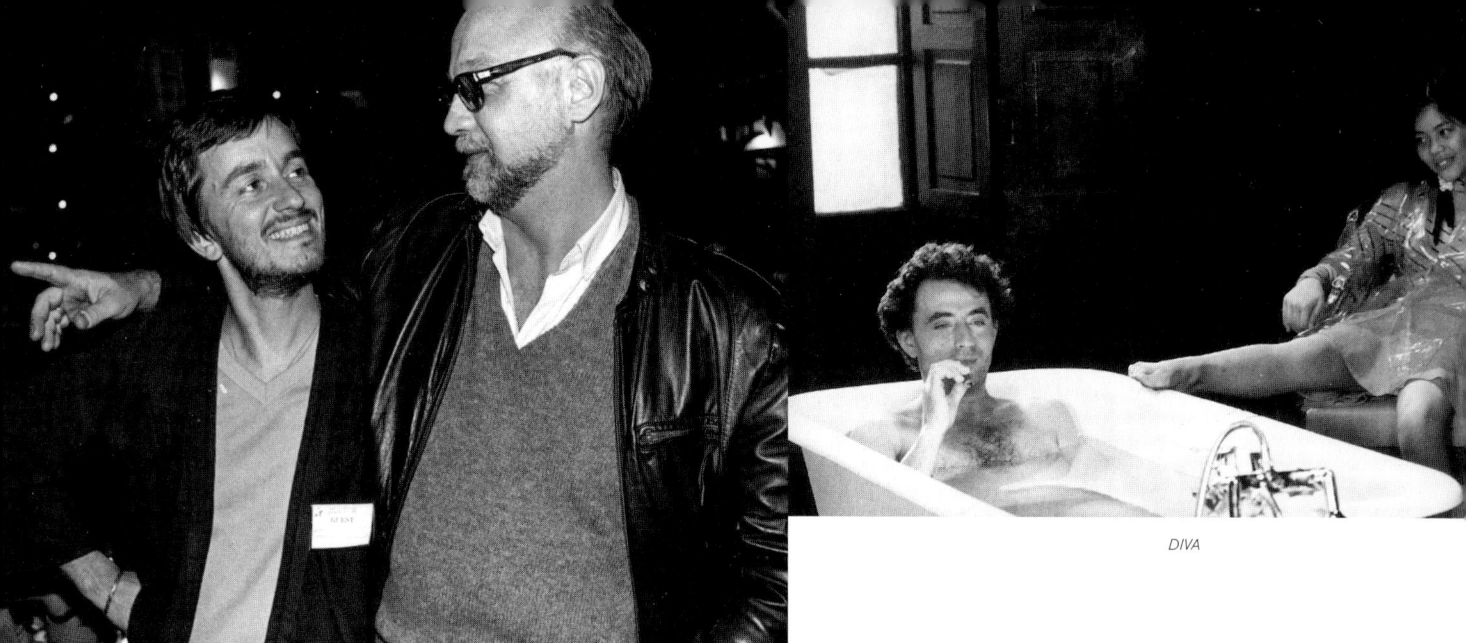

DIVA

JEAN-JACQUES BEINEIX AND OVERBEY

PHOTO: GAIL HARVEY

liked the film enormously. He sent Serge Silberman a telegram saying: 'Serge, you promised to give me the film a few months ago. And now you're refusing. But do you remember that I interviewed you on the subject of Luis Buñuel, and at that time you said something marvelous about Luis Buñuel, which is that he was a man of his word. *Will you be able to follow the example of Luis Buñuel?*' All of a sudden, Serge Silberman gave me the authorization to go to the Toronto festival. And I remember very well at this time certain French producers saying, 'You're going to Toronto? Where's that? There's a festival in Toronto?'"

Beineix arrived in Toronto the day *Diva* was to screen at the festival. "I introduced the film in *un anglais approximatif*," he recalls, "then I left with David to a bar nearby, and we had a few beers." When he returned to the theatre for the closing credits, to see the audience standing and cheering, he couldn't believe it. "It was six in the morning for me, I was totally jet-lagged—I showed up in this theatre and people were on their feet. It was *extra-or-di-naire*. I was *born* on that day, that night," says Beineix. "I was standing in front of this room and I didn't know what was happening. I'd never experienced anything like it. People were coming up and shaking my hand. Women were looking at me. I thought, 'It's six in the morning, I must surely be in my bed dreaming, having a nightmare.' Then we went out to a party, the hostess wouldn't let go of me." The party was at the French ambassador's house, where the guests included David Gilmour, who has fond memories of drinking with Beineix. "The ambassador's wife," says Gilmour, "got terribly, terribly drunk and came on to me, and then came on to him in such an outrageous fashion that the maid was finally dispatched to pull us out of the party. My memory is of leaving the party and seeing Beineix being smothered by this French ambassador's wife."

Beineix remembers getting back to his hotel close to dawn. "I was exhausted. I'd been up for twenty-four hours. But then in the hotel corridor I saw this *fille ravissante* smiling at me. I turned around. I thought she was looking at someone behind me. Then she said, 'Your film was wonderful, I want to talk to you,' etc. I said, 'Okay, let's go to the hospitality suite.' But the suite was closed. I said, 'Listen, I know this isn't done, but I'm going to suggest we go to my room. The festival has given me a bottle of wine. We can drink it together.' So we drank the bottle and did a lot of other things."

She wasn't the only one trying to seduce Beineix. After the screening, he was besieged by distributors wanting to buy the rights to *Diva*. "Earlier Serge Silberman had shown the film to the Americans at screenings in New York," he says, "and the same people said, 'Yes, it's not bad, but how are we going to market it?' This horrifying line that we're still hearing today—*how can we market it?* We should bring the death penalty for those who utter such nonsense in cinema! The Toronto festival created an extraordinary response to this idiotic question: *ask the audience*.

"So I owe Toronto some marvellous memories," Beineix concludes. "It was in Toronto that I became a director with an international audience." *Diva* was bought by U.A. Classics and became an art-house hit in North America and around the world. Remarkably, the film was also re-released in France, where it had initially bombed, and the second time around it scored commercial and critical success, winning four Cesars. This was an astonishing turn of events: a festival in Toronto picks a movie from the dumpster of French cinema, resurrects it, and sends it back to France in triumph.

Diva is very much a film of its time. *Miami Vice* would resynthesize pop culture by blending cops and robbers with hot colours, cool drugs, high fashion and pop music, but Beineix did it three years earlier in *Diva*. The film's haywire plot concerns a young postman on a moped named Jules (Frédéric Andréi), who makes a pirate recording of his soprano idol (Wilhelmenia Wiggins Fernandez), which gets mixed up with a tape of incriminating evidence from a dead prostitute. As the postie, Andréi has the ingenuous appeal of a nouveau Jean-Pierre Léaud. As his black American diva, Wiggins Fernandez is a good singer who demonstrates, in painful French, that she is a bad actress. But Beineix directs with such flash and wit that even the flaws take on a naive charm. With a highly controlled palette, he creates a carnival of visual puns. He is the master of the Pop Art sight gag. He lets his camera linger, for no reason, on the image of a crumpled white Rolls Corniche. He introduces a Vietnamese nymph in a pink cellophane dress shoplifting records. Her boyfriend works on a jigsaw puzzle of the sea in an electric-blue loft adorned with kinetic sculptures of shifting water. The comic-book plot climaxes with a virtuoso chase scene in the Paris Métro that is as imaginative as any ever shot by Hollywood—a marathon sequence of Jules racing his moped up stairs, down stairs and through a moving train.

Comparing *Diva*'s visuals to "the pristine, surreal clarity of Magritte," Jay Scott hailed the movie as "the most impressive debut from a French director since Godard's *Breathless*." Roger Ebert predicted that "if Beineix can continue at this level of achievement he'll be the best French director of his generation." With hindsight, it could be argued that Beineix's filmmaking was a novelty act, a seductive coup of style over substance, and that he literally painted himself into a corner with *The Moon in the Gutter* and *Betty Blue*. But *Diva* lit up the eighties zeitgeist in neon, revived North American interest in French cinema, and vividly demonstrated that art could be as carefree and irresponsible as trash.

Despite *Diva*'s cheery blast of Euro decadence, much of the 1981 programme was dominated by a new generation of bleak, visceral dramas about the disenfranchised. Charles Burnett's *Killer of Sheep*, another Overbey selection, still stands as a landmark of working-class realism on the frontier of American film. Set in South Central Los Angeles, where Burnett grew up, it is an acutely observed drama about emotional erosion in a black ghetto. Without pathos or preaching, Burnett draws a stark portrait of hope and frustration in a community in the aftermath of the Watts riots. Shot in 16-mm black and white, the episodic narrative centres on Stan (Henry Gayle Sanders), who slips into depression and slowly climbs out of it while holding down a hellish job in a slaughterhouse. For Stan, poverty is a relative concept. "We ain't really poor," he says. "We even give things to the Salvation Army. You can't do that if you're really poor."

Working on weekends, and mostly with unprofessional actors, Burnett made *Killer of Sheep* as a $10,000 student feature while studying film at UCLA. He finished it in 1977, but it wasn't discovered until 1981, when it shared the top prize at the Sundance festival, Robert Redford's new showcase for American indie cinema. I finally met Burnett at the 1999 Toronto festival, where he was premiering a small feature called *The Annihilation of Fish*, starring Margot Kidder. And as I talked to this soft-spoken African-American, who was still a struggling filmmaker two decades later, it became clear that his was not the typical film-student success story. "At UCLA," he recalled, "there was this atmosphere of protest and civil rights. A lot of the kids lived in Bel Air and were making films about working-class people, which was fine, but they were romanticizing the subject. I came from a different environment, and I wanted to make a film that expressed the things I knew about. I wanted to do it in a black community. I wanted it to have the appearance of a documentary. And I didn't want it to have a sense of a plot—a beginning, middle and end—although there was a subtle narrative."

Cinq et la pea
the man findi
charged the c

The critics who discovered *Killer of Sheep* at the festival included future director Atom Egoyan. In *the newspaper*, a campus rag at the University of Toronto, he reviewed Burnett's feature debut with a poignant diagnosis. "There is a certain amount of sadness involved in writing a review for a film that will probably never receive commercial distribution," he began. *Killer of Sheep* "never transcends the limitations imposed on it by its minuscule budget." But Egoyan went on to call it "one of the most compelling portraits of poverty and human endurance ever committed to the present-day American screen. Director Charles Burnett shows how even in the most adverse of social conditions, where a person must suspend sensitivity in order to preserve sanity, a sense of moral order can still be kept intact."

KILLER OF SHEEP

Egoyan—nurtured by Canadian funding for the arts—would achieve international prominence as a non-Hollywood director, while Burnett would become frustrated by the market-driven agenda of American movie-making. "At UCLA, they encouraged you to develop your own vision," Burnett told me. "They were hostile if you came up with anything they'd seen before. They were anti-Hollywood. That sort of shaped you. Even to this

bout a man finding himself in Manila, but what upset the censors was
bar girl who picks up a Coke bottle without using her hands. Clarkson
rs with "attempting to destroy this festival"

day I have problems because of this uncompromising attitude. You want to impose your values on the subject matter. It's not about entertainment so much as getting it right. But if you talk in a meeting about the social elements of the film, they're not interested. It has to be the common denominator kind of thing. If you want to do something about life in Mississippi, you can forget about it. It has to be about a murder, or something you've seen before."

Burnett belonged to a new generation of filmmakers using verité techniques to portray oppression on an intimate scale. In political terms, the era of revolutionary upheaval was the late sixties and early seventies. But its repercussions were still echoing through film schools, and filmmaking, for at least another decade. It was a global phenomenon. From the slums of the Philippines to the barrios of Brazil, socially aware directors took their cameras to the ghetto. They hired non-actors. They made the world their set. And they dramatized economic desolation, political repression, child prostitution and street crime with unvarnished realism. The antithesis of Hollywood escapism, these were films that offered no exit.

Hector Babenco's *Pixote*, another Overbey choice, shocked festival audiences in 1981 with its raw look at street kids in the slums of Sao Paulo, Brazil. By the age of ten, its title character has lost his innocence to a prostitute, witnessed a rape, committed a murder and become a hardened criminal. Other jolts of Latin American realism included Colombia's *Gamin* (Ciro Durán), a documentary about children living on a highway divider in Bogotá, sniffing fumes from gasoline cans, and Bolivia's *Chuquiago*, a drama about an Indian peasant boy struggling to survive in La Paz. The 1981 festival also included a spotlight on dissident Turkish director Yilmaz Güney, who was at the time serving an eighteen-year jail term on trumped-up murder charges. The festival showed five of his films, notably *Hope* (1971), an autobiographical tale of a horse-drawn-taxi driver whose horse is killed by a car—which was banned in Turkey—and *The Enemy* (1980), a grim saga of an unemployed father, which Güney directed from jail via a highly detailed shooting script. The Turkish government pressured the festival to prevent *The Enemy* from being shown. "I was told to hide the print somewhere," recalls Martin Heath, "because secret agents might show up to try to steal it." Heath hid *The Enemy* with his private collection of prints.

Toronto, of course, had its own art police. Since 1978, when the Ontario Censor Board had slashed the innocuous *In Praise of Older Women* and saved us from Brooke Shields by banning Louis Malle's *Pretty Baby*, censorship was an ongoing issue in the province. At the festival certain films acquired outlaw status, and Overbey's selections were especially vulnerable. But wading through hundreds of films in just two weeks to root out evil proved too much, even for Ontario's fastidious guardians of public morality. So instead of demanding to see every film programmed, in 1981 the censors agreed to a documentation system—the festival would provide background on the films, and the censors would ask to see the ones that intrigued them. "One year they said they wanted to see this British film about a sailor who comes back after three years at sea and finds his true love," recalls Wayne Clarkson, who struck the deal with the board. "I said, 'What do you want to see that for?' Anyway, up goes the print. And in the film, the sailor comes back from sea and the first thing he does is go to a massage parlour and get a hand job. Total hard-core sex. They insisted on cutting it." The festival had always let the filmmaker decide whether or not to show a censored print. "I remember calling the censor with the filmmaker right beside me," adds Clarkson, "and saying, 'You can't do this. Please let us run the movie.' But they said there was no question about it. It was an erect dick, and she was masturbating him. We can't have erect dicks open to the public. In that instance the screen went black. We didn't run the film. We didn't run any film in its place. We put a sign up saying that due to the Ontario Censor Board the film will not be shown."

The censors were unpredictable. The same year, they asked to screen Dusan Makavejev's *W.R.: Mysteries of the Organism*, a surreal extravaganza about sex, Stalinism and Wilhelm Reich. The movie includes a scene of *Screw* founder and publisher Al Goldstein being immortalized on the verge of orgasm by the Plaster Casters—an instance of erect dickdom that the board somehow found permissible. The year's biggest censorship controversy, however, concerned the National Film Board documentary *Not a Love Story: A Film About Pornography*, Bonnie Sherr Klein's moralistic tour through the porn trade. The board decided to allow just one festival showing of the film, in which hard-core footage was tempered by sobering interviews with Margaret Atwood and Kate Millett. When the festival tried to meet popular demand with a repeat screening, the board refused—bringing the curious logic of a peep show to its censorship policy. Now you see it, now you don't.

In 1981, the censors also banned *Pixote*, then reversed their decision. The next year they demanded cuts to Lothar Lambert's *1 Berlin-Harlem*. And Overbey clashed with them over *Cinq et la peau*, directed by Pierre Rissient, a French filmmaker and rival programmer of Philippine cinema. Calling Rissient "a genuine pain-in-the-ass" in his programme note, Overbey swallowed his pride and hailed *Cinq et la peau* as "the most original French film in years." It is about a man finding himself in Manila, but what upset the censors was a scene of the man finding a bar girl who picks up a Coke bottle without using her hands. Rissient argued that cutting the scene would destroy his film. Clarkson, after losing his appeal to the board, charged the censors with "deliberately attempting to destroy this festival." The movie was not shown and again a sign was put up outside the empty theatre to explain why.

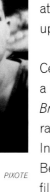

PIXOTE

Censorship tormented the festival throughout its first decade. In 1983, when it mounted a David Cronenberg retrospective, the board insisted on retaining its 1979 cuts to *The Brood*. And in 1986, Mary Brown, the board's infamous chair, objected to foreign entries ranging from Brazil's *Ganga Zumba*, which showed Portuguese colonists hacking up an Indian woman tied to a tree during a seventeenth-century slave revolt, to Marco Bellocchio's *Devil in the Flesh*, with its fleeting glimpse of fellatio. "Silly old Mary Brown filled some theatres with some pretty tame stuff," says Helga Stephenson, who took over the festival the following year. "The ranting and raving was a very good way to get the festival into the minds of the public, but internationally it was hugely embarrassing. And it filled the theatre with the wrong people, because they came looking for nothing but blow jobs, and they found themselves in the middle of a long, hard, boring film waiting for a few seconds of a grainy image showing something that looked vaguely like a male sex organ."

Occasionally, attempts to ban festival films had comic results. In 1985 Mary Brown and her censor board drew attention to Jean-Luc Godard's *Je vous salue, Marie* (*Hail Mary*) by approving it for one festival screening only. The film, which depicts Mary as a French high-school student and Joseph as a taxi driver, provoked Catholic protests. "We started getting phone call after phone call," recalls Stephenson. "And I couldn't figure out what was going on. Then I discovered someone had posted my name and the press office number over all the holy water fountains in Catholic churches." A crowd of one hundred protesters showed up at the University Theatre where *Hail Mary* was showing. Some were on their knees praying, others were weeping. But because the *Hail Mary* print was delayed, there was a last-minute change in the schedule. And as people left the theatre and ran into these weeping protesters, they wondered what on earth was going on—they had just come out of *Mishima*, which is about the famous Japanese author who

NOT A LOVE STORY: A FILM ABOUT PORNOGRAPHY

committed hara-kiri.

Wayne Clarkson relates another absurd scenario. Having led the battle against censorship while at the festival, he was still on the front lines after leaving to head up the newly formed Ontario Film Development Corporation in 1986. Lily Munro, then Ontario's new Liberal minister of culture, invited him to discuss the issue at her ministry's staff retreat. "I'd been in the job for all of a month," recalls Clarkson, "and she said, 'Would you screen a film with us and enlighten us on the issues surrounding censorship in the province?' I said, 'Yeah, sure.'" Clarkson showed them *Sweet Movie* (1974), a Canadian film directed by Yugoslavian iconoclast Dusan Makavejev—and banned in Ontario. Memorably, a naked Carole Laure gets coated in chocolate. There are no graphic sex scenes. There are, however, scenes of Reichian therapy in which a regressing patient defecates all over himself. Clarkson screened it for Munro and her ministry at the genteel Millcroft Inn. "I said, 'Okay ladies and gentlemen, here's the issue you're grappling with. Here is one Canadian film, financed by the Canadian Film Development Corporation, run at festivals around the world, heralded as a great movie by a great filmmaker, commercially released in Quebec and banned in Ontario. You are not allowed to see this movie. You now are responsible for a film agency called the Ontario Film Development Corporation. Where do you stand?'"

"Well," laughs Clarkson, shaking his head, "I'd forgotten how raw it was. It was so overwhelming—and complicated. If it had been *Pretty Baby*, that would be one thing. But this wasn't about fucking. It was about pissing all over yourself, and shitting yourself. They couldn't handle it. It was difficult to even talk about it."

With the new Liberal government committed to a more progressive policy, however, in 1987 Ontario's censors finally gave the festival a blanket exemption. The festival would be treated as an adult. By then, the whole notion of transgression—sexual, political and artistic—had become part of the festival ethos. Seeing something that you couldn't see elsewhere, for whatever reason, was why a lot of people went to the festival in the first

CATHOLICS PROTESTING THE SCREENING OF GODARD'S* HAIL MARY *OUTSIDE THE UNIVERSITY THEATRE

PHOTO: GAIL HARVEY

MARY

place. But there were also those who were looking for the thrill of the familiar, who wanted to take part in something grand and glorious. And in 1981, the year of *Diva*'s success, they found their champion in a film that was as stereotypically English as *Diva* was French. Overbey was furious when *Diva* did not win the award for most popular film; instead the prize went to a dignified challenger called *Chariots of Fire*.

Sweet Chariots. Big Chill

PHOTO PREVIOUS PAGES: GAIL HARVEY

THE MUSIC IS WHAT YOU REMEMBER, THE BRIGHT PIAN

AND SPRINTING SYNTHESIZER KEEPING PACE WITH A TEAM

runners on a beach. Without the Vangelis score, the movie is unima

nable. And the music is what remains, a simple riff conjuring

clichés of hope and glory. Chariots of Fire *is the quintessent*

triumph-of-the-human-spirit picture, a tale of two heroes winning

footrace for God and king and country. A paean to vanishing ideals

honour and virtue, it's the sort of sterling period piece that only the English can pull off with a straight face. Hard to believe that it came from the same cinema that has produced the red-brick realism of Mike Leigh and Ken Loach, for here was a British movie that beat Hollywood at its own game.

Playing fast and loose with a true story, *Chariots of Fire* is about an English Jew and a Christian Scot, rivals who overcome the odds to win gold at the 1924 Olympics in Paris. Harold Abrahams (Ben Cross) is the stubborn Jew, defying racism and snobbery at a Cambridge ruled by John Gielgud—and who violates the amateur ethic by hiring a professional trainer, an Italian no less, played with scene-stealing panache by Ian Holm. Eric Liddell (Ian Charleson) is the devout Scot, the goody-two-shoes track star who postpones a missionary career in China to become an Olympian, creates a national scandal by refusing to run the 100 metres on a Sunday, then goes on to win the 400 metres instead. The movie is a hymn to British underdogs who buck the system and leave a bunch of glamorous Americans in the dust. Which is more or less what happened

PREVIOUS PAGES, GLENN CLOSE, WILLIAM HURT, KEVIN KLINE AND JEFF GOLDBLUM, 1983

to the film. After creating a sensation at the Toronto festival, this feature debut from an unknown director, Hugh Hudson, and two unknown stars went all the way to Hollywood's Olympics, the Academy Awards, where it stole Best Picture from the favoured American contenders, *Reds* and *On Golden Pond*. Inaugurating a trend that would lead to such triumphs as *The English Patient* and *Shakespeare in Love*, this was the first in a series of David-and-Goliath victories for independent cinema at the Oscars. The David in question was David Puttnam, the British producer whose career includes such milestones as *Midnight Express*, *Local Hero*, *The Mission* and *The Killing Fields*.

Puttnam offers to meet me at 8:30 a.m. in the dining room of Claridge's Hotel in London, where he has been coming for breakfast for some thirty years. Announcing that his stomach is a little off, he orders bacon and grilled tomatoes, no eggs. Impeccably dressed in a dark suit, like a banker, Puttnam speaks with brisk, understated efficiency, as if there could not possibly be enough time in the world to say or do everything there is to be done and said. He has fond memories of the Toronto festival. Alan Parker's *Midnight Express*, which he co-produced, was the closing gala in 1978. With its infamous "Turks are pigs" epithet, the film had created a sensation in Cannes, where it polarized critics and was snubbed by the jury. Toronto re-ignited the controversy, and served as a hot launch pad for the North American release.

With *Chariots of Fire*, Puttnam followed the same one-two punch. Once again the Cannes jury ignored the film and the critics were divided, with the loudest denunciations coming from the Europeans. "The French critics were extraordinarily sniffy," recalls Puttnam. "But that helped a good deal, because a lot of the other critics, especially the Americans, were outraged. They voted their own Palme d'Or, and awarded it to *Chariots of Fire*. Roger Ebert, Kathleen Carroll, Charles Champlin, about four or five of them. We knew from Cannes where our audience was." The movie went from Toronto to the New York Film Festival, then straight into release, zooming to number one at the box office in the first week. "There was a theory in those days that Toronto was too soon to make a run for the Oscars," adds Puttnam, "and that you should come out of the box in late October, early November. *Chariots* very impressively defied that. Toronto was a very good platform for the picture."

The Toronto gala had the kind of magic that happens only when an audience finds itself on its feet, applauding a movie about a heroic legend onscreen in the presence of its real-life legacy (something that would happen again with *The Hurricane* in 1999). Runner Eric Liddell had died in a Japanese concentration camp in 1945, while doing missionary work in China. His widow, Florence Hall, who had settled in Stoney Creek, Ontario, showed up at the premiere with their three daughters. "It was a very emotional evening," Puttnam recalls, "because we were up onstage with his whole family, one of whom had been born after he died, two of whom had never known him at all. One of the daughters turned to me and said, 'You've given me my father back. I always wondered what he was like.'"

As a maverick producer of mainstream movies—who had a brief fling running Columbia Pictures—David Puttnam has a curious place in the indie movement. We tend to think of independent films in terms of *auteurs*—writer-directors who put a distinctive signature on their work. But Puttnam behaves like an *auteur* producer. It is his name, not Hugh Hudson's, that we associate with *Chariots of Fire*. And while Hudson, who went on to make *Revolution*, *Greystoke: The Legend of Tarzan, Lord of the Apes*, and *I Dreamed of Africa*, has never lived up to the promise of his directorial debut, *Chariots* was just another jewel in the crown for Puttnam. "All the films I've ever done that I'm remotely proud of started with me," he says. "I have genuine paternity. *Chariots* started with an idea that I read in a book. *Local Hero* started with an idea from a couple of newspaper articles I read, *Killing Fields* with an article I read in *Time* magazine. And in every single case I commissioned the screenplay. The germ of it started in my brain and no one could ever take that away from me. That wasn't true of *Midnight Express*. But the films that I regard as my core work, which would include *The Mission*, are things that I feel I found."

'Wayne's genius was to combine good commercial material with dr
have thought he was bringing a different kind of cultural experience
real impact was doing the reverse. He legitimized relatively mains
kind Merchant Ivory make, the kind that I produce. He gave us a cul

In a world of cinematic fashion that favours the postmodern, Puttnam has old-fashioned ideas about the mission of making movies, which he feels must bridge the distance between challenging art and commercial entertainment. "The real trick, the real talent of the filmmaker, is to stake out that middle ground. *Local Hero* precisely does that. It's a human film. There isn't a single original shot in the whole picture. But it ends up informing you about what it is to be a human being, which I happen to think is the principal purpose of the motion picture. A motion picture is not theatre. Theatre offers a different experience. Cinema is about the transference of personality from the person sitting in the audience to the person on the screen." A lot of festivals, notably Cannes, did not warm to the kind of movies that Puttnam liked to make. But Toronto was another story. "One of the attractions of the Toronto festival early on," he says, "is that it felt like a people's festival. It wasn't auteuristic. It didn't spring from the loins of the British Film Institute. It was very, very unpretentious. In Berlin I always felt intimidated. I always felt you were there because [its director] Moritz de Hadeln decided to tip his hat to a certain area of commercial cinema, but you weren't wanted, you weren't part of the core."

Although Toronto's director, Wayne Clarkson, came to the job with serious academic credentials, and supported the esoteric slant of programmers such as David Overbey, Clarkson appreciated the power of a crowd-pleaser in a town crazy about movies. "Toronto had one of the best cinema-going audiences in the world," Puttnam acknowledges. "It was a rock-solid movie town. Films there consistently out-performed other cities of comparable size. And in its own odd way the Toronto festival altered film festi-

CHARIOTS OF FIRE *PRODUCER DAVID PUTTNAM WITH ACTOR BEN CROSS, 1981*

vals. Wayne's genius was to combine good commercial material with discoveries. He may have thought he was bringing a different kind of cultural experience to Toronto, but his real impact was doing the reverse. He legitimized relatively mainstream movies—the kind of films Merchant Ivory make, the kind of films that I produce. He gave us a cultural legitimacy, whereas most festivals, maybe all festivals prior to Toronto, concentrated on giving commercial legitimacy to small films. In that sense he performed a very important act. He pulled the two threads of cinema together."

Wooing the Hollywood studios became an essential part of Clarkson's strategy. And he had help from Canadian directors who had found a home in the studio system. In 1978, Ted Kotcheff's *Who is Killing the Great Chefs of Europe?* brought a Hollywood press junket to the festival for the first time. Then in 1979, after living in Europe for nine years, Norman Jewison made his Toronto homecoming with the premiere of *...And Justice for All*, a somewhat heavy-handed satire of the legal system starring Al Pacino, who would get an Oscar nomination for his flamboyant turn as a lawyer defending a judge accused of rape.

eries. He may ronto, but his n movies, the legitimacy"

Jewison had been reluctant to give the festival the movie, which wasn't opening until late fall. "I thought it was awfully early," he recalls. "But Dusty was on the phone and Wayne was on the phone. Everybody was pushing me. I thought, 'Aw, they're right. I should support the festival.' So I prevailed upon Columbia and I rushed my post-production to get the picture ready." Jewison insisted that critics hold their reviews. All but one complied. The media previewed *...And Justice for All* at a press screening the day before Saturday's closing-night gala. On Saturday morning, Jewison and the Columbia executives flew in on the studio jet, and the first thing they saw was a front-page review in *The Toronto Star* panning the movie before its premiere. For Jewison, it was a bitter homecoming, although the audience gave his film a warm reception. "I was embarrassed for my country and embarrassed for my city," he says. "And embarrassed that people didn't keep their word. All it did was reinforce my opinion that they're never going to give me a break. The same thing happened with *In the Heat of the Night*. Look up the Toronto reviews of that—saying, 'What does Jewison know about the South?' Canadians have never supported their own." But the director was impressed by the scale of the festival. "It was so professional," he says. "For the first time I experienced that respect they had for film in this city, which I never knew existed. I took for granted that we had a kind of mid-western mentality, like Chicago or Cleveland. Then I realized how sophisticated it was, and how knowledgeable people were. And the enthusiasm, my God, was exactly what I didn't expect. There was this tremendous passion."

PHOTO: ©EVA EVERYTHING 1981

While Jewison and Kotcheff worked with Hollywood studios, back home Canadian cinema was still struggling, at least in English Canada. By the eighties, the tax-shelter boom had ended. In 1981, the festival showcased a final flurry of homegrown movies: *Ticket to Heaven*, *Heartaches* and *Threshold*. Four years would pass before the premiere of another high-profile English-Canadian feature.

PHOTO: ©EVA EVERYTHING 1981

JEFF BRIDGES AND PETER FONDA AT THE CUTTER'S WAY GALA, 1981

The '81 festival opened with *Ticket to Heaven*, a fact-based drama about freeing a young Toronto man (played by Nick Mancuso) from a Moonie-like cult in San Francisco. The cast showcased some notable talents from the Toronto theatre scene, including R.H. Thomson as a scary deprogrammer. And the film delivered its anti-cult message with a certain diligence. But with former CBC journalist Ralph Thomas directing, *Ticket to Heaven* remained trapped in the pedestrian mindset of a TV movie. Here was a story of reality versus delusion that never transcended the facts—a classic example of Canadian cinema unable to see beyond its documentary tradition. That did not prevent a mob scene on opening night. Several hundred angry patrons, many of them with tickets, were shut out of *Ticket to Heaven*'s over-crowded premiere. Torontonians had clamoured to see taboo sex at the riotous opening of *In Praise of Older Women*; now they were fighting for a peek at taboo religion.

Heartaches appeared to have a perfect pedigree. With veteran Don Shebib at the helm, Margot Kidder was home from Hollywood, leaving Lois Lane in the dust by playing a white-trash loudmouth with yellow hair, taking Annie Potts under her wing as a shy, pregnant girl on the run from her husband. *Heartaches* tried to be the comic flipside of *Goin' Down the Road*—two girls going down the road in a Greyhound bus and landing in a Toronto mattress factory. But it had a ring of contrivance, the sound of a screenwriter spinning his wheels. And the raging fights on the set between Shebib and Kidder didn't

help. The director never wanted Kidder in the first place. He said he wanted someone unknown and ugly and fat. But he needed a star to raise the financing, and after Bette Midler and Stockard Channing turned him down, he was stuck with Kidder even though he said he found her appalling as an actress and a human being. *Heartaches* wore the ills of our film industry on its sleeve.

Threshold, which closed the '81 festival, was a healthier collaboration. It starred Donald Sutherland as a famous, iconoclastic heart surgeon (modelled on Denton Cooley), Jeff Goldblum as a schizophrenic colleague who invents the first artificial heart, and Mare Winningham as the patient who receives it. Sutherland, who has a talent for playing surgeons, went to unusual lengths to prepare for his role, hanging out in the operating room with Cooley, who let him put his hand into the open chest of a ten-year-old child and feel the beating heart. (Later, on the set of *Bethune: The Making of a Hero* in China, Sutherland told me he came to realize that taking his research that far was an unforgivable violation.) *Threshold* ended the era of tax-shelter debacles on a redeeming note. Its Canadian producers had taken the tax-shelter route after failing to persuade a studio that anyone would want to watch open-heart surgery. Consequently, the film was shot in Toronto, though set in Los Angeles. The director, Richard Pearce, and the writer, James Salter, were both American. But with its lean, compelling drama, *Threshold* proved the exception to the rule that mongrel productions make for bad movies.

PHOTO: ©EVA EVERYTHING 1982

The festival had become keen on opening with a Canadian film whenever possible. In 1982, Clarkson had his heart set on launching the festival with *The Wars*, directed by Stratford's Robin Phillips and adapted by author Timothy Findley from his own novel. Clarkson, who adored the film, waged a long battle with the myriad of interests controlling it, including its producers, Torstar and the NFB, and its distributor, International Spectrafilm, which was run by his friend Linda Beath, the festival's first programme coordinator. Beath refused to give him the movie. "I fought literally to the last minute," says Clarkson. "I even tracked down the head of the National Film Board on his yacht on holiday. But I lost the battle, and I'd pushed it way too long. I got carried away. There was no Plan B."

The Big Chill
They knew th
want The Big
people my ag
it's not comm

Hastily, he enlisted Australia's *We of the Never Never*, a bland outback adventure, for the opening-night gala. The morning of the premiere Jay Scott dismissed it in *The Globe* as "a nice, unassuming, proficient picture, the sort of film that makes culture vultures proud and that puts people on the prowl for challenge or innovation asleep." Clarkson was furious, betrayed first by Linda Beath and then by Scott. He called up Scott and found himself yelling at the top of his lungs. "Jay, how could you do this? We haven't

WENDERS AND DERIC FORREST, 1982

opened the movie yet." Remembering the incident, Clarkson says, "I'd never screamed at anybody like that. And we were pals, good friends. We were the same age. We'd come to Toronto at the same time. I just lost it."

For Clarkson, 1982 was a hellish year. He began to see the festival unravelling and felt powerless to do anything about it. He also lost a fight to stage a gala premiere of *The Grey Fox*, Phillip Borsos's splendid epic about train robber Bill Miner, which now stands as a classic of Canadian cinema. The distributor, once again Linda Beath, was worried that giving away so many free seats at a splashy Toronto premiere would erode the movie's box-office potential in its key market. So instead she slipped *The Grey Fox* into the Montreal festival without fanfare. Clarkson also saw a scheduled gala of *The Executioner's Song*, the Norman Mailer adaptation, fall through at the last minute in negotiations with the Screen Actors' Guild. And he faced a staff mutiny over the VIP paranoia surrounding Robert De Niro's appearance at a tribute honouring Martin Scorsese.

There were some consolations. To replace the Mailer film, the festival snagged Robert Altman's scrappy adaptation of *Come Back to the 5 and Dime, Jimmy Dean, Jimmy Dean*. And Jeremy Irons graced the closing-night premiere of Jerzy Skolimowski's *Moonlighting*, a slapstick tragedy in which England's most urbane actor got away with playing a Polish construction worker. The festival also culled some gems from Cannes and Venice: Antonioni's *Identification of a Woman*, Fassbinder's *Veronika Voss*, Margarethe von Trotta's *Marianne and Juliane*, Peter Greenaway's *The Draughtsman's Contract*, Bertrand Tavernier's *Coup de torchon*—and Paul Mazursky's *Tempest*, which was voted most popular film.

The international critical elite, meanwhile, was falling in love with the festival. "The secret of Toronto's success," wrote Dave Kehr in *Chicago* magazine, "lies in its diversity—the kind of contradictions that would tear another festival apart hold Toronto together. It isn't

one of those movies that left studio executives scratching their heads wrence Kasdan was hot stuff, they wanted Kasdan, but they didn't "Everybody turned it down," Kasdan recalls. "The young executives uld say, 'I love it, it's funny, it's sad and I'll be the first one in line, bu l. It doesn't have a hook' "

the size that makes Toronto my personal favorite among film festivals: It has a sense of warmth and intimacy. For the length of the festival, the audience becomes a kind of community; there is an atmosphere of shared interest, shared enthusiasm and (when the occasion demands) shared disgust unlike any other festival I've ever attended."

THRESHOLD

But the festival was having a hard time snaring important world premieres, of either Canadian or Hollywood movies. A year later, *The Wars* had still not opened commercially, and Clarkson told the distributors, Linda Beath and Bahman Farmanara, that he wanted it for the 1983 opening gala. They told him they'd have to think it over. "Well, I figure I can't go through this again," says Clarkson. "So I go down to L.A., meet with the folks at Columbia and they say, 'We've got a film we'd like you to consider for opening night. *The Big Chill*. We'll fly up the cast. You'll have the world premiere.' The film wasn't finished, but they showed me a clip. This is a no-brainer. So I go back and announce we're opening with *The Big Chill*. And who phones and gives me living shit?—*'How could you do that? We were negotiating!'* I said, 'Are you kidding? There's blood on the floor about *The Wars* from last year.'"

When a Hollywood studio has a movie that it doesn't know how to market, a movie that it doesn't even understand—something arty—it often turns to a festival. *The Big Chill* was one of those movies that left studio executives scratching their heads. They knew that its director, Lawrence Kasdan, was hot stuff. This was the same Lawrence Kasdan who had scripted *Raiders of the Lost Ark* and two *Star Wars* sequels, and who had launched his directing career with *Body Heat*, a steamy tale of fatal attraction. The studios could relate to that. But all of a sudden this guy was trying to make a movie about a bunch of people sitting around talking.

Every studio in town wanted Kasdan, but they didn't want *The Big Chill*. "Everybody turned it down," the director recalls. "The young executives, people my age, would say, 'I love it, it's funny, it's sad and I'll be the first one in line, but it's not commercial. It doesn't have a hook.'" Finally, Johnny Carson's production company took the bait, and dragged Columbia into the deal. "It was tortuous," adds Kasdan. And when the Columbia brass saw the results, "they sat there cold and silent. They just didn't get it." But when previews in Seattle and San Jose went through the roof, "that changed everything. So the studio knew what to expect by the time we got to Toronto. And from that point on, they were trying to figure out how to open it. Toronto was a great launching. It was a fantastic reaction." In 1999, returning to Toronto for the premiere of *Mumford*, Kasdan stood in Roy Thomson Hall and said, "I opened *The Big Chill* here sixteen years ago and won the Labatt trophy [for most popular film]. I didn't even know what that was. But it did big things."

JEFF GOLDBLUM AND CATHERINE O'HARA, 1983

The Big Chill, which made $56 million in North America, became a generational landmark. Like a grander, pop version of *Return of the Secaucus Seven*, which John Sayles had launched at the 1980 festival, it was an ensemble piece about seven survivors of the radical sixties: a reunion of thirtysomething college pals who are brought together by the funeral of a friend and spend the weekend talking about how their lives have changed. Its cast of rising stars included William Hurt, Glenn Close, Jeff Goldblum, Kevin Kline, Tom Berenger, Mary Kay Place and Meg Tilly—not to mention the uncredited Kevin Costner, whose moment as the corpse at the funeral was cut. This was not an independent film. It was a movie that escaped, like a prodigal son, from the heart of Hollywood. If *Star Wars* changed the way America made movies, *The Big Chill* was the dissenting voice from within the Empire, about people remembering how they once

PHOTO: GAIL HARVEY

wanted to change the world.

"The people who control Hollywood—their goals are really the jackpot goals," said Kasdan when he visited Toronto in 1983. *Star Wars* "transformed the balance sheets of an entirely publicly held company, so that became the new goal. The amazing thing is, even given the attention they have focused on making blockbusters, they haven't got a clue as to how to do it. They don't understand that a blockbuster always comes from one person's crazy idea." And Kasdan no longer wanted any part of it. "George Lucas is a very good and close friend of mine," he added, "but I don't think we would work together again. The kinds of movies I make, they're really my business, you know. As soon as you start doing that, there's not really much you can do for each other. I would not write another *Star Wars* movie."

Kasdan kept his word.

For the festival, *The Big Chill* marked an appropriate watershed. Its success parallels that of the festival itself—a countercultural echo that strikes a chord in popular culture. And it established Toronto as a place to launch smart movies that the studios don't know what to do with. "To me," says George Anthony, "*The Big Chill* was the festival's biggest turning point. It was Hollywood saying, 'We're going to Toronto because that's where it's happening.' After that, it was never tin-cup time. There were still pictures the festival couldn't get. But it never had to beg."

As the festival courted Hollywood, however, it found itself in the dicey business of babysitting celebrity guests. Today when stars show up at the festival they are cocooned by layers of handlers, from studio flacks to personal publicists. But back then, festival staff often ended up handling the talent directly. Rosie Levine, who ran the guest office for four years with a staff of young volunteers, recalls the ordeal of trying to get Karen Black out of her room. It was 1983, she had come for the premiere of *Can She Bake a Cherry Pie?* and it was time to go home. "We had a car waiting and she had a flight to catch," says Levine. "But she was having a really hard time packing. She was a mess and so was her room. We sent a volunteer up to help her pack, and the room was literally covered with chocolate bar wrappers."

Everyone found Black a little bizarre. Brian Linehan remembers her stopping tape during a TV interview to smear Vaseline under her eyes to give them a lift. "I thought, 'Fine, you're lovely, you're talented and you live on Pluto,'" he recalls. When Bruce Kirkland talked to Black, he tried to break the ice by mentioning her previous visit to the festival, with *In Praise of Older Women*. "She drew a blank," says Kirkland. "She had absolutely no recollection of it."

It was customary to have some flowers and a bottle of liqueur waiting for a star in the hotel room. After Glenn Close showed up for *The Big Chill*, a volunteer named Heather Blurton was dispatched to her room. "It was her first day on the job," says Levine. "She

e festival found itself in the business of babysitting celebrity ests. Karen Black “was having a really hard time packing. She was ness and so was her room. We sent a volunteer up to help her, and room was literally covered with chocolate bar wrappers”

knocks on the door with a vase of flowers in her hand. The door opens and the girl is startled. She says, ‘Oh, I thought you were a *man*!’ And Glenn Close goes completely ballistic—‘Don’t you know who I am? What kind of festival is this? Why are you doing your job if you don’t know what you’re doing?’” The volunteer comes back to Levine in tears. “Well, I guess I’m fired,” she says. “I just insulted this major movie star. She screamed and yelled at me. I’ll just pack up my things.” Levine tells her to stay put. An hour later, Close shows up at the guest office. “I introduce myself,” says Levine, “and take her directly over to Heather. ‘I would like you to meet Heather Blurton, our volunteer. This is her first day on the job.’ And Glenn Close, to her credit, says, ‘I came in to apologize. I am so sorry. I had no right to do that.’”

As the festival braved the Big Chill of celebrity, it had to develop a whole new class of hospitality. And there would be no hospitality suite big enough to contain it. The boys were coming to town: Marty, Bobby, Francis, Warren and Jack.

Goodfellas

SEPTEMBER 13, 1982. THE DAY OF THE FESTIVAL'S TRIBUTE

MARTIN SCORSESE. SCORSESE WAS DOWNSTAIRS IN THE LOBBY OF T Plaza II, discussing his wardrobe for the evening with his mother, Catheri and Roger Ebert. "What should I wear?" he asked. "Well, Gene and I are t presenters," said Ebert, "so we have to wear tuxedos, but you are t guest, so you can wear anything you want." "Maybe I'll wear my b eans," said Scorsese, who had not yet entered his Armani phase. "Marti his mother chimed in, "you wear your tuxedo." "And that was the end c that," recalls Ebert.

In the early 1980s, the festival was transformed from a contender to a player. As it became known as a place to discover films, and filmmakers, it was being discovered in its own right by Hollywood. Over the years, the studios would come to dominate the

PREVIOUS PAGES, CATHERINE AND CHARLES SCORSESE WITH ROBERT DE NIRO AND MARTIN;

LEFT, ROBERT DUVALL AT HIS 1983 TRIBUTE

media spotlight with gala premieres, leading to complaints that they were taking over the festival. But this was a courtship that the festival initiated and avidly pursued, as it went out of its way to solicit stars by staging a series of gala tributes honouring Martin Scorsese in 1982, Robert Duvall in 1983 and Warren Beatty in 1984—events that would have a dramatic impact on the festival's style and status.

"The festival was at a crossroads," says Bill House, who produced all three tributes. "It had to make a quantum leap into the consciousness of the public and the industry." It was Dusty Cohl's idea to stage a tribute. He approached his friend Roger Ebert, who agreed to co-host a gala evening with Gene Siskel. They chose to honour Scorsese. "I had met him very early on," says Ebert, who had favourably reviewed the director's feature debut, *Who's That Knocking at My Door*, at the Chicago Film Festival in 1967. "So he agreed to do it. He was happy to have his work recognized—because it hasn't been all that easy for him. He's a great director, but there were times when Hollywood had no interest in him at all. I think he has felt, from time to time, like a guy out there in the darkness."

In fact, Scorsese was on the ropes. Despite the brilliance of *Mean Streets*, *Taxi Driver* and *Raging Bull*, Hollywood had written him off. Critics' polls would proclaim *Raging Bull* to be the best movie of the eighties, but it was knocked out in the early rounds at the box office and defeated at the Oscars by *Ordinary People*. "When I lost for *Raging Bull*," Scorsese told author Peter Biskind in his book *Easy Riders, Raging Bulls*, "that's when I realized what my place in the system would be, if I did survive at all—on the outside looking in." Along with George Lucas, Francis Coppola and Steven Spielberg, Scorsese was part of the New Hollywood, the wave of fiercely independent directors who changed the face of American movie-making in the seventies. And although he'd won critical acclaim, he longed for the commercial success that the others had enjoyed. When Scorsese arrived in Toronto, he was struggling to finish *The King of Comedy*, a movie that he'd directed as a favour to Robert De Niro and had come to regret. His health had been ravaged by a dangerous mixture of asthma medication and cocaine. His marriage to Isabella Rossellini had just broken up. He was about to turn forty. He was a man in need of a tribute.

The event was staged as an upscale *This is Your Life*, with De Niro and Harvey Keitel headlining the list of surprise guests. It was a logistical nightmare trying to keep their presence a secret, and they were hustled up the service elevator to a suite at the Plaza II Hotel, where they were to remain hidden. The tribute itself was a success, although it stretched into a three-hour marathon. With fifteen hundred people packed into the University Theatre, the show unfolded as a series of film clips interwoven with onstage interviews by Siskel and Ebert. One by one, the surprise guests arrived to pay homage, from Scorsese's long-time editor Thelma Schoonmaker to his mentor, director Michael Powell. Finally, Harvey Keitel stepped into the lights and brought the crowd cheering to its feet. Everyone was wondering the same thing. There was only one person missing. "Then Robert De Niro came down the aisle and the roof went off," reported Jay Scott.

PHOTO: GAIL HARVEY

GENE SISKEL AND ROGER EBERT HOSTING THE WARREN BEATTY TRIBUTE, 1984

"Mutt had been restored to Jeff, Laurel had been restored to Hardy, yin had been restored to yang. The evening was complete."

De Niro, of course, is a famously recalcitrant interview subject. "He doesn't like talking about himself," says Ebert. "There were a couple of questions that we asked that seemed to really blindside him. We were talking about Catholic symbolism in *Mean Streets* and *Taxi Driver*. Scorsese had talked about the overhead shots in *Taxi Driver* as being emblematic of the priest's eye view of the altar, and De Niro, as I recall, looked at us during those questions as if he couldn't think of a possible reason in the world why they should be asked or answered." But even when asked a straight question about whether he planned to make more movies with Scorsese, De Niro just grinned and stammered. "Yeah, I would imagine . . . I mean we have ideas now to do things. Some we will do. It's a complicated thing . . . life. Who knows what will happen?"

The week of the Scorsese tribute, the festival also honoured another great American director, John Cassavetes, with a far less glamorous retrospective. No slight was intended, and Cassavetes gamely attended Scorsese's night, but the disparity between the two events was embarrassing. "It was shoddy on our part," admits Anne Mackenzie, then the festival's managing director. "The Cassavetes tribute was at the tacky little

EARTHA KITT AND DIRECTOR CHRISTIAN BLACKWOOD, 1982

PHOTO: ©EVA EVERYTHING 1982

Backstage theatre. And Cassavetes did notice Scorsese was swanning around next door in limos. Naturally he felt he had been honoured, and then to see that just down the block there was this much bigger tribute to another director—it was a hideous mistake, and Wayne and I were just sick about it. Because we really *meant* it for Cassavetes." Mackenzie laughs at the memory. "We had such crushes on him and Gena Rowlands that they could hardly get us out of their hotel suite. Gena was so beautiful, and Wayne was so in love with her—we're talking a high, high cinema crush."

The *faux pas* seemed especially resonant because, as a pioneer of raw American realism, Cassavetes had a profound influence on Scorsese. Among the New Hollywood directors, he was the first to offer an American answer to the *verité* drama of the French New Wave. And it was seeing Cassavetes's *Shadows* as a teenager in 1960 that "made

"We had such crushes on Cassavetes and Gena Rowlands that th could hardly get us out of their hotel suite. Gena was so beautiful a Wayne was so in love with her—we're talking a high, high ciner crush"

me realize that *I* could make a movie," Scorsese told Biskind in *Easy Riders, Raging Bulls*. When Cassavetes saw Scorsese's first student feature, *Who's That Knocking at My Door*, he actually told him it was better than *Citizen Kane*, according to screenwriter Jay Cocks. "John meant it," says Cocks, "and from that day on, he loved Marty like a son." In fact, when Scorsese was snorkelling through life in a blizzard of cocaine during the late seventies, Cassavetes angrily berated him for ruining his talent, although he himself was a notorious drunk who would die from cirrhosis of the liver.

CLARKSON WITH CASSAVETES AND ROWLANDS AT THE CASSAVETES TRIBUTE, 1982

After the tribute, Scorsese, De Niro and Keitel partied late into the night. With the bars closing at 1 a.m., and the hospitality suite unable to keep up with the demand, friends of the festival had discreetly arranged for an illegal after-hours bar to be set up in a modern dance studio on Yonge Street. With live music every night, it was run by Toronto actor Michael Copeman, who charged $20 at the door. The night of the tribute, he says, "Catherine O'Hara walked in and said, 'Do you mind if a few friends of mine come in, and would you not charge me?' I said okay. And in walked Jeremy Irons, Harvey Keitel, Martin Scorsese and Bobby De Niro. Of the bunch Jeremy was definitely the tallest."

John Allen, the theatre manager at the University, had spent the night handling the overflow crowd at the tribute. He showed up at about 3:30 a.m. "I go in and see De Niro and Keitel stoned out of their minds with these two bimbos," he says. "Just two days earlier, as part of my job, I'd pulled one of them off some guy she was blowing in the hospitality suite." Copeman recalls that he guarded the washroom for De Niro and one of the girls for about ten minutes. But after a while, Copeman and Allen realized that they had to get the stars out of the club. "They were so wrecked it was unbelievable." says Allen. "It wouldn't be too great for an illegal booze can to have to call an ambulance for Harvey Keitel or Robert De Niro."

Allen approached them and suggested it was time to go. "It was like talking to a deaf person," he says. "'*We . . . have . . . to . . . leave. . . . You . . . can't . . . stay . . . here*.' Finally, I get them into the limousine. I'm about to close the door and De Niro puts his arm out so I can't close it. And he says, 'Get me those girls! Get me those girls!' So I had to go up and get the girls and bring them down to the car. I went from theatre usher to pimp in one night."

Scorsese was still upstairs. "So I go back up," says Allen, "and Marty is whacking back his inhaler by the gallon and gabbing to everybody. He's crammed with coke, and he offers me a hit. It's four o'clock in the morning and I'm afraid we're going to get busted. He's talking a mile a minute—'I-don't-wanna-get-out. I-like-it-here. This-is-fine. I'm-talking-film. This-is-a-French-director.' He wouldn't leave. He was there till 6:30 in the morning."

Oh well, at least he didn't wear his jeans.

It was hard to keep the festival booze can a secret with limousines lined up outside, and a couple of nights later it was raided. The club was jammed with about three hundred people. About twenty uniformed police came in and started busting patrons, including several producers and distributors.

One of them was New York–based distributor Ira Deutchman. He says he had gone there after receiving "an invitation to what looked like an official festival party—we didn't realize it was for an illegal after-hours club. People were dancing and having a good

THE SCORSESES (DAVID CRONENBERG IS SITTING BEHIND THEM), HARVEY KEITEL AND CASSAVETES, 1982

time getting wrecked. Suddenly the lights went on. We heard some whistles and a siren. And before we knew it there were a bunch of cops piling into the room." The police divided the patrons into groups of ten and busted one person in each group. In Deutchman's group, they picked the dishevelled producer's rep and party animal Jeff Dowd (who became the basis for the character of "the Dude" played by Jeff Bridges in *The Big Lebowski*). When the police asked Dowd for ID, he tried to persuade them he'd lost it in a cab, which was true. Then Deutchman jumped in and offered them *his* ID, not realizing he was volunteering to be busted. The police wrote him a ticket and let him go. He charged the fine to the festival. But then, to his friends' delight, *Variety* ran a story saying that Cinecom's Ira Deutchman had been busted in a Toronto nightclub on a "morals" charge.

After the raid, the police confiscated all the booze in the club. "Of course, everybody had emptied their pockets into the various potted plants," says Copeman, "and there were drugs all over the place by the time it was over. We really cleaned up after they left." The seized liquor included a black-market supply of Dom Perignon champagne salvaged from a western theatre tour. "One big burly sergeant was walking out the door with all our stuff," Copeman recalls. "He looked at the sign: 'Dom $50 with two glasses'—for fifty bucks you'd get two glasses and the bottle in an ice bucket—and he said, 'Fifty dollars? You're really gouging them.' I looked at him and said, 'Yeah, when was the last time you drank Dom Perignon? If you ever had, you'd know it was $51.40 in the liquor store.' What I didn't tell him is we'd bought it for $26.40 in Saskatoon." The after-hours club re-opened the next night with live entertainment by the Clichettes, a popular cabaret trio of lip-synching women. "After people had heard De Niro and those guys were there," says Copeman, "we had people lined up around the block."

It was all terribly exciting. But for those who worked at the festival, 1982 was a stressful year. They were handling major stars, without knowing quite how to go about it. Anne Mackenzie, who served as Wayne Clarkson's managing director, had taken it upon herself to commandeer the talent. She was the organizational nerve centre of the festival. Kay Armatage remembers first working with Mackenzie on the women's film festival in 1973: "She was the major researcher, the one who found the only print in America of *The Blue Light*. She could talk on the phone to anybody. She could find out anything about anything. And she used that skill tremendously at the Toronto festival. She was on the front lines most of the time, and it was an incredible skill. She could talk to people in a way that totally charmed them, and solicited information and got tremendous concessions from them. It was no small thing."

A tall, vivacious woman with the high-cheekboned look of Kate Hepburn, Mackenzie had a sharp intelligence and a quick laugh. Whether dining with Warren Beatty or clearing a path for Robert De Niro, she negotiated the hysteria of celebrity wrangling with brisk authority. But now, looking back on those heady days, she admits the festival was

PHOTO: ©EVA EVERYTHING 1982

out of its depth. "We were not used to that stuff," she says. "None of us were. Now I can't think of what the fuss was about. But it probably would have been better if those people were looked after by people who knew what they were doing." The tribute, says Clarkson, "was a huge strain on everybody and Annie was carrying the brunt. She delivered the components. And she got incredibly territorial. Rosie Levine and the entire guest office quit on me the day after the tribute." Why? It was all about not getting into a party—which is about the worst thing that can possibly happen to you at the festival. Levine, who ran the guest office, showed up at a soiree for Scorsese and was barred at the door by Mackenzie, who was strictly enforcing De Niro's directive that *no one* should be allowed in. George Anthony recalls getting the same reception at the door: "I remember laughing and saying, 'Annie, that's what they all say. They don't mean it.'"

"Something happened to the festival around 1982," says novelist David Gilmour, who had been hired by Mackenzie, his ex-wife, to edit the festival programme book and was later fired by her for drunken proofreading—on overproof rum. "The whole tenor of the place changed," he says. "Where the doors had always been open before and everyone would sit around after work with their feet on the table drinking beers, suddenly this odd hierarchical situation insinuated itself. Suddenly doors were being shut. It ceased being something that all of us were putting together and became this corporation."

"If you wanted something done, Annie was the one who got twenty-four elephants in front of the Canadian Film Centre i Annie is the person I would get to do it"

Perhaps that was inevitable. The festival wanted to attract stars, and stars require unusual levels of privacy, luxury and security. By its very nature, says Mackenzie, the festival "is an event that is given to secret dinners and secret parties." She eventually learned that the secret to taking care of celebrities was getting other people to do it. "You need really good drivers who know really good dealers," she says. "If you have enough limo drivers, things get taken care of. And you don't have to do it. It's all very amusing to see that play out, everybody 'taking care' of everybody." Helga Stephenson, the festival's chief publicist at the time, learned in the early eighties that the festival could no longer babysit the stars. "I basically insulated the festival from it," she says. "I

PHOTO: GAIL HARVEY

-ne. If I wanted
-nty-four hours,

PHOTO: ©EVA EVERYTHING 1982

ANNE MACKENZIE AND CLARKSON AT THE JEWISON PICNIC IN THE CALEDON HILLS, 1982

BEAU BRIDGES AND BONNIE BEDELIA, 1983

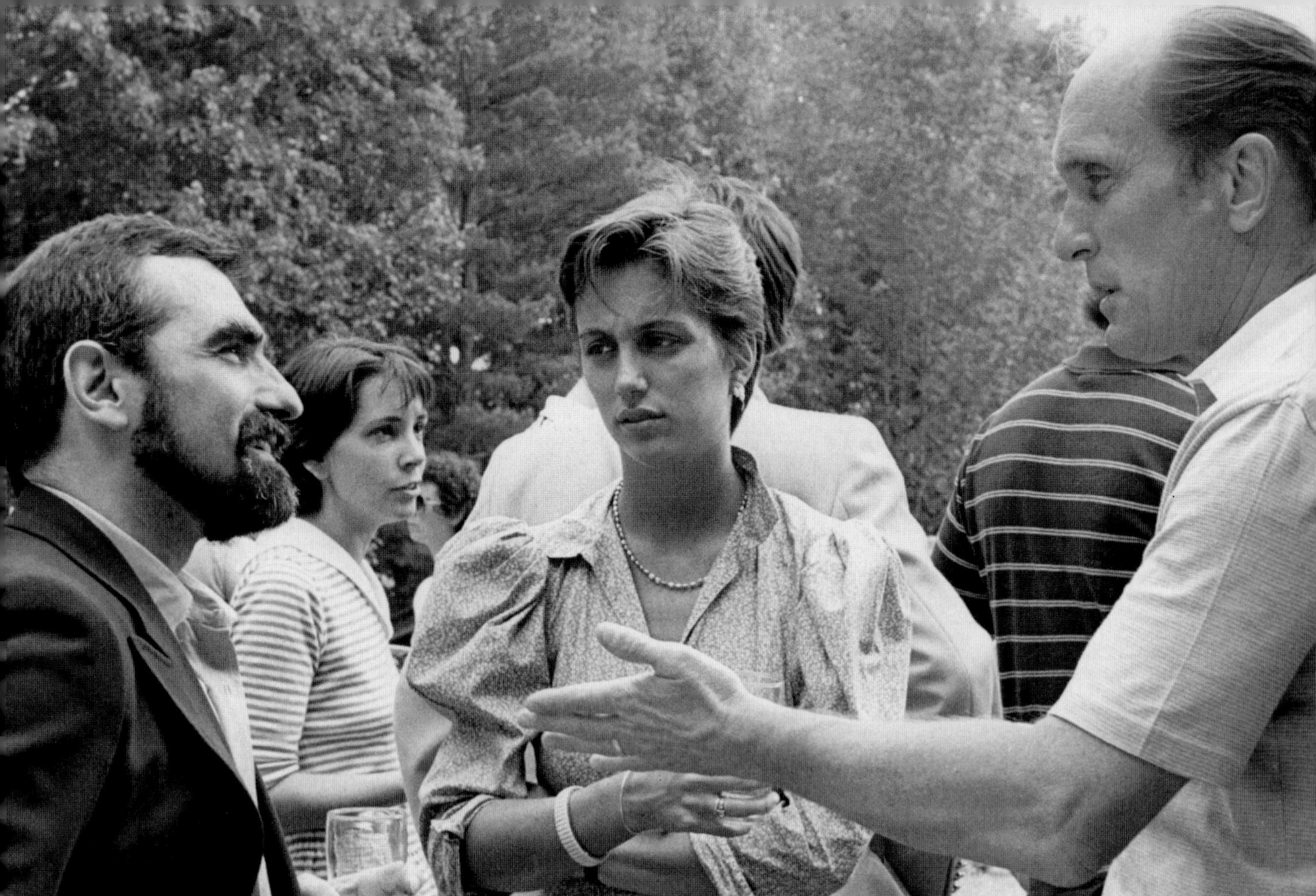

PHOTO: ©EVA EVERYTHING 1982

SCORSESE, DEBBIE SCHINDLER AND ROBERT DUVALL AT THE JEWISON PICNIC, 1982

learned the hard way that if there's the studio and the star and the festival pipsqueak . . . you guess who gets blamed. So I said to Wayne and Annie, 'We can't deal with star X. When problems happen, we're going to lose every single time. There's only a downside. The studios have their people, so why don't we let them take care of their own talent and we'll ask for what we need. We need public appearances for the screenings, we need press access, we need a press conference, and if a sponsor is having a party, maybe they could pass by.'" What that meant, says Stephenson, "is that the stars were better taken care of, and it was cheaper for us."

One star who clearly needed no babysitting was Robert Duvall. The 1983 tribute to Duvall was less crazed than the Scorsese event. Again, the idea was to honour someone whose talent had not received its due in Hollywood. Although he'd been nominated for three Oscars and was adored by critics, at the age of fifty-two Duvall felt he was not getting the roles he deserved. "I'm not one of the five or six most bankable names in Hollywood, and I've had two projects whisked away from me to go to a bigger name," he told the tribute audience. Again, Siskel and Ebert moderated, and Canadian editor Robert Boyd cut together an opening montage of clips from 35-mm prints of Duvall's films. It began with his performance as Arthur "Boo" Radley in *To Kill a Mockingbird*, and featured his roles as a self-effacing Mafia lawyer in *The Godfather*, a faded country singer in *Tender Mercies* and as the manic colonel in *Apocalypse Now*—the famous "I

PHOTO: GAIL HARVEY

love the smell of napalm in the morning" scene in which Duvall does not even blink as a mortar shell explodes right behind him. "It was an incredible montage," says House. "We screened it for Duvall in the cutting room—we showed the cut prints on the flatbed, the Steinbeck—and he cried. He was very, very happy. He thanked us profusely. We practically passed out we were so thrilled."

MICHAEL CAINE, JULIE WALTERS, GARTH DRABINSKY AND PAUL GODFREY, 1983

At the tribute, a standing ovation greeted Duvall as he arrived in a white tuxedo to the sound of Wagner's "Ride of the Valkyrie" from *Apocalypse Now*. He listened to praise from director Ulu Grosbard (*True Confessions*) and screenwriter Horton Foote (*Mockingbird*, *Tender Mercies*), who said the actor "has an enormous instinct for the truth, an incessant appetite to find the exactness of a person." Duvall, meanwhile, entertained the audience with ruminations on acting, and imitations of Marlon Brando in *The Godfather*. Francis Coppola, he said, reminded him of "a kid with an all-day sucker in his mouth, whatever he wants he gets"—apparently unaware that Coppola was waiting in the wings as a surprise guest. Then, with another blast of "Ride of the Valkyrie" and another standing ovation, Coppola, looking like a cartoon Godfather in a black suit, orange tie and white fedora, stepped onstage and gave the actor a bear hug.

The tribute was followed by a lavish party in a series of model condo suites at Queen's Quay. The developer was trying to sell them and thought the festival crowd would be a good target market. It was Barb Hershenhorn's first year on the job as the festival's party organizer (a role she still plays), and she had the suites tricked out with movie themes. *The Godfather* suite had a Sicilian motif; the *Apocalypse Now* room looked like a jungle; a saloon was set up for *Tender Mercies*; waiters in priests' robes served wine with communion wafers in the *True Confessions* suite.

Early in the evening, when Hershenhorn arrived to supervise the set-up, she found two hookers in the lobby dressed in tacky evening gowns. "Can I help you?" she asked.

"We're singers with the band."

"Well, that's funny because I booked the band and it has no singers—it's a three-piece with piano, upright bass and soft drums."

Hershenhorn asked the women to leave, and when they refused, she called security. One of the women insisted she first had to go to the bathroom, and the only bathrooms were upstairs in the suites. Hoping to hide out until the party started, she spent over an hour in the bathroom. When she finally emerged, a security guard escorted her out of the building. Two hours later, after the party was under way, she showed up completely redone, in a new outfit with a blonde wig. At that point, said Hershenhorn, "I thought she'd gone to so much trouble she deserved to get in." A few years later, the woman returned to the festival—as a gold patron—and she's been back every year since. "She's still a hooker," says Hershenhorn. "I've thrown her out of parties because she's tried to crash VIP areas."

With each tribute, wrangling celebrities became more complicated. Coppola was actually a bigger star than Duvall, and snaring him for the evening was a logistical nightmare. The director was in New York, shooting *The Cotton Club*, and had to be back on the set at 7 a.m. the next day. "This was at the height of Coppola fandom," recalls Mackenzie. "The insurers on the film almost didn't allow him to come. And those were the days when everyone was so medicated they couldn't think straight—I mean, when did you last see *The Cotton Club*?" Mackenzie managed to borrow an executive jet from Alfred Powers of Noranda Mines. "He had a Gulf Stream II and was kind enough to lend it," she says. The next year, for the Warren Beatty tribute, two private jets were arranged to fly in Beatty with Diane Keaton from Los Angeles and Jack Nicholson from New York. Each year, the tributes became more elaborate and more expensive, culminating with the Beatty event. It cost more than $100,000. It ushered the festival into a new stratosphere of celebrity politics. And it made perfectly sane people show signs of dementia.

PHOTO: GAIL HARVEY

Brave

New Whirl: 1984

N WARREN BEATTY, THE FESTIVAL MET ITS MATCH. AFTE
THE TRIBUTES TO SCORSESE AND DUVALL, HONOURING BEATTY IN
manner that would make him feel comfortable required an entirely d
erent order of diplomacy. Scorsese was a great director, Duvall was
great actor, and Beatty was a bit of both. But he had something th
was beyond their reach: the glamour and power of Hollywood royalty

PHOTO PREVIOUS PAGES: GAIL HARVEY

Beatty was a movie star who had carved his own niche squarely between Old and New Hollywood. Although he'd been discovered under the studio system, with *Splendor in the Grass*, he was a child of the sixties, intent on translating the freedoms of the counter-culture into a new kind of cinema. He made his breakthrough with Arthur Penn's 1967 landmark, *Bonnie and Clyde*, worked up a promiscuous lather of sex and politics in Hal Ashby's *Shampoo*, chased Julie Christie through the mud and murk of Robert Altman's *McCabe & Mrs. Miller* and won an Oscar for directing *Reds*, Hollywood's first socialist epic. Beatty was the ultimate insider, the cautious Hollywood liberal who had struck his own canny compromise between the studio system and artistic autonomy. He was a producer. He was also a control freak, a political animal with an acutely developed sense of his power and influence. And he was not about to take a passive approach to his own tribute. Warren wanted no surprises.

"The Beatty thing was strange," says Ebert, "because Warren was very conflicted and ambiguous about being there. He's a person that likes to be in control of things and a tribute, by its very nature, is something that he wouldn't be in control of." Ebert was on good terms with Beatty. He had met the actor around the time of *Bonnie and Clyde*, and championed the film when many critics had dismissed it. "I thought it was a great, great film," says Ebert, "the best American film of the year, and it got off to a rocky start. So he was kind of grateful for friends at that point."

Beatty exerted meticulous control over the tribute through David MacLeod, his Toronto-born cousin. This is the same David MacLeod who had been Bill Marshall's wrangler in the festival's first, abortive attempt to recruit Hollywood stars—and who would be found dead fourteen years later in Montreal as a convicted pedophile on the lam. Back then, MacLeod had some friends around the festival, notably David Gilmour. "We got high together," says Gilmour, meaning "high" in every sense of the word. "We did Mandrax and went skydiving—he and one of his little Indian boys, Ronnie, a real pretty-boy Indian. We did a whole lot of Mandrax because I'm afraid of heights. It's a major tranquilizer with a kick to it. David was a serious pill boy, and I was too in those days. I used to get it for him because I had a 'scrip with a very disreputable doctor who would sell his name. We did a lot of pills together.

"David MacLeod was a consummate backroom boy. He manipulated people by the promise of contact with the higher powers. I remember MacLeod turning up once and saying, 'Come on up to my house if you want to meet Julie Christie,' and sure enough there was Julie Christie sitting in his mother's living room. Once he phoned up and said, 'I'm having dinner with Diane Keaton tonight. Do you want to come?' By this point I was sufficiently furious about my own lack of secular recognition, I couldn't bear the notion of actually having a life that was about going to dinner with people simply because they were famous. My self-esteem wouldn't allow it."

MacLeod's fall from grace came as a shock to those close to him. James Toback, who wrote and directed MacLeod's production of *The Pick-Up Artist* (1987), was one of his best friends. The last time they saw each other was in Toronto in 1992, when Toback presented *Fingers* in a Cinematheque Ontario series programmed by Geoff Pevere. MacLeod, who was on the lam, suddenly materialized in the lobby of the director's hotel. "Later that night, we went walking around the streets, looking left and right in a state of serious paranoia," recalled Toback, whose memory of the incident was jogged when Pevere met him again at the '99 festival. "We finally ended up in some little restaurant at midnight that was about to close. Somebody came in and he said, 'We got to get out of here right away.' He didn't know who it was but he had a bad feeling. We said goodbye around two in the morning." Toback dismisses the police account of

PHOTO: GAIL HARVEY

Beatty exerted meticulous control over the tribute through David MacLe his Toronto-born cousin, who would be found dead fourteen years la n Montreal as a convicted sex offender on the lam

MacLeod's death. "Who's going to choose suicide by swallowing lighter fluid? What is far more likely is that he was killed." The whole business left Toback angry and haunted, but he decided there was no point in pushing for an investigation. "It's too bad," he says. "MacLeod was bright and smart and charming and people liked him. He didn't get away with something that a lot of guys in Hollywood get away with. A lot of famous and powerful people are as addicted to exactly that or more but they didn't get caught. Or they bought their way out."

The whole episode left Beatty with "a sense of tremendous frustration," says Toback, who co-wrote *Bugsy* for the actor in 1992. "Beatty does not like failure. Not that it's his failure. It's just that the whole thing was a disaster. MacLeod was like a brother for him. I mean, MacLeod basically ran his life for twenty years. The only person who knew exactly what was going on with Beatty was MacLeod."

MacLeod hovered over every detail of the Beatty tribute. He had attended the Duvall event, which had dragged on far too long, "and was very concerned about Siskel and Ebert going on and on," says Bill House. "He wasn't wrong about that." Once again, Robert Boyd cut an opening montage of clips, but, through MacLeod, revision after revision was sent to Beatty in Hollywood. "They wanted to control the images," says House. "They made us cut a scene from *Splendor in the Grass*, the scene near the end of the movie with Natalie Wood against the lockers, the prelude to a kiss. They didn't want that because of whatever notions there were about Beatty and women. And it was important for them to have the politics, the liberal politics, front and centre in all of this, which we also wanted to accommodate."

Just how much was required to accommodate Warren Beatty became apparent when he showed up for a run-through at the University Theatre on the afternoon of the tribute. John Allen remembers standing onstage with him, dealing with exhaustive questions about how to get out of the theatre after the show. "We'll take you down these stairs, and then we can go down the alley to your limousine in the back," said Allen.

"How far is it?" Beatty asked.
"I don't know. About 30 or 40 feet."
"Let's find out."

At this point, as Allen recalls, "Beatty jumps down off the stage and starts counting the number of feet, putting one foot in front of the other toe-to-heel, doing this kind of tightrope walk all the way back to the car. He comes back and says, 'It's 47 of *my* feet. But I think my foot is not quite a foot. Let's call it 40 feet. How long do you think that will take me?' I said, 'Will you be with other people?' He said, 'Let's do it two ways, one with me walking by myself, and one with other people.' So he walked all the way back by himself and we timed it. And then we had to get everyone else to do it. We all traipsed along with him and we timed it again. It was a little longer. He said, 'You're right, it slows down with other people.'"

With the Beatty tribute, the strange paranoia of Hollywood protocol began to rub off on festival organizers. "There was a feeling that we were doing God's work here," said Allen. "There was the Normandy invasion, and then there was putting on the tribute. It was like the world was sitting on the head of a pin. For some reason we had RCMP at the tribute. Bill House kept bugging them, saying, 'Is this going to be a security zone? I want the lobby to be a security zone.' Finally one of the cops said, 'Mr. House, you want this lobby to be a security zone?'

STRANGER THAN PARADISE

At the party, a Globe and Mail *reporter held up a note pad on whi
she'd written, "Want to dance?" Jack leaned across the table to read
mouthed, "No thank you," then said, "Pity she used the wrong verb*

PHOTO: GAIL HARVEY

"'Yes, I do.'

"'Do you realize we would have to terminate anybody who moves into the security zone?'

"'Terminate them?'

"'Yes, we'll shoot them. Is that what you would like? Would you like us to shoot your patrons as they move into the lobby?'"

But House was only reflecting Beatty's fastidious concern. "There was this aura around him," House says. "It was like a version of paranoia, a fear of the public. There was an enormous security arrangement that had to be made around Beatty. We had plain-clothes cops all through the venue. I couldn't quite figure out why that had to be. I was thinking, this is Toronto, what are you guys talking about? Then when I met him, there was this sense of fear, as if there were people who hated him because he slept with a lot of women, because his politics were left, because he was so good-looking—whatever. It was like you were guarding against some kind of attack, or assassination. And I don't think I'm being dramatic."

Even Siskel and Ebert were spooked by Beatty. "We both looked at all of his movies because we were really insecure about how prepared we were," says Ebert. "We felt that he was putting so much pressure on us—not pressure, but he was so involved that we thought we better be ready—and we locked ourselves into the Plaza II Hotel with all these cassettes of his movies."

The tribute itself followed a different format than the others. There were no surprise guests. Instead of sitting onstage for hours while others talked about him, Beatty would remain in the audience, and Ebert had been given no indication whether or not he would even go onstage. Looking dapper in horn-rimmed glasses and a tan suit, the forty-seven-year-old actor sat with Diane Keaton and MacLeod while one by one the guests arrived to pay homage: *Bonnie and Clyde* director Arthur Penn, *Shampoo* screenwriter Robert Towne, novelist Jerzy Kosinski and then the night's biggest star, Jack Nicholson. "I don't usually tell stories about Warren Beatty because you get trained not to," said Jack, who played to the crowd, ducking the earnest line of questioning from Siskel and Ebert. When the critics asked about *The Fortune*, an expensive flop in which he co-starred with Beatty, Nicholson joked that the character in the movie was based on Beatty himself—"a mean guy who'd murder his wife for a nickel."

As the critics persisted with questions about *The Fortune*, Jack reached into his pocket and put on a pair of lime-green sunglasses. "I got them in Los Angeles, where everything this colour grows," he drawled, eating up the crowd with his crocodile grin. The audience went wild. I was there that night, having spent the day delivering films. Seeing that one simple gesture—Jack putting on those shades—I understood what it meant to be a movie star. You had to act like one. And in that one moment it became clear: this must be the Big Time. Finally, the festival had made it. We could all relax, because this was as good as it gets. Warren and Jack—Hollywood's Mick and Keith—made the dream come true eight years after Bill Marshall played bad tennis at Beatty's house on Mulholland Drive.

Like Coppola at the Duvall event, Jack upstaged the guest of honour. Beatty, the master of noblesse oblige, seemed an anti-climactic presence at his own tribute. But eventually he did rise from his seat and make his way to the stage. He turned to Siskel and Ebert and suggested a remake of *The Fortune* with the two critics in the roles played by himself and Nicholson, and Pauline Kael in the part played by Stockard Channing. Beatty went on to praise the Toronto festival, the first film festival he had attended in about fifteen years. "I used to go all the time, to Cannes and Venice," he said, "but the stories I could tell you about that would be too lurid for this august gathering. They don't have anything to do with film." The actor also paid tribute to Diane Keaton, calling her "the finest actress in America" and "the most profound influence on my work for the last six or seven years." But the actress chose to remain in the audience.

Beatty said he had written an eight-page speech on the plane comparing the crisis in American liberalism to the plight of the progressive filmmaker. Although he didn't read it, he delivered the gist. "Films in their pursuit of demographics," he declared, "have come to the same point as American liberals. If a political leader now wanted to pay attention to the concerns of the Third World, he'd need a combination of Steven Spielberg and George Lucas to get elected." Beatty said he had screened *Reds* at the White House for Ronald Reagan. "I don't want to take a cheap shot," he told the crowd. "He was very nice about it and said he had hoped it would have a happy ending. He's a likeable and an amiable man and I happen to detest his politics."

Fifteen years later, Warren Beatty would flirt with the idea of running for president. But even back then, he acted as much the statesman as the star, fastidious about controlling his image. He allowed only one festival photographer into the tribute and insisted on approving the pictures, which had to be developed and then rushed to him at the party afterwards to meet newspaper deadlines. He also prohibited any cameras from the party, a bash for fifteen hundred at Yorkville's Copa nightclub, where he was sequestered in a roped-off VIP area—a concept that was anathema to festival veterans but would become standard practice with visiting stars. At one point, *Globe and Mail* reporter Susan Ferrier MacKay, unable to get around a table to talk to Nicholson, held up a note pad on which she'd written, "Want to dance?" Jack leaned across the table to read it, mouthed "No thank you." Then, turning to Toronto financier David Perlmutter, he said, "Pity she used the wrong verb."

Later that night, Nicholson moved on to an all-night coach-house party hosted by Michael Budman, the co-owner of Roots. Pioneering the synergy between celebrity and merchandise that has since become the engine of pop culture, Budman went out of his way to cultivate celebrity friends, and worked his connections to make the Roots brand fashionable. "We were always interested in having music, sports and entertainment figures exposed to Roots," he says, "but the festival really helped." Budman, who sat on the festival board, hung out with a high-flying elite of guests and patrons. And his coach-house parties, white nights in which no one had trouble staying awake, were legendary. "The hippest party I ever hosted," he says, "was after the Warren Beatty tribute." Beatty didn't show up, "but every other celebrity in town did. And Jack was there all night, until six or seven in the morning." Lorraine Segato, who had played the Copa party with The Parachute Club—a band she had formed in 1982 to play an opening-night party at the festival—was among the guests. "It was odd," she recalls. "I met Jack for a brief second. But he was upstairs most of the time. There was always kind of a going off into a corner, into a room. Even though you were at an exclusive party there was still that sense of untouchableness."

The Beatty event would be the last of the tributes. They had accomplished what they were designed for—to raise the profile of the festival. They had become prohibitively expensive. And the whole idea of importing a couple of American critics to play host to Hollywood stars rubbed some people the wrong way. Toronto critic Martin Knelman had

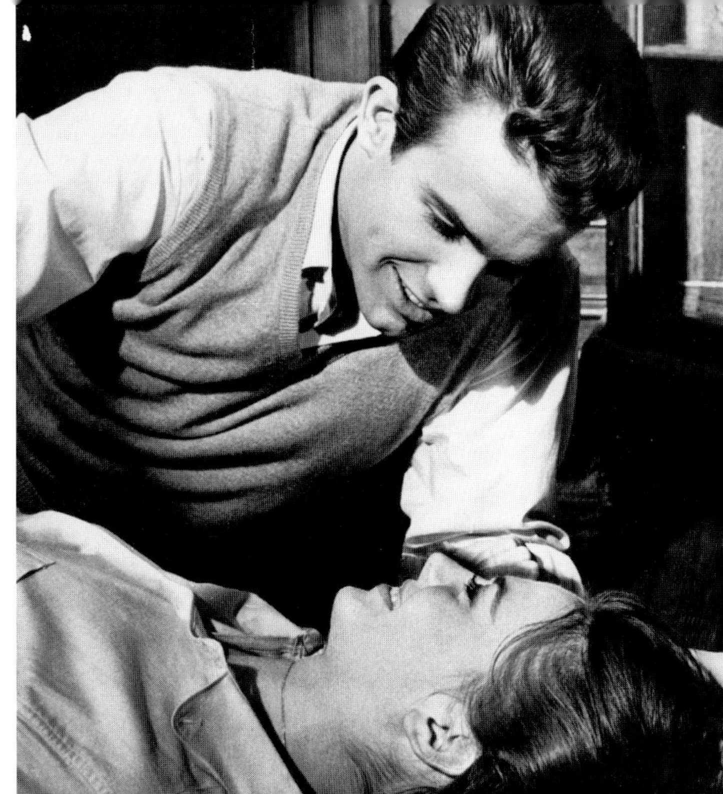

ney wanted to control the images. They made us cut a scene from lendor in the Grass, *the prelude to a kiss. They didn't want that be* *ɹse of whatever notions there were about Beatty and women"*

been miffed a few years earlier when, without telling him, the festival had Ebert take over Buried Treasures, which Knelman had originated in 1977. "I'd assumed my programme was just a one-shot thing," says Knelman, "but to my astonishment Buried Treasures reappeared the next year with Ebert's name on it." Siskel and Ebert received a rough ride in the local press after all three tributes. Jay Scott wrote that Beatty acted "as if he were graciously making an appearance on The Tweedledum and Tweedledumber Show." Ebert, however, now says he understands the sentiment behind some of the criticism. "There was a feeling," he says, "that maybe Canada had some movie critics who could be doing this, that it wasn't necessary to bring in two people from Chicago, as if Canada didn't have enough critics of its own. And there's a lot to be said for that point of view." In fact, Citytv's syndicated celebrity interviewer, Brian Linehan, was chagrined that he wasn't called upon to host the event. "I would like to have done it," he says, pointing out that he established a good relationship with Beatty over several interviews. According to Anne Mackenzie, however, without Siskel and Ebert, the stars might never have agreed to come. "The reason these people showed up," she says, "had nothing to do with the festival. It had everything to do with Roger and Gene."

Although some saw the Beatty tribute as a kind of Faustian pact with Hollywood, for one of the festival's most rigorous cinephiles, future director Piers Handling, it was a means to an end. That year he coordinated Northern Lights, the massive Canadian retrospective. "We were all concerned with creating a profile for an event that would have a trickle-down effect," he says. "The tributes allowed you to do a bunch of other things at the same time. Having that excitement allowed me to do the Canadian retrospective. It allowed Wayne to take the risk. He could deliver Beatty and Nicholson to his board, and to the corporate sponsors, so they could ignore the fact that there were 150 Canadian films off to one side." But the Beatty tribute "almost bankrupted the festival," adds Handling. "The board paid attention after that and put the brakes on Wayne for a year. After that it started to turn into a business-like board."

Clarkson had tried to get sponsorship for the Beatty tribute. American Express bought in to the tune of $35,000. But two days before the press conference to announce the details, Clarkson remembers getting a call from managing director Anne Mackenzie: "Wayne, we got a problem. Warren Beatty won't do the tribute if it's sponsored by American Express—not because he's got anything against American Express, but he doesn't want to be seen to be endorsing it." Scrambling to hang onto the money, Clarkson offered American Express Carlos Saura's *Carmen*, the closing night gala at the University Theatre. A subtitled Spanish opera movie doesn't have the pizzazz of Warren Beatty. But, banking on a guest appearance by Placido Domingo, Wayne persuaded American Express to buy in—for the same $35,000.

After the *Carmen* gala, as Clarkson was heading over to the Courtyard Café to dine with Domingo and his agent, he ran into Yos Winter, the president of American Express Canada. Would he and his wife like to come for dinner with them? "This is totally improvised," explains Clarkson. "Their jaws drop. We go across the street. We sit them down, with his wife right next to Placido Domingo. And American Express financed the festival for the next three or four years." Clarkson ran into Winter a decade later. "Wayne," he said, "my wife and I have never forgotten that night in 1984. Wait till I go home and tell her I ran into you. We still reminisce about that incredible evening when Placido

PHOTO: NANCY ACKERMAN

Domingo sat next to her."

If there was one year when it all came together, when the festival was everything it was supposed to be, it was 1984. This was the dream festival, the ideal balance of indie breakthroughs, Canadian content and Hollywood glitz. It presented the feature debuts of no less than five major directors, forerunners of a new movement in independent cinema. The Coen brothers kick-started their career with the diabolical *Blood Simple*; Jim Jarmusch floated his first offspeed pitch across the plate with *Stranger Than Paradise*; Stephen Frears revealed his knack for character-driven drama with *The Hit*; Luc Besson made a post-apocalyptic splash with *Le dernier combat*; and a twenty-four-year-old hometown boy named Atom Egoyan etched his first family-Gothic portrait with *Next of Kin*. The same festival also launched John Sayles's *The Brother from Another Planet*, Wim Wenders's *Paris, Texas*, Neil Jordan's *The Company of Wolves*, Alan Rudolph's *Choose Me* and Robert Altman's *Secret Honor*.

PARIS, TEXAS

Even more remarkable, half of the four hundred films programmed in 1984 were Canadian. It was the largest retrospective of Canadian cinema ever assembled and it attracted sell-out crowds. This was also the year that a seventeen-year-old Toronto actor named Kiefer Sutherland made his first screen appearance in the opening-night premiere of *The Bay Boy*. And another native son, Norman Jewison, introduced a shyly charismatic newcomer named Denzel Washington at the premiere of *A Soldier's Story*, Jewison's most powerful drama since *In the Heat of the Night*.

The festival's perennial quest for star power paid off as never before, and not just at the Beatty extravaganza. Steve Martin and Lily Tomlin kibitzed with director Carl Reiner at the launch of their identity-flipped farce, *All of Me*. Sally Field graced the premiere of Robert Benton's *Places in the Heart*, which was voted the festival's most popular film—and would later give Field the opportunity to accept her second Oscar with the most memorable line of her career: "You like me, you really like me!" Even the pope inadvertently figured in the picture. A visit by Pope John Paul II happened to coincide with the festival, and the Catholic bishops hosting his tour suggested that two National Film Board documentaries had been programmed deliberately to embarrass the pontiff. For some, however, the festival was so all-consuming, they weren't even aware the pope was in town. Rob Salem remembers walking out into a big crowd on Bloor Street with Harry Dean Stanton, possibly the shiftiest-looking actor in the movies. Stanton couldn't figure out why all these heavy-looking men were eyeing him so strangely, until he realized that they were plainclothes security on the lookout for potential assassins on the Popemobile's parade route.

For Kay Armatage, the coolest star in town that year was not Warren Beatty or Pope John Paul, but David Byrne, who showed up with the Talking Heads for the world premiere of Jonathan Demme's *Stop Making Sense*. Armatage, who had joined the festival

LILY TOMLIN AND STEVE MARTIN, 1984

TALKING HEADS TINA WEYMOUT AND DAVID BYRNE AT THE STOP MAKING SENSE *PRESS CONFERE* 1984

in 1982, was the only woman on the programming team, and its most avant-garde curator—David Overbey notwithstanding. If Overbey was the gay iconoclast oblivious to fashion, Armatage was the cool feminist with a conscience and a sense of style, forever one step ahead of the newest new wave. A sexy academic who teaches film and women's studies at the University of Toronto, she was the only programmer who had actually made films—arresting documentaries ranging from *Strip Tease* (1980), a creative portrait of women who dance naked, to *Artist on Fire: Joyce Wieland* (1987), a naked portrait of a creative woman. To truly appreciate Kay's curatorial flair, you have to visit her Haliburton cottage: she has transformed a glorified shack into a funky paradise, with a sun porch of faux-zebra-covered Barco loungers overlooking the lake from a steep hillside that she has landscaped with rocks and wildflowers. She has also had an interesting choice of boyfriends. She lived with Joe Medjuck, an academic film theorist who left Canada to produce Hollywood movies with Ivan Reitman. And she raised a daughter with Bill House, the festival manager who became an executive at Telefilm Canada, then at Alliance Atlantis.

Armatage was a fan of both Talking Heads and Jonathan Demme before most people had heard of them. When she and Medjuck were living in London during the seventies, they had dinner with Demme, who had just co-written *The Hot Box*, a bimbo B-movie about nurses who bust out of jail to become guerrillas in the jungle. And she had saved Talking Heads posters from the band's early fringe gigs in Toronto, at A Space and the Ontario College of Art. At the '84 festival, after introducing the Heads to a cheering crowd at the Elgin theatre, Armatage had Byrne sign the posters over dinner. Demme, who collected Heads memorabilia, requested copies. Later that night, there was a party for the film at the Manulife Centre. I remember seeing David Byrne walk through the room alone, with no handlers or entourage, as invisible as a rock star could be. But people noticed. They pretended not to stare. Among the guests that night was Atom Egoyan, then premiering his first feature, *Next of Kin*. "It was amazing seeing someone like David Byrne in the flesh," he recalls. "It was my first contact with glamour. I remember watching him walk into the middle of the room. People made a clearing for him. He just sized up the place, and he left. I thought that was the coolest thing I'd ever seen."

A cool guy in a cool movie. *Stop Making Sense* is the postmodern antidote to rock 'n' roll delusions of grandeur. Byrne walks out onto a bare stage with an acoustic guitar, sets a boom-box down beside himself, and performs "Psycho Killer" using the absurdly small machine for accompaniment. The band is slowly assembled in modular units as the musicians are wheeled onto the stage, one by one, with their equipment. Byrne moves like a scarecrow dancing his way out of a straitjacket, chicken-twitching some strange semaphore. He is the Thin Man in the Big Suit, backed by a nine-piece funk band that works like a semiotic windup toy, filtering African rhythms through theories of suburban alienation. The camera registers the show without comment. There is nothing to add. No vicarious glimpses backstage, no cutaways to delirious audience members. The show continually exposes its own artifice. And as the music plays, slides of images and words run interference behind the band, like Godardian flash cards.

BLOOD SIMPLE

STOP MAKING SENSE

PHOTO: GAIL HARVEY

the extravagant eighties, as pop music got fat and Hollywood got stupid op Making Sense *was the sound of a sardonic resistance. And ir nerican cinema, Byrne's deadpan edge found an equivalent in the ark, self-conscious style of the new film noir*

This was before people got bored with irony, when it was still possible to be *genuinely* ironic. Which is perhaps why the film still holds up today. In the extravagant eighties, as pop music got fat and Hollywood got stupid, *Stop Making Sense* was the sound of a sardonic resistance. And in American cinema, Byrne's deadpan edge found a cinematic equivalent in the stark, self-conscious style of the new film noir. It would show up in the staccato existentialism of Jim Jarmusch and the gentle absurdism of Alan Rudolph, in the surreal nightmares of David Lynch and the hep-cat capers of Quentin Tarantino.

In 1984, the most startling example was *Blood Simple*, which Joel and Ethan Coen wrote, directed and produced. This low-budget gem mixes film noir and graphic horror with unprecedented nerve. A serpentine plot begins with a private eye double-crossing the sleazy owner of a Texas roadhouse, who has hired him to kill his wife and her lover. Through a series of ingenious twists, an inexorable momentum sets in. As the plot thickens, along with the blood, it is like Edgar Allan Poe on acid. The horror is all about guilt, and the impossibility of cleaning up after a murder, of burying a telltale body without a trace. And in the gathering dusk of Barry Sonnenfeld's cinematography, a fluid conspiracy of blood and sweat and smoke, nothing will ever come clean.

Because no one had ever seen anything quite like *Blood Simple*, the Coens had trouble persuading people that anyone would want to. Before the Toronto premiere, all the distribution companies had turned them down. Producer's rep Jeff Dowd remembers

PHOTO: DOUG MACLELLAN

LEFT, ATOM EGOYAN AND ARSINÉE KHANJIAN, 1991

showing the movie to Paramount executive Frank Mancuso: "He just thought it wasn't a commercial film. Unlike *Halloween*, you didn't have a victim you could identify with." Only when the distributors saw *Blood Simple* with a festival audience in Toronto did the industry finally catch on. "If you saw it in a screening room," says Dowd, "the black humour didn't work. When he's dragging the body across the field, and trying to bury it—when you show that with an audience, people laugh." After the festival screening, half a dozen distributors, the same ones who had rejected the film earlier, jumped into a bidding war for the film. "The unique thing about the Toronto audience," Dowd explains, "is that it's the closest thing you'll get to a regular Friday-night audience in a theatre. That's not the case with Sundance or Telluride or even the New York festival."

Toronto became known as a festival where the audience would *get it*. Something similar happened the same year with a very different kind of picture, *A Soldier's Story*. Based on the Charles Fuller play, this drama of racism and murder on a Louisiana military base stands out as a milestone in Norman Jewison's career. The Canadian director has made his best movies about black America, from *In the Heat of the Night* (1967) to *The Hurricane* (1999), and *A Soldier's Story* was groundbreaking in its own way, as a drama about racism, not just between blacks and whites, but among blacks. It was a Hollywood movie that Jewison made on what was, for him, a shoestring—less than $6 million. "It was an extremely small film that nobody wanted to make," the director recalls. "Nobody was paid anything but scale. And nobody expected it to do any business. But Toronto went crazy for it. The impact from that screening in New York and Los Angeles was unbelievable." The picture opened commercially after the festival, platforming from a few major cities to wide release. "Before you knew it, you had this hit," says Jewison. "And it all started here at the University Theatre. Of all my films, the one that this festival helped most was *Soldier's Story*."

That year, Jewison and his wife, Dixie, invited two hundred festival guests up to their spread in the Caledon Hills for a Sunday picnic. It was the forerunner of an event that has since grown into the festival's biggest shmooze, sprawling over the grounds of the

Canadian Film Centre, which Jewison founded in 1988. But at the director's farm, the picnic originated as a relaxed and rather exclusive event, an escape from the festival rather than an addition to it. In 1984, the guest list included an eclectic mix: Stephen Frears, Judd Hirsh, John Malkovich, David Cronenberg, Garth Drabinsky, Irene Cara and Tony Bennett. Food was laid out under a blue-and-white-striped tent. A string quartet played as guests picnicked on the grass. "You'd see directors and actors talking, having a drink, strolling across the green lawns," recalls Jewison. "There was something elegant and Canadian about it. People were going down to the barn to turn on, actors. One of the farm lads noticed they were smoking pot down there and got alarmed."

With each festival, the brunch grew. The first year, people found their own way there. Then there was a bus, then two buses, then three. Finally, says Jewison, "it got too complicated. We had everybody wandering through the house, and all of a sudden we were missing stuff. We had to have cops watching people. I thought it should be a bigger production, and that's when I thought of having it at the film centre. The festival was very disappointed. They didn't think it would work." The annual "picnic" now attracts a mob of twenty-five hundred to the film centre.

Self-doubt, as Jewison is fond of pointing out, seems to be endemic to the national culture. There were a lot of people who thought a Toronto film festival wouldn't work. Never mind a festival where Canadians would flock to see Canadian movies.

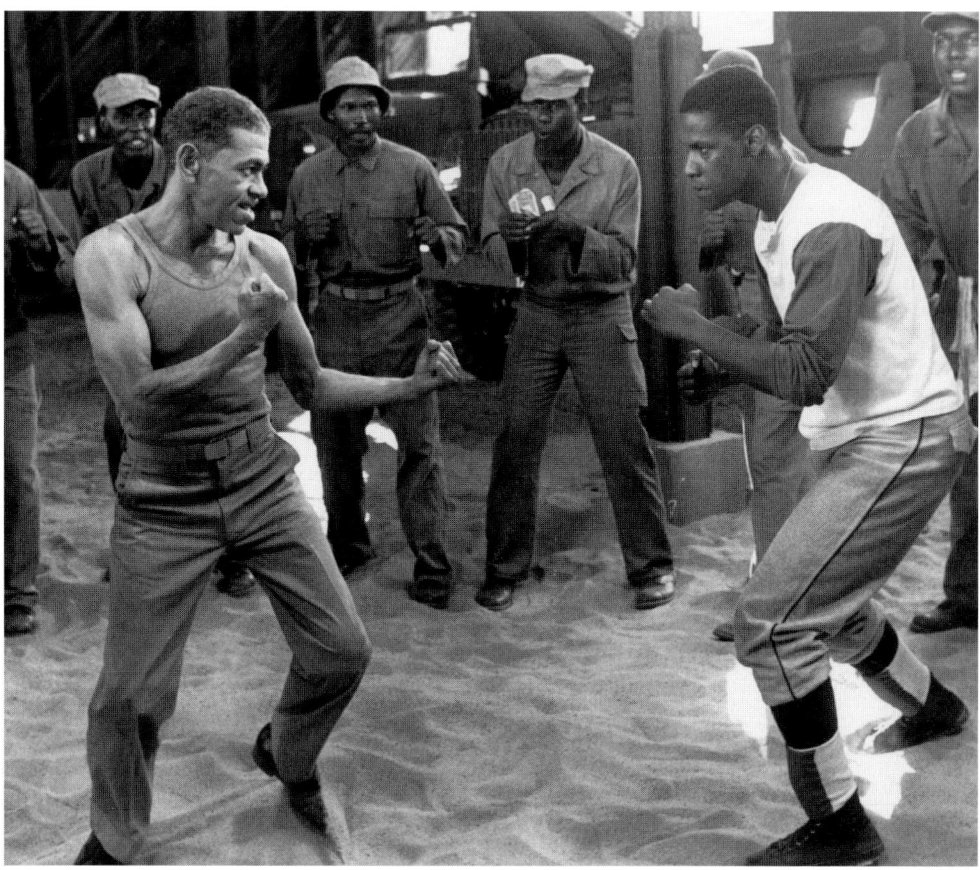

A SOLDIER'S STORY

American Cousin
American Empire

NORMAN JEWISON CAME TO TAKE HIS PLACE AS T *GODFATHER OF CANADIAN CINEMA, AN ODD STATUS CONSIDERI that he continued to direct all his pictures for American studios. founder of the Canadian Film Centre, he would help nurture a n generation that would do things differently. But was there an audie*

PHOTO: GAIL HARVEY

NORMAN AND DIXIE JEWISON, IN THE CALEDON HILLS, 1984

9

GOIN' DOWN THE ROAD

for Canadian cinema? Even if it could get films financed, distributed, promoted and exhibited, would anyone go to see them? Canadians, after all, were not in the habit of watching their own movies. In the late seventies, programmer Peter Harcourt explained it this way: "Canadian cinema is a foreign language in Canada. We do not know it. It's as foreign to us as French cinema. So you have to educate people." And that's what the festival set out to do—to build an audience that would feel at home in the foreign and often forbidding land of Canadian film.

The initiative can be traced back to the Canadian Film Institute in Ottawa, which has incubated a variety of festival talents, including Wayne Clarkson, Linda Beath, Michèle Maheux and Piers Handling. Handling joined the CFI as a microfilm clerk in 1971 and was one of the country's leading authorities on Canadian cinema by the time he joined the festival in 1982. In the seventies, he had watched a couple of film students at Carleton University, John Sharkey and Steve Bingham, draw sellout crowds to monthly screenings of Canadian movies. With Canada Council money, they would bring directors to town with the films and do heavy promotion. "They were brilliant marketers," says Handling, who hired the pair to do the same thing for the CFI's National Film Theatre,

LES BONS DÉBARRAS

while increasing the programme to 30 per cent Canadian content. "We were a struggling arts organization, and our executive director thought this was suicide. The previous regime had run only 10 per cent." But the programme was a success and Handling came to Toronto convinced that, with the right approach, an audience would materialize for Canadian films. He pitched the idea to Clarkson, who not only agreed but opened the floodgates. In 1983, Harcourt put together a series of sixty Canadian documentaries while Handling curated an ambitious Cronenberg programme—gearing up to the massive Canadian retrospective and the launch of Perspective Canada, a programme devoted to Canadian directors, in 1984.

With a lineup of two hundred films spanning eight decades, Northern Lights was the most comprehensive programme of Canadian cinema ever assembled. It seemed like a huge risk, especially since the documentary series had bombed the year before. "But Wayne was smart," says Handling. "He said we should run the films in small cinemas and create the illusion of mass interest and panic—have them banging down the doors. Which is what we did." The Northern Lights programme also had a gimmick: the festival polled hundreds of critics, academics and filmmakers all over the world to come up with Canada's Ten Best, an all-time honour roll:

1. *Mon oncle Antoine* (1971)
2. *Goin' Down the Road* (1970)
3. *Les bons débarras* (1980)
4. *The Apprenticeship of Duddy Kravitz* (1974)
5. *The Grey Fox* (1982)
6. *Les ordres* (1974)
7. *J.A. Martin photographe* (1976)
8. *Pour la suite du monde* (1963)
9. *Nobody Waved Good-bye* (1965)
10. *La vraie nature de Bernadette* (1972)

MON ONCLE ANTOINE

"The list was a fantastic marketing hook," says Handling. "If people didn't want to buy into the rest of the programme, there were ten films they could run off and see." The festival struck fresh prints, which later toured across Canada and the United States.

Meanwhile, nine programmers had scoured the country for more obscure Canadian fare. "We screened our little eyeballs out," says Handling. "And even for us, the so-called Canadian experts, we found material we hadn't been exposed to before." Among the buried treasures unearthed at Ottawa's National Film Archives were four movies by Larry Kent, a sixties renegade who drew a sobering portrait of the counterculture. In the semi-improvised *Bitter Ash* (1963), shot in the gritty style of Cassavetes's *Shadows*, a Beat playwright betrays his wife for a selfish fling; *High* (1967), which had been banned in Ontario, climaxes with two hippies making out in the shadow of a tree against which they've propped a freshly killed corpse.

But the sixties generation of English-

CLAUDE JUTRA

Canadian filmmakers—Larry Kent, Don Shebib, Don Owen—never lived up to its promise. There was no real industry to sustain them, and with the end of the tax-shelter era in 1979, local production was drying up. By the mid-eighties, English-Canadian cinema had yet to find its voice. Tellingly, more than half the features on the festival's top-ten list were from Quebec, as were the best of the twenty-one new films launched that year in Perspective Canada's inaugural programme : Léa Pool's *La femme de l'hôtel* and Micheline Lanctôt's *Sonatine*, two movies from women writer-directors who both employed a poetic formalism to arrive at an emotional truth.

La femme de l'hôtel, which won the prize for 1984's best Canadian feature, sounds precious—a film about a filmmaker making a film. But Pool's remarkably assured directing debut was the real thing. It's a kind of triangular *Persona*, a dramatic riddle about three women who converge as different aspects of the same psyche. Paule Baillargeon portrays a director shooting a movie in a hotel where she meets a mystery woman who is recovering from a nervous breakdown—played by the formidable Louise Marleau. The woman's life eerily parallels that of the movie's heroine. And as the director pursues this elusive figure, trying to use her as an inspiration for the character she has created, the actress cast in the role (Marthe Turgeon) is caught in the middle.

Unlike many films-within-films, *La femme de l'hôtel* doesn't come across as a postmodern conceit. It's a detective story about the essence of authorship. Dealing in emotion, not irony, it unfolds as a slow dance of strangers surrendering identity across a vast solitude, a city of empty spaces. And in the role of the reluctant muse, Marleau is a ravishing enigma, a woman whose life is stranded between an asylum and a hotel. Her haunting presence becomes synonymous with the city itself. As a refracted portrait of the artist—a riddle of women moving in and out of each other's movies—Léa Pool's debut feature is reminiscent of Jeanne Moreau's first film, *Lumière*. It examines the same fear of losing one's identity to art, and it salvages the same sense of female solidarity out of despair. For Pool, a Swiss-born immigrant in Quebec, *La femme de l'hôtel* reflected her own transience as a stranger passing through, an outsider in a culture of outsiders.

Micheline Lanctôt arrived at alienation from the opposite end of the telescope, as a Québécoise whose career took her to the heights of Hollywood and back. She started out as an animator in the monastic obscurity of the NFB, then became a celebrated actress and moved to California after starring in two movies on Canada's Ten Best list, *The Apprenticeship of Duddy Kravitz* and *La vraie nature de Bernadette*. Lanctôt describes *Sonatine* as a response to the dire alienation she felt as a Québécoise living in Los Angeles with *Duddy* director Ted Kotcheff in the late seventies: "Being a woman, being somebody's wife in L.A., is just about the worst position you can imagine, and it almost destroyed me."

Like Pool, she portrays Montreal as an alien landscape and constructs her film in three-part harmony—*sonatine* means "little sonata." Tracking the lives of two teenage girls

THE APPRENTICESHIP OF DUDDY KRAVIT

MORDECAI RICHLER, JACK WARDEN AND RICHARD DREYFUSS ON THE SET OF THE APPRENTICESHIP OF DUDDY KRAVITZ

drifting through an indifferent world, the narrative unfolds in three movements, each linked to a mode of transportation. In the first, one of the girls develops a relationship with a suburban bus driver; in the second, her best friend gets to know a Bulgarian sailor aboard a ship; in the third the two girls announce their impending suicide with placards in a Metro station. Lanctôt admits that *Sonatine* is an obstinately personal piece of work. "It doesn't tell a story," she says. "You can't relate to the girls as normal girls. There's no point of contact with the audience, so you can only identify with what the director wanted to say. As such, it's really an *auteur* film."

Quebec filmmakers could afford to be misanthropic. They had an established audience, with a tradition of popular *auteurs*, from Claude Jutra to Gilles Carle. But English-Canadian cinema was still trying to find itself, and its ambition was torn in two directions—spelled out in 1985 by two radically different films: *Joshua Then and Now* and *My American Cousin*.

With a budget of $11 million and a distribution deal with Twentieth Century Fox, *Joshua Then and Now* was, at the time, the most expensive Canadian movie ever made. It can be seen as a composite portrait of all the inharmonious forces then converging on the country's film business, which had become an industry driven by television. With the CBC and the newly formed Telefilm Canada donating $4.7 million of *Joshua*'s budget, director Ted Kotcheff was forced to shoot a three-and-a-half-hour mini-series alongside his feature—which he resented. Phillip Borsos would face a similar conundrum a few years later with *Bethune: The Making of a Hero*. "TV by its nature has to be more timid," said Kotcheff. "By investing in TV, the government is protecting its downside while compromising the upside." But for producer Robert Lantos, who was on the verge of creating Alliance Entertainment, *Joshua* was a coup, a prestigious marriage of public funding and Hollywood clout. And for Kotcheff, the man who brought Rambo into the world with *First Blood*, it was a chance to come home, to work with author Mordecai Richler and hopefully reproduce the magic of their first collaboration, *The Apprenticeship of Duddy Kravitz*.

JAMES WOODS WITH HIS MOTHER, MARSHA DIXON, 1985

PHOTO: SUSAN SHAW

With a script that went through nineteen drafts, the creative process was as complicated as the deal. And so was the casting. James Woods brought his acerbic edge to the role of Joshua Shapiro, a Montreal Jewish writer; Alan Arkin provided a sharp counterpoint as his father; and French-Canadian actress Gabrielle Lazure, a Quebec cabinet minister's daughter, played the WASP princess he falls in love with. Actors are in the business of playing people unlike themselves. But Lazure's Gallic intonation presented an insurmountable problem. As Lantos explains, "Her English was okay but she kept on hitting the wrong syllable, the wrong note, and she had a very high voice. In the heavy-duty dramatic scenes, her voice was way up there." At the last minute, Lazure's scenes were dubbed by another actress, Susan Hogan, who had originally auditioned for the part along with virtually every other Canadian actress of her generation. Lazure didn't discover that her voice had been stripped from the film until just two hours before the movie's red-carpet premiere in Cannes. "Ted was supposed to tell her; he didn't tell her," shrugs Lantos. "She took the news surprisingly well. We made a deal that she could dub herself in the French version."

Joshua won no awards in Cannes. But Lantos was thrilled just to be on the red carpet: "I'd always had that dream of walking up those stairs in Cannes," he says. "Nothing was quite as heady as that again." Seven years after Lantos had ridden a horse and buggy down Yonge Street for the premiere of *In Praise of Older Women*, a French honour guard finally accorded him a level of attention commensurate with his ambitions. This aspiring mogul, who played a mean game of water polo in his youth, was building an empire with a competitive instinct that would leave his rivals struggling for air. As Bill Marshall drolly observed, he is "the essential water polo player: grace above the water, kicking and gouging beneath." With *Joshua Then and Now*, Lantos emerged from the fray as the broker who could play both sides of the game, selling the nation's cultural mandate to politicians or swimming with the industry sharks. They were all at the opening-night gala in Toronto, including Ontario's new minister of culture, Lily Munro, who made Richler wince as she referred to the movie as *Joshua Here and Now* in her speech. The

JOSHUA THEN AND NOW

With a budget of $11 million and a distribution dea with Twentieth Century Fox, Joshua Then and Now *was at the time, the most expensive Canadian movie eve made. It can be seen as a composite portrait of all th inharmonious forces then converging on the country' film business*

premiere, however, was a rousing success. The crowd cheered James Woods, who escorted his mother to the event, and afterwards the stars joined a nightclub bash where guests feasted on 135 kilograms of smoked meat and 600 cheese blintzes.

But there was the sense that a culture's entire sense of self-worth was riding on the movie's fate. As Richler grumbled, "*Joshua* has assumed an importance way beyond the worth of the film itself, with everybody looking over our shoulder to see if we'll fall on our asses." In fact, the film made an unembarrassing $1.7 million in Canada, but died in the United States. In the middle of production, the head of Twentieth Century Fox had been fired and his replacement, Barry Diller, did his best to dump the movie. "We tried to get him to look at it, but he never saw the film," says Lantos. "The U.S. marketing campaign was a disgrace. The budget for launching it in New York was $25,000, which

MY AMERICAN COUSIN

"Moses Znaimer asked me if we were going to sleep together th night and I said no. He told me the red lights on the CN Tower were h And I said, 'How nice for you'"

bought one of those one-inch ads in the *Village Voice* every day and a one-line ad in *The New York Times*. It played in one theatre."

The night after *Joshua's* premiere, a much smaller picture scored a more clear-cut victory for Canadian cinema. *My American Cousin*, which opened Perspective Canada, was a first feature from an unknown director and unknown actors. Made for $1.2 million, about one-tenth of *Joshua*'s budget, it was a home movie in every sense of the word. Vancouver director Sandy Wilson created *My American Cousin* from her own coming-of-age story, as a girl growing up in the Okanagan Valley in the fifties. She shot the film at her childhood home, a 642-acre ranch overlooking Okanagan Lake. And she cast her next-door neighbour Margaret Langrick, who had never acted before, to play her younger self.

Sandy is a precocious twelve-year-old who is bored by paradise until the view is brightened by the arrival of a California cousin, Butch, who rolls up in a cherry-red Cadillac convertible. Played by newcomer John Wildman as a cartoonish James Dean, Butch sends Sandy's older friends into fits of giggling adulation, but she tries to act cool, dismissing him as "conceited and immature." While he picks cherries at her father's orchard, she nurses her crush through the summer, as astute in her naïveté as he is myopic in his American chauvinism. "They only play rock 'n' roll on Saturday afternoons," she says as he tries to punch some life into the car radio. "In the States," Butch boasts, "we got rock 'n' roll all day long."

SANDY WILSON AND MOSES ZNAIMER, 1985

No one had great expectations for the movie. The Canadian distributor wouldn't even pay for publicity photos. But at the festival the film struck a chord. Its seasoned producer, Peter O'Brian, who had worked on *Outrageous!* and produced *The Grey Fox*, remembers the magic of the premiere. During the opening scene, which shows Sandy scrawling "Nothing ever happens" repeatedly in her diary, the theatre erupted in laughter and prolonged applause. "I hadn't expected that," says O'Brian. "I didn't know what was going on. It was like you wanted to check your fly or something. And it just went from there. Everything worked. Everything was received and loved."

Sandy Wilson's memory of the event is less rosy. She was terribly nervous. Showing up at a cocktail reception beforehand, she met director Paul Cox, who advised her to drink a fat slug of Scotch, which she did. She then was put into a convertible to ride to the theatre, where she was astonished to see a lineup. She recalls getting up to introduce the film. "Then all of a sudden the Scotch hit me as I looked at the crowd. I realized I was drunk." As she watched the movie, the audience was so attentive she thought something was dreadfully wrong. "There would be a burst of laughter and then everybody would go really quiet. I remember examining the stitching on the seats in front of me and wanting to die. I broke into a cold sweat. It was excruciating. I thought, that's it, it's over. It's a bust."

Wilson soon realized that her movie was a hit. She found her groove as a festival star and dressed the part. At a sex shop on Yonge Street, she picked up a pair of condom-snug leotards adorned with cherries and wore them to the Variety Club lunch, where she cozied up to Cineplex czar Garth Drabinsky. She persuaded him to book *My American Cousin* into the Okanagan drive-in where she hung out as a teenager.

Like her persona in the movie, Wilson was still keeping a diary. "I'd never seen so many limos and stars and famous people," she wrote. "It was all about sex. For me, newly separated and all dressed up with a new film, I was travelling in brand new territory. I met [Citytv president] Moses Znaimer, who invited me out one night and had his camera crew follow us around. We went to a party in a penthouse full of black marble and pink shag wall-to-wall, with a bathtub filled with ice and champagne. Glenn Close, Mary Steenburgen and Harry Dean Stanton were there. Moses Znaimer asked me if we were going to sleep together that night and I said no, and then he cooled considerably until the cameras arrived and the lights went on. He had his psychic read my palm. He told me the red lights on the CN Tower were his. I said, 'How nice for you.'"

One afternoon, as Wilson was rushing off to introduce the repeat screening of her film, an extremely tall black stranger stopped her on the sidewalk—basketball star Wilt Chamberlain. "Girl, where you goin' in such a hurry?" he asked.

"Looking for the theatre where my film's playing."
Chamberlain looked her up and down. She was wearing the cherry leotards.
"Girl, where you staying? I got to get in touch with you."

Wilson was sharing a room with her fourteen-year-old ingenue, Margaret Langrick. "I'd come home and Margaret would say, 'Saaandy, Mr. Chamberlain's been calling.'" Eventually Wilson agreed to meet him for breakfast. "And that's what happened with Wilt," says Wilson. "He was a different kind of American cousin. It didn't come out until later that he'd had so many women."

While Wilson was courted by Chamberlain (who died in 1999), the young Langrick attacked the Big City in style. A gossip columnist duly noted her presence at all the late-night parties, "guzzling wine and smoking tons of cigarettes," while wearing blonde streaks in her hair, "enough pancake make-up to serve the entire cast of *Cleopatra* and a week's supply of black kohl under her eyes." Clearly, the girl made an impression. So did the movie. Local audiences were thrilled to see a film that seemed so young and fresh and unselfconsciously Canuck.

The 1985 festival was the first that I covered as a critic for *Maclean's*. The previous year I'd driven films around in a van, and now I was reviewing them—a job that seemed less crucial but still got me into the parties. It was the festival's tenth anniversary, and the glitz had geared up a notch. Hollywood chef Wolfgang Puck was flown in to recreate Spago's menu at Sutton Place for ten days. To fête the documentary *Les Canadiens*, Roots boys Michael Budman and Don Green recreated the Toe Blake Tavern at the Squeeze Club, where Tony Bennett shared the limelight with Maurice "the Rocket" Richard and Guy Lafleur. The Roots duo also helped stage the first annual George Christie lunch, hosted by the influential columnist from *The Hollywood Reporter*. The following year, the Four Seasons stepped in to sponsor it—currying Christie's favour for the opening of the new Four Seasons hotel in Beverly Hills—and his lunch has since become the most coveted invitation at the festival.

Delivering stars to the lunch is always a priority. One year, publicist Gino Empry dragged singer Eartha Kitt to the event, and "she was not a happy camper," Christie recalls. "She was a little snarly, so I sat her next to Dusty Cohl, who can get a rock fired up. Then, boom. She was among the last to leave. We always give favours, and we were giving out these beautiful leather-bound agendas from Roots. People had gone to the washroom or were in the foyer, and Eartha went around and picked up about ten of these off the tables. I said, 'Eartha, you can't do that. You have to put them back.'"

In 1985, the hot party was the *Kiss of the Spider Woman* celebration at the Bamboo on Queen Street, an Indian-summer crush of sweat and music and glittering women. Helen Shaver preened for the cameras with Sonia Braga. Rock divas Carole Pope and Lorraine Segato compared notes. Sandy Wilson and Margaret Langrick worked the crowd on the outdoor terrace where the guests included Brigitte Berman, a Toronto director premiering her documentary, *Artie Shaw: Time Is All You've Got*. "There was such a buzz of excitement in the air," Berman recalls. "Everywhere you turned were extraordinary personalities." At parties like this, as Canadian hopes and Hollywood dreams all swirled together in a mirage of glamour, you felt anything could happen. And

By the time
premiered in
in Beverly Hil

it did. Six months later Berman ended up at the Oscars with the stars of *Spider Woman*—accepting the prize for best documentary feature.

I remember getting caught up in the delirium around *My American Cousin*, imagining that its producer, Peter O'Brian, would take Canadian cinema to the next level. Fifteen years later, he is still trying to make it happen. O'Brian had hoped *American Cousin* would usher in a new wave of Canadian movies aimed at a popular audience. "But that is not the mission," he says now, arguing that the government funding agencies have pursued a policy of favouring high art over entertainment. "Not enough people have made it their mission to provide a popular cinema. Our filmmakers somehow don't want to meet with the Americans head-on." Sandy Wilson's sunny view of adolescence was an anomaly. In the eighties, English-Canadian film was heading in quite another direction, into the darkly interior landscapes of directors like Egoyan and Cronenberg, directors who would make the kind of European movies Europeans didn't make any more. If cinema was the art of light, English-Canadian cinema would be afflicted, for better or worse, by seasonal affective disorder.

In 1986, English Canada's two strongest films were Anne Wheeler's *Loyalties* and Leon Marr's *Dancing in the Dark*, two grimly feminist dramas of domestic discontent by first-time directors. *Dancing in the Dark*, based on the Joan Barfoot novel, featured the immaculate Martha Henry as a mad housewife who spends her days obsessively cleaning and who, after twenty years of listless marriage, stabs her dull and adulterous husband. But he was a sweetie compared to the man in *Loyalties*, the story of a British couple starting a new life in the remote Alberta village of Lac La Biche. It climaxes with the husband (Kenneth Welsh) raping his Métis housekeeper's daughter while his wife

FAR RIGHT, DENYS ARCAND AND RENÉ MALO, 1986
THE DECLINE OF THE AMERICAN EMPIRE

PHOTO: NANCY ACKERMAN

ecline of the American Empire *opened the festival in 1986, it hac s to rave reviews, and its director had been sharpening his tennis skills h studio executives urging him to remake the movie in English*

(Susan Wooldridge) is out celebrating her birthday with the housekeeper (Tantoo Cardinal). Melodrama shattering the dead calm of sexual repression: this is a syndrome that would come back to haunt English-Canadian cinema again and again.

Quebec, however, had its own agenda. Gothic scenarios belonged to its past, especially Gothic scenarios freighted with colonial angst. And by the mid-eighties Quebec filmmakers were moving towards more cosmopolitan terrain. Making his feature debut at twenty-five, Yves Simoneau, a former TV news cameraman, dazzled the festival with *Pouvoir intime*, a claustrophobic thriller about an armoured truck heist that leaves an armed guard holed up in the truck. Breaking the tradition of Quebec cinema, Simoneau would leave the French language behind at the first opportunity—shooting an English-Canadian feature, *Perfectly Normal*, which opened the 1990 festival, and then emigrating to Hollywood to make movies of the week.

DANCING IN THE DARK

But the most dynamic re-invention of Quebec cinema came from Denys Arcand. By the time *The Decline of the American Empire* opened the Toronto festival in 1986, it was already a success. Arcand's urbane sex comedy had premiered in Cannes to rave reviews, was a hit in Quebec, and its director had been sharpening his tennis skills in Beverly Hills with studio executives who were urging him to remake the movie in English. *Decline* would go on to win an Oscar nomination. "Success is the most unpredictable thing in the world," Arcand told me over lunch in Montreal. When he was scrambling to finance *Decline*, he hadn't made a feature in twelve years, not since *Gina*, his bleak drama about a gang of snowmobilers raping a stripper. "I had a long and difficult relationship with Telefilm at that point," he says. "They'd taken a film [*Maria Chapdelaine*] away from me and given it to someone else. And when I began writing *Decline*, they said, 'It's boring. It's just intellectuals talking. There's no action.' The readers' reports were unanimously negative." Telefilm and the NFB ended up financing most of *Decline*'s $1.8-million budget. "But I remember showing the film to six or seven people in Montreal before going to Cannes. People looked at me and said, 'Yeah, I guess it's okay.' They reacted quite indifferently. So I went to Cannes not expecting anything." The film was accepted by the Directors' Fortnight after Cannes festival director Gilles Jacob had turned it down for the main competition. "He diddled and dawdled about it for a month," says Arcand. "He had my cutting copy and I was desperate to get it back. He kept showing it to people not knowing what to think about it."

Arcand still wonders why *Decline* struck such a chord. For him it was a personal film, "a film about people that I really know." And it marked a watershed in Quebec cinema, a move away from dramas of taverns and guns, of murders, suicides and dying fathers. There is not a single reference to Quebec. Fifteen years after *Mon oncle Antoine* had a sled dragging a coffin through the snow, *Decline* has a group of sophisticated women driving a BMW from an urban health spa to a luxurious cottage, where a gang of male intellectuals are preparing a gourmet meal and talking dirty—tales of adultery, serial monogamy, sado-masochism, erotic massage, and anonymous gays getting it on. Arcand intercuts the conversations as a crisp symphony, from the slice of Nautilus machines to eggs in a Cuisinart. But as the party sours and betrayals come to light, convivial satire gives way to the sad vacancy of the human condition.

Despite the title, *The Decline of the American Empire* did not start with a concept. "It was tacked on after the fact," says Arcand. "You don't make films with an idea. You make them with dark unconscious drives and fears. Then hopefully you give all of this some kind of coherence afterwards. I'm always very practical, very down to earth. I had a very specific job to create something on a very small budget. How could I manage given my abilities? With people talking. What's interesting when people talk? When they talk about sex."

Decline has been described as "*The Big Chill* with a PhD," a comparison that irritates Arcand. No wonder. The film, which he based on his own experiences and those of close friends, is not derivative. And its satirical bite owes as much to Buñuel's *The Discreet Charm of the Bourgeoisie* as to Kasdan. Still, the zeitgeist has a way of levelling all originality, and you can see Arcand take his place in the lineage. Like Kasdan—or, more seminally, like *The Secaucus Seven*'s John Sayles—here was a filmmaker of a certain generation taking stock, wondering about his friends, exploring the desires that lurk behind successful careers, and asking the question: what on earth are we doing with our lives?

Judging by the most prominent Canadian movies in the mid-eighties, the answer could have been: going to the cottage. In *Joshua Then and Now*, Montreal's Anglo bourgeoisie while away the summer on vast cottage lawns overlooking the water. *My American Cousin* opens with a picturesque shot of Okanagan Lake at sunset, with Sandy's ranch house perched on the shore. *The Decline of the American Empire* winds down with melancholy views of a grey lake at dawn, outside a luxury chalet in Quebec's Eastern Townships. And *Loyalties* offers the colonial version of rural escape—a British couple escaping to the edge of the wilderness with their secrets and lies. All these films are, in some sense, summer-cottage movies, stories of individuals who find themselves at loose ends by a lake, distrusting paradise. And in more ways than one, Canadian cinema was still a cottage industry. The view was beginning to improve, but there was something terribly familiar about it. *Joshua*, *American Cousin*, *Loyalties*, *Dancing in the Dark*, even *Decline* . . . these films all view the world from an instructive distance. Although they are dramas, you can feel the vestigial tick of the documentary eye. And it's never hard to identify the enemy—the WASP anti-Semite, the arrogant American, the colonial child-abuser, the faithless husband. The pathology is familiar, almost comforting.

Canadian cinema would learn to live dangerously soon enough. In this country, where culture has clung to the institutional preserves of the CBC and the NFB, we have developed a reassuring mantra: our stories should reflect Canada to Canadians. But our most compelling pictures often reflect something alien to our experience, as a new generation of directors was about to demonstrate by making perfectly foreign films without ever leaving home.

Dances

WHEN DIRECTORS START TO MAKE MOVIES THAT FE

FOREIGN, EVEN IN THEIR OWN COUNTRY, A NATIONAL CINEMA C

start to get interesting. We don't think of the eighties as an especia tumultuous decade, but cinematic revolutions follow their o timetables. And by the mid-eighties, the festival was overwhelmed evidence of film cultures around the world braving new frontiers—a often taking on each other's identities. Japanese director Juzo Ita

PHOTO: NANCY ACKERMAN

DIRECTORS ELISEO SUBIELA, FRANCISCO NORDEN, FERNANDO BIRRI, PAUL LEDUC AND ALBERTO DURANT, 1986

with Strangers

shattered his country's taboos around rituals of death with *Ososhiki* (*The Funeral*), a saki-drenched satire about the Buddhist funeral of a family patriarch who owns a brothel; the priest pulls up in a white Rolls-Royce. By contrast, American director Paul Schrader enshrined Japanese tradition in *Mishima*, a ritualized epic about the samurai author who disembowelled himself while having his head chopped off. In France, Bertrand Tavernier cast saxophonist Dexter Gordon as an alcoholic musician in *Round Midnight* to create perhaps the finest film ever made about the distinctly American idiom of jazz. In *Kiss of the Spider Woman*, Brazil's Hector Babenco spun fantasies of Hollywood kitsch from the friction between a homosexual dreamer (William Hurt) and a Marxist revolutionary (Raul Julia) in a South American prison cell.

World cinema was beginning to converge as a carnival of promiscuous identity, and it was finding its way into the mainstream. With *Kiss of the Spider Woman*, Hurt became the first actor to win an Oscar for playing a raging queen. Then in *Children of a Lesser God*, which premiered at the festival the following year, his co-star Marlee Matlin became the first actor to win an Oscar for a performance signed in the language of the deaf. On the horizons of independent film, meanwhile, the landscape was darkening. At the 1986 festival, we watched David Lynch's *Blue Velvet* in shocked disbelief, like witnesses at a crime scene. The severed ear found lying on the grass in the perfect American suburb. Dennis Hopper furiously sucking back nitrous oxide, eyes bulging, as he throws Isabella Rossellini to the floor and drives himself to a horrific orgasm. Rossellini—who was married to Lynch at the time—stripped naked and somehow made ugly as she staggers through the frame in an unforgiving light. *Blue Velvet* was one of those movies that changed the rules of engagement. It led the way for the shock-art of Quentin Tarantino, for the giddy brutality of *Reservoir Dogs* and *Pulp Fiction*. It suggested that anything was permissible in the name of irony.

While America opened up new horizons in noir escapism, England was making edgy films grounded in social realism. With *My Beautiful Laundrette*, Stephen Frears cracked open conflicts of race and class in Thatcherite Britain, sealing them with a homosexual kiss between a Pakistani and a neo-Nazi skinhead. In the deliriously nihilistic *Sid and Nancy*, Alex Cox plumbed the depraved romance between Sid Vicious and Nancy Spungen, punk rock's Romeo and Juliet. And eleven years before making *Four Weddings and a Funeral*—which would become the most successful independent film in history at the time—British director Mike Newell showed up in Toronto with a small, grim tale of infatuation and doom called *Dance with a Stranger*, starring an unknown actress named Miranda Richardson.

Written by Shelagh Delaney, who had co-written *A Taste of Honey* at nineteen, the movie was based on the true story of Ruth Ellis, a platinum-blonde nightclub hostess who fell for an indolent, upper-class playboy in the fifties. She was a bitch; he was a brute. And as their sexual obsession spiralled into self-destruction, she became a victim of his abuse. Eventually she shot him. In 1955, she earned her place in history as the last woman hanged for murder in England. "I had a great deal invested personally in *Dance*

MY BEAUTIFUL LAUNDRETTE

with a Stranger," Newell told me. "I was very, very close to the writer. And the fate of the film hung on the casting of Ruth Ellis. I was unwilling to give it to anybody that I'd ever heard of. There was a neuroticness and suppressed hysteria in the character, which was difficult to find in a real person. Most people manage to cover that up by the time they get to their mid-twenties. I just kept looking—way beyond the point where anybody could see reason in what I was doing. We had got to the bottom of the barrel. And then somebody said there's this girl in a local repertory theatre, in Lancaster. She came down to see me. As she came into the room, it suddenly filled with the sound of a siren, a police car driving very fast down the street. She bounced across to the window, not taking any notice of me, and said, 'Oh, I like a bit of trouble.' And I thought, for all sorts of reasons, 'That's interesting.' Then she read, and of course she's a God-given actress. I went down one floor to the producer, who was on the phone, and wrote on a piece of paper: 'I've got her.'"

Before casting Rupert Everett as the playboy, Newell "agonized over choosing between him and Dan Day Lewis. Rupert was a much more commercial name at the time. But he had this other thing that was extraordinary about him, which is that you believed him as someone utterly perverse, you believed he would drive her mad by his vacillation and lack of commitment and cruelty."

After playing in London and at the Directors' Fortnight in Cannes, *Dance with a Stranger* had its North American premiere at the Toronto festival. "I remember standing at the back of the theatre, and it was the first time I had heard foreign applause, as it were, and I wasn't sure if it was real or not. This was the first time I had been aware of any non-English response. I didn't know whether there would *be* a non-English response. The film seemed to be so rooted in the injustices of England in the fifties. I wondered if it would travel at all. The big thing for me was to see that there was something wider there, that there was this nub of universality in the film. And that was a discovery I made at Toronto, which was very exciting. I was there for three or four days. I watched other films. It wasn't like Cannes, which was kind of crazy and rather grand. This was very relaxed. And everybody was very young and very sweet. They looked after you and at the same time they didn't crush you. I remember this sense of it being very young. I adored that."

The festival became known as a friendly place to do business, a stop on the international circuit where the growing community of indie producers and distributors began to feel at home. Tom Bernard, who runs Sony Classics with Michael Barker, says he would argue with Wayne Clarkson every year over who would pay for their filmmakers to come to the festival. Finally, Bernard challenged him to a game of tennis, and the winner would pay the shot. "I thought I'd negotiate to his ego," says Bernard. "Here's a guy who prided himself on his athletic ability." For three years, they played tennis to settle their account. Once they even found time to do it during the festival, hopping a fence into a private court. "And one year," adds Bernard, "we played in Manhattan Plaza by the Lincoln Tunnel, and Wayne was overcome by fumes. I won. I always won."

KISS OF THE SPIDER WOMAN

DANCE WITH A STRANGER

"As she came into the room, it suddenly filled with the sound of a siren, a police car. Miranda bounced across to the window, not taking any notice of me, and said, 'Oh, I like a bit of trouble'"

As distributors began to treat Toronto as a source for discovering films, an informal market took root. In 1983, *The Fourth Man*, by Dutch director Paul Verhoeven, arrived at the festival without a distributor. The buzz around it persuaded Spectrafilm's Linda Beath to snap up the North American rights, and Verhoeven went on to become the Hollywood sensation behind such blockbusters as *Total Recall* and *Basic Instinct*. In 1985, nobody knew much about Stephen Frears. But when Bernard showed up at the festival that year, he asked his tennis buddy what was hot, and Clarkson said he'd heard good things about *My Beautiful Laundrette*. "We watched it on tape in a hotel room," Bernard recalls, "and we scooped it for the world. Everybody else thought we'd gone to London to buy it. But we'd sat in a hotel room on Wayne's advice and saw this amazing movie and snatched it up. No one had great expectations for it."

After the 1985 festival, Wayne Clarkson stepped down from his post as director to take command of the newly formed Ontario Film Development Corporation. He was a hard act to follow. As Jay Scott wrote in an article on his successor, "Clarkson's taste in film was superior to that of most film critics; his political instincts were the envy of aldermen; and his personal charisma matched that of many of the movie stars he attracted to Toronto." The festival was at a difficult crossroads. Leonard Schein, the man chosen to succeed Clarkson, looked good on paper. He had created the Vancouver International Film Festival out of nothing and ran it for five years, putting it in the black. He also operated a successful rep cinema. To the festival board, he was a dream candidate, and they offered him a two-to-three-year contract. Schein took the job, but not the contract, feeling—"naively" as he said later—that he wouldn't need one.

Schein reported to work on April Fool's Day, 1986, and didn't take long before he had alienated much of the staff. It was his style as much as anything else. Before taking the job, he righteously told the board's search committee that the staff was pilfering booze donated for parties and he was going to put a stop to it. Clarkson was incredulous. "Stealing the *liquor*?" he says. "The booze was Vat 69. It was sponsored. We had boxes and boxes of this stuff and we couldn't *give* it away. We couldn't pour it down people's throats. The Toronto festival has always had more booze than it knows what to do with." Alcohol was also one of the rewards for working ridiculous hours in an underpaid job—Anne Mackenzie had faithfully kept the office fridge stocked with free beer. At his first production meeting, Schein's first order was to turn off expensive coffee makers.

At the Cannes festival in May, he showed up at functions in Birkenstocks and wool socks with a baby in a backpack. While Clarkson, representing the OFDC comfortably shmoozed at the Hotel Majestic, ordering exorbitant rounds of drinks for filmmakers and journalists, Schein would show up for a brief visit, pay for his own Perrier, then leave. That may not seem like scandalous behaviour. But remember, this was Cannes. And it was the eighties.

By the summer, the festival's staff morale was disintegrating. Mackenzie, who had stayed on as managing director, quit, and the rest of the office was on the verge of mutiny. Each year, as September loomed closer, the staff worked out the festival

PHOTO: SUSAN SHAW

SISSY SPACEK AND DIRECTOR TOM MOORE, 1986

PHOTO: DAVID CHAN

schedule with index cards on a big board. "It was a huge logistical operation that everyone took part in," explains former programmer David McIntosh. "Everybody looks at the cards going up and throws ideas around. One day, Leonard went in by himself and unilaterally changed everything around. David Overbey came in and changed it all back again—and taped all the cards down so they couldn't be moved." With or without Schein, the stress in the cramped Yorkville headquarters would become almost unbearable as the festival deadline approached, and at one point it drove an employee to a nervous breakdown. "She just flipped," says McIntosh. "She was just shaking and flailing and had to be wrapped up in a warm blanket and carted off to the hospital."

Ten days after the close of the 1986 festival, in a long and acrimonious meeting, the board voted to dump Schein, who then announced his "resignation." In retrospect, his nine-month tenure was just a hiccup in the festival's history. But it offers some insight into what the organization had become. The hostile reaction against Schein revealed just how jealously the festival's guardians, from within and without, would defend it. And in their eyes, perhaps his worst offence was parochialism. If there was one thing the festival did not want to be, it was parochial. Also, Schein never grasped the collective nature of the enterprise. He liked to refer to it as *his* festival, something his predecessors had never done. "You always had to use 'we,'" says Helga Stephenson. "But Leonard was an 'I' guy. He'd stand up at a gala and talk about 'my festival' in front of an audience of stakeholders—patrons and government people. That was a mistake."

Stephenson, who had become Schein's deputy director, manoeuvred to inherit his job, and ended up imposing her personality on the festival far more forcefully than he had ever done. But she did it with style. She also had the good sense to divide up the duties. For eight years, Clarkson and Mackenzie had worked as a team, with Clarkson out front as the diplomat and master programmer, and Mackenzie running the organization in the backroom. With Piers Handling, Stephenson formed another kind of marriage. While she would run the festival—guiding it to new levels of foreign prestige, Hollywood glamour and corporate support—he would provide the cinematic backbone as its artistic director. Together they would turn the Toronto festival into a truly international event.

As types, they could not have been more different. Stephenson was a flamboyant extrovert, Handling a shy cineaste. But both were insatiable cosmopolitans, children of the sixties who had spent their youth travelling the world and could never get enough of it. Piers grew up as an army brat in Canada, Germany and Pakistan. From his first movie memory—of seeing Charlie Chaplin eat his shoe at an outdoor screening of *The Gold Rush* in Pakistan—he had cultivated an enviable pedigree in film appreciation. But while Piers spent his life immersed in movies, Helga lived her life as if it were a movie, from managing a rock band in Japan to running a bar for American fly boys in Laos on the edge of the Vietnam War. She was a larger-than-life character, the kind of woman who, like Madonna or Cher, had no real need of a last name. In film circles around the world, she would be known simply as Helga.

RICHARD GERE AND JOHN ALLEN AT THE JOHN SCHLESINGER TRIBUTE, 1986

Our

Gal in Havana

'VE ALWAYS SEEN THE WORLD AS MY OYSTER, AS A
)TENTIALLY FRIENDLY, INTERESTING PLACE—I DON'T REALLY SEE
as foreign." Growing up Catholic in an enclave of English Montreal
elga Stephenson felt the lure of foreign affairs ever since the mis
onary nuns showed up at her school with slide shows. In fact, he
st ambition was to become a missionary nun, as far from the
mforts of home as possible. She grew up in the elite Town of Moun

HELGA STEPHENSON AT CANNES

PIERS HANDLING, JUSTO PÉREZ AND HELGA STEPHENSON, HAVANA, 1986

Royal, pearl of the Liberal Party, home riding of Pierre Trudeau. Her family was not rich, but it was connected. Her mother, a Toronto-born Catholic, did PR for the fashion industry, bore four children and served as a Liberal Party organizer. Her father, an Icelandic alcoholic from Winnipeg, was a department-store executive with Eaton's. Helga hopscotched through a myriad of Catholic schools, private and public, and polished her French with a year at the University of Fribourg Switzerland. Then, this well-bred Catholic girl, the product of Quebec's convent education system, underwent her own Quiet Revolution.

A paragon of the Trudeau era—bilingual, nomadic and curious—she ran around Europe with her friends. She traded her cardigan and pearls for Carnaby Street colours and miniskirts. Then, at McGill University, "I turned into one of those daughters you hope you never have," she says. "The hair went down, the bra came off, the shaving stopped." McGill in the late sixties was an exciting place to be. Louis Dudek's poetry classes. Expo '67. The inflammatory fun and games of the student left. Rioting in the streets. Helga got a taste of tear gas and hung out with a crowd of radical young journalists—from future CBC commissar Mark Starowicz, who raised Marxist hell at the *McGill Daily*, to boulevardier Nick Auf der Maur, who held court at the Bistro, smoking Gauloises and reading *The Peking Review*.

Piers and Hel
"It became c
facilitator and

In Montreal, bars were places where people went to change the world. And it was in a bar that Helga got wind of an opportunity that would change her world for good. It was 1970. She had just graduated from McGill and was working as a model. One night, after a showroom gig involving fur coats, she and the girls went to a bar where she met Yves Michaud, a legendary Quebec sovereigntist, who engaged her in a heated debate about bilingualism—and mentioned that his wife was in charge of hostesses at the Canada pavilion of the Osaka World's Fair. Before long, Helga was taking a crash course in Japanese and flying off to work as a hostess. In Osaka, she met a Canadian folk-rock band, the Rosewood Daydream featuring Sneezy Waters, and became their manager. She toured the Rosewood Daydream—or the Plywood Nightmare, as they were known on bad nights—through Bangkok, Hong Kong and Laos. They broke up in the Laotian capital of Vientiane, but when the others went home, Helga stayed.

She sailed the Mekong river with her sarong and her Little Red Book. She hung out with war correspondents and pilots and spies. She was a twenty-three-year-old woman in a Humphrey Bogart movie, a demimonde of ceiling fans, opium dens and aperitifs with French Foreign legionnaires left over from Dien Bien Phu. Helga taught English to a clientele that included the chief of the Laotian secret police. At nights, she worked as a bartender in a club owned by a pilot for Air America, the CIA's unofficial charter airline. Next door was the notoriously seedy White Rose, where strippers smoked cigarettes without using their mouths. At the Air America bar, Helga fell in with a gang of crack fly boys from West Virginia who pooled their money to buy her a ticket out because it was no place for a young woman. It was dangerous. There was a war going on. One night at work she got an ingratiating visit from the man who ran the Purple Porpoise, the heavy

PHOTO: COURTESY OF PIERS HANDLING

ited Rio and Havana to prepare a huge Latin American retrospective hat we had a pretty smooth partnership," says Helga. "I was the slator. Piers was this exquisite cinema brain"

CIA bar on the Mekong. "You've made yourself very welcome in this town," he told her. "You've made a lot of friends from a lot of different places. You know, Helga, a girl could feather her nest quite nicely here."

That's when she realized it was time to leave. She chose Ottawa, because it was Trudeau's town. Helga poked her head into External Affairs, but the building felt all wrong. Then she walked into the National Arts Centre, which felt right, and forged a new career as a publicist in the high end of show business. Her boyfriend, Patrick McFadden, was a film critic, so she saw a lot of movies. Then, in the winter of '74, her life turned into a movie once again when she took a cheap flight to Cuba. From the moment she arrived, riding in from the airport through the ruined beauty of Havana, she says, "my heart soared—I thought, before I die I want to be in love in this city."

So be it. Helga joined CUSO, took a crash course in Spanish, and spent a year teaching English in Havana to engineers and architects. A fling with a guitarist provided an entree into the richness of Cuban culture. "In twenty-four hours," she recalls. "I was back in with painters and filmmakers and musicians. And I had more fun than you are allowed to have." Moving to Toronto in 1975, Helga resumed her career, establishing a high-powered public relations company (Stephenson, Ramsay and O'Donnell Ltd.), with clients such as the National Ballet of Canada, the Moscow Circus, Bill Marshall's movie productions and the Festival of Festivals. In 1982, she joined the festival as director of communications. The same year, she married Bill Marshall. It seemed

ENTRE TINIEBLAS (DARK HABITS)

highly unlikely that these two promoters—the man who put the festival on its feet and the woman who taught it to dance—could co-exist as husband and wife. And it was.

Early in their marriage, they had a custody battle over festival resources. One day Marshall noticed that his festival VISA card was missing. It had been years since he'd actually worked for the organization, but he still retained the card, which proved useful in liquidating his bar tab at Club 22 in the Windsor Arms. Helga had quietly taken it from his wallet and cut it up. "There, you don't have anything more to worry about," she announced, tossing the pieces onto Wayne Clarkson's desk. "I should have had her up on charges for theft," Marshall grumbles. "What kind of behaviour is that for a wife, I ask you?" (But her petite act of vandalism pales in comparison to what one of Marshall's previous girlfriends had done—the spurned lover who sliced one of his Riopelle paintings into very small pieces and deposited them in his new mailbox. "The painting was worth about fifty grand," sighs Marshall. "It was in the well-known series on that grey paper with the Jackson Pollock splotches. Later, she apologized all over the place. So I got some value out of it, but all things considered I'd rather have the picture.")

Bill's marriage to Helga was over almost before it began. "George Anthony says he's had lunches that lasted longer," says Marshall. In fact, they split up after two years and remain friends to this day. As the festival's pioneer promo man, Bill has a respect for Helga's acumen that remains undiminished: "She is *such* a promoter. I would blush to say the things she says. On my best day I would never have the nerve to kiss up and suck up in the shameless way that she does. She is far and away the best at that business." Helga disagrees: "Bill was a much better promoter. He was always yards ahead of me. The only difference is I kept at it."

PROGRAMMER RAMIRO PUERTA; (BELOW) ON STAGE WITH RAMIRO'S LATIN ORCHESTRA AT A FESTIVAL PARTY, 1987

Helga knew how to promote her own passions. In 1984, Clarkson sent her to the Rio de Janeiro film festival, asking her to see what it would take to program a Latin American retrospective. "I was completely lost there," she says, "but I saw the beginnings of a network, and everyone said you have to go to Havana." The Cubans had just set up the Foundation for New Latin American Cinema, headed by Gabriel García Márquez, and the Havana Film Festival had become the hub for a new movement of filmmakers from the region. As soon as Helga got back from Rio, she began agitating to go to Cuba. Clarkson refused to send her. "Fuck you, I'm going," she said, and bought her own ticket. She wasn't disappointed. "It was the apex of Latin American cinema," she says, "and it was hopping. They had these huge parties and all the best bands in Cuba playing there. You just partied and drank yourself to death."

The next year, Stephenson and Handling visited both Rio and Havana to prepare a huge Latin American retrospective for the 1986 festival. At the Havana festival, they made their pitch to a room full of the world's leading Latin American directors, persuading them to cooperate. Helga and Piers ended up screening some five hundred films for the program. On the road, they realized that they made a good team. "It became clear that we had a pretty smooth partnership," says Helga. "I was the facilitator and translator. Piers was the screener, this exquisite cinema brain." Together, they also dreamt up future scenarios for the Toronto festival, including the concept of running it as joint directors. "It's a traveller's disease," adds Helga. "You go into utopian mode. Certainly the idea of creating a cinematheque and attaching it to the festival was born there—during that time when Piers and I started to noodle about where this organization could end up."

Their program, Winds of Change, was a remarkable feat. With ninety-six films from thirteen countries, ranging from 1951 to 1986, it was the largest retrospective of Latin American cinema ever mounted anywhere. Its richness and diversity were stunning. And it shattered any preconceptions that Latin American movies might be homemade or crudely militant. The styles ranged from neo-realism to magic realism, from agitprop burlesque to Brechtian cabaret.

From the 1920s to the 1940s, Brazil, Argentina and Mexico had commercial film industries to rival Hollywood's. Then, in the wake of political upheavals, just as the New Wave swept through Europe, Latin American cinema underwent a revolution. Many of its directors, from Argentina's Fernando Birri to Cuba's Tomás Gutiérrez Alea, studied in Italy in the fifties and came back imprinted by neo-realism. Filmmakers took the camera into the street and into their dreams, finding the vein that runs between politics and poetry. After Castro came to power, like Lenin, he proclaimed the importance of the moving image. He created a state film agency, the icalC, and Cuba flowered with a cinema as vivid and sophisticated as its music. In Brazil, *cinema nôvo* exploded in the early sixties. In Argentina, the *joven cinema* group led the way. And Allende's Chile erupted with cinematic expression in the years leading up to the 1973 coup.

PHOTO: DOUG MACLELLAN

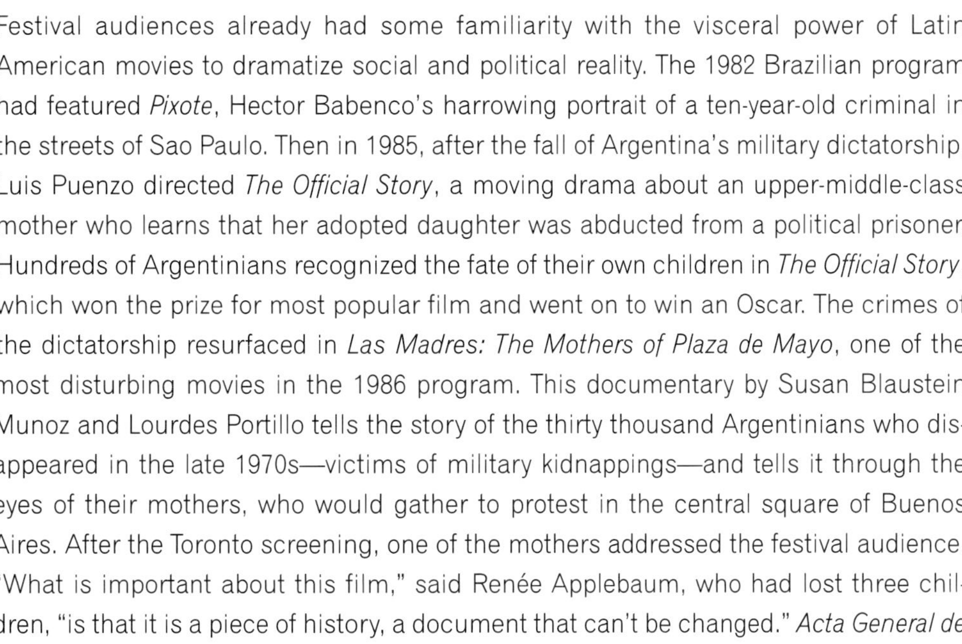

Festival audiences already had some familiarity with the visceral power of Latin American movies to dramatize social and political reality. The 1982 Brazilian program had featured *Pixote*, Hector Babenco's harrowing portrait of a ten-year-old criminal in the streets of Sao Paulo. Then in 1985, after the fall of Argentina's military dictatorship, Luis Puenzo directed *The Official Story*, a moving drama about an upper-middle-class mother who learns that her adopted daughter was abducted from a political prisoner. Hundreds of Argentinians recognized the fate of their own children in *The Official Story*, which won the prize for most popular film and went on to win an Oscar. The crimes of the dictatorship resurfaced in *Las Madres: The Mothers of Plaza de Mayo*, one of the most disturbing movies in the 1986 program. This documentary by Susan Blaustein Munoz and Lourdes Portillo tells the story of the thirty thousand Argentinians who disappeared in the late 1970s—victims of military kidnappings—and tells it through the eyes of their mothers, who would gather to protest in the central square of Buenos Aires. After the Toronto screening, one of the mothers addressed the festival audience. "What is important about this film," said Renée Applebaum, who had lost three children, "is that it is a piece of history, a document that can't be changed." *Acta General de*

LA TIERRA PROMETIDA

With ninety-six films from thirteen countries, Winds of Change shattered that Latin American movies might be homemade or crudely militant. The neo-realism to magic realism, from agitprop burlesque to Brechtian

Chile, meanwhile, made history with a four-hour, clandestine portrait of Chilean life under the rule of General Augusto Pinochet. Director Miguel Littin shot the documentary at great risk by sneaking into Chile and working in disguise. Littin, who visited the festival, recalled that one day, while he was getting a haircut, the barber remarked on his plucked eyebrows—part of his disguise. Deflecting the danger of being discovered, Littin snapped, "Do you have something against homosexuals?"

The weight of history could be felt behind the most personal stories, but by the mid-eighties there was much more to Latin American cinema than politics. Music, for instance. Swirling through pain, laughter and whimsy, *Tangos: The Exile of Gardel*, by Fernando E. Solanas, spun an atmospheric tale of Argentine exiles trying to stage a musical in Paris. *Opera do Malandro*, by Brazil's Ruy Guerra, married Bertolt Brecht and Busby Berkeley in a musical about a zoot-suited hustler who takes revenge in a cabaret after the 1941 attack on Pearl Harbor. It was Brazil's first musical in three decades. And in *Patakin*, Cuba's first musical ever, director Manuel Octavio Gómez parodied socialist realism with a delirious sequence of choreographed tractors wheeling through fields of singing workers: Communist high camp.

Meanwhile, Argentina's Eliseo Subiela won the Critics' Prize at the festival for *Hombre mirando al sudeste* (*Man Facing Southeast*), the story of a patient in an insane asylum who believes he is from another planet. Reminiscent of the space alien in *The Man Who Fell to Earth*, the inmate is a knowing naïf with uncanny powers and an unblinking gaze. A nebular savage, he spends hours on end staring into space, a man without feelings who can work miracles of compassion. If he is an alien, he is divinely alienated. He has no desire to be cured. Putting psychiatry on trial, he defends his claim of extraterrestrial intelligence with razor logic until he is on trial himself, to be crucified with medication prescribed by his doctor, a Pontius Pilate swayed by the system.

Audiences expecting moral tales of anti-colonial realism discovered that Latin American cinema had gone far beyond that. It was *out there*. Even among the classics presented in Winds of Change, there were wild flights of imagination, notably in the work of Cuba's Tomás Gutiérrez Alea. Watching his *Memories of Underdevelopment* (1968) is like falling through a rabbit hole of history, and finding yourself in some lost epicentre of revolutionary thought, a time capsule where sex, art, history and politics all converge in a lucid dream. Shot in black and white, the film is set in 1961. It unfolds through the eyes of Sergio, a bourgeois intellectual who has chosen to remain in Havana after the revolution. He surveys the city through a telescope on his apartment balcony, looking for answers that aren't there. He picks up a coquettish eighteen-year-old from a working-class family, seduces her with an offer of dresses left by his ex-wife, and ends up absurdly charged with the girl's rape. Lamenting his country's underdevelopment, and paralyzed by the depths of his own intelligence, Sergio drifts in and out of reverie, a character in a European movie dismayed to find he's not in Europe. Alea creates an existential landscape worthy of Antonioni, yet pierced with documentary glimpses of political reality—Batista's torture victims, the Missile Crisis, the Bay of Pigs. The frontiers of intellectual angst have never seemed so transparent.

preconceptions
s ranged from
ret

Five years after Winds of Change, in 1991, the festival created a permanent showcase, Latin American Panorama. Ramiro Puerta became its programmer. That year, the guests included Tomás Gutiérrez Alea, who was trying to drum up support for making *Strawberry and Chocolate* (1993), one of the first Cuban films to break into the American market. Alea approached Puerta with a special request. His wife, actress Mirta Ibarra, needed a spare part for her bicycle. "He hands me this thing wrapped in a handkerchief," recalls Puerta, "this weird sprockety part. I said, 'I don't know the vaguest thing about bicycles, but I know somebody who does.'" He took the Cuban director to Cinecycle in Kensington Market, the eccentric enterprise operated by the festival's Martin Heath where bikes were repaired by day and films shown by night.

Heath's jaw dropped when Tomás Gutiérrez Alea walked into his shop. "I love your films," he said. "In fact, I have a copy of *Memories of Underdevelopment*."
"You have a copy on video?" asked Alea.
"No, I have a 35-mm print subtitled in English."
"You *do*? How did you get that? *Nobody* has that, not even the Film Institute in Cuba."
Martin, who has seen a lot of festival prints pass through his hands over the years, changed the subject.
"So, what can I do for you?" he asked.
When Alea showed him the spare part he needed, Heath recognized it at once.
"Oh, yes, it's from a Czechoslovakian bicycle—I have one here," he said, hauling down a bicycle. "You can take it if you want."
"I can't take a bicycle on the plane."

"Sure you can. It folds up like this."
The director accepted the gift of the bicycle, rode all around the festival on it, then took it back to his wife in Cuba.

Ramiro Puerta first showed up at the festival in 1986, the year of the Latin retrospective. He was hired to do simultaneous translation of films that arrived without English subtitles. One of them was the four-hour Littin documentary, *Acta General de Chile*. There was no written translation provided with it, and the film was dense with narration. "There were four of us taking turns translating," Puerta recalls. "We'd take ten minutes each. Then one fellow began to cough and wouldn't stop coughing. He was sent away. Then another guy went for coffee and never came back. So then we were two. We were just burning. At one point, my colleague lost it. You could just see him short-circuit at the microphone. And I continued all by myself. When the credits came up, my tongue could not move another inch. And that's when Piers comes in and says, 'Good job, guys. Can you translate another film?'"

Before becoming the Latin American programmer in 1990 (as well as a bandleader and filmmaker), Puerta worked as a driver, clearing films through customs at the airport. It required a certain touch. "I effectively greased everyone's palms with free passes and T-shirts," he says. "That way I could skip the lineup. But when the people in line see me and find out I'm Colombian, well, there could be certain associations." One day customs officials had no record of a print that Puerta was positive had arrived. He persuaded them to let him look for himself. As he went into the back room, the dogs were sniffing for cocaine. Suddenly he saw one of the dogs start to go crazy over a shipment, and sitting right beside it was a box labelled with the title of the film he was looking for. "Here's my film!" he cried. But he couldn't get near it. The dogs were tearing apart the package next to it, splattering cocaine everywhere.

Puerta never encountered any contraband in film cans. But he did become a vital connection for smuggling Cuban films to festivals in the United States. For years, an embargo prevented Cubans from doing it directly. So they would send the films to Ramiro. He would put a "costume" on the package, a fake label with no Cuban identification. "I did that for four or five years," he says proudly, "my own little private endeavour. I loved it. Out of thirty-odd attempts we only got one returned."

The Latin connection has worked its magic on the festival in strange ways. For Piers Handling, it offered a chance to meet the woman of his dreams. Reserved and cerebral, Handling is not one to be easily star-struck. But ever since seeing *Darling* as a teenager, he had been mad for Julie Christie. And in 1986, she showed up at the festival as the star of *Miss Mary*, directed by Argentina's Maria Luisa Bemberg. Christie plays a decidedly

JULIE CHRISTIE AND PIERS HANDLING, 1986

PHOTO: NANCY ACKERMAN

PHOTO: NANCY ACKERMAN

A WINTER TAN

FAR LEFT, JACKIE BURROUGHS

As Maryse, a female Lowry, Burroughs animates every frame, her dance body revealing sudden angles that defy glamour and redefine beauty

unsexy role, as a prim English governess hired by a wealthy Argentine family that is afflicted by madness and threatened by the rising tide of Peronism. Since the days of *Darling* and *Dr. Zhivago*, Christie had retreated from the limelight. After *McCabe & Mrs. Miller*, *Don't Look Now*, *Shampoo* and *Heaven Can Wait*, she'd had her fling with the New Hollywood, and her affair with Warren Beatty. At forty-five, she was an outspoken feminist living on a goat farm in Wales with a British journalist, and acting in the occasional low-budget film. As this no-nonsense woman in white slacks and a black-fringed jacket talked with journalists in Toronto, she delivered impassioned critiques of Hollywood ideology, American ignorance and the injustice of Thatcher's England. Perhaps no screen goddess has ever analyzed her glamour with such bittersweet candour:

"I regret that I didn't enjoy my looks," she told Jay Scott. "I did use them enormously, in very manipulative ways, of course, as all people thought to be good-looking do, but now that I am getting older and see young, beautiful people on screen, I get such pleasure from it. I was resentful, annoyed, frightened with being used as 'a face.' I wish I had realized what pleasure it *does* give people to look at what they consider beautiful."

Behaving more like a citizen than a star, Christie threw herself into the festival. She went to movies and parties, and Piers Handling was thrilled to bits. "I remember seeing her for the first time," he says. "It just took my breath away. It was in a cinema. She wanted to get into a film, and I walked her in. She was so real, very easy to get to know. She hung out with everyone and we had a lot of great evenings together." Christie even stayed for the awards brunch. Then, before leaving Toronto the next day, she phoned Handling at the festival office in Yorkville. He was asleep on the couch. "Don't wake him up," she said. When Handling finally woke up, someone said, "Oh, Julie Christie phoned." He was mortified. "I couldn't *believe* they would not wake me up," recalls Handling, who had her paged in the airport but failed to reach her.

In later years, Latin American movies presented at the festival, such as *Like Water for Chocolate* and *Central Station*, would win mainstream recognition. Meanwhile Helga Stephenson's Havana connection played a role in the production of a Canadian movie in Mexico, an erotic odyssey called *A Winter Tan*, starring Jackie Burroughs, which must be one of the most audacious pictures ever made with public money. "*Winter Tan* was a hospitality suite production," says Stephenson. Well, not entirely. But Mexican contacts that she made in Havana were crucial. Distributor Jorge Sanchez handed over his offices in Mexico City for casting and location scouting, and his wife, director María Novaro, travelled with the crew as their translator. The film was made for $220,000 by a collective of five directors: Louise Clark, John Frizzell, John Walker, Aerlyn Weissman—and its star, Jackie Burroughs. The idea of five people directing a movie was unheard of, but there has never been a movie quite like *A Winter Tan*.

Based on the libertine letters of New York professor Maryse Holder, an erotic adventurer who was murdered in Mexico, it is the portrait of an artist surrendering herself to the world, a lyrical essay in self-destruction. With Burroughs giving a tour-de-force performance as Holder, the film unfolds as a virtual one-woman show. The script consists largely of monologues from Holder's letters, burlesque rants saturated with sun, sex, smoke and liquor. "I'm on vacation from feminism," Maryse proclaims, as she throws herself at young brown men on the Mexican coast. By turns satirical and tragic, profane and elegiac, *A Winter Tan* is about a woman at a land's end of desire. The c-word flows like warm beer. Maryse is a female Lowry, an impossible romantic writing and fucking her way south in a cunt-centric search for "one night of perfect dark love."

The sex is mostly in the words. But the film is also a figure drawing of a woman in a landscape, this gaunt, tawny Viva who wears her tan like a tightening drum. Burroughs animates every frame, her dancer's body arched between narcissism and self-loathing, revealing sudden angles that defy glamour and define beauty in unlikely ways. Maryse swims through Mexico as a sexual tourist. She worships tan skin and turquoise water. And, yes, she objectifies the natives. She's jailed for seducing a fourteen-year-old Indian boy, "this lovely child sucking at my lips like a guppy." It's no surprise the movie was controversial. Writing in *Cinema Canada*, Cameron Bailey, who later created the festival's Planet Africa series, declared: "*A Winter Tan* suffers from a profound, unthinking racism . . . this film isn't just politically incorrect; it's politically dangerous." But the film doesn't canonize Maryse Holder as some sort of post-feminist role model. She is an expatriate tramp who goes looking for youth and finds death, a female version of all those male derelict writers who go sculling into the heart of darkness. "Jackie and I thought Maryse Holder was the funniest woman alive," says Frizzell, who originated the project with Burroughs. "At no point did we take her seriously. The notion that what she was doing was sexually imperialistic was lost on her. But we felt we couldn't indict her. We'd let the audience judge. We decided not to have cutaways of Third World agony, of the poverty on the streets. This woman spent two years in Mexico and never once mentions poverty."

A Winter Tan marked a breakthrough precisely because it was dangerous. It signalled the dawn of a new sexual maturity for Canadian cinema. As a film about an American in Mexico, *A Winter Tan* also marked a departure from narrowly defined Canadian content. And along with Patricia Rozema's *I've Heard the Mermaids Singing*, it ushered in a breed of small, unorthodox pictures financed by the new Ontario Film Development Corporation—under the direction of Wayne Clarkson. "It was like connective tissue," says Frizzell. "Wayne had this very canny knowledge of what made a festival picture. And if independent films in Canada were going to succeed, they had to be festival pictures. It was the only way they were going to get credibility, perspective and publicity. So he chose to support films that would work on the festival circuit."

A Winter Tan's festival premiere was a night of chaos. The movie started an hour late. Then, after fifteen minutes, the second reel came on upside down and backwards. Burroughs bolted from her seat, ran to the booth, and started throttling the projectionist. "She had her hands around the guy's throat," recalls Frizzell. "I literally had to pull her off and take her outside. We were both sobbing uncontrollably until it occurred to us that people would leave. Then we manned the doors and begged them to stay." Almost the entire audience stayed, waiting forty-five minutes for the film to resume. Afterwards, because the filmmakers couldn't afford a party, Helga handed over the hospitality suite. "The vodka was moved in," says Frizzell. "We have no idea who paid for it or how it got there. The party was half Latin, half Canadian, a fabulous mix. You'd see Helga move through the room with a tray of something over her head. She was fantastic—sexual and funny and political all at the same time. She was everything Canadians wanted to be like."

DAVID CRONENBERG, 1981

A Winter Tan was a festival hit. It picked up American distribution. And it travelled to other festivals around the world. At the Berlin Festival, Frizzell used travel expenses to take a dozen international journalists—as well as Jay Scott and David Overbey—out on the town. "I took them to a little Turkish hustler bar," he recalls. "It had no sign over the door, just a little slot where they look at you and decide whether to let you in. I bought everybody prostitutes—I paid for the 'strudel.' It was expensive. But it was an extremely savvy way to spend the money, far better than taking them to dinner. We got great publicity."

First we take Havana . . . then we take Berlin. The summer-cottage school of Canadian cinema was over.

Dead Ringers

PHOTO: BOB VILLARD

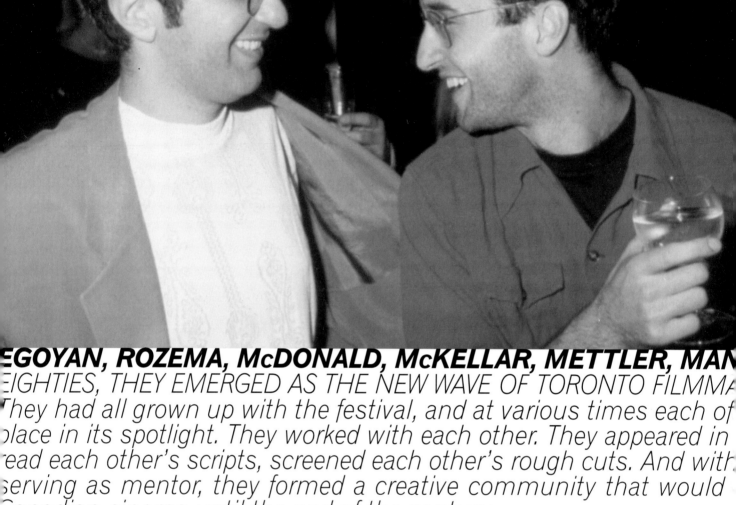

EGOYAN, ROZEMA, McDONALD, McKELLAR, METTLER, MAN

EIGHTIES, THEY EMERGED AS THE NEW WAVE OF TORONTO FILMMA

They had all grown up with the festival, and at various times each of place in its spotlight. They worked with each other. They appeared in read each other's scripts, screened each other's rough cuts. And with serving as mentor, they formed a creative community that would Canadian cinema until the end of the century.

PHOTO: SAM BARNES

The first time Atom Egoyan and Bruce McDonald premiered films at the festival, they showed them on the sidewalk. It was 1982. The festival had rejected Egoyan's *Open House* and McDonald's *Let Me See*, short films that they had made as students at Ryerson Polytechnical Institute. "We were crushed," recalls Egoyan. "So we rented a generator and got a 16-mm projector and set it up on the sidewalk outside the University Theatre. We were told to move it, and ended up one store down from the ticket window." Atom and Bruce wore tuxedos and white gloves. As it got dark, they began rolling their films, hoping to catch the crowd coming out of the Fassbinder gala. A couple of cops came along, looked them over, then grinned and said, "We're going for a long coffee break." Figuring they didn't have much time, the filmmakers phoned Citytv, and Jeannie Becker showed up with a camera crew. A festival staffer came by and gave them a fistful of free passes. That year, Atom and Bruce saw their friend Peter Mettler, another Ryerson film student, get his feature debut accepted in the festival. "We were all so

SCISSERE

PHOTO: SUSAN SHAW

FAR LEFT, ATOM EGOYAN AND DON MCKELLAR, 1981; LEFT, BRUCE MCDONALD, 1987

N THE LATE S. THE GANG. *n would find a other's films, 'd Cronenberg nate English-*

impressed—I'll never forget the thrill of having someone you *know* in the festival," recalls Egoyan. "At that point," says McDonald, "getting a film into the festival was the only definition of success. I was pissed when mine didn't get in. But we probably got more press out of that sidewalk screening than Peter did."

Mettler was twenty-four. His movie was *Scissere*, an experimental feature made for $14,000. During the early years of the Toronto festival, he had worked as a limo driver. He'd landed the job by meeting a Canadian coterie at the Cannes festival, where he bummed around as a wannabe filmmaker, sleeping on the beach and sneaking into movies with a fake pass. As a limo driver, Mettler enjoyed a privileged relationship with filmmakers and stars. "I'd babysit them and get them their drugs and take them to parties—whatever they had to do," he remembers. "I was a pretty boy, and I turned down several offers to get into bathtubs and beds." Mettler has many surreal memories of the film festival: steering Henry Winkler through a sea of fans who had plastered love notes all over the car windows; driving Robbie Robertson to strange places late at night with strange women; scoring dope to help Peter O'Toole stay off the booze, then watching him smoke it at a party in the Forest Hill home of the American consul.

Four years later, Mettler was on the other side of the looking glass, drawing critical raves for *Scissere*—a non-narrative collage of sounds and images focused on a young man deciphering the world after his release from a mental hospital. He also served as cinematographer for Egoyan's feature debut, *Next of Kin*. Egoyan was so thrilled when it was selected for the festival he still has the answering-machine cassette on which programmer Peter Harcourt gave him the news. The premiere itself was anti-climactic. The audience was packed with friends of John Frizzell, who had shown up to see *Neon*, a short film he had scripted. After *Neon* played, Frizzell left the theatre to host a party for it, and more than half the audience left with him. "John had this image of me from '84 of having this corduroy suit and ridiculous haircut," Atom recalls. "He was the doyen of the cool scene and he didn't want anything to do with me." But when Egoyan returned to the festival in 1987 with *Family Viewing*, and heard Frizzell's unmistakable laugh cueing the audience to the film's dark humour, he felt he'd made it. "That night was electrifying," recalls Egoyan, who went on to win the prize for best Canadian feature. "The whole climate of independent film had changed. People had begun to sense there was a gold rush. It was five years after Bruce and I had set up a projector outside, and suddenly we felt very much inside."

The 1987 festival marked a turning point for Canadian film. Fresh from acclaimed premieres in Cannes, Jean-Claude Lauzon and Patricia Rozema presented their debut features, *Night Zoo* and *I've Heard the Mermaids Singing*, to resounding enthusiasm. *Mermaids* opened the festival, and there was a sense that its success stood for more than a single filmmaker. It is, after all, a story of an artist struggling for recognition within the cultural establishment—a photographer, played by Sheila McCarthy, working as girl Friday for a cold-hearted gallery owner. And as this skittish dreamer takes flight into a world of unfettered imagination, it could just as well be Rozema leaving behind the sad baggage of the Canadian film industry. *Mermaids* was not some producer's hyped concoction, but a breakthrough for a new generation of directors who were changing the rules.

It was a supportive community. Rozema remembers seeing *Next of Kin* and having "the sensation that there was another kind of Canadian cinema, a personal voice that dared to break from the formula." She didn't know Egoyan, but she phoned him in Victoria, where he was on vacation, and found out all she could from him about making movies. Rozema did the same with Mettler. "People were always bringing his name up. He was one of the guys everyone was talking about." She also connected with Cronenberg, working as third assistant director on *The Fly*: "That taught me a lot. I learned that you can be absolutely gracious on set and get everything you need, which is not what I experienced working on more Americanized features."

David Cronenberg was the first Canadian director to be lavishly showcased by the Toronto festival. In 1983, it mounted a complete retrospective of his work up to that point, including *Stereo*, *Crimes of the Future*, *Shivers*, *Rabid*, *The Brood*, *Scanners* and *Videodrome*. Meanwhile, Cronenberg programmed Science Fiction Revisited, a selection of thirty-five films that did not fit conventional notions of sci-fi. *The Shape of Rage: The Films of David Cronenberg* was published the same year. Edited by Piers Handling, this book of opinionated essays—which included Handling's "A Canadian

I'VE HEARD THE MERMAIDS SINGING

FAMILY VIEWING

Cronenberg"—revealed that the director had become the most fiercely debated subject in Canadian cinema.

Martin Scorsese provided the commentary for the retrospective in the programme book. He first encountered Cronenberg's work at the 1975 Edinburgh Film Festival, which had opened with *The Parasite Murders* (*Shivers*). "I thought I didn't like it," said Scorsese. "But a year later, I found myself thinking about it and talking about it to anyone who would listen. To be blunt, there were a lot of people who wouldn't listen. Cronenberg was a strange name, and my friends were dubious about Canadian cinema anyway. Still, I kept talking, maybe as a way of exorcising Cronenberg's images. Well, I've never exorcised any of them. The last scene of *The Parasite Murders*, with the cast going out to infect the entire world with sexual dementia, is something I've never been able to shake. It's an ending that is genuinely shocking, subversive, surrealistic and probably something we all deserve."

In 1978, when *The Last Waltz* screened in Toronto, Scorsese tried to connect with this bizarre Canadian. He said, "I told my friend Robbie Robertson, who was at the Canadian Film Awards as a juror (a pretty amusing concept in itself), to invite Cronenberg." After Cronenberg didn't show up, Robertson told Scorsese "they couldn't find him." Now, as Cronenberg recalls, "I do remember Scorsese being in town and there was some deliberate sleight of hand so that I wouldn't get to meet him. I'm actually not paranoid, despite my movies. But there was a moment when they didn't want me out there representing Canada . . . I was too disreputable." (*They?* It's hard to imagine now. But at the end of the seventies, Cronenberg had not won the respect of the Canadian film establishment; his reputation still hadn't recovered from the infamous broadside by *Saturday Night*'s Marshall Delaney—a.k.a. Robert Fulford—depicting him as the B-movie pariah of public film financing.) Eventually, however, Cronenberg looked up Scorsese in New York and they became friends. "The man who showed up at my apartment looked like a gynecologist from Beverly Hills," recalls Scorsese (in an oddly prescient reference to the man who would make *Dead Ringers*, featuring a twin gynecologist named Beverly). "We had a pleasant dinner, even though there was a certain tension on my part, probably originating in my expectation that David's veins would run open and his head would explode. Later, as a birthday gift, David sent me a copy of the uncut *Brood*. He said it was his version of *Kramer vs. Kramer*."

In the landscape of Canadian cinema, so imprinted by the realism of the documentary tradition—and its subjugation of the self *to* landscape—Cronenberg's work was a seismic event. His horror always comes from within. Reflecting on *Rabid* and *Shivers* in "The Word, the Flesh and David Cronenberg," an essay in *The Shape of Rage*, John Harkness wrote: "These are not horror films that delight in dark corners concealing lurking menace. Instead they are composed around rigidly controlled visual frames and taut Apollonian environments—sterile modern apartment buildings and hospitals, clean Canadian shopping centres and subways." But for Cronenberg, the operative landscape is the flesh. And on some level, all his movies concern eruptions of the flesh, itself a metaphor for the uncontrolled mind, for unconscious desires and fears. Treating the human body as a mutation in progress, Cronenberg dramatizes the intercourse between biology and technology as an existential mating game. In his early horror films—*Shivers*, *Rabid* and *The Brood*—the id literally explodes from the body in creature form. But later he abandoned genre films to create tragedies of sexual identity—*Dead Ringers*, *M. Butterfly* and *Crash*—which explore fantastic scenarios within the bounds of existing technology.

In programming Science Fiction Revisited, Cronenberg foreshadowed his move away from the horror genre to less obvious forms of sci-fi. He included titles such as *Taxi Driver*, *Don't Look Now*, *Duel*, *Performance*, *Hour of the Wolf*—and *Satyricon*, which Fellini had described as a science-fiction film projected backwards into an almost unimaginable past. "The idea of what people think is real on film is a joke," says Cronenberg. "How real is it? Coloured light on a screen. So let's get a little more metaphysical about it." He did a lot of research to create the programme; his criteria were "totally subjective," he adds. "It was just an ambiance. *Don't Look Now* or *Taxi Driver*—how realistic are those films? They're not. To me alternate realities and alternate societies also count as science fiction."

Cronenberg's Rubicon was *Dead Ringers*, which opened the 1988 festival. It was his first horror movie that was not a horror movie. And it changed the course of his career and that of his star, Jeremy Irons. Cronenberg proved that behind the shock-meister there was a legitimate artist, while Irons proved that behind the dashing good looks there was a serious actor. Together they mustered the nerve and the talent to pull off a movie about drug-addicted, suicidal twin gynecologists.

Dead Ringers *is not just about twin gynecologists, but twin dire*
has always been fascinated with the Other, and here he draws a scal
tissue connecting his dual identities: the scientist and the poet

Of the Mantle twins, Beverly is the sensitive one who works in the lab, "slaving over the hot snatches." Elliot is the slick bastard who makes the speeches and softens up the women. Irons creates them as distinct characters even though they're joined at the hip—or the head at least—as Siamese psyches. Genevieve Bujold's Claire is the actress who comes between them. The movie plays as a darkly comic descent into hell. Sliding into druggy paranoia, Beverly sees mutant women wherever he looks. With missionary zeal, he has a sculptor forge gynecological tools in surgical steel, devices that look like medieval torture instruments, or modern art objects. In the operating theatre, the director appears in a cameo among a team of doctors who wear red gowns, like cardinals of some carnal church. *Dead Ringers* is not just about twin gynecologists, but twin directors. Cronenberg has always been fascinated with the Other, and here he draws a scalpel through the soft tissue connecting his dual identities: the scientist and the poet.

Like the Mantle twins, comedy and tragedy are conjoined. As the medical and sexual

. Cronenberg
rough the soft

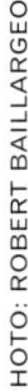

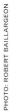

PHOTO: ROBERT BAILLARGEON

FAYE DUNAWAY AT THE BARFLY PRESS CONFERENCE, 1987

horrors unfold, dry English wit is the dominant mode. But in the end, comedy's mortal coil is shuffled off. Tragedy is all that remains as one twin disembowels the other, falls asleep, then takes a walk. At that moment, Cronenberg executes one of the saddest landscape shots in Canadian cinema, panning from a concrete building, past a grey line of skeleton trees, an old church and a spiral parking structure, to a Plexiglas phone booth. Beverly dials, hangs up after hearing Claire's voice, then walks back into the building to kill himself. Inside, in the ruined lab, in the aftermath of the twins' birthday-party suicide pact, the camera lingers over congealed surfaces—operatic falls of candle wax—until it comes to rest on the entwined, naked bodies of brothers in arms: the *Pietà* meets Narcissus.

CHOOSE ME

Cronenberg recalls the opening-night premiere as being "pretty intense." Bujold was especially nervous. "She was sitting next to me and holding my hand. She was terrified—she's an emotional girl. I remember her just hanging onto me, with [his wife] Carolyn on the other side." Premiering a movie as disturbing as *Dead Ringers* to a corporate audience on opening night was cause for some concern. "I was worried, but it actually went over rather well," says the director. "I was very happy with the movie. I knew it was very emotional, which a lot of my movies aren't in the traditional way. Even though Jeremy's performance has often been criticized as cold and aloof, I had an inkling this could be a breakthrough for him."

I catch up with Jeremy Irons at the airport in Nice in May of 1999. He is on his way to the Cannes film festival, being flown in as a surprise guest at the opening ceremonies for Cronenberg, who is heading the jury. The actor looks every bit like one of his ravaged characters, the bohemian from *Stealing Beauty* or the ruined man from *Damage* after he has fled England. He appears in a tan linen jacket and spooky little sunglasses, a battered leather bag slung over his shoulder. His face is pale and alarmingly gaunt. As we wait by the baggage carousel, there is a steady stream of fans seeking autographs, and he obliges them with an impressionist signature that sprawls across the page like an

*"I've been around a bit, you know, and I thought I'd seen some cre[e]
[t]hings go on in the movie business." — Genevieve Bujold as actr[e]
[C]laire Niveau, upon discovering that she has been sharing her [b]
[w]ith twin gynecologists*

extended sigh. As we begin to talk, Irons meticulously handcrafts a cigarette with a rolling device. He remembers Cronenberg tracking him down in a London hotel and giving him the script for *Dead Ringers*. "I didn't much want to do it when I read it, because I thought it would be technically difficult, and that would get in the way of what I like to do—which is apparently doing nothing. I didn't like many of his other films. I liked *The Fly*. I didn't like *Videodrome*. I found it a bit creepy. But then I find *Dead Ringers* creepy when I watch it now. I don't like watching it very much really."

PHOTO: CATHY JOHNSON-CAMPBELL

Cronenberg has a reputation as an intellect who shocks audiences with images and ideas, but actors who end up in his movies talk about him in the warmest terms as an actor's director. "He's not a puppet master in any way," says Irons. "He never came with an agenda. He allows you to feel it's yours, which is probably why actors are so loyal to him. He really shares the work, which is not the same for all filmmakers." Like Scorsese, Irons discovered that this maker of monsters seems exceptionally well-adjusted in person. "He's such a normal guy, a man who loves racing cars more than anything. We would look forward to the end of the day if we were at the studio, and he'd drive me back in the Morgan or his Ferrari, and that would be the high point of both of our days."

When Irons won the Oscar for *Reversal of Fortune*—which premiered at the Toronto festival—he specifically thanked Cronenberg. "I thought it was more than half for *Dead Ringers*, that award," he told me. "I got a lot of reaction from Hollywood that I hadn't been nominated for *Dead Ringers*. People said that's crazy, you should have been. So there was an enormous amount of goodwill by the time they decided to mount an Oscar campaign for *Reversal*. Without that goodwill, I probably wouldn't have won."

Irons has been a frequent visitor to the Toronto festival, with films that have submerged his Brit persona in various international guises—as a Polish construction foreman in *Moonlighting* (1982), a Parisian Jew in *Swann in Love* (1984), a German wife-killer in *Reversal of Fortune* (1990), and a French diplomat in Cronenberg's *M. Butterfly* (1993). "I like the Toronto festival more than any others," he says, "because it seems to pull in the city more. I've always enjoyed my time there. Cannes is just madness. It's more about

RONENBERG AND JEREMY IRONS

PHOTO: PAM GAWN

TINY TIM, 1988

deal-making than loving films, whereas Toronto is really about people who love going to see films which they might not see otherwise."

As for Cronenberg, the festival has played a vital role in his career. It was there in 1984 that he first met British producer Jeremy Thomas, who helped him bring *Naked Lunch* and *Crash* to the screen. "He was with some Rastafarian friends," recalls Cronenberg. "He was a little stoned—he was in party mode. But he definitely had his eye on me as someone he wanted to work with. We talked about *Naked Lunch*. He's the one who connected me with William Burroughs. And we first talked about *Crash* at the festival." The festival also launched *M. Butterfly*, although it was not one of Cronenberg's best-received films. At the opening-night premiere, he says, "I remember we were sitting behind Kim Campbell, who was the prime minister at the time, and she was in tears by the end of the movie. I thought it went very well. But then I started to hear rumblings that people didn't like it. That was my first inkling that the movie would have trouble. We didn't have critical support, and Warners just dropped it. I remember I was very worried about *The Crying Game* because people would say Jaye Davidson was a better woman than John Lone, and that became the focus. Little did I know that *Farewell My Concubine* would also appear. How often do you have two movies about homosexuality and the Peking Opera?"

MATTHEW MODINE, 1987

PHOTO: DOUG MACLELLAN

Don McKellar was working as a theatre manager at the festival in 1989 the first time he met Cronenberg, who was chairing the Canadian film jury. Cronenberg came running out of the Uptown One and started yelling at him. "This is appalling to have Canadian films projected in such poor quality," he said.

"Sir, I couldn't agree with you more," replied McKellar.

In fact, the air-conditioning was broken, there was a hole in the screen, and although McKellar didn't tell this to Cronenberg, there were raccoons in the house. Yes, raccoons. "The Uptown was literally falling apart that year," says McKellar. "And the projectionists were a disaster. Projectionists . . . how should I put this? Well, to be charitable, as a profession they are prone to alcoholism."

The festival has had its share of disastrous screenings. One night at the New Yorker theatre, in 1986, German director Cristel Buschmann's melodrama, *Now or Never*, became even more melodramatic when part of the ceiling caved in during a torrential downpour. And on the opening night of Perspective Canada in 1989, Atom Egoyan was horrified to see that the reels of *Speaking Parts* had been stuck together in the wrong order by the lab. He was beginning to wonder if the film was cursed: after watching it literally melt on the screen at the Directors' Fortnight in Cannes, he'd run up to the booth to find celluloid spooling onto the floor and flames shooting out of the projector. In Toronto, Egoyan begged the audience to be patient, then rushed home in a taxi to get another print. "It was a hot, humid night," he recalls. "I went barrelling downstairs and found a cab. This Rastafarian guy was driving, and I kept imploring him to go faster. I told him eight hundred people were in a theatre waiting to see my film. Of course, he thought I was delusional—'Yeah mon, eight hundred people.' We finally got to the house, and I threw the

M. BUTTERFLY

LEFT, VALERIE BUHAGIAR AND MCKELLAR, 1989

PHOTO: SAM BARNES

Don McKellar was working as a theatre manager when Cronenberg of the Uptown One, yelling at him. The air conditioning was broken. he screen. And there were raccoons in the house. Yes, raccoons

other copy into the trunk. At that point, I think he sensed that I wasn't completely crazy. When I got back to the theatre, I was shocked that people had waited. There was this round of applause when I walked in. I'd thought it was going to be a really glamorous night. I'd thought I'd arrived. And I ended up being drenched in sweat like a pig."

McKellar spent that festival engaged in a running feud with a new Famous Players district manager, until finally getting himself banned from the Uptown. But on the closing night of Perspective Canada, McKellar returned to the theatre and marched triumphantly past the manager—as the writer of Bruce McDonald's feature debut, *Roadkill*, in which he plays an aspiring serial killer. The film, a black-and-white comedy about a rock band going AWOL in northern Ontario, was finished just in the nick of time. McDonald delivered the print to the theatre straight from the lab. After the premiere, he partied until 5 a.m. Then someone dragged him out of bed ordering him to go to the awards brunch, where he listened in disbelief as Cronenberg's jury awarded *Roadkill* the $25,000 prize for best Canadian film, beating out Denys Arcand's masterpiece, *Jesus of Montreal*.

For Arcand, who took the International Critics' Award, the abyss between English- and French-Canadian cinema must have seemed wider than ever before. But there has been an unofficial tradition of giving the Canadian award to novice directors who tend to blurt out bizarre acceptance speeches. Besides, McDonald looked like he could use the money. Hungover and dishevelled, with a cigarette in his hand, he clutched the prize and said it's "gonna buy me a big chunk of hash." What did he spend it on? Well, among other things, McDonald now recalls that he "did buy a nice big chunk of black hash . . . and a black winter coat." The prize also helped McDonald sell his movie to Germany, Japan and Australia. "Without a lot of marketing and distribution," he says, "a prize is enough to turn a mutt into a show dog."

McKellar, meanwhile, quit the festival staff at the end of that year. He has since written or directed half a dozen films that have shown at the festival—including two with performances by Cronenberg, who plays a porn magazine addict in *Blue* and a gas company supervisor in *Last Night*. If anyone has served as a common denominator among Toronto filmmakers, it is McKellar: as a director, actor or writer, he has worked with Cronenberg, McDonald, Rozema and Egoyan. Which is oddly fitting, considering the years he spent trying to accommodate filmmakers in his self-described role as "a glorified usher" at the festival. "My first experiences with almost everyone in Canadian film," he says, "was with them panicking or running out of the theatre with some problem."

e running out
was a hole in

He also had some odd brushes with celebrity. The premiere of *The Princess Bride,* McKellar recalls, "was one of the first times we had a big influx of Hollywood publicists. They gave me instructions about how Andre the Giant had to be handled. He required a chair exactly double the size of a normal theatre seat. We had to build it—this big bench made of orange vinyl. They warned me he was very big, and he was. His hand was the size of my head." At the premiere of Gus Van Sant's *Drugstore Cowboy*, to avoid the crush at the Varsity Cinemas, McKellar had Matt Dillon and Kelly Lynch delivered to the loading dock. "It was more like a garbage dock," he recalls. "They rolled up in a limo. I was waving at them from behind a dumpster. They were all dressed up and I led them through this minefield of refuse, apologizing all the way. I told them it was just a short ride up the freight elevator. Then it got stuck between floors. We weren't stuck that long, but the audience was waiting, and there I was making small talk while trying to reach someone on the emergency phone."

Sometimes, it's the star that gets stuck. Or stuck up. McKellar had an especially hard time getting Richard Gere onstage to introduce the premiere of *Miles from Home*. Gere was more interested in tinkling away at a piano backstage. "He was playing this really irritating jazz tune," recalls McKellar. "It just went on and on and sounded like it was never going to end. I kept going, 'Okay, we should be going now . . . we really should be going.' He kept saying, 'Relax, what's the problem?' 'Well, I've got 1,250 people out there who have been waiting for half an hour.' I just wanted to slug him."

Then there were the run-ins with Garth Drabinsky—and Lynda Friendly, his PR executive and frequent companion. As CEO of Cineplex Odeon, Drabinsky controlled many of the theatres used by the festival, and, after the closing of the University Theatre, it was his idea to use Roy Thomson Hall for galas. Garth had offered his production of *The Glass Menagerie*, with Paul Newman and Joanne Woodward, as the closing-night gala in 1988. But he was not about to let his stars traipse into the grungy old Uptown. So his Cineplex team created a state-of-the-art screening system for Roy Thomson Hall, which eventually would serve as the festival's prime gala venue.

It was pouring rain for *The Glass Menagerie* premiere. The photographers were not allowed in the lobby, so McKellar had them wait outside the front door, promising that they would get their shots of the stars arriving at the red carpet. The stars were late. And when they finally showed up, Lynda Friendly decided to whisk them in by the artists' entrance in the back to avoid the crowd. "The photographers were really not happy," says McKellar, understating the case. "And I was very, very mad."

He had another run-in with Garth and Lynda at the 1989 opening-night premiere of Norman Jewison's *In Country*. It was at the Eglinton Theatre. There was a mob outside the door. Again the stars were late. McKellar was in the manager's office, frantically manning a portable phone the size of a tank walkie-talkie, trying to contact limousines carrying Bruce Willis and Ontario's lieutenant-governor. "I was panicking," he says. "Then Garth came through the door with Lynda Friendly. They wanted to use the office. I said, 'I'm waiting for a call that's quite important.' He said, 'Do you know who I am?' or something to that effect, and he finally left in a huff." The next day Drabinsky demanded a written apology. McKellar refused to provide it, and remains puzzled to this day as to why Drabinsky felt he had a right to use an office in a theatre that was not even part of his chain.

But it would be understandable if he felt he had the right to throw his weight around. In providing his theatres as an exhibitor, and his films as a distributor, Drabinsky played a vital role in giving the festival a home and establishing its prestige. Although he rubbed a lot of people the wrong way, the festival may not have survived without him. Besides, when you hear war stories from the front lines of the festival in the 1980s, you have to remember the atmosphere of those premieres, which was often one of barely controlled hysteria. "People would just go insane about seeing a movie," recalls McKellar. "They would use any excuse. They had a friend inside. They were sick. Could they please use the washroom? One lady tried to push her way through me. Another was in hysterics because she'd broken a nail."

Keeping people from entering a packed theatre is one thing. Trying to get them out once they're in is another. That was the situation at the premiere of *In Praise of Older Women* in 1978. And that happened again, on a smaller scale, in 1989. McKellar got a call that there was trouble at the Royal Ontario Museum Theatre. He arrived to find people sitting in aisles and on top of each other. Ushers using counters at two separate entrances had let in twice the capacity of the room by mistake. McKellar was trying to clear people out. I'd managed to get in by tagging along with the director, whom I'd met on the street, and I wasn't about to leave. It was the first time I'd ever seen McKellar perform. I remember him looking terribly officious as he stood in front of the crowd and asked in that shy, halting manner of his, "Would some of you please leave?" No one moved. The occasion was the premiere of a funny little movie called *Roger and Me*.

The premiere
had a big infl
the Giant hac
theatre chair.
me he was ve

PHOTO: SUSAN MORROW

ANDRE THE GIANT AND MCKELLAR, 1987

he Princess Bride, *McKellar recalls, "was one of the first times we Hollywood publicists. They gave me instructions about how Andre be handled. He required a chair exactly double the size of a norma had to build it—this big bench made of orange vinyl. They warned g, and he was. His hand was the size of my head"*

Roger, Me and th
Documentary Eye

AS MICHAEL MOORE ROLLED UP TO THE BORDER CROSSIN
AT THE BLUEWATER BRIDGE IN SARNIA, ONTARIO, HE THOUGHT
might as well be honest. So when the Canada Customs official asked if
had anything to declare, he mentioned the Roger and Me *baseball ca*
and T-shirts that he was bringing to the Toronto festival. Then he point
o the big carton of lint rollers, about five thousand of them. "They cou
understand the T-shirts and ball caps, but lint rollers—what is this?"

ROGER AND ME

13

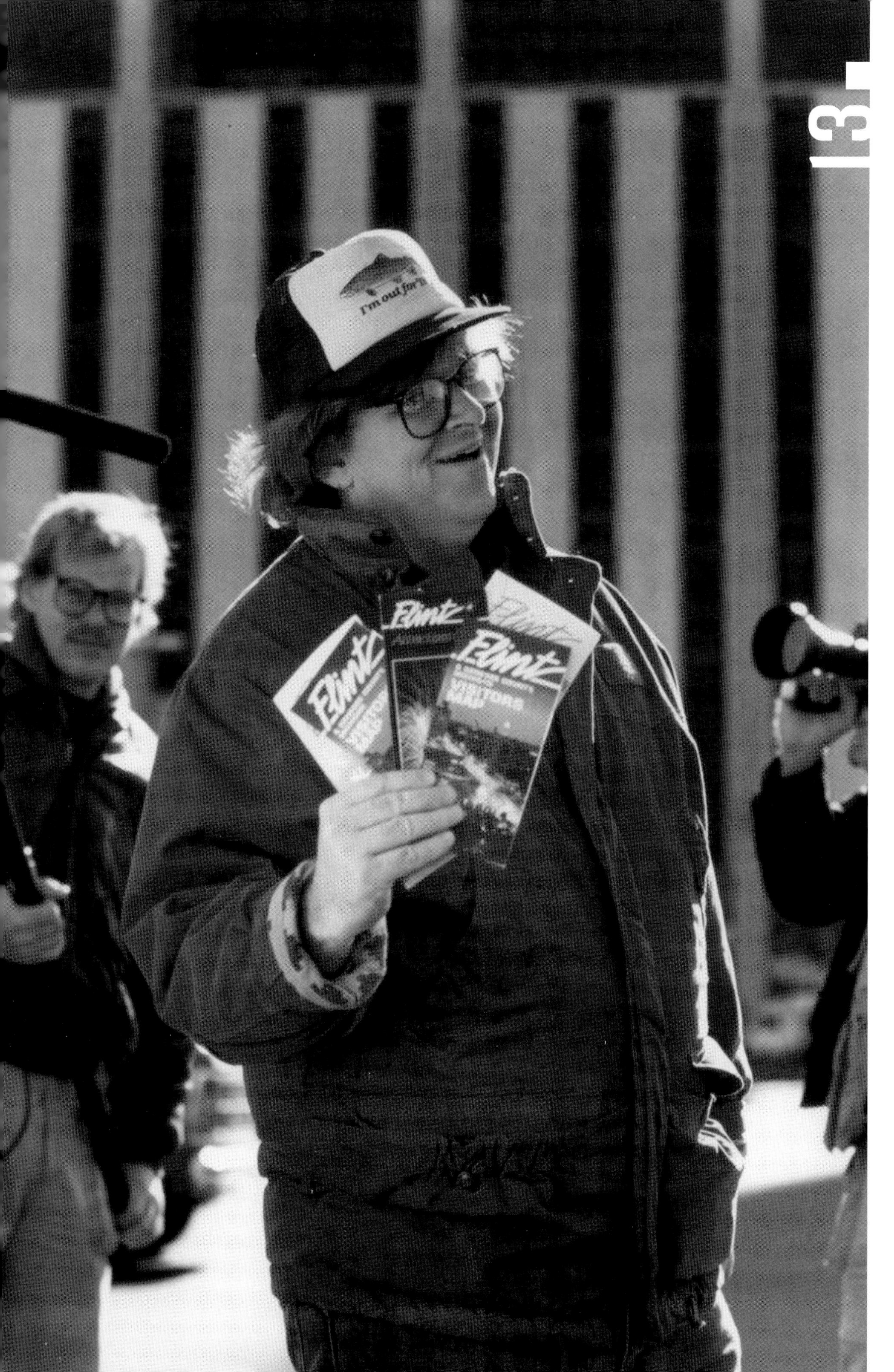

Errol Morris's landmark documentary was the first movie mystery murder, and is credited with overturning the conviction of Randall A death row. But when it came out "it was criticized because it brok documentary and journalistic conventions"

Moore starts to tell them about his movie, and how it's about his hometown of Flint, Michigan, the birthplace of General Motors, and how it's been devastated by GM's elimination of thirty thousand jobs, and how the film shows a GM lobbyist saying that even if the company leaves Flint altogether, people can still make lint rollers, because that's the other thing Flint is famous for: manufacturing about 90 per cent of America's lint rollers. And that, said Moore, is why he was taking five thousand Flint lint rollers stamped with *Roger and Me* to Toronto. Two hours later, after a great deal of bureaucratic wrangling, Canada Customs finally let Moore, and his lint rollers, into the country. "I thought they were going to say, 'Look, the country is already clean enough,'" he says.

Roger and Me—a darkly satirical portrait of a town trying to put a happy face on the Rust Belt blues, framed by Moore's guerrilla quest to buttonhole GM chairman Roger Smith—became the top-grossing documentary in history. Moore, the blue-collar comedian from Flint, became North America's most famous socialist. And it all started with a call to the Toronto festival. Moore was broke. To raise the $270,000 budget of *Roger and Me*, he had sold his house, held yard sales and organized weekly bingo games in Flint, but he was still $100,000 in debt. While editing his film in a fleabag hotel in Washington, D.C., he phoned the festival. Noah Cowan answered and told him he had missed the deadline for submissions by a week. Moore talked him into bending the rules, and agreed to hook up with programmer Kay Armatage, who was in New York. He showed up with a rough cut of his film on reels in a gym bag. Armatage ended up viewing it on an old Steinbeck editing machine in a friend's apartment on the Upper West Side. "It was missing music, and some narration," says Moore. "There was no sound mix. But she sat there amazed and laughing and in tears. When she was finished, I said, 'What's the process from here?' She said, 'Are you kidding? This is in the festival.' We were just stunned." Armatage took them around the corner to a fancy seafood restaurant, where Moore, who had never earned more than $17,000 a year, ate the best meal of his life.

After the film was accepted by Toronto, the Telluride festival wanted to see it, and immediately accepted it. *Roger and Me* screened in Telluride in late August, and by the time Moore arrived in Toronto, there was an industry buzz around the film. The premiere was pandemonium. Among those jamming the aisles in the ROM theatre was Matt Dillon with the gang from *Drugstore Cowboy*, and distributors such as Tom Bernard of Orion Classics, who had applied his college football skills to barge through the door. The fire marshall was ready to shut the screening down. Finally Armatage managed to persuade those without seats to leave with a promise of tickets to another screening. The next day the *Sun* reported a riot at the ROM, "which I always thought was kind of funny," says Moore, "because what a Canadian would call a riot, we'd just call moving forward. For a riot in the U.S., you have to have some gunfire and arson going on. You can't just nudge people."

tually solve a
, who was on
h all kinds of

Soon after the premiere, Moore found himself in the middle of a heated bidding war. He fielded offers from all the independents and one studio—Disney offered him $1 million for the movie plus a five-picture deal. But he turned it down because Disney would not guarantee the number of theatres in which it would release the film. "I didn't make the movie to make money or to get a Hollywood deal," Moore explains. "I made it because I wanted people to see what was going on in my town."

Meanwhile, Harvey Weinstein of Miramax collared Moore in his hotel corridor. "He was

TROY HURTUBISE OF PROJECT GRIZZLY

PHOTO: MOTTY LEVY

in his pyjamas," recalls Moore, "and the pyjama top had a big Mickey Mouse on it, although this was before Disney owned Miramax. He invited us into his hotel room, where he had already ordered breakfast for me and my friends. And he made his pitch. He told us how he and his brother grew up in working-class Queens. They felt they came from a similar place. We immediately connected with them. But we wouldn't sell Harvey the film right then and there; he literally chased us down the hallway, with scrambled eggs on his Mickey Mouse pyjama top." Harvey topped the Disney offer, matching Universal with a $1.5-million bid. But about a month after *Roger and Me* won the People's Choice Award at the festival—the first documentary to do so since Ira Wohl's Oscar-winning *Best Boy* in 1977—Warner Bros. eventually purchased it for $3 million. *Roger and Me* has since grossed $12 million worldwide but failed to get an Academy Award nomination: apparently, the conservatives drawing up the list felt that Moore's showmanship violated the decorum of documentary film.

Moore came back to the festival with *Pets or Meat: the Return to Flint* in '92, and *Canadian Bacon* in '95. Then in '97 he launched *The Big One*, a chronicle of his renegade book tour to promote *Downsize This!* By that point, Moore had refined his guerrilla comedy to a savvy stand-up act. With *The Big One*, he delivers a sharp critique of corporate America, while skewering everyone from his Random House "media escorts" to Nike CEO Phil Knight, who invites Moore to interview him then ends up coming off like the Scrooge of the sneaker racket. At the festival, Harvey Weinstein landed *The Big One* for $600,000, plus a promise to give $100,000 in grants and scholarships to the people of Flint. At the premiere, I saw Harvey plunk himself into the reserved seat in front of me almost halfway into the film. Moore was sitting in front of him. Before the film was even over, Harvey made his move. He grabbed Moore by the collar—"C'mon I want to buy this film"—and took him out to the lobby.

"People are applauding," Moore recalls. "I'm missing this great moment with the audience. He's dickering on the money, and the festival people tell me I've got to get onstage." Moore left the deal in the hands of his BBC co-producer, telling him, "Don't give away the store, and don't stick him up. Just get this thing distributed." Before going onstage for the Q&A, Moore quickly ducked into the washroom. One of the smaller distributors followed. "He stood at the urinal next to me and didn't even unzip his fly," says Moore. "He just whispered, 'I'll offer you more than Harvey. Whatever he says I'll give you more.' I said, 'Do you mind? I'm trying to relieve myself.'"

Documentaries, an endangered species in the world of theatrical distribution, have found a high-profile haven at the festival. And a glance through some of the non-fiction hits—*Best Boy, Soldier Girls*, *Burden of Dreams*, *P4W: Prison for Women*, *Stop Making Sense*, *Hearts of Darkness: A Filmmaker's Apocalypse*, *The Thin Blue Line*, *Cane Toads*, *Let's Get Lost*, *Twist*, *The War Room*, *Hoop Dreams*, *Crumb*, *Project Grizzly*, *Sick: The Life & Death of Bob Flanagan, Supermasochist*, *The Big One*, *Mr. Death: The Rise and Fall of Fred*

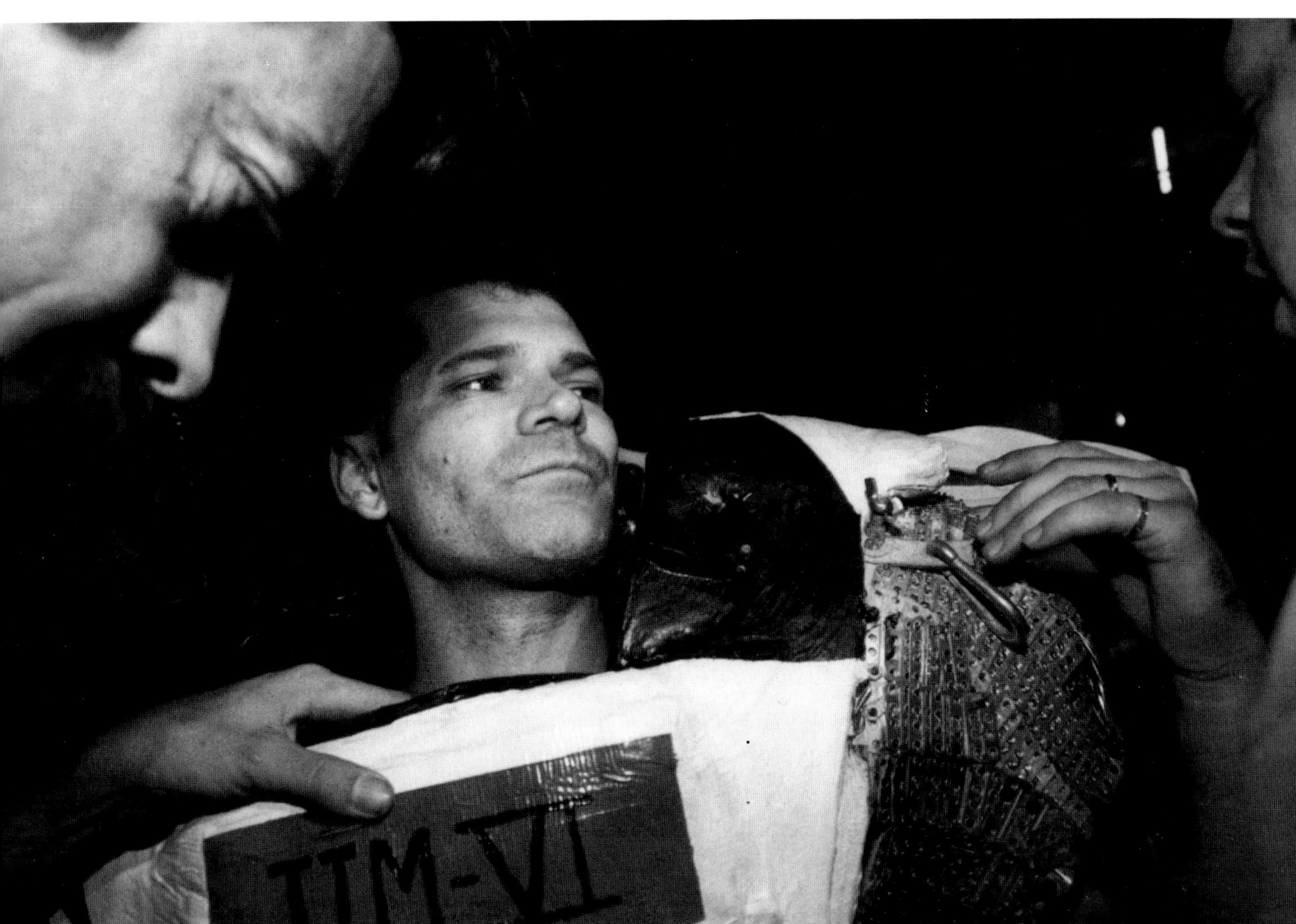

Project Grizzly, *the story of a man's quixotic mission to build a*
ar-proof suit of armour, Peter Lynch lets his subject run wild on camera
a kind of Canuck Davy Crockett doing performance art

A. Leuchter, Jr.—shows that creative non-fiction is infinitely elastic. It can be satirical, poetic, musical, investigative, political, epic or intimate—possibly all at once. Just as the New Journalism shattered the objectivity myth by revealing the writer's point of view, the documentary has adopted dramatic techniques to create new forms of personal filmmaking.

In *Roger and Me*, Michael Moore is the *auteur* as amateur, a filmmaker learning on the fly. He is the working-class clown in a baseball cap, with a deadpan persona that is as fictional—or not—as Woody Allen's. In making a home movie about capitalist decay, Moore essentially made a movie about making a movie. British director Nick Broomfield follows a similar formula in several of his films—telling the story of not getting the story. His *Tracking Down Maggie: The Unofficial Biography of Margaret Thatcher* (1994), in which he spends the whole film trying to talk to his subject, could be called *Maggie and*

Me. Like Moore, he does guerrilla verité, sticking the camera in unsuspecting faces. But he has less to say, and over the years Broomfield's lazy, laconic shtick starts to wear thin. Besides, with postmodern videographers rampant on television, the device of the disingenuous investigator stumbling into people's lives with a camera rolling begins to lose its allure.

A lot of documentary filmmakers don't like the word "documentar
't's not sexy, it spells death at the box office, and it suggests dry reporta
as opposed to creative filmmaking

Not all personal documentaries involve first-person escapades with the filmmaker mugging on camera. Take *The Thin Blue Line*, Errol Morris's landmark of documentary expressionism, which premiered at the 1988 festival. Perhaps the first movie mystery to actually solve a murder, the film is credited with overturning the conviction of Randall Adams, who was on death row for the 1976 roadside murder of a Dallas police officer. But what is extraordinary about *The Thin Blue Line*, aside from the evidence it uncovers, is how it casts a spell by using formal devices to explore the nature of subjectivity. Morris's circling inquiry is measured with stylized dramatizations—repeated close-ups of a red flasher on a squad car, the revolver firing in the night, a police flashlight shattering on the pavement, a Burger King milkshake spilling in slow motion. The interviews float on a Philip Glass score, which ebbs and flows through the film like the sound of destiny idling. Morris lets the truth creep up on the viewer. It slowly becomes apparent that the real killer is David Harris, who incriminated Adams in exchange for immunity. On Death Row for a second murder, Harris sits in his orange dungarees and recalls with psychopathic calm how his younger brother drowned when they were kids. Morris intercuts his words with family snapshots of the two boys splashing in a wading pool. Then, in a chilling epilogue, the camera moves in on a small tape recorder as it plays one final interview with Harris, saying he's sure that Adams is innocent. We hear the director asking how he can be so sure. Then Harris, coldly: "Because I'm the one that knows."

The film was controversial because Morris dared to frame his evidence with dramatic re-enactment, a device that has since been cheaply imitated by tabloid TV. But Morris's re-enactments were deliberately stylized. "In *The Thin Blue Line*, you never had the feeling they were an illustration of what really happened," he told me eleven years later. "They were dreamscapes, intended to take you deeper into the mystery of what happened. They had, for better or worse, the function of metaphors. They illustrated what people *said* happened. And it was always clear what they said happened was wrong. Of course, I was very much concerned with what happened. But my way of exploring that was to take you into all these crazy, contradictory accounts that were given at the trial. When *The Thin Blue Line* came out—and it's a film that I still like after all these years—it was criticized because it broke with all kinds of documentary and journalistic conventions. There's this idea that if something's real it has to be presented to us according to certain stylistic rules, as if the answer to the Cartesian riddle of what's out there is going to be settled once and for all by just following a style manual."

To understand Errol Morris, it's worth noting that he began his interviewing career as a graduate philosophy student at Berkeley—talking to mass murderers, their friends and families for a PhD thesis on the insanity plea that he never completed. He became a filmmaker instead. "I'm a surrealist and an absurdist interested in true stories," he says. "Call me a have-your-cake-and-eat-it director." His subjects have ranged from the pet cemeteries of *Gates of Heaven* to the mole rats and robots of *Fast, Cheap & Out of Control*, but his work is most compelling when he's tackling the Big Questions.

In the '99 festival, Morris premiered *Mr. Death*, a fascinating portrait of Fred A. Leuchter Jr., a Massachusetts engineer who became the Florence Nightingale of Death Row, intent on designing more humane execution systems. Leuchter was commissioned by Toronto neo-Nazi Ernst Zundel to conduct a forensic investigation to "prove" that no cyanide gas was used at Auschwitz and that the Holocaust never happened. The film shows Leuchter, the most rational of madmen, chipping away at the rubble of Auschwitz and slipping brick samples into baggies. But Morris does not just refute the engineer's report with obliterating evidence. Lyrical images of a chisel chipping at stone keep coming up like a recurring dream. And Leuchter, eagerly talking to the

NICK BROOMFIELD

camera, paints his own portrait as a ridiculous man whose life is ultimately ruined by his obsessive quest. "It becomes this quixotic, deeply empty enterprise in the void," says Morris. "It has this Beckett/Kafka quality about it. There's something so starkly, nakedly absurd about the whole thing." Morris makes mysteries. In *Mr. Death* the mystery is not whether the Holocaust happened, but how a rational man could become so consumed with trying to prove that it didn't. "All my movies—and I think this makes them *anti*-documentaries, if anything—are designed to take you into a mental landscape," says Morris. "They take you into a subjective world, rather than the world as such."

A lot of documentary filmmakers don't like the word "documentary." It's not sexy, it spells death at the box office, and it suggests dry reportage as opposed to creative filmmaking. But the camera is never a passive observer: its gaze is selective and intense. Even in Canada, home of the documentary tradition, non-fiction filmmakers have developed exotic hybrids of meditative inquiry and expressive investigation. In *Picture of Light* (1994), Peter Mettler shows a metaphysical sense of the absurd not unlike Morris's as he tries to film the aurora borealis in shutter-freezing temperatures. When a blizzard strands his crew in a motel room for three days, he fires a bullet through the wall to see if a snow-drift will form on the floor. And in *Project Grizzly* (1996), the story of a man's quixotic mission to build a bear-proof suit of armour, Peter Lynch lets his subject expose his own laughable frailty on camera as a kind of Canuck Davy Crockett doing performance art.

As the first of his generation in the city to make movies and launch ther the festival, Ron Mann was a pioneer of what some have ambitiou called the Toronto New Wave. Three budding directors worked for h on Poetry in Motion. *Atom Egoyan was in charge of finding che accommodation for the talent; Peter Mettler was the focus puller; Bru McDonald was a production assistant*

In a more serious vein, Canadian directors began to explore social conditions by turning the camera on the emotional reality behind the issues. With *P4W: Prison for Women*, which premiered at the '81 festival, Toronto filmmakers Janis Cole and Holly Dale presented an intimate portrait of female inmates at an antiquated Kingston jail. Making a videotape for her daughter, a murderer plays guitar and sings a song then reads *The Tale of Peter Rabbit*. Another inmate fondles a Mother's Day card from children she hasn't seen in years. Stereotypes collapse as we meet women who have been dragged into crime through years of abuse. The movie makes no argument and offers no solution; it is an act of compassion.

Sturla Gunnarsson's riveting *Gerrie & Louise* is a more political documentary, yet once again empathy is more crucial than exposé. In Gunnarsson's film, which played the '97 festival, the camera becomes a confessor, drawing candid memories from Gerrie Hugo, a former intelligence officer from South Africa's death squads who broke rank and fell

in love with an anti-apartheid journalist. Hugo casually reminisces about torture, about electrodes in the mouth and pins in the fingertips. He remembers seeing a man "necklaced" (set ablaze with a burning tire) and being surprised that a human body had so much fat in it. And as he talks, there is a nervous glint in his eye that is hard to decipher. Gunnarsson does not just document the sins of apartheid. Like Errol Morris, he tries to fathom the banality of evil. "The things that Gerrie perpetrated were so often hideous," he says, "but the man himself seemed to be so ordinary. We go out looking for monsters and when we find them they have a human face."

One filmmaker whose documentaries do involve a degree of literal documentation is Toronto's Ron Mann, cinema's pop culture and counterculture historian. In films such as *Twist* and *Grass*, Mann compiles a blitz of archival footage to chronicle, respectively, a dance craze and the war on drugs. With aggressive editing, animation and music, Mann creates dense collages of image and sound, working his material so assiduously that his filmmaking is as much a deejay mix as a record of the times.

TRACKING DOWN MAGGIE

Perhaps more than any other filmmaker, Mann is a child of the festival. He has used it to launch all of his documentary features—*Poetry in Motion*, *Imagine the Sound*, *Comic Book Confidential*, *Twist* and *Grass*. And they have all gone on to theatrical distribution, making him one of just half a dozen filmmakers in the world who consistently make documentaries for the big screen. In his early teens, even before the Toronto festival was founded, Mann would skip school to attend the Stratford (Ontario) International Film Festival every September. Its director, Gerald Pratley, would sneak him in through the back door. At eighteen, Mann started going to Cannes, sleeping on the beach and filching party invitations from journalists' mailboxes. There, he met legends such as Werner Herzog and Elia Kazan, and he hung out with the community that would form the nucleus of the Toronto festival. He first met David Overbey when Overbey tried to pick him up on the beach. In the early years of the Toronto festival, Mann would persuade Wayne Clarkson to give him free passes, and gorge on movies from morning till night. Then, at twenty-three, he premiered his first documentary feature there, a portrait of vintage jazz musicians called *Imagine the Sound* (1981). It was reviewed internationally, and Jonathan Rosenbaum called it one of the ten greatest jazz films of all time. Although "jazz" and "documentary" are two of the least commercial niches imaginable, Miramax agreed to distribute it in the United States. And it was one of the first five movies to baptize the Carlton Cinema as Toronto's new art-house multiplex.

"Since that moment," says Mann, "my career as a filmmaker has been linked to the festival." In fact without it, Mann might never have finished a film. Using the festival as his deadline, he is notorious for tinkering up to the last minute. "The editing never ends," he says. "It just stops. *Poetry in Motion* was hand-delivered to the theatre dripping wet from the lab half an hour before the screening."

As the first of his generation in Toronto to make movies and launch them at the festival, Mann was a pioneer of what some have ambitiously called the Toronto New Wave. Three budding directors worked for him on *Poetry in Motion*, his anthology of poets performing their work. Atom Egoyan was in charge of finding cheap accommodation for the talent; Peter Mettler was the focus puller; Bruce McDonald was a production assistant. "And it was all because they saw *Imagine the Sound* at the festival," says Mann.

During the early eighties, Mann found a mentor and "a second father" in Emile de Antonio, the maker of such radical U.S. documentaries as *Underground* and *Year of the Pig*, who taught him that "history is the outtakes of television." He also told him never to use documentaries as a stepping stone to dramatic features. Mann attempted a dramatic feature, *Listen to the City* (1984), with little success. Then he spent two years in Los Angeles working as a screenwriter with expatriate Canadian Ivan Reitman (*Ghostbusters*). By day he would shoot a promotional video of Robert Redford for Reitman's *Legal Eagles*, and by night he worked on *Comic Book Confidential*. Spearheading the movement to take comic-book art seriously, *Confidential* is a kaleidoscopic history that mixes animation and graphics with interviews of twenty-two artists, from Art Spiegelman to Stan Lee, who also read from their work. A number of them showed up for the premiere at the '88 festival, including pioneer Will Eisner, who said, "We don't have to apologize about comic books any more." The film, which went on to become an international art-house hit, also drew celebrity comic-book fans out of the woodwork—at the festival, Mann arranged a special screening for Keanu Reeves.

One of the movie's subjects, Robert Crumb, was very shy about being filmed. After seeing his images ripped off left and right, from "Keep on Truckin'" coffee mugs to Ralph Bakshi's film of *Fritz the Cat*, Crumb had a deep suspicion of the media. By persuading him to go on camera for the first time in *Comic Book Confidential*, Mann paved the way for *Crumb*, Terry Zwigoff's extraordinary documentary portrait, which was launched at the '94 festival. (Zwigoff spent six years filming the artist for *Crumb*, a masterpiece that so impressed Woody Allen he asked Zwigoff to make a movie of his jazz band European tour. Zwigoff turned down the opportunity when Allen would not grant him final cut—and the job passed to Barbara Koppel, who made *Wild Man Blues*.)

In 1989, Mann took *Comic Book Confidential* to the Sundance Festival and found himself rooming with Steve Soderbergh, who was there with *sex, lies, and videotape*. "I was the guy who had worked in Hollywood and had four feature films, so I was giving *him* advice," Mann recalls, chuckling at how absurd that now seems. So what advice did he give him? "I asked him to change the title . . . I have no commercial sense."

But he knows how to please a crowd. In the 1992 festival, after organizers had to bump Woody Allen's *Husbands and Wives* from the closing-night gala to an earlier spot, *Twist* was chosen to replace it. As far as Mann was concerned, that gave him another week to edit it. One night in the thick of the festival, after Mann had finally finished the sound mix, Jay Scott—who was gravely ill with AIDS—interviewed him until 5 a.m. over a bottle of vodka then wrote an article that began with him fretting about Mann's health. Mann called *Twist* "the first movie about rock-and-roll dancing," showing how it grew

CRUMB

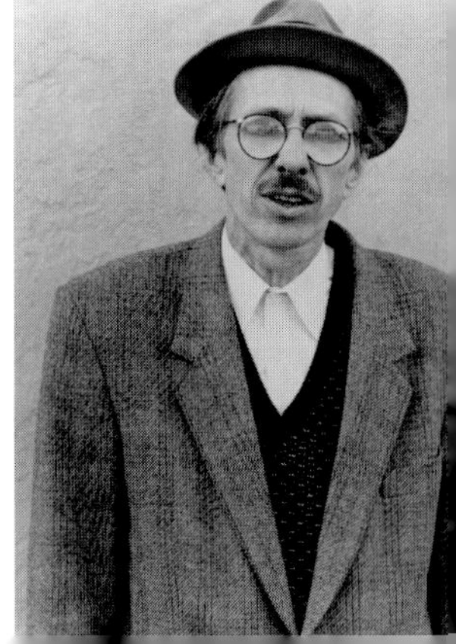

Mann watched people dance in the aisles, he felt "it was all a dream, airy tale. I hadn't slept in three nights. It was like taking psychedelic ushrooms. I was in my own movie"

out of jazz vernacular dance, and "how we went from squareness to awareness." The director took three days to film interviews for *Twist* and three years to edit them with archival footage. As usual, he delivered the film in the nick of time. At the Elgin theatre, as Mann basked in a standing ovation and watched people dance in the aisles during the closing credits, he felt "it was all a dream, a fairy tale. I hadn't slept in three nights. It was like taking psychedelic mushrooms. I was in my own movie."

That night Hank Ballard, the American musician who created the twist, performed at the party. Who would ever have imagined that the most festive closing-night gala in the history of the festival would be a Canadian documentary?

Sex, Lies and

14 Reservoir Dogs

RESERVOIR DOGS

LEFT, PETER GALLAGHER, MATT DILLON AND GUS VAN SANT, 1989

PHOTO: DEAN GOODWIN

PATRICIA ROZEMA WAS STILL REELING FROM THE NEW
THAT CANNES HAD SELECTED I'VE HEARD THE MERMAIDS SINGI
for the Directors' Fortnight when she got a call from some guy nam Harvey. A distributor. He wanted to see the film before it went to Cann In fact, he told her she had to show it to him in advance—it was "stand industry practice." Rozema insisted he wait and see it with everyone els

Harvey phoned back, again and again, hounding her with calls every other day. Then in Cannes, as Rozema arrived for her premiere, who was lying in wait for her on the steps of the Palais? Harvey. "He just hustled us," she says. "Everywhere I went, there was another bottle of Dom Perignon." And when Rozema and her novice producer, Alexandra Raffé, finally sat down to negotiate with this Harvey character, "it was like haggling with a rug merchant. He'd say, 'I'll make you an offer, but you have to respond before leaving this room,'" recalls the director, "and in our innocence we'd think, 'Oh, is that how it's done?'" The filmmakers had half a dozen offers on the table, and they were being advised to go with one of the bigger names, such as Orion Classics. Back then, no one had really heard of Harvey Weinstein and Miramax. "But he was so damn aggressive," Rozema recalls. "I thought, if he's going to be that aggressive, he really wants it." He also came up with the best offer, US$350,000, which seemed a lot for a film that cost C$350,000 to make. But *Mermaids* went on to gross $6 million. Harvey Weinstein knew what he was doing. And over the next five years, mining the festival circuit like prospectors, he and his brother, Bob, would revolutionize the business of independent film.

If the story of the Toronto festival is one of spinning the counterculture into a mainstream phenomenon, the Weinstein brothers are its entrepreneurial equivalent. They grew up as lower-middle-class kids in Queen's, New York, sons of Max, a diamond-cutter, and Miriam, a housewife—whose names were used to form "Miramax." Harvey and Bob were film buffs from their early teens, from the day they stumbled into a screening of *The 400 Blows* thinking they were going to see a porn film. They dropped out of college to promote rock concerts in a dilapidated theatre in Buffalo, and on off nights they showed movies, the kind that appealed to an audience in an altered state of consciousness, from Stanley Kubrick's *2001: A Space Odyssey* to Frank Zappa's *200 Motels*. In 1979, Harvey and Bob made their first jaunt to Cannes, and bought their first movie, *The Secret Policeman's Other Ball*. A decade later, they were the hottest game in town.

For the Weinsteins, and the indie movement, the 1989 festival marked a watershed. Miramax released no fewer than six films that were hits at Toronto that year: *Cinema Paradiso*; *sex, lies, and videotape*; *My Left Foot*; *The Unbelievable Truth*; and *The Cook, the Thief, His Wife and Her Lover*. Releasing *Cinema Paradiso*, says Harvey, was "the defining moment of our company." Essentially, he forced the film on the multiplexes—by bundling it with *The Grifters*, which premiered as the closing-night film at the 1990 Toronto festival. With the gradual success of *Cinema Paradiso*, the Weinstein brothers convinced exhibitors that subtitled movies could find an audience if given a chance. And they got their first taste of Oscar glory when it went on to win best foreign film. Meanwhile, Steve Soderbergh's *sex, lies, and videotape* became an indie landmark. After signing a distribution deal for a $1-million advance and a hefty slice of the gross, Soderbergh wrote in his diary: "There are some who think Miramax went overboard. We'll see. I don't know if it can make the kind of money they need to return their investment." Who knew? The movie, which cost $1.2 million, was the surprise winner of the Palme d'Or in Cannes and has since grossed $25 million in North America.

For Soderbergh, *sex, lies* was the ultimate calling-card film. It opened up a career that has allowed him to shift from esoteric detours like *Schitzopolis* to Hollywood escapades with George Clooney and Julia Roberts, who batted in the director's first major-league hit with *Erin Brockovich*. Ten years after the premiere of *sex, lies*, Soderbergh was in Cannes with *The Limey*. I asked him why his feature debut had become such a milestone. "Timing," he said. "It's lightning in a bottle. Pure chance. I have a very strong feeling that if *sex, lies* had been made a year earlier or a year later it wouldn't have hit in the same way. It was a very modest film with very modest aspirations that happened to be something people wanted to see right then—in a way that I obviously haven't been able to duplicate. [He had yet to make *Brockovich*.] It seemed very unlikely that I would ever again be the recipient of such unified acclaim. A lot of people never get it. For me to get it for my first movie was almost comical. You had to laugh." Then he added, "If that film had made half a million dollars, nobody would be talking about it today. It made a ton of money and it cost a little. And that was news. Suddenly everybody went, 'I want that to happen to my film, or my company, or whatever.' It was all driven by the money. I knew that while it was going on. Everything that flowed from that, in terms of what happened to me and the movement, was all based on racing after this perceived cash that people hadn't seen out there before."

SEX, LIES, AND VIDEOTAPE

As Denys Arcand had discovered with *The Decline of the American Empire*, talking about sex is a cheap way of getting people to sit up and take notice. And for a generation of aspiring filmmakers, *sex, lies* became a Seinfeldian model for creating something out of nothing. The opening shot is a strip of pavement scrolling under the camera, like film stock. The opening line of dialogue is "Garbage," as Ann (Andie MacDowell) tells her therapist how she worries about finding a home for all the trash. *Sex, lies* appreciates the dramatic value of emptiness. Basically it's four people in rooms talking: two sisters, a philandering husband and an enigmatic stranger who gets his kicks videotaping women's sexual confessions. What is left unsaid carries as much weight as what is said. The operative moment is the awkward silence. It's the erotic distance between Ann and Graham (James Spader) as he explains that he is impotent except when alone. Or the innuendo between Ann and her sister, Cynthia (Laura San Giacomo) after Cynthia confesses that she took off her clothes while being videotaped by Graham:

Ann: Did he touch you?
Cynthia: No.
Ann: Did you touch him?
Cynthia: No.
Ann: Did anybody touch anybody?
Cynthia: Well . . . yes.

Like Atom Egoyan's *Family Viewing*, which came three years earlier, *sex, lies, and videotape* concerns a voyeur and his home-video archive. Again, videotape is cut in and out of the film as if its ephemeral grain is the substance of alienation, a disembodied flicker of human existence. For Egoyan—in both *Family Viewing* and later *Speaking Parts*—videotape is layered to create an entire architecture of memory and loss. In *sex, lies*, it serves more as a narrative device. But what is so striking about *sex, lies* is its grasp of time, its luxurious expansion of the moment. Soderbergh magnifies intimacy with a theatrical sense of actors relating in real time. Egoyan does a similar thing in his early films, but his performances are so self-consciously attenuated that they beg disbelief. Soderbergh simply creates space around his actors—the one thing a Hollywood budget can never seem to afford—and they come up with exceptionally naturalistic performances.

Although we tend to think of independent cinema in terms of transgressive themes and stylistic innovation, what really distinguished the new American directors is that they allowed actors room to act. Take *Drugstore Cowboy*, another hit from the 1989 festival. It's an unusually authentic drug movie, an inside story based on the true-life experiences of a convict who robbed pharmacies. And William Burroughs lends it his Beat blessing with a sepulchral cameo as a defrocked junkie priest. But what stands out in *Drugstore Cowboy*, amid Gus Van Sant's dreamy scenes of getting high and hallucinating, is the acting. Just as David Cronenberg found an untapped vein of creepy talent in Jeremy Irons, Van Sant took a Hollywood pretty boy, Matt Dillon, and sent him out to explore the frontiers of love, paranoia and addiction. Drugs play tricks with time, and as the drama tries to simulate pharmaceutical warps of perception, it seems almost elastic

SCREAMIN' JAY HAWKINS, 1989

PHOTO: DAVID MALTBY

both the zen rhythms of Jarmusch and the truth-or-dare dialogue o derbergh, there is an arresting intimacy, a real-time zone of consciousness ere it seems that anything, or nothing, might happen

to the actor's touch.

When it comes to toying with real time, Jim Jarmusch led the way in his first three films, which all played the festival: *Stranger Than Paradise* (1984), *Down By Law* (1986) and *Mystery Train* (1989). All I remember from first seeing *Stranger Than Paradise* is how it was so seductively fresh and odd. Looking at it again, a decade later, I'm struck by its warmth, by the sweetness of these two gentle louts in fedoras tracking down the cute Hungarian cousin in Cleveland and having no idea what to do with her. From the screen's P.O.V., we watch them watch a kung fu movie in a deserted theatre. They study the blankness of a frozen Lake Erie as if it were a scenic view. And once you get beyond the film's deadpan style—the cool music, the wintry black-and-white photography, the offbeat blackouts—you realize that it is so well acted you haven't even noticed.

In both the zen rhythms of Jarmusch and the truth-or-dare dialogue of Soderbergh, there is an arresting intimacy, a real-time zone of consciousness where it seems that anything, or nothing, might happen. Hal Hartley pushed for the same effect, to the point that his characters were unpredictable from one moment to the next, and Jarmusch was a major influence. "I was inspired by the simplicity of Jim's first couple of films," says Hartley, who premiered his feature debut, *The Unbelievable Truth*, in Toronto in 1989. "They really, really affected me. I admired Jim's calmness and his resolution to not rush things. He has such an interest in people, and that people exist in time. There's a patience, a restraining of what he feels he wants to say, which is very different from my work. There's no subtlety in *The Unbelievable Truth*. There's a lot of subtlety in Jim's work. If anything, I look back on everything before *Flirt* [Hartley, 1993] as hyperventilating—as if I'm so desperate I won't have an opportunity to get something across that I have the

PHOTO: JOHN MEDLAND

LEFT, STEPHEN FREARS AND JOHN CUSACK AT THE PRESS CONFERENCE FOR THE GRIFTERS, 1990

actors submit their instincts and feelings to almost a pre-determined vocabulary. I think that's the basis of all those dialogue scenes in the earlier films where people are talking at cross purposes, but acting as though they're having a conversation with each other. They're actually talking in tangents. Dialogue only interested me as action. I wrote the dialogue as a diagram for physical action."

Hartley's tangential dialogue pushes plot in apparently random directions with quick, water-bug thrusts. It's a deliberately stilted rhythm. And his concept of narrative as dialectical discourse owes much to Godard. When he was making *The Unbelievable Truth*, Hartley immersed himself in a Godard retrospective at Film Forum in New York. "I was also influenced by the newer stuff," he says. "When *Hail Mary* came out, I could not pretend to understand it, but I knew to the depths of my body that this was important, and that if there was a way forward for me to move I would have to start a relationship with this work."

Via festival culture, watching films became an integral part of making them. Every director was, on some level, a critic. What made this new generation of directors unique is that they were film-literate not just about the European New Wave, but about the filmmakers influenced by it. Soderbergh's diary of making *sex, lies, and videotape* is filled with references to movies he saw while he was editing it, from *Wings of Desire* to *Dead Ringers*. And in both *sex, lies* and Hartley's *Unbelievable Truth*, the protagonist could be a stand-in for the filmmaker-as-watcher—an outsider confounding mainstream America with blunt observation. Both films revolve around a mysterious man in black who shows up in his hometown after a long absence and poses a sexual threat. The parallels are coincidental—the two directors made their films concurrently. But when Hartley was struggling to find a distributor, he would use Soderbergh's prize-winning movie as ammunition. "The person who gave me the money for *The Unbelievable Truth* was a little concerned that nobody was biting," he recalls. "I remember using *sex, lies, and videotape* as an example—'Well, here's a little film, and it's made here in America.'"

Hal Hartley was one of the festival's genuine discoveries. Kay Armatage picked *The*

Unbelievable Truth from the slush pile of unsolicited films sent to her on video. She spends every summer sifting through stacks of tapes. "Many of them are absolutely without merit," she says. "You watch them and you think, 'Why was this film made and why was it sent?' And you see so many films that it's hard to believe it when you finally see something good. You think you're just getting dizzy." Armatage held off programming *The Unbelievable Truth* until the last minute. Then just before the programme book went to press, she decided, "This is the film that's stayed with me—I'm going to show this bloody film."

Hartley, who had trotted *The Unbelievable Truth* around to all the distributors without a single offer, was thrilled to be accepted, even though he knew nothing about the festival. "I was just happy that it was going to be seen anywhere," he says. By the time he arrived in Toronto, press screenings had already generated a buzz. "When I checked in at the guest office, everyone was talking about my film. And the audience responded really well. We made a U.S. sale right away to Miramax, which boosted the interest in it around the world. My head was spinning."

Miramax paid $200,000 to distribute *The Unbelievable Truth*, which cost $65,000 to shoot. Hartley's idiosyncratic work is a perfect example of the kind of niche cinema that the festival could discover—and that a new breed of independent distributor was eager to market. The festival went on to show all Hartley's features, including *Trust*, *Simple Men*, *Amateur*, *Flirt*—and *Henry Fool* (1997), which premiered in Toronto before playing in competition in Cannes. "Hal's films are unusual, they have integrity, and they're original," says Armatage. "They're not to everybody's taste and they don't have huge commercial potential. He's not like Quentin Tarantino. He has his own thing, his own voice and his own shtick."

Of all the new American directors, there was no more studious, and hyperbolic, fan of movies than Tarantino, the video-store clerk who would be king. Hartley remembers first meeting him in an elevator at the 1992 festival. Tarantino was presenting his feature debut, *Reservoir Dogs*, and Hartley was there with *Simple Men*. "Quentin told me he had watched *Trust*, like, one hundred thousand times in order to make *Reservoir Dogs*," says

TRUST

PHOTO: DAVID MCLEOD

MIRA SORVINO AND QUENTIN TARANTINO, 1995

f the new American cinema was all talk, Quentin Tarantino was t director who turned talk into a semi-automatic weapon

Hartley. "And he came to see *Simple Men* more than once. I remember him sitting there in the third row, and when I was doing my Q&A, he had lots of questions. He was asking really practical things, like how I'd have the actors move. He had that enthusiasm for filmmaking—watching everything more than once, and really scrutinizing how it's done. At one point, I introduced him to the audience: 'Ladies and gentlemen, Quentin Tarantino.'"

Mr. White: I need you to be cool. Are you cool?
Mr. Pink: I'm cool.
Mr. White: Are you cool?
Mr. Pink: Yes, I'm fucking cool.

In 1992, no movie was cooler, or nastier, than *Reservoir Dogs*. Who can forget Steve Buscemi as the querulous Mr. Pink, weaseling through his rationalizations of why he doesn't tip waitresses? Or Tim Roth as Mr. Orange, the undercover cop bleeding to death in real time on a warehouse floor after the botched diamond heist. Or Michael Madsen as Mr. Blonde, dancing to "Stuck in the Middle with You" with a razor in his hand as he prepares to slice off an ear—"I don't give a good fuck what you know, I'm going to torture you anyway." If the new American cinema was all talk, Quentin Tarantino was the director who turned talk into a semi-automatic weapon. Gangsters had never talked so much, or with as much menace, as they did in *Reservoir Dogs*. The movie, which unfolds as a vicious game of Truth or Consequences, became notorious for raising the threshold of cruelty onscreen. And Tarantino's dialogue, foreplay to physical violence, plays as a kind of savage bebop, syncopated with the word "fuck."

When I met Tarantino at the festival, I asked him how he distinguished his violence from the violence in Hollywood movies. "Mine's tougher," he said without hesitation. "It goes further. I'm not worried about alienating the audience. My characters do what they do and they say what they say. With a lot of the bigger action films, as wild as they are, it's safe carnage, cartoon-fun violence. I try to make it disturbing." The intimate scale of a low-budget film like *Reservoir Dogs* brought with it an inherent theatricality. "It was very much like a play," Michael Madsen told me. "Having a time constraint, and only so much money to spend, creates a tension, and in a film like *Dogs* tension was essential." As Tarantino explained, "The whole thing was to keep you up close enough so there really wasn't a third wall, so you were trapped in that room with them, which is what would happen in theatre. The movie's set in real time. The story takes an hour to happen. It takes longer than an hour to see the movie, because the story keeps going back in on itself. But when you're in the warehouse, every second for them is a second for you; every minute for them is a minute for you. Cinema doesn't intrude and move things along or shave off time. You're there with them. I wanted you to feel claustrophobic. I wanted you to feel their paranoia."

Talking to Tarantino at the festival was like meeting one of his films in the flesh. He chewed off his words like a starving man tearing his way through a steak. He was a human amphetamine, surfing fatigue with the exhilaration of someone who had stayed up half the night consuming films and parties and people. He moved through the festival with a posse, with Madsen, Buscemi, Harvey Keitel, Tim Roth—and Robert Rodriguez, the *El Mariachi* wunderkind whom he had just met in Toronto. Tarantino plunged into the life of the festival like no filmmaker before or since. And it was there he met his idol John Woo, the Hong Kong director of *The Killer*, which had left a clear imprint on *Reservoir Dogs*. Woo was in Toronto with his new thriller, *Hard-Boiled*, and Tarantino was so blown away by it he immediately promised to write a script for Woo within a month. (The project never came to fruition.)

Three years later, Tarantino came back to the festival to premiere the misbegotten *Four Rooms*. At a screening of Wong Kar-wai's *Fallen Angels*, he hooked up with Mira Sorvino, who was in town for the premiere of *Mighty Aphrodite*. Later that night, at Bistro 990, Tarantino and Sorvino joined a dinner hosted by Harvey Weinstein for directors Wayne Wang and Paul Auster, who had just premiered *Blue in the Face*. "Mira was trying to pick up Quentin," Wang recalls. "They weren't really an item yet. Mira was making her move and Quentin was playing hard to get. All through dinner that was going on." But

Greg Gatenby, director of the Harbourfront International Authors Festival, was seated across from Sorvino as Auster's guest, and he remembers it the other way around. "Quentin was making moon eyes at her, trying to get her interested," says Gatenby, "and she was playing Mistress Domina, paying no attention at all. She was stuck with me, which was driving her nuts. Mira Sorvino was bored by me from the moment she sat down. Her eyes just glazed over when she realized that I'm not in the film business. She left early. Quentin and I ended up talking all night. Harvey hardly spoke. He just kept feeding us tremendous white wine until I was so smashed at four o'clock in the morning I could barely stand up."

Gatenby was no stranger to festival protocol. He was Helga Stephenson's boyfriend for two years, from 1986 to 1988. But even he was shocked by how assiduously Tarantino was protected by his handlers. "A television producer I knew came up and whispered in my ear, 'I'll do anything if you could introduce me to Quentin Tarantino.' Within seconds, a young woman came over and put her hands firmly on the shoulder of the person squatting beside me and said, 'I'll have to ask you to move along because Mr. Gatenby is in conversation with Mr. Tarantino.' It was like military intelligence. The security was so efficient they knew I was okay, my date was okay, but this woman wasn't—*and* they knew how to pronounce my name."

By then, Tarantino was a player. But in his debut year, when he showed up with *Reservoir Dogs*, he behaved like a fan. The director became an ardent devotee of Midnight Madness, the festival's programme of genre films. "He met this really cute girl who told him to meet her at *Tokyo Decadence*, the Sunday-night show," recalls Noah Cowan, the programme's coordinator at the time. "He brought Steve Buscemi and they were blown away. They just kept coming back night after night." When Tarantino received the festival's first annual FIPRESCI award for best first feature—voted by a jury of the International Federation of Film Critics—he said that he would have given the prize to *Man Bites Dog*, a Belgian movie in Midnight Madness that received the Metro Media Award from the festival's accredited press: *Man Bites Dog* is a blood-soaked black comedy about a documentary crew that becomes enamoured of a serial killer.

Noah Cowan, who programmed Midnight Madness for a decade, traces his own taste for the horror genre back to childhood memories of his mother, actress Nuala Fitzgerald, who appeared in David Cronenberg's *The Brood*: "She came home from work one day and said she'd spent the afternoon being bludgeoned to death by midgets in green snowsuits." Midnight Madness was inaugurated in 1988 to show movies that were too extreme, or simply too trashy, for "normal" festival audiences. Movies about cannibals, vampires, alien monsters and heavy-metal bands. "Nobody else wanted to show any of this stuff," says Cowan. "By 1988, the midnight movie had died. The concept was confined to *The Rocky Horror Picture Show*. But the risk paid off, because after three years almost every other festival in North America started midnight movies. One of the

things about the Toronto festival that sets it apart is that there's always been a sense of genre challenge, that cinema comes in many flavours, and the festival's duty has always been to show them all. The idea behind Midnight Madness was to seek quality in genre cinema in the same dogged way the rest of the festival does in art cinema."

The precursor to Midnight Madness can be found in the '78 festival, for which Toronto film theorist Robin Wood and three other critics put together The American Nightmare, a marathon of six horror movies a day at the Bloor Cinema. A separate twenty-five-dollar pass bought the entire series plus a book of essays by the programmers. In Wood's view, there was a lot more at stake than cheap thrills. "The horror film," he said, "provides the possibility for the radical critique of our civilization. The central concept within the genre is of the monster as the dramatization of all our cultural represses in order to construct its idea of the moral."

The first Midnight Madness menu in 1988 ranged from Penelope Spheeris's campy rock documentary, *The Decline of Western Civilization Part II: The Metal Years*, to Tony Randel's psycho splatter movie, *Hellbound: Hellraiser II*. In 1992, with titles such as *Braindead,*

Romper Stomper, *Tokyo Decadence*, *Candyman* and *Swordsman II*, "the programme hit an incredible peak," says Cowan. "Virtually every film in that programme has had an impact on critical thought about transgressive filmmaking."

TOKYO DECADENCE

The whole idea of using elevated terms like "transgressive" and "genre film" to describe a movie about a zombie cannibal mom with monkey venom in her veins seems perverse in itself. But midnight movies have acquired the cachet of art. Brian De Palma, a festival regular, can often be found at Midnight Madness. It is John Sayles's favourite programme. And *Time*'s Richard Corliss says he tries to attend at least two midnight movies each festival to renew his "faith in cinema." At a festival that gains respectability with each passing year, Midnight Madness provides a bohemian heartbeat. It keeps the festival's ear to the street, with a higher ratio of single-ticket admissions than any other programme. And there is a party atmosphere to the screenings. "People are there to have a good time or to be really spooked out," says Cowan, "and it sets down a daunting challenge to you as a programmer."

It is only fitting that the current Midnight Madness programmer, Colin Geddes, who succeeded Cowan in 1998, started out as a fan. Like Tarantino, he apprenticed in a video store, and as an early devotee of Midnight Madness, he met Tarantino in a festival lineup. I met Geddes in the lineup for *Summer of Sam* in Cannes. And as I listened to him talk about extreme cinema, it was like hearing someone describe hang-gliding or rock climbing. You immediately want to go out and try it yourself. Geddes was especially keen on director Dario Argento, the cult legend of Italian horror, who has been a frequent visitor to Midnight Madness since bringing *Opera* to the festival in 1989. Many of his films feature a black-gloved killer. In *Opera*, which was recently enshrined by Argento's Profondo Rosso museum in Rome, the killer ties up a diva and forces her to watch him brutally murder her lover—literally forces her by putting pins under her eyes. Argento came up with the idea after seeing viewers cover their eyes at his movies. But in Ontario, censors often did the job for them by cutting his most gruesome scenes

ntroducing a film, Argento said, "Last night I had a dream. I saw t names of the board of censors, and each one died a horrible death at t hands of this black-gloved killer"

PHOTO: FITZROY BARRETT

before allowing his films to be released commercially. "One night at the Bloor," recalls Geddes, "Argento was introducing a film and said, 'Last night I had a dream. I saw these black-gloved hands, and I saw the names of the board of censors, and each one died a horrible death at the hands of this black-gloved killer. Was that a nightmare . . . or just a dream?'"

A clear line can be traced from film noir, through the exploitation movies of the seventies, to the genre fetishes of the nineties. And as Tarantino ushered in America's new cinema of cruelty, he was not alone. At the same festival, James Foley presented his serrated adaptation of David Mamet's *Glengarry Glen Ross*, a drama of cutthroat competition among real-estate agents who pitch property over the phone. Al Pacino plays the ace, Jack Lemmon the Willy Loman loser whose life is on the line with every call. In *Glengarry Glen Ross*, the bloodshed is less literal than in *Reservoir Dogs*, but it is another clubhouse tale of dishonour among thieves, a game of chicken played with zip-gun profanity, eviscerating dialogue and an arcane code of ethics—*Real Estate Dogs*.

Also in 1992, Robert Rodriguez offered comic relief with his Tex-Mex shoot-'em-up, *El Mariachi*, one of the first micro-budget novelties to be acquired by a major studio. And Abel Ferrara weighed in with *Bad Lieutenant*, an excoriating drama in which Harvey Keitel improvises a sexual shock scene that made Dennis Hopper's gas-mask routine in *Blue Velvet* look like a cheap carnival trick: as a married cop who is addicted to gambling, booze and rock cocaine, but who is desperately trying to do the right thing, Keitel's character lets off a little steam by getting two young girls to watch him masturbate as he blasts them with obscene invective. Apparently he improvised it in one take.

It's enough to make you want to get out of town. And for that, Robert Redford offered the '92 festival an elegiac excursion into thirties Montana with *A River Runs Through It*. Based on the spare, stoic novella by Norman Maclean, it's the story of two estranged brothers who find communion in the silent art of fly fishing. Redford created the Sundance Institute, where Tarantino developed the script for *Reservoir Dogs*, but it would be hard to find two men exploring male ritual from more opposite ends of the culture. Tarantino, who would go on to make *Pulp Fiction*, was a young renegade on a collision course with Hollywood without even knowing it; Redford was a Hollywood icon in retreat, looking for a patch of still water removed from the fray. *A River Runs Through It* was his psalm to Montana, to fly fishing, and to the silence that runs deep within rural families from the American West.

FAR LEFT, DARIO ARGENTO, 1990

It is always interesting, a little exciting, to meet movie stars of the old school. I met Redford that year at the festival and was not disappointed. He was iconic in a way that the current generation of stars will never be. It wasn't just that he looked the part—although he did, in cowboy boots and blue denim, with wheat-gold hair and cerulean eyes that had the uncomplicated clarity of a Montana sky. What was striking about him was the directness of his presence, the way his gaze connected and his words made sense. He seemed luxuriously ordinary. We talked about the lost value of silence, in families and film. In both his family and the one in *A River Runs Through It*, he said, "silence was used as a weapon and a strength. Words did not play a big part unless they were taught through school, or through stories being told. Now, of course, words are everywhere. They're flying like shrapnel around us."

"But when words do break the silence in your movie, they have power," I said. "The moment of tragedy is not even shown. It's described in a sentence. Just like in the book."

"That suited me just fine," he said. "I'm quite happy to see film used in a different way, and not slam people over the head. We've got enough of that. Not that it's bad. It's just that we've got enough of it. Technology is so advanced now that we can slam people in the face pretty well. But we don't have a lot of the other use of film, the use of silence as a power, and the use of nature to speak its own language."

While Redford, through Sundance, became the gold patron of American independent cinema, John Sayles is often considered its godfather. He, too, is known for straightforward storytelling, a kind of blue-collar narrative integrity. But his example has inspired some unlikely admirers, such as Todd Solondz, director of *Welcome to the Dollhouse* and *Happiness*. "There wasn't a role model until John Sayles came along with *Secaucus Seven*," Solondz told me. "Here was someone making an intelligently crafted story that could have been made by Hollywood—and was in fact made by Hollywood three or four years later [as *The Big Chill*]. After him, came Susan Seidelman and Jim Jarmusch and Spike Lee. A movement was created, and with the success of the Soderbergh movie it became very attractive to distributors. I look at John Sayles as someone who made a career out of doing his own stories, doing it his way, and they weren't so-called art movies. They were very successful. I think he is very much the shaper in spearheading this whole movement. Esthetically he was very conventional, and yet what was very unconventional was his method."

At the '92 festival, as Redford romanced fly fishing, Sayles premiered *Passion Fish*, another lovely film set in a rural backwater. It tells the story of a New York soap-opera writer (played by Mary McDonnell) who returns to her childhood home in the Louisiana bayou after a car accident leaves her paralyzed from the waist down. It is a seductive drama, plainly told, that recedes from melodrama to subtle magic.

THE BAD LIEUTENANT

Sayles had been to the festival before, with *Return of the Secaucus Seven*, *The Brother from Another Planet* and *Matewan*. "It's one of the few festivals where I get to see movies," he told me one sunny afternoon in Cannes, as we enjoyed a strangely unhurried interview on a hotel terrace before his premiere of *Limbo* in 1999. "I'll see whatever I think is not likely to open in the States. I usually end up going to the midnight ones. I

ROBERT REDFORD AND BRAD PITT, 1992

PHOTO: SAM BARNES

What was striking about Redford was the way his gaze connected and the words made sense. He seemed luxuriously ordinary

saw the *Swordsman* movies there. The nice thing about Toronto is that there isn't the thing that there is in Sundance where everyone is desperate to get discovered. Sundance has turned into a Hollywood festival despite itself. I'm sure that's not what Redford had in mind when he started it. Toronto, and to a certain extent Seattle, are both festivals where people come to like the movie. You get a lot more civilians."

With *Passion Fish*, Sayles used the festival not just to premiere the film but to sell it. "We hadn't shown the movie to anybody," he said. "Rather than get into the thing where each of the independent distributors watches it in a separate screening, or watches it on video while taking phone calls, we said, 'Look, we're going to show it here. If you're interested in this movie, see it here.' We showed it in Toronto. Miramax saw it. We made a deal, and they said, 'We want this out right away because we think the actresses could be up for Academy Awards, and we want to do a campaign.' Within two months we were on the screen."

But at the same Toronto festival where it acquired *Passion Fish*, Miramax also launched *The Crying Game*. And the phenomenal success of that movie would propel the company into another league. Just five years after taking a gamble on *I've Heard the Mermaids Singing*, Harvey and Bob had carved out a small empire. While maintaining autonomy, they would sell Miramax to Disney. Other studios would follow suit, buying up boutique distributors. And the reckless spirit of independent film, like that of the festival itself, would begin to be eclipsed by the shadow of corporate culture.

The Buying Game

THE GUESTS WERE SO INTENT ON TALKING MOVIES AN DEVOURING FOOD—OYSTERS, ROAST PHEASANT, RACK OF LAM *salmon, pike, pâté, crepes and cakes—that at first hardly anyone n ticed there was a sword fight going on. High overhead, on a balco under a Gothic arch in the University of Toronto's Great Hall, two m in medieval dress were putting on an energetic display of swashbuc ling while a damsel screamed in mock distress. They lunged. Th wrestled. They performed acrobatic flips. Briefly, people looked up watch, as if another movie was vying for their attention, then we back to the feast, and to the endless business of discussing film*

The occasion was a party following the festival's North American premiere of *Cyrano de Bergerac*, Jean-Paul Rappeneau's opulent rendering of the Edmond Rostand classic, starring Gérard Depardieu. Shot in a burnished candle-chrome, with poetic subtitles by Anthony Burgess, this was a foreign film with the patina of an Old Master. And at the restored Elgin theatre, on a screen surrounded by rococo gilt and red velvet, it was framed like a canvas at the Louvre. "It was a magnificent theatre," Rappeneau recalled as we sat in his ornate Paris apartment, which itself resembles a small museum, with high ceilings, antique furniture and landscape paintings that take up entire walls. "The sound was extraordinary. It was the best audio reproduction of the film I'd ever heard, even better than in Cannes." Although *Cyrano* received two prizes in Cannes, Rappeneau expressed distaste for the French festival. "Filmmakers are continually being martyred—there's an atmosphere of cannibalism. In Toronto, people don't come to destroy, but to see films. And when my film was so warmly received there, that's where I first understood it meant something for the North American audience."

That's also where Rappeneau met the distributors from Orion Classics who had bought the North American rights and had big plans for it. "They had this idea in their heads that *Cyrano* would get the Oscar for best foreign film," he says. "Myself, I hadn't even thought about it." As it turned out, although the film didn't win the Oscar, it did get five nominations, including a Best Actor consideration for Depardieu's career-capping performance. And the wave of North American acclaim for *Cyrano* began with the Toronto gala—and the fact that the festival audience voted it most popular film.

The festival's greatest asset, aside from its programming, is its audience. When you talk to the directors, producers, distributors and sales agents who descend on Toronto each September from around the world, they all rave about the audience—how it is devoted, astute and unnaturally enthusiastic. New York producer Ben Barenholtz, who gave the festival its very first film, *Cousin, cousine*, in 1976, and subsequent offerings such as *Blood Simple*, says, "Audiences in Cannes go to a film to dislike it—you have to make them like it. In Toronto it's just the opposite. I've seen some very bad films get polite applause." Jim Jarmusch premieres his films in Cannes then brings them to Toronto. But there is no question which he prefers. "Cannes is such a zoo," he told me at a party for *Ghost Dog: The Way of the Samurai* in Toronto. "Here it's about films. I go to Cannes only because my films are financed in Europe and the investors want me to. It's like showing your work to two thousand hairdressers from the Riviera. It's not as honest a reaction as you get here. This is so much more pleasant and real."

The Toronto audience is the product of a well-cultivated love affair between the festival and the city. When Helga Stephenson took over the festival in 1987, she says she had two goals. First, she wanted to "internationalize it big time." Second, she wanted the city to fall unconditionally in love with it. "Toronto *liked* the film festival," she says, "but I wanted Toronto to take this film festival to its bosom and *love* it. I wanted it to become like motherhood. Unassailable. So that even if you didn't want to see the latest Russian epic, you thought it was a good thing for the city." Stephenson's two goals neatly coincided. Toronto's poly-ethnic fabric was tailor-made for an international festival. And as she and Piers Handling broadened the event's global reach, she assumed the role of festival queen. But it didn't happen overnight. "It took a couple of years," she says. "One day David Overbey said, 'Helga, get your hair cut and start looking like a festival director.' He'd got tired of my leather skirt. My mother had come from the shmatte trade and I'd been a model. So I knew how to do this. And I became fanatical about supporting Canadian designers."

Helga also brought an avid entrepreneurial style to the job. She nurtured an informal market by subsidizing foreign sales agents (who sell distribution rights) to come to the festival. Carol Myer, from the Sales Company in Britain, was one of them. "I wasn't very keen to go," she recalls. "I thought I needed another market like a hole in the head. And I always loved going to Venice, so I wasn't very keen to jump on a plane right after and go to Toronto." But Toronto turned out to be an important stop for Myer, whose roster of festival hits include *The Crying Game*, *Orlando*, *Priest*, *The Snapper* and *Antonia's Line*. "For me, Helga really opened up the North American presence," she adds. "Helga brought in a lot more foreign buyers, people who now would never miss the Toronto festival. It became absolutely essential for people trying to sell into North America. For years, the only access to North America was the very restricted New York Film Festival, and Sundance, which was primarily for American independents. So if you were sitting there with a really good French or Italian movie, the one place you could take it where you were assured there would be buyers was Toronto."

Since 1987, Piers Handling had made a concerted effort to woo French cinema, which meant going toe-to-toe with the rival Montreal festival, a more obvious North American beachhead. "France has the second most important national cinema in the world," says Handling, "and we became very focussed on bringing it on board. But it hasn't been easy. The French are not prepared to get down and dirty fighting for North American publicity. We said you've got to fight fire with fire—you've got to bring out the stars." And they did. The Depardieus and Deneuves made their way to Toronto and the festival established itself as a North American gateway for directors such as Rappeneau, Patrice Leconte, Bertrand Blier and Oliver Assayas. Veteran French distributor Alain Vannier remembers bringing *Europa Europa* to the festival in 1990. Agnieszka Holland's film, the story of a Jewish boy who masquerades as an Aryan to escape the Holocaust, had already been released in Europe. "It hadn't had the success we'd expected," says Vannier, "but the Toronto screening was exceptional. Afterwards, Michael Barker from Orion Classics was so moved, he came up to Agnieszka Holland and embraced her. I told him, 'It's not enough to embrace the director, you have to buy the film.'" Barker bought *Europa Europa*. And the film, which its French distributor had given up for dead, was sold around the world, then got a second wind in Europe with a re-release. It went on to receive an Oscar nomination and a string of American critics' awards.

PASSION FISH

The explosion of independent film in the late eighties brought with it a new breed of entrepreneur. By the end of the decade, there were myriad small distribution companies

JIM JARMUSCH, 1997

PHOTO: TYRONE KERR

"Cannes is such a zoo. I go to Cannes only because my films are financed in Europe and the investors want me to. It's like showing your work to two thousand hairdressers from the Riviera. This is so much more pleasant and real"

created by a sixties generation of film enthusiasts. Among them was Tom Bernard, who together with Michael Barker formed UA Classics, Orion Classics and Sony Classics. When I met Bernard at his cramped office in Sony's modernist cathedral in Manhattan, he pulled out a thick wad of snapshots containing almost two decades of memories. For him, the festival has never been just business. It's the story of his generation. "Toronto has become much more corporate now," he says, reminiscing about the days when you could fit everyone who mattered into the hospitality suite. "Like all good things, in the early years there was more camaraderie. The buyers and the sellers and the talent all mingled. People worked the festival till four in the morning every night. It was a great mix for ideas and cinema. It's what Sundance always tried to be and never succeeded—this primordial mixing ground." Bernard discovered art films when he was playing football for the University of Maryland. One night he stumbled upon a campus programme of movies selected from the titles shown on the psychedelic Ken Kesey bus that Tom Wolfe immortalized in his book *The Electric Kool-Aid Acid Test*. Soon Bernard was borrowing projectors and screening Kenneth Anger films in a student union room. As he graduated into the distribution business, "it was a great thing to be involved with," he says. "The movies had an impact on people. They changed their lives, and it was your job to get them out there."

JEFF DOWD AND B.J. MCQUEEN

PHOTO: DOUG MACLELLAN

Toronto has become more corporate now. Like all good things, in t early years there was more camaraderie. The buyers and the sellers a the talent all mingled. People worked the festival till four in the morn every night. It was a great mix of ideas and cinema

---

The hard currency of a film festival is buzz. And the most notorious buzz merchant to haunt the Toronto festival is Jeff Dowd, the producer's rep known as The Dude. The films that he has helped put on the map include *The Black Stallion*, *Blood Simple*, *Chariots of Fire*, *Hoosiers* and *The Blair Witch Project*. He also helped Robert Redford create the Sundance Institute. But his greatest claim to fame is that he was the model for the stoner character of The Dude played by Jeff Bridges in the Coen brothers' *The Big Lebowski*. "That's Joel and Ethan deciding what I would have been like if I'd been frozen in time," says Dowd, who has survived into the new millennium by being somewhat more abstemious than the character he inspired.

The Dude first gained notoriety at nineteen, as a member of the Seattle Seven, a group of activists who were charged with conspiracy to destroy federal property after an anti-war demonstration in 1968. The defendants, who drew support from Donald Sutherland and Jane Fonda, eventually saw their charges dropped in a mistrial. Although Dowd did not serve time, he was convicted of contempt of court. On the day of his sentencing, he smuggled into the courtroom a huge Nazi flag—made the night before by a local theatre designer—and unfurled it across the judge's desk declaring, "You're acting like a good German."

Dowd, who sees the Toronto festival as "the best of the sixties hippie ethic mixed with the best of entrepreneurial capitalism," is a walking embodiment of both. A gregarious bear of a man with curly hair, moustache, and his shirt half untucked beneath his sports jacket, he sweats his way through the festival each year hoisting a briefcase spilling with publicity material. Roger Ebert, who devoted two generous columns to him during the '99 festival, said Dowd passes on tips "like a racetrack tout." That year he was pitching *Goat on Fire and Smiling Fish*, a $40,000 first feature by a charming young NYU graduate named Kevin Jordan, who paid off the production's suppliers with lobsters from his family's Brooklyn lobster farm. In Toronto, Dowd organized a beer-and-lobster bash to promote the movie, which went on to win the new Film Discovery Award voted by the media for best first feature.

No one works the angles like Dowd. He finds his way to all the parties, and tracks them by obtaining a copy of Piers Handling's daily schedule, which he photocopies for his cronies. Over the years, Dowd has accumulated his own personal folklore of festival stories. In 1985, when he was representing Donna Deitch's lesbian romance, *Desert Hearts*, he was dating its Toronto star, Helen Shaver, and kept being photographed with her on his arm, which irritated the hell out of Deitch, who felt she was getting left out of the picture. One night during a high-profile directors' dinner at Bemelman's, Dowd recalls, "Donna just exploded—'What are you doing with my film, now it's the Helen Shaver film, what about me?' I said 'Donna, that's the *angle* in Toronto.' And we just went at it. It was like *Who's Afraid of Virginia Woolf?*" The directors sitting around the table included Mike Newell, Fred Schepisi and Volker Schlondorff. "Half of them were writers," says Dowd, "and it got so wild some of them started taking notes."

Then there was the time The Dude flew back to the States with Jack Lemmon after premiering *Life in the Theatre*, in 1993, and had the nerve to ask Lemmon to smuggle some Cuban cigars for him in his luggage. "I called ahead to avoid the hassle at customs, and we got the whole VIP treatment," says Dowd. "They just walked us through. Jack was the mule. He's a great actor, certainly good enough to fool the guys at customs."

One of Dowd's most memorable stunts occurred after a long night of drinking near the end of the '87 festival. He spent an evening in the bar at the Windsor Arms with Faye Dunaway, Brian Dennehy—and a woman he'd never met before. "I drink more in Toronto in ten days than in any season anywhere else," says Dowd. "And Brian can really drink. So I meet this woman, and we end up making out in the curtains of the Windsor Arms. We walk back to my hotel, up to the room, and we're kind of swinging from the rafters. Then she tells me she has a better room." So, at 4:30 a.m. she leads Dowd up to a lavish suite, which looks untouched, with no sign of luggage.

"What's the deal?" he asks.
"I work for the hotel," she says.

As it turns out, Dowd has a problem with his hotel bill. Each night after the hospitality suite closed, he would invite the hangers-on back to his room, and by the end of the festival he had racked up a $1,800 room-service and mini-bar tab. The festival was paying for the room but despite Dowd's protests, Helga refused to pay the incidentals. Now, suddenly finding himself in the arms of a hotel employee, Dowd explains his problem. "Come with me," she says, escorting him down to the office. "Then she goes into the computer and it's just like that scene in *War Games*—$1,800 becomes zero."

While Dowd's maverick style hasn't changed a lot over the years, the industry has. And Stephen Woolley, the British producer behind such Neil Jordan films as *The Crying Game*, has followed it from the fringe to the mainstream. He first hooked up with Jordan when he distributed the director's first feature *Angel*, which showed at the festival in 1982. It had been made for television by Britain's Channel Four. "They had no plans to release it theatrically," says Woolley, "and I spearheaded this move to release their television films in cinemas, which led to Channel Four doing that." In fact, Britain's TV industry, unlike Canada's, would nurture a whole generation of film directors, from Ken Loach to Mike Leigh.

"Our company was ostensibly a sex, drugs and rock-'n'-roll thing," says Woolley, remembering his early days with Palace Productions in London. "We would work passionately, twenty-four hours a day, but it would be fun. The Toronto festival was kind of like that." Sitting in his London office, with shoulder-length hair and black leather coat, Woolley still doesn't look remotely corporate, but he works at arm's length with a corporate world, producing mainstream pictures like *Michael Collins* and *The End of the Affair* with money from major studios. "Toronto is a terrific barometer," adds Woolley, who first showed up with *The Company of Wolves*, Jordan's second feature, in 1984. "You get audiences that really like movies. New York is very arid. Sundance I don't see as a festival. It's a marketplace, and it's mostly American independents. Sundance gets huge press, but it's about agents and studios discovering talent." Unlike Sundance, Telluride, New York or Cannes, Toronto offers a civilian audience. "But they go in pretty much biased toward the film. You have to be aware of that—and if they don't like it you're in trouble."

Not a single N
as a universa
this idea of n

That's what happened when Miramax's Weinstein brothers took their production of *The Big Man*, by David Leland, to the 1990 festival. "Bob and Harvey used, and still use, Toronto as a sneak preview environment," explains Woolley. "*The Big Man* got lukewarm reviews—two stars. And Miramax can't live with that. So after Toronto, it was recut, against my will. The major thing they cut was the affair that Joanne Whalley's character was having with a young doctor. Bizarrely, the unknown actor playing the young doctor was Hugh Grant. So Miramax cut Hugh Grant out of the movie because of the response from Toronto. Of course, if they were seeing it now, they would insist we shoot another two weeks with Hugh Grant."

Woolley dealt with Miramax again over *The Crying Game*, the product of an exceptionally difficult shoot. "It was a nightmare," he says. "Everything that potentially could go wrong was going to go wrong with this film. And Neil did not stop complaining throughout the whole thing. It was cold. We had no money. I was using my credit card to finance it. We brought it through kicking and screaming without any American funds. And after our three-picture deal—*The Big Man* flop, *The Miracle* flop, *The Pope Must Die* flop—Miramax was washing their hands of us [Palace Productions] like a really bad smell."

GLENGARRY GLEN ROSS

When the Cannes film festival's Gilles Jacob rejected *The Crying Game*, Jordan and Woolley were devastated. They showed it to him again, with subtitles this time, but to no avail. "Then we screened it in L.A., and a strange thing happened," says Woolley. "I showed it to all the studios, and they were totally intrigued. They were saying, 'You guys have made a really strange movie. This is the kind of thing we wish we could make.' I'd decided I wasn't going to screen it for the independents, and of course that caused a huge fuss—'What's going on? How come we can't see it?' Finally Harvey saw it and loved it. There was a bidding war. Harvey won in the end, and we laid out extremely hard terms with him. He couldn't touch a frame of the picture. He couldn't touch the title. He couldn't preview it. Two days before we signed the contract, we changed the title from *The Soldier's Wife* to *The Crying Game*. They said, 'We like the old title. Please let us call it *The Soldier's Wife*.' They begged us. We said no, we want to call it *The Crying Game* because that's what the song is called. We'd got Boy George at the last minute and stuck the song on the end of the movie."

After a screening at Telluride and a rave review in *Variety*, the movie premiered before a gala audience in Toronto. Jordan recalls the thrill of seeing the film work for a large crowd: "When it came to the moment that they realize Jaye Davidson is a male, there was this strange, audible gasp from the audience. People came out of the film quite shocked. It was very satisfying. When we'd showed it in Britain, the reception to the movie was occluded by the issue of the IRA—a portrait of a sympathetic terrorist was very disturbing to the British press. But the minute I showed it in North America, in Canada, I felt they were seeing the story for what it is, a story about identity in all forms. It struck a chord."

American critic gave away the twist. The Crying Game *secret worked from the dinner party to the factory floor. And it all began in Toronto ing the secret away*

I remember walking into a festival press screening of *The Crying Game* that year and being handed a sheet of paper asking me not to reveal the movie's secret. That strategy turned out to be the secret of the movie's success. "It was my feeling that we should ask the initial wave of reviewers to talk about the movie without giving away too much of the plot," says Jordan. "Then it became the talking point of the movie. It became a marketing thing, and it got a bit scary after a while. It reached the ludicrous stage when Jaye Davidson was nominated for an Oscar for best actor, and the secret was still going around."

Not a single North American critic gave away the twist. *The Crying Game* secret worked as a universal joke, from the dinner party to the factory floor. "And it all began in Toronto, this idea of not giving the secret away," says Woolley. "Telluride was the spark. Toronto was the fire, and it just went from there. Miramax threw everything at it. *Sex, lies, and videotape* had shown that they were terrific distributors. *The Crying Game* was the film

Harvey and Bob stood on and said, 'Look, this is what we can do.' It was the film where they realized that if they knocked hard enough, the door would open, the film that led directly to *Shakespeare in Love*. Harvey and Bob just kept pushing."

The Crying Game grossed about $80 million, beating the British record set by *Chariots of Fire* a decade earlier. And on the strength of its performance, the Weinsteins sold Miramax to Disney. The other major studios followed suit, each setting up an indie boutique operation. Time Warner bought New Line Films; Universal acquired October Films; Sony, Fox and Paramount now all have classics divisions. The Weinsteins, meanwhile, have gained a reputation as bulls in the china shop of fine film. Harvey has been dubbed Harvey Scissorhands for his habit of re-editing movies he has acquired. "Our unorthodox style has always had its kibitzers because we don't do it by their rules," Harvey once told a journalist. "We set our own pace, set our own rules and actually don't care how anybody else does it. We're blue-collar guys with white-collar taste who believe that art is for everyone."

But some of his competitors feel Miramax has upset the ecology of independent film. "Two people raised the cost of doing business," declares Tom Bernard. "Harvey Weinstein and Garth Drabinsky." Like Weinstein, Drabinsky was a throwback to the moguls of old Hollywood, a domineering impresario fuelled by a righteous passion for the product. "Garth was the American Canadian," says Bernard. "He was always carrying the Canadian flag with a hammer. He'd come to our office in Los Angeles and say, 'I want to give you $700,000 for all your movies in Canada. I want to play you exclusively.' I'd say, 'Garth, you can't do that.'" In the 1980s, when Drabinsky was building his Cineplex empire, he would overpay for art-house cinemas, adds Bernard. "Word got around, 'Garth's coming, let's ratchet up the price.' Then he would transfer the cost of the theatres into the deal you made with him when he played your movies."

Harvey, meanwhile, chased box-office numbers by giving movies like *Cinema Paradiso* to theatres at a discount if they played them longer, according to Bernard. "That put a dent in the profits of specialized distribution." Harvey also bid for films with a tenacity that left competitors in the dust. Tom Bernard remembers watching *Il Postino* at the Toronto festival in 1994, and feeling his heart sink as the film got better and better. "It was the first screening," he says. "I was sitting next to Tom Sternberg, the sales agent, and I kept getting more angry, because I knew how much money it was going to take to buy the picture. And he was giggling with glee, knowing that he was going to whip it into a huge bidding war, which he did. Every time we bid, Harvey Weinstein bid higher." In the Monopoly game of independent film, Harvey is the guy who ended up with all the railroads plus hotels on Boardwalk and Park Place. Yet even his rivals have a grudging admiration for him. "You can say a million things about Harvey, most of it ugly," says former October Films executive Bingham Ray, "but he knows movies and he's a brilliant marketing guy. He and his brother have always had that killer instinct. You can learn it and master it, but it's best when it comes right out of the gut. And with Harvey it comes out of the gut."

JEFF DOWD AND
HARVEY WEINSTEIN

PHOTO: CATHY JOHNSON-CAMPBELL

e Weinsteins gained a reputation as bulls in the china shop of fine film. e set our own rules and don't care how anybody else does it. We're e-collar guys with white-collar taste who believe that art is for every-

Ray has a favourite Harvey story, which may be apocryphal. Harvey is a chain-smoker; his leased Miramax jet is nicknamed the Flying Ashtray. As the story goes, Harvey is flying from New York to Los Angeles when he realizes that, among all the Miramax staff on board, no one has a light. So Harvey gets the pilot to make an unscheduled landing, in some place like Minneapolis, to pick up matches. "I don't know if the story's true or not," says Ray, "but that's Harvey in a nutshell."

Perhaps the gulf between Harvey and The Dude is not as wide as it would seem. Although their successes are on a vastly different scale, both are shameless self-promoters, buccaneers who chased their passions out of the sixties and elbowed their way into the marketplace with sheer force of personality. After the '99 festival, no one was more incredulous than Jeff Dowd when he turned up as the subject of a glowing four-page article in *Fortune* magazine. The piece introduced him in deep conversation with Miss Canada, trying to persuade her to see the two movies he was representing at the festival. Why Miss Canada? As *Fortune* explained, "Because a celebrity at your movie means press coverage; press coverage means buzz; buzz means a sale."

Bill Marshall couldn't have put it any better himself.

Women

on the Verge

MIDNIGHT DINNER FOR CLINT EASTWOOD. HE'S HOLDING
URT AT A TABLE WITH CRITICS ROGER EBERT AND REX REED AFTER
e premiere of White Hunter, Black Heart*. Nearby, Liza Minnelli*
locked in conversation with Sheila McCarthy, who has skipped
t of the post-premiere party for White Room, *her second feature*
h Patricia Rozema, to attend Clint's soiree. If the festival has a
on society, this is it: an inner circle of influence and glamour.

Helga Stephenson breezes through the room. Earlier in the evening at the Elgin theatre, after presenting Eastwood to the audience before his premiere, she walked him over to St. Michael's Hospital to pay a surprise visit to her mother, a huge fan, who was dying of cancer. He made her day. I am introduced to Clint by Jay Scott—who is on familiar terms with the actor after hanging out on his set, then on his yacht in Cannes, and who joined the French critical elite in anointing Eastwood as a serious *auteur*. "Jay was one of the people they chose to cultivate," Helga explains years later. *They?* Clint's handlers. "We were all cultivated. When it came time to get Clint accepted as a director, serious festival directors were romanced. It wasn't that difficult a courtship because, generally speaking, people believed in his talent."

Clint extends a warm handshake. We exchange pleasantries. When I meet a movie star at a party, rather than an interview, I feel just as flummoxed as anyone else does. And Eastwood is one of those rare movie stars who appears larger than life off screen as well as on. He actually seems taller in person. Less threatening, though. Softer around the edges—almost feminine, if that's possible. In *White Hunter, Black Heart*, he plays a thinly veiled version of director John Huston on a quest to shoot an elephant while preparing to shoot *The African Queen*. This was Eastwood's brave but strained attempt to explore the Hemingway persona of the macho American artist, a tortured genius on safari, and there was something vaguely incestuous about it: Hollywood's iconic tough guy directs himself as the iconic tough guy of Hollywood directors.

PHOTO: JOHN MEDLAND

SHEILA MCCARTHY AND LIZA MINNELLI, 1990

PATRICIA ROZEMA AT THE WHITE ROOM PRESS CONFERENCE, 1990

PHOTO: STEVEN ROBINSON

While entire esthetic theories have been erected on the voyeurism female directors of prominence are rare, and in Hollywood almost no Toronto festival is one place where women's cinema has thrived

At the festival that year, there was no shortage of men playing tortured geniuses—Donald Sutherland as a crusading Communist doctor in *Bethune: The Making of a Hero*; Tim Roth as Van Gogh in *Vincent & Theo*; Gérard Depardieu as a ventriloquist lover in *Cyrano de Bergerac*; Jeremy Irons as evil genius Claus von Bülow in *Reversal of Fortune*. Movies, of course, are an overwhelmingly male preserve. There are more heroes than heroines. While entire esthetic theories have been erected around the voyeurism of the male gaze, female directors of prominence are rare, and in Hollywood almost non-existent. But the Toronto festival is one place where women's cinema has thrived.

In 1990, the festival's sleeper hit was *The Company of Strangers*, Cynthia Scott's serenely improvised National Film Board drama that cast elderly, non-professional actors to portray themselves getting stranded in the countryside. Audiences voted it the third most popular film after *Cyrano* and *The Long Walk Home*, a civil rights drama starring Whoopi Goldberg and Sissy Spacek. The same year, Jane Campion—who had been driven to tears by an abusive audience at the premiere of *Sweetie* in Cannes—won the International Critics' Award in Toronto for her compelling second feature, *Angel at My Table*, adapted from author Janet Frame's life story of being misdiagnosed as a schizophrenic. Also in 1990, an enthusiastic response in Toronto salvaged Agnieszka Holland's *Europa Europa* from European indifference. And Ann Hui, one of the world's most prolific female directors, revealed there was more to Hong Kong cinema than kinetic visuals with *Song of the Exile*, a delicate story of a daughter (Maggie Cheung) unravelling the trauma of her Chinese-Japanese roots.

The following year saw an explosion of women's cinema. Although *The Fisher King*—another tale of a wigged-out male visionary—was voted most popular film in 1991, female directors had such a strong presence that Martha Coolidge, on hand for *Rambling Rose*, dubbed the event "the Toronto Women's Film Festival." Also, the biggest stars that year were women, from chameleon-savant Lily Tomlin, who unveiled her one-woman show, *The Search for Signs of Intelligent Life in the Universe*, to the immortal Sophia Loren, who reduced veteran journalists to abject fans when she glided through town with Lina Wertmüller's *Saturday, Sunday and Monday*. Fifteen female directors made their feature debuts at the '91 festival. Leading the brigade was Jodie Foster, who launched her directorial debut, *Little Man Tate*, in which she plays the working-class mother of a child prodigy. With twenty-six movies and two Oscars to her credit at the age of twenty-eight, the former child star was something of a prodigy herself. And now she was emerging as a poster girl for Hollywood's new feminism, standing up for the uncelebrated valour of common motherhood long before becoming a mother herself.

e male gaze,
stent. But the

"What female actors, and certainly women in history, have to fight against," Foster told me, "is not so much the obvious things—victimization, etc.—but just being *ignored*. A real hero to me is a woman who has five kids and no money and takes care of them and survives. That's a heroic feat." Foster said she moved into producing and directing because she had trouble finding even one decent role a year amid the deluge of scripts she was sent: "Female roles are not written like human beings. They're written like stereotypes or functions of the plot. So instead of sitting around and waiting for it, I try to make it happen." In the end, she found directing easier than acting. "So much of acting is letting go of what you think and accommodating other people. And that, to me, is much more emotionally exhausting than directing. Being given all the information and having the ultimate voice is relaxing."

Meanwhile, Foster's co-star from *The Accused*, Kelly McGillis, used the '91 festival to launch her first foray into producing—Mary Lambert's *Grand Isle*, based on Kate Chopin's 1899 feminist classic, *The Awakening*. McGillis also starred in this pet project, playing a married woman who undergoes an erotic awakening during a languid summer on the Louisiana seaside. Martha Coolidge offered a curious companion piece with *Rambling Rose*, another period tale of sexual repression in the Deep South, which reunited *Wild at Heart*'s mother-daughter team, Laura Dern and Diane Ladd. And two movies offered backstage views of filmmakers by their wives. With *Jacquot de Nantes*, Agnès Varda bade a bittersweet farewell to Jacques Demy. And in *Hearts of Darkness: A Filmmaker's Apocalypse*, Eleanor Coppola's home movies from the set of *Apocalypse*

Now presented an absurdist portrait of the artist as a mid-life madman—yet another tormented genius, but one whose sandbox included Marlon Brando and enough firepower to start a small war.

Of the many feature debuts by female directors in '91, the film that generated the greatest buzz was *Proof*, by Australian writer-director Jocelyn Moorhouse. This odd story of a blind photographer in a love triangle had played at Cannes. "But we couldn't get a fix on the audience for it there," said Ira Deutchman, who finally bought it for Fine Line at the Toronto festival. "It wasn't until we saw the film with audiences and the press in Toronto that we perceived a groundswell of support for it." Another popular favourite was *Antonia and Jane*, Beeban Kidron's odd-couple tale of a frumpy misfit and a conformist beauty—one of those wafer-thin, semi-precious gems that acquired a unique lustre in the festival setting.

VARIETY'S *DIRECTOR BETTE GORDON, AND PRODUCER, RENEE SHAFRANSKY, WITH KAY ARMATAGE, 1983*

The person who has been the most ardent champion of women's cinema at the festival is Kay Armatage. For many years, she was the only female programmer aside from Helga Stephenson. In 1989 she curated Surfacing, an ambitious retrospective of thirty-six films by Canadian women. It began with *Back to God's Country* (1919), featuring the intrepid Nell Shipman as a dog-sled heroine who saves her husband, a silent film that Armatage considers "as significant to Canada as *Birth of a Nation* is to America." The programme also covered animation, experimental films, documentaries and the new generation of features ushered in by Mireille Dansereau's *La vie rêvée* in 1972. Long before joining the festival, Armatage championed the feminist cinema as part of the collective that organized Toronto's Woman and Film International Festival in 1973. It shocked an audience at the St. Lawrence Centre with a screening of American director Anne Severson's *Near the Big Chakra*, a forty-minute silent montage of female genitalia, vaginal portraits of every description, from girls in infancy to ninety-year-olds. The screening was accompanied by a live commentary from a group of women in the projection booth—Deanne Taylor, Linda Beath, filmmaker Freude Bartlett, and Warhol protegé Viva. "We were all tremendously thrilled with ourselves," recalls Armatage. "The only thing I remember from the commentary is someone saying, 'There's a big clitoris,' and Viva saying, 'When my daughter was born she had a *huge* clitoris—of course I showed her how to masturbate.'"

Along with David Overbey, Armatage carved out a singular niche at the Toronto festival. Combining academic authority with an eye for style, and transgression, she has helped keep the festival on the edge. It was Armatage who discovered Germany's Monica Treut, who became a fixture in Toronto with her kinky, post-feminist experiments. Armatage plucked Treut's first feature, *Seduction: The Cruel Woman*, from the 1985 Berlin festival—an archly stylized, utterly avant-garde film about sado-masochism. The opening images show what looks like a flooded parking garage, an industrial Styx where a man in a white dress and bobby socks crawls through plastic car-wash fronds, licking the floor.

)verbey was the gay iconoclast oblivious to fashion, Armatage was the ol feminist with a conscience and a sense of style, forever one step ead of the newest new wave

We meet a dominatrix who runs a "gallery" of torture with an ensemble of artists, lovers and slaves. In her dungeon cabaret, genteel spectators watch this sweet-faced tyrant carve a heart into a woman's back with a hunting knife. Everything is bathed in a Berlin-blue light. Between the lines of ritual submission, a romance flickers between two women, who embrace roughly against a wall or wrestle on a raft in the harbour amid burning debris—or laugh at a man pointing a gun as one licks blood from a fresh bullet wound in the other's hand.

After seeing *Seduction* in Berlin, Armatage approached Treut and her co-director, Elfi Mikesch, in a café and invited them to the festival. "They were completely thrilled," she says. "They thought nobody would see their film outside of a few people in Germany. In Toronto, the two of them showed up in black leather from head to toe. I was in a white linen suit. Their film got picked up by an American sleaze distributor—Monica's films

-oster moved into producing and directing because she had troubl
decent role a year amid the deluge of scripts she was sent: "Female r
ike human beings. They're written like stereotypes or functions of the
sitting around and waiting for it, I try to make it happen"

PHOTO: PETER BREGG/MACLEAN'S

have always been picked up by sleaze distributors—and I just continued showing them. People love her movies. They come up to her with their eyes shining, so excited to have been introduced to people they didn't know were human beings. Transsexuals and dominatrixes who look like your mom."

On a more refined plane, Armatage also championed Sally Potter's early work. When she screened *The Gold Diggers*, Potter's 1983 movie with Julie Christie, she says the audience consisted of "about twenty-five of my closest friends." Nine years passed before Potter showed up with her next feature, *Orlando*, an exquisite warping of gender and history starring Tilda Swinton as an immortal aristocrat who changes from a man to a woman over the course of four centuries. *Orlando* is a pivotal film about the properties of class and gender, about being possessed, and dispossessed, by love and destiny.

LEFT, JODIE FOSTER, 1991

With her pale sweep of orange hair and her ethereal eyes wide open to the world, Swinton is never really credible as a man, which only makes her masquerade more provocative. She wears her gender as a costume. Sometimes a movie is crystallized in a single image. With *Orlando* it is the macabre vision of a woman frozen under the Thames during the Great Frost of 1610, suspended in a window of ice as she is caught falling with a basket of apples—a deep frieze, if you will—while members of the court, clad in jet-black and glinting silver, skate on the river amid pearl tents and tapestries. In this conjured world, Orlando the Elizabethan lord falls for a French Muscovite princess in a black fur hat with a Bujold mouth. They kiss, only to be distracted by the sight of a peasant woman crossing the ice, insect-like, under a bundle of sticks three times her size.

As an intimate epic, *Orlando* now stands out as a rigorous antecedent to the flowering of Renaissance women usurping men's roles in *Elizabeth* and *Shakespeare in Love*. Gender-bending was clearly in the air—*Orlando* surfaced in the same festival as *The Crying Game* and Derek Jarman's *Edward II*. And for Potter, *Orlando* was a triumph, a thoroughly modern period film. "I'd always been a supporter of Sally's," says Kay, "and whenever I'd gone to London I'd have tea with her or whatever. So when I heard *Orlando* was ready halfway through the summer, I invited it sight unseen. It went to Venice, and by the time it got to Toronto, the word was out. Everyone was scrambling for tickets, and all the filmmakers were in the audience. Tilda Swinton was there, wearing the fabulous embroidered shoes that she wore in the movie, and Sally looked absolutely fantastic. At the end of the film there's this standing ovation that goes on for minute after minute after minute. The response was huge. I went to the front with Sally and Tilda and—remembering *Gold Diggers*—I said, 'Sally, isn't this *great*? Did you ever imagine that this would happen?' And Sally turned to me coolly and said, 'Well, actually this happened four times in Venice already.' Sally has become known as the Duchess on the festival circuit ever since."

ling even one
re not written
So instead of

It is getting harder and harder to discover films. But occasionally a hit sneaks in under the radar of advance buzz, and in 1994 that's what happened with Antonia Bird's *Priest*. It is the story of a young Catholic priest who is tormented by two secrets. First there is his homosexuality—one night he strips off his collar, picks up a man in a gay bar and spends the night with him. Then he is tempted to break his vow of confessional silence after a young girl tells him that she is locked in an incestuous relationship. Both Cannes and Venice had rejected *Priest*. The film's British sales agent, Carol Myer, had reservations about it. And Piers Handling, who programmed it, had only viewed it late one night on video. "He thought it was interesting," says Myer, "but none of us knew that I had a very successful movie."

The night of the premiere, after the film was introduced, Myer escaped from the festival with Helga and Piers to attend the swanky black-tie opening of the Barnes Exhibit at the

ABOVE, ANTONIA BIRD ON THE SET OF MAD LOVE; DREW BARRYMORE IN THE DRIVER'S SEAT

PRIEST

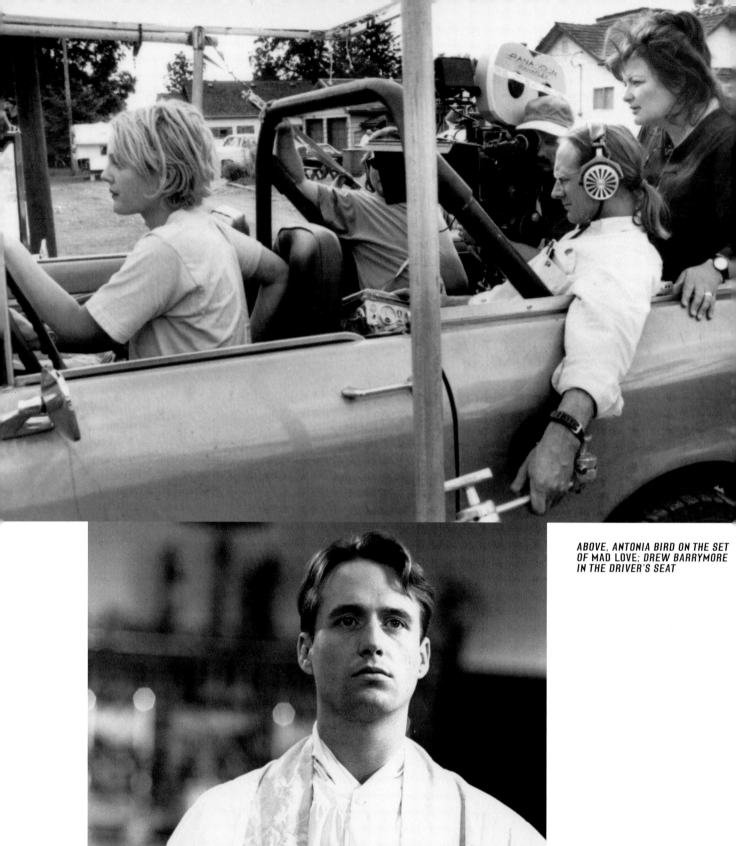

Art Gallery of Ontario. When she returned to her hotel, she bumped into Trea Hoving from Miramax in the lobby. "Carol, what a film!" said Hoving.

"Which film?" asked Myer, still under the spell of the paintings in the Barnes. "*Priest*—you've had a huge response."

Myer went up to her room and found twenty-two messages on her voice mail. *Priest* had played to a rapturous standing ovation. "Everyone wanted to buy the movie," she says. "It was a huge uproar. People were chasing me all over town not knowing which restaurant I was eating dinner in, not knowing I wasn't eating dinner anywhere." Miramax won the bidding war. And *Priest* won the People's Choice Award for the festival's most popular film. As it turned out, it didn't do that well in North America. "Harvey and Bob thought it was going to be a big scandal in the U.S.," says Myer, "but the Catholic Church was very wise and didn't rise to the bait." However, the film was a hit in Europe, notably in Germany, where a real-life controversy involving a naughty priest provided some timely free publicity.

Getting attention for an obscure, potentially controversial film requires a certain talent. But stirring up a scandal around a film that is not in the least controversial calls for serious sleight of hand. Dutch director Marleen Gorris had made some provocative feminist films in her time, notably *A Question of Silence*, in which three women kick, stab and genitally mutilate an annoying man to death in an orgiastic frenzy. But there was nothing incendiary about *Antonia's Line*. This warm-hearted saga wends its way through four generations of matriarchy in a Dutch village without great consequence. Gently feminist, and by turns elegiac and cheerful, the narrative follows practical women and thick men through seasons of birth and death, romance and misfortune, and it's all imbued with the common-sense, life-affirming spirit of Antonia, the matriarch looking back on her life in her dying hours.

Carol Myer knew she'd need a gimmick to get anyone to notice it. The movie had been rejected by the official selections at both the Cannes and Venice festivals. So she decided to show it at a market screening in Cannes—to women only. "This was the first time anyone had ever advertised a screening that only women could go to," she says, "and Marleen accused me of being incredibly old-fashioned. I told her I thought everything had changed so much that people didn't remember when we were all fighting for women's rights in the film business, and sure enough I never got so many column inches for free."

I meet Gorris for coffee at the train station in her hometown of Amsterdam. At fifty, she's a shy, skittish woman with a guarded intelligence. She speaks immaculate English with a mild Oxbridge accent. When Myer first told her about her gimmick for *Antonia's Line*, she recalls, "I said, 'Carol, you'll make me an extremely unhappy woman, because I'm going to be vilified for that action forever. They'll think it was my idea and they'll think it was all wrong.' And in Holland this was the case. They disliked the idea intensely. But it was a very good idea, because that's what got the film noticed."

At a film festival, there is no better way to draw attention to a movie than to create a situation where people can't see it. In Cannes that year, camera crews were waiting outside the Ambassades cinema, where absolutely no men were being allowed in, which was news. "It was such fun in the lobby," says Myer. "It had a terrific atmosphere. I'd planned a lunch afterwards, and there were all these women standing in a queue, still crying from the film, waiting to get into the restaurant." Finding two hundred powerful industry women to fill the cinema had not been easy. Among the distributors, "there are very few women who make the decisions. Some countries had no buyers at all who were women. So I invited the wives. I sold Switzerland on the basis of the wife's say-so. The man never saw it; he just bought it. It was a huge money earner in Switzerland." Although men were invited to subsequent market screenings in Cannes, the only North American distributor that bid for it was First Look Pictures, where two women were in charge of acquisitions. "The women at Miramax saw it," adds Myer, "but then one of the men saw it and told Harvey it wasn't good enough."

By the time *Antonia's Line* got to Toronto for its first public screening, it had been sold around the world. When Kay Armatage asked Gorris to introduce the film, however, she resisted. "She was incredibly nervous," recalls Armatage. "Her previous film had been denounced as a man-hating feminist film. I just kept saying, 'No, this is what you're here for.' I had to cajole her right up to five minutes before the screening." *Antonia's Line* turned out to be immensely popular at the festival. It won the People's Choice Award. It won the Oscar for best foreign-language film. And it was a hit in some of the least likely places, including such patriarchal societies as Japan and Brazil. The only country where it did not do well, strangely enough, is Holland. Canadian filmmakers can take solace in knowing that they are not the only ones under-appreciated in their own land. "This is a terrible country for films," says Gorris. "Dutch films don't get screens. And Dutch people simply don't go to see Dutch films."

The success of *Antonia's Line* allowed Gorris to make *Mrs. Dalloway*, a Virginia Woolf adaptation starring Vanessa Redgrave, which played at the '97 festival. And the Oscar led to the inevitable Hollywood courtship. But negotiations to direct a studio picture with Richard Gere broke down after a couple of months of trying to cast a female lead. Gorris wanted Cameron Diaz or Renée Zellweger. Diaz passed, and the studio insisted Gorris choose from a narrow field of A-list actresses that did not include Zellweger. "In the end," says Gorris, "they came up with somebody I didn't want to work with, so I said, 'I'm sorry, I can't do this.' You don't want to turn down a wonderful offer, but I thought it was too early for me to go for a big Hollywood movie when I thought the result would be disastrous."

Although Hollywood talent scouts do not have the same piranha presence in Toronto

ORLANDO

ANTONIA'S LINE

"This was the first time anyone had ever advertised a screening that only women could go to. And Marleen accused me of being incredibly old-fashioned"

that they do in Sundance, occasionally a feeding frenzy can converge around a new talent. In 1995, Armatage got a letter from a fifteen-year-old Rhode Island girl, Susanna Fogel, who had made a seven-minute short. "It was completely amateurish," says Armatage, "but it had a certain charm, so I put it on. The festival then put out a release saying she's the youngest filmmaker in attendance, so the press just descended on her. It was the first year of cell phones. All the agents and producers were swarming in the lobby of the Sutton Place. Like vampires sucking this sweet, young flesh. It was disgusting." A high-powered agent took Fogel to lunch. Her film got invited to Berlin. "And she had a wonderful ride," Armatage recalls, "but in Berlin she got absolutely trounced. They were merciless."

Undeterred, Fogel returned to the Toronto festival two years later with another short film titled *Words of Wisdom*—a satirical story of a young female director braving her first film festival.

17

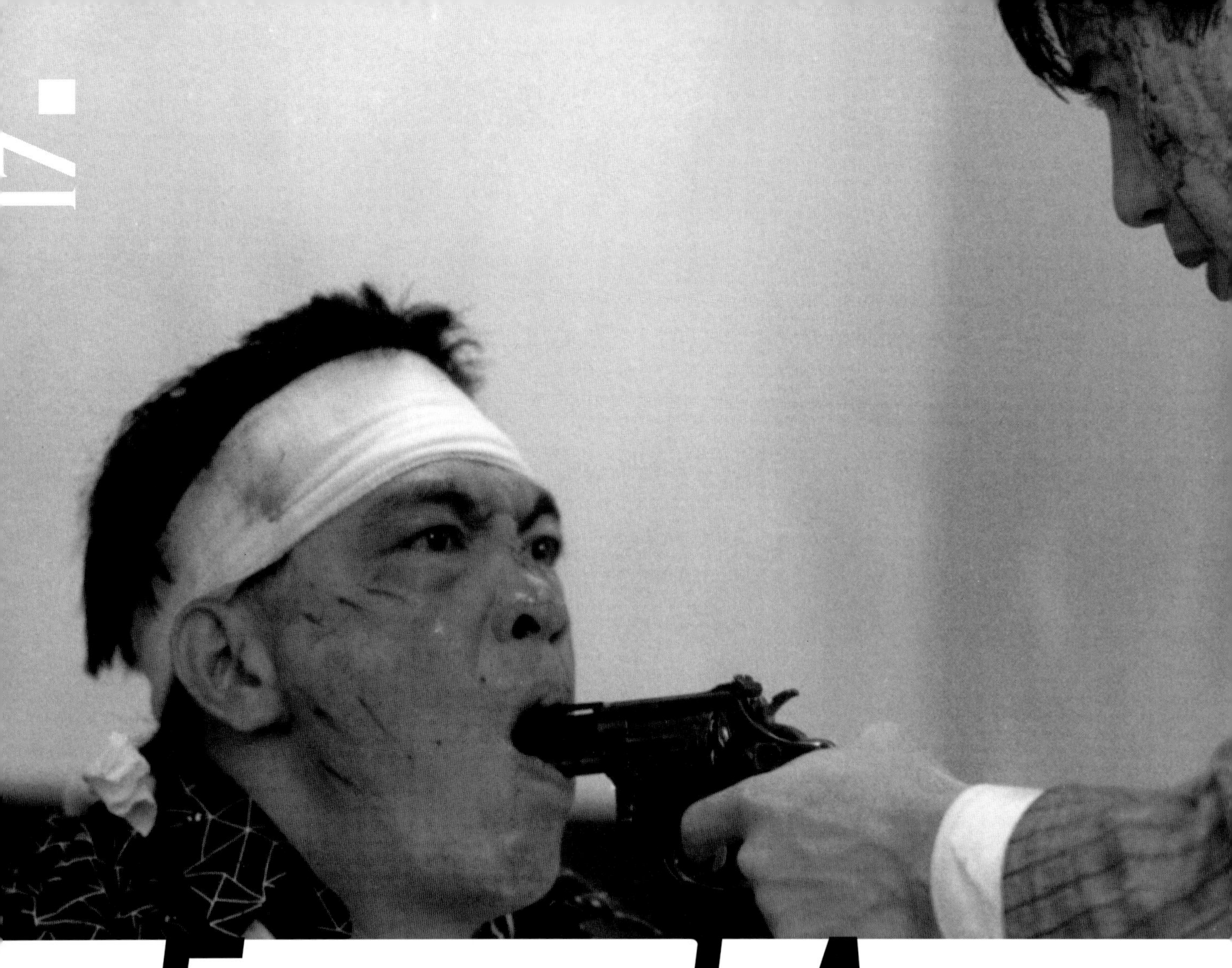

Far and Away

JOHN WOO IS ON THE PHONE FROM LOS ANGELES. HE
N THE THICK OF POST-PRODUCTION WITH TOM CRUISE (
Mission: Impossible-2*, but he's more than willing to make time to t*
about David Overbey, the late festival programmer who was h
riend and mentor. Tom Cruise and David Overbey. I try to put the
men together in my mind, but can't even imagine them in the sar
oom—Cruise, Hollywood's top gun, and Overbey, the gay iconocla
of world cinema. Yet through Woo's career, which has passed fro
Hong Kong to Hollywood, they are oddly connected.

Woo gives Overbey full credit for discovering him and introducing his work to North America. It was 1989. Woo had just finished *The Killer*, a Hong Kong action-melodrama that pushed the already exaggerated conventions of the genre into romantic overdrive, and he was completely demoralized. "People weren't paying any attention to the film," he says. "They were saying, 'This kind of movie won't work for the audience. It's too new and too stylish.' I was feeling pretty down and lonely. I felt there was no hope. Then all of a sudden, David came to the office and watched the film. Afterwards, I saw him in the corridor. It was an unforgettable moment. He came up to me with a big smile and hugged me. He said, 'John, this is a wonderful movie. This film must go to Toronto.' I said, 'Not many people like it.' He just kept saying, 'It's fantastic.'"

The Killer was cheered with a standing ovation at the festival, "and because of that screening," says Woo, "it got a lot of great attention from everywhere. I was so grateful to David. He restored all my pride and made me feel dignity. He helped me find myself. After that, we became really close friends. He was very supportive. He made a great contribution to Hong Kong movies and introduced them to people all over the world."

Like a parent whose child can do no wrong, Overbey even supported films that Woo was embarrassed by. "Sometimes I made a bad movie, like *Once a Thief*," he says, "but he still took it. I said, 'No, no, no, this is not a movie for the festival. It's very commercial.' I was so afraid the fans would be disappointed. But he insisted—'John, you're going to be fine.' Then after the screening, when people really liked it, he phoned me right away." Overbey didn't much care for Woo's first Hollywood outing, *Hard Target*. "But he was so humble," the director recalls. "He'd say, 'This wasn't John Woo's best movie, but it was still interesting.'" Woo last talked to Overbey a month before his death, in 1998. "I said, 'David, I'm going off to shoot *Mission*. What do you think?' He said, 'Oh, good luck.' Then we talked about Hong Kong movies. He was always hoping I would make more Hong Kong movies."

In 1994, the Festival of Festivals changed its name to the Toronto International Film Festival. The idea was partly to reflect the new reality of the event, which began as a festival of films from other festivals and evolved into its own venue for world premieres. But the new name also reflected a mandate to show challenging international fare, despite the escalating Hollywood presence. From Hong Kong to Helsinki, Bombay to Burkina Faso, the festival has scoured the frontiers of world cinema. And in the process, it has introduced a number of major filmmakers to North America, including Pedro Almodóvar, Krzysztof Kieslowski, the Kaurismäki brothers, Nanni Moretti and Wong Kar-wai.

Almodóvar was unknown on this continent when programmer Piers Handling ran across *Law of Desire*, the director's sixth feature, at Berlin. Handling had heard some buzz about it but had missed all the screenings. "On the last day of the Berlin festival," he says, "as they were dismantling the market, they sat me in front of a video machine at the Spanish stand. That's where I saw *Law of Desire*, with all this noise going on around me. And on the basis of that, I said, 'Let's do a spotlight on Almodóvar.'" In 1987, Toronto showed all six of his movies, a carnival of anarchist nuns, transsexual mothers and love-struck homosexuals. Swinging from campy farce to dire melodrama in the twinkling of a sex change, Almodóvar celebrated the freedom of post-Franco Spain with a pop surrealism all his own. Each movie played as a flamboyant seduction in progress, with a repertoire of actors who were all overtly carnal creatures, from the Picasso-angled Carmen Maura to doe-eyed Antonio Banderas. The following year, a festival gala launched *Women on the Verge of a Nervous Breakdown*, the Oscar-nominated breakthrough that put Almodóvar on the map. (It had been turned down by Cannes, which did not show an Almodóvar film until *All About My Mother* in 1998.)

The year of the Almodóvar spotlight, Handling also discovered the obscure pleasures of Finnish cinema. He was new to international programming, and because David Overbey and Kay Armatage had specific territories staked out, he says, "I was stuck with the leftovers. The last thing they would do is see a Finnish film." Handling saw Aki Kaurismäki's *Shadows in Paradise* at the Directors' Fortnight in Cannes and invited it to Toronto. The following year, he programmed a spotlight on Aki and his brother, Mika, showing eight of their movies. The Kaurismäki brothers work separately, but both tend to make films about rebels and misfits, a disenfranchised class of dishwashers, cab drivers, shop assistants and garbage collectors. In 1988, Mika's most recent film was his first English-language feature, *Helsinki Napoli All Night Long* (1987), an offbeat gangster movie with some of his favourite directors in the cast—Wim Wenders pumping gas, Jim Jarmusch in a pool-hall shootout, and Mika's mentor, American B-moviemaker Samuel Fuller as a drug lord. Aki, meanwhile, presented *Hamlet Goes Business*, recasting the Danish prince as a middle-aged oaf who reads comics, plays with his computer and is trying to buy into the rubber-duck industry.

In Toronto, Aki's films found North American distribution for the first time. The Kaurismäki brothers never caught on commercially, but as characters they charmed the festival, especially Aki. "Aki was drunk all the time," says Handling. "He's famous at other festivals for drinking beer until he's pissed as a newt and then introducing his movies. But in the Q&A's, I've never seen a filmmaker who speaks a foreign language grab an audience so quickly. He's like a stand-up comic. In thirty seconds, he had them eating out of the palm of his hand." Aki decided he had to drive to Manitoulin Island in the middle of the festival. He rented a car and spent four days there with his wife, scouting locations for co-productions. On his return, he reported that they'd had a terrific time—and that Manitoulin Island looked just like Finland.

Nanni Moretti, another idiosyncratic talent that Handling ushered into North America, has often been described as Italy's Woody Allen. He is a writer-director who stars in his

PHOTO: DOUG MACLELLAN

JOHN WOO AND BERENICE REYNAUD, 1990

elt there was no hope. Then David came to the office and watched the n. Afterwards, he came up to me with a big smile and hugged me said, 'John, this is a wonderful movie. This must go to Toronto aid, 'Not many people like it.' He just kept saying, 'It's fantastic' "

own films, mixing zany physical comedy with a cerebral wit. But while Allen's universe seems ever more circumscribed by his own neuroses—an infernal spiral of sexual guilt and artistic failure—Moretti's ego is leavened by a giddy political perspective. In his exhilarating *Palombella rossa* (1989), he plays a Communist intellectual with amnesia who conducts a perplexed inquiry into the future of Communism, and the futility of language, while playing an antic game of water polo. There are absurdist intrusions that take your breath away—as when Bruce Springsteen's "I'm on Fire" brings the game to a halt and the whole crowd reverently sings along, or when hundreds of spectators mill around a television set to watch the final scene of *Doctor Zhivago*, cheering on the separated lovers. A screwball revolutionary torn between Karl Marx and the Marx brothers, Moretti makes movies that seem forever on the verge of turning into musicals. And sometimes they do: in *Aprile* (1998), he cast himself as a frustrated filmmaker trying to make a musical about a Trotskyist pastry chef.

Moretti can be as whimsical in person as onscreen. The year after his festival spotlight, 950 people packed the Uptown One for *Caro diario*—a surreal mix of confession, manifesto and travelogue in which Moretti rides a Vespa to Pasolini's grave, cruises the Aeolian Islands, and conducts a Byzantine quest to cure a mysterious disease. But he didn't get to Toronto in time for the screening, or even the repeat screening on the final day of the festival. He finally showed up the day after the festival, during the Sunday awards brunch. Spotting Piers Handling, he ran across the hotel lobby, slid up to him on his knees and pleaded: "Will the director of the festival please forgive me?"

LEFT, KIESLOWSKI

PHOTO: DAVID MALTBY

"I walked Krzysztof into the theatre and the entire house stood up. I've never seen people so spontaneously rise. That was one of the most extraordinary moments—to see how you can create an audience for a filmmaker in ten days"

Of all the festival spotlights on international filmmakers, the most dramatic was the one devoted to Poland's Krzysztof Kieslowski. Before his death in 1996, he would become famous for his stunning *Three Colours* trilogy, *Blue*, *White* and *Red*. But when Handling and Dimitri Eipides brought him to Toronto in 1989, he was virtually unknown in North America. The cornerstone of the spotlight was *The Dekalog*, a magisterial series of ten one-hour films that Kieslowski had loosely based on the Ten Commandments, setting each film in the same Warsaw housing project. Two of them, *A Short Film About Love* and *A Short Film About Killing*, had been expanded into features. Combining the intensity of Hitchcock with the moral weight of Dostoevsky, *The Dekalog* explores the big questions of free will, fate and death without offering easy answers.

The festival began showing *The Dekalog* on a Friday. The theatre was half empty. The second day it was two-thirds full. By the end of the festival, hundreds of people were lined up on a Saturday afternoon to see *A Short Film About Killing*. "I walked Krzysztof into the theatre," Handling recalls. "We walked down the aisle and the entire house stood up. I've never seen people so spontaneously rise. He was just blown away. That was one of the most extraordinary moments I've ever had in a festival—to see how you can create an audience for a filmmaker in the course of ten days."

Eastern Europe had never been Toronto's forte. Serge Losique of the rival Montreal festival had built up close relations with the various state film agencies in the Eastern Bloc and would annually invite their bureaucrats, and their films, to Montreal. But in 1988, scouring English-subtitled prints from around the world, Toronto mounted Kino Eye: Soviet Cinema from Stalin to Glasnost, the largest Soviet retrospective ever assembled. Spanning thirty years, the survey shattered stereotypes of socialist realism and, as programmer Ian Christie pointed out, underscored a paradox: "Soviet cinema has often been at its boldest during periods of political repression or stagnation." Conversely, with the collapse of Communist bureaucracies—and their state film agencies—Eastern Bloc cinema is now politically unshackled but impoverished.

Also in 1988, Piers Handling recruited programmer Dimitri Eipides, a Greek expatriate who had left his homeland after the colonels' 1967 coup and co-founded Quebec's Festival du film et du nouveau cinéma. In contrast to Overbey, Eipides is a shy, self-effacing cinephile who remains an enigma to many of his colleagues. But he played an essential role in expanding the festival's international horizons. In 1988, he programmed *Damnation* by Hungary's Béla Tarr and *The Cannibals* by Portugal's Manoel de Oliveira—introducing Toronto to two major directors who would both be featured as Spotlight directors in later years. Eipides also helped discover Iranian cinema for North America. In 1989, he brought the festival its first Iranian film, Amir Naderi's *Water, Wind, Sand*. The following year, he gave Toronto its first glimpse of Abbas Kiarostami, with *Close Up*, a documentary-like yarn about an imposter who insinuates himself into a family by trying to pass himself off as celebrated Iranian director Mohsen Makhmalbaf. Then, in 1992, Eipides curated an Iranian retrospective. In a programme note—explaining how "the total elimination of sex and violence from Iranian cinema after the Islamic revolution has drawn filmmakers towards visual poetry and formal research"—he apologized for showing only eighteen movies, and for choosing more than one each from Kiarostami, Makhmalbaf and Naderi. "Future opportunities and my deep belief in the vigour and warmth of Iranian cinema should help to exonerate me," he concluded with an odd defensiveness. Eipides was prescient: by the end of the century, Kiaorostami and Makhmalbaf were two of the world's most universally admired directors.

The Eastern Bloc became another priority for Eipides. As a champion of the new Russian cinema, he brought Aleksandr Sokurov to Toronto in 1990 with *Second Circle*. And he opened a window onto the Balkans. Cinema that arises from civil strife and political repression can have a dramatic power surpassing anything manufactured by Hollywood or imagined by the stylists of independent film. And what is often staggering about these films is not the weight of war and oppression, but the burlesque imaginings that erupt under the pressures of historic conflict. That's been especially true of Balkan cinema, which was the subject of a timely retrospective at the festival in 1997. The programme went all the way back to *W.R.: Mysteries of the Organism* (1971), Yugoslavian director Dusan Makavejev's incendiary essay about Stalinism and sexual repression, involving a red-haired heroine promoting sexual revolution, a Soviet thug of a figure skater, a giant bust of Karl Marx sailing the Danube, and the plaster-casting of an erect penis. The carnival spirit that infused Makavejev's work re-emerged in *Underground* (1995), Emir Kusturica's riotous escapade through a half century of Yugoslavian history. Its baroque plot had partisan fighters going underground in the Second World War and re-emerging in the Bosnian war. I'll never forget the opening scene, of a Nazi bombing raid that hits a zoo and sends lions and zebras fleeing through the explosions to roam the burning rubble of the city streets. Or the final scene of a brass band playing mad gypsy music on a piece of coastal land that calves from the shore like an iceberg and floats away. Somewhere between the European New Wave and the social realism of the Communist Bloc, the Balkans forged its own cinema of revolutionary extravagance, a kind of social surrealism.

In 1998, before a packed house at the Uptown, Serbian master Goran Paskaljevic presented *The Powder Keg* (later released as *Cabaret Balkan*), which follows a maze of fractured lives through the black-market terror of war-torn Belgrade. The director asked how many people in the audience were from the former Yugoslavia: about two-thirds of them raised their hands. It was a reminder that the "foreign film," treated so often as highbrow exotica, is the flesh and blood of someone else's culture. Toronto's immigrant community has provided an organic constituency for the festival's international programming. That's been especially true with Asian filmmakers such as Taiwan's Hou Hsiao-hsien and Hong Kong's John Woo and Wong Kar-wai—all championed by David Overbey. When Wong Kar-wai first came to Toronto with *Fallen Angels* in 1995, he was amazed to see that more than half the audience was Chinese. "It was kind of strange," he recalls, "and very warm. It felt like Hong Kong."

Unlike Woo, Wong has never crossed over to Hollywood, which is remarkable in light of his virtuosity. There isn't another filmmaker in the world possessed with a more kinetic visual style. Using the urban landscape as his palette, Wong paints the screen with the camera. He improvises his script on the set, drawing out his actors, so that shooting the movie becomes a form of unconscious writing, spinning a tangential narrative that often doesn't come together until the cutting room. His storylines side-swipe each other in a choreographic blur of image and sound reminiscent of music video, but altogether different. "Music video," says Wong, "is a form that you can see anytime, anywhere. It has become part of the visual imagery that surrounds us, like trees or flowers. It's around you, and somehow you just pick it up."

Wong Kar-wai records the beauty of chaos. In *Fallen Angels*, Hong Kong is a fish-eye vortex, with trains and escalators streaming through the frame like fast-moving rivers. A restaurant massacre explodes as a refracted ballet of slow motion and freeze-frames. Beyond the visual delirium is the sweet romance of chance encounter and missed rendezvous. The hit man and his agent, a woman in a black vinyl dress, are potential lovers on parallel vectors. As in *Chungking Express*—where a young woman keeps sneaking into a stranger's apartment and rearranging his decor—they live alone with their daydreams, freefall commuters in the auto-erotic rush hour. The way Wong uses infectious pop songs ("California Dreamin'" playing over and over in *Chungking Express*) suggests that he is one of cinema's great untapped commercial talents. But he is not about to surrender control to a Hollywood studio, and the emotional commitment in his films, the visceral romance, cuts deeper than the surface style would indicate. His influence, however, does rub off. With *Fallen Angels* serving as a date movie for Quentin Tarantino and Mira Sorvino at the Toronto festival, it is hard to say where Hong Kong ends and Hollywood begins.

Like John Woo, Wong Kar-wai owes much of his North American exposure to David Overbey. Toronto is the only festival that has played all his movies, and he, too, came to regard the programmer as a friend and mentor. "When I first met him," says Wong. "I was a new director and he would always give me advice, which I really appreciated." Overbey held court at Bemelman's restaurant, where he monopolized the festival's contra in free drinks and food. He had the waiters stash open bottles of wine in the planters on the patio so they could drink after last call. Sylvia Chang, a writer-director and star of Hong Kong cinema, visited Toronto as the subject of a festival spotlight in 1992, but remembers little. "All we did was drink," she says. "It was the first time I had to throw up at the airport, and all the way back to Hong Kong." Overbey later told her she had met Quentin Tarantino and John Malkovich, but she has no memory of it. "I never realized how many people I met in Toronto," she adds, "because I was always drunk with David. He was a lot of fun. It's like he never cared about anything but having fun."

Overbey's predilection for picking up teenage boys in Asia, however, did not sit well with some of his colleagues. "He fucked young men in the Philippines and brought them here," says former festival programmer Cameron Bailey. "He picked out boys from very poor backgrounds. I didn't like that part of David. But he is someone I could never

h Fallen Angels *serving as a date movie for Quentin Tarantino anc*
ra Sorvino at the festival, it is hard to say where Hong Kong ends
d Hollywood begins

THE WEDDING BANQUET

condemn harshly, because he was so honest. He was the only PhD I knew who admitted to trying crack. David would never get hired at the festival today. He's just too much of a wild card. The thing I most admired about him is that he was such an advocate for his filmmakers." Some of them would show up with no money and no reputation, adds Bailey. "And David would protect them and celebrate them to the death. David fed his directors. He got them interviews, he probably got them drugs and got them laid."

"David was something of a pasha," allows programmer Noah Cowan, who joined Overbey in curating India Now in 1995. "But one of the reasons he's been so loved internationally is he really treated people from all over the world equally—with great delight when they were involved in great cinema, and with total sarcasm and disdain towards anything that didn't live up to his standard." Travelling through India, the world's most prolific film-producing nation, Overbey and Cowan saw hundreds of movies. "David taught us all the value of looking under every rug for gems," says Cowan. "That's especially true of India where you have sub-genres and regional cinemas that rarely emerge in the West. It was a nightmare, going through dozens of cities and, frankly, seeing a lot of appalling movies. But the jewels in the rough made it worthwhile."

Africa was the last unexplored continent on the festival horizon. In 1991, Cameron Bailey and Piers Handling made their first trip to Burkina Faso for the biennial Pan-African Film Festival of Ouagadougou. They flew straight from the Berlin festival, leaving the snow of a bleak European winter at 5 a.m. and landing in Africa half a day later. Handling remembers stepping off the plane into a wall of heat, lugging his winter clothes into town, and lining up for hours to discover his hotel reservation had vapor-

AKI KAURISMÄKI, 1988

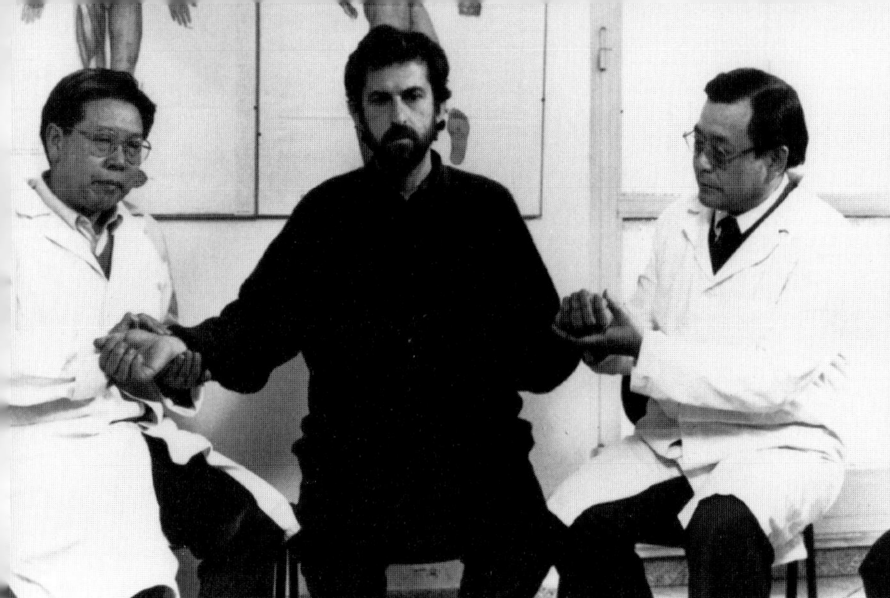

CARO DIARIO

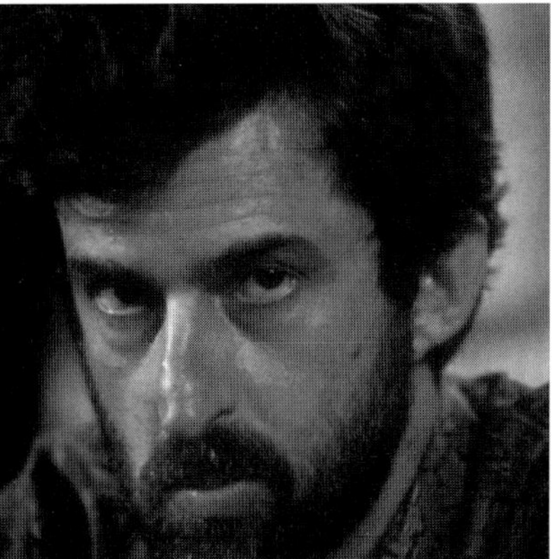

PHOTO: BEN MARK HOLZBERG

NANNI MORETTI, 1993

ized. He found himself in a taxi heading out of town, following an unpaved highway through a pall of dust, past people cooking at fires by the roadside under a darkening sky. "It was hallucinatory," he says. "I felt like I was in *The African Queen*. We drove into this little motel with five keys hanging there. We opened the door to the room and all you could hear was the scurrying of a gazillion cockroaches. I looked around, got into the cab and drove back to the festival headquarters."

Handling finally got settled, and survived Burkina Faso despite a severe sunburn. Bailey also had to fight his way through chaos. But as an African-Canadian raised in Barbados and visiting Africa for the first time, he felt strangely at home. He rented a motor scooter. He had budding dreadlocks, and kids in the street kept mistaking him for an African pop star. Films played in open-air screenings as well as in theatres. Bailey has memories of sitting on a concrete bench at dusk with a local audience, watching bats scatter past a full moon as images of British race riots played on the screen. "I kept having a great time," he says. "It was partly the films, but it was also the whole vibe, to come from Berlin, which is so regimented, and to fall into this world where you're staying out really late and dancing in these great African clubs, where there's this mix of distributors and filmmakers and local prostitutes and bad boys. Then seeing films at 8:30 the next morning still a little delirious from the night before."

Africa's cinema did not really get started until 1966, with Ousmane Sembene's *Black Girl*, and its filmmakers still face tremendous hardship. Many work in exile. Burkina Faso, meanwhile, is one of the world's poorest countries. But every two years, its festival takes over the capital. On opening day, forty thousand people pack a stadium for an Olympian ceremony with drummers, dancers and fireworks. At the 1995 opening, Bailey found himself sitting behind Winnie Mandela and her entourage. "South Africa had just been welcomed back into the fold," he says, "and it felt like this was the place to be in Africa that night. There were people from all over the continent and the world, all of them interested in African film. The fuzzy idea of pan-Africanism suddenly felt real."

PHOTO: ROB TETERUK

HAV PLENTY (LEFT); LAW OF DESIRE

That year, Bailey inaugurated the Toronto festival's first Planet Africa series. The permanent programme would showcase films from Africa alongside work by Africans wherever they lived—Jamaica, Birmingham or Brooklyn. Cameroon director Jean-Pierre Bekolo (*Quartier Mozart*) ended up living in Toronto for a spell, and got a job editing one of those 976-pick-up-the-phone shows about how to meet women. He used the facilities to cut his second feature, *Aristotle's Plot*. The British Film Institute commissioned it as a documentary about the history of the African film industry. But Bekolo, deciding he couldn't film a history of an industry that didn't exist, turned it into a wild satire—the tale of a vigilante cineaste in a southern African town taking on a group of wannabe gangstas who model themselves on Hollywood action heroes.

Although Planet Africa is one of the festival's less commercial sections, several titles have sent a buzz through the industry. Christopher Scott Cherot's *Hav Plenty*, a nervy romantic comedy set in Washington, D.C., premiered to a sensational response at the '97 festival. Afterwards, the filmmakers were having dinner at the Bellair Café when Miramax honcho Harvey Weinstein walked in, brandishing a fat cigar. Weinstein is not one to make a subtle entrance, and recognition rippled through the room. "He makes a big point of pulling Chris aside," recalls Bailey. "He stands him up, and the two of them talk for about ten minutes. Chris comes back, sits down at the table, and he's just glowing. Finally he whispers that they've pretty much made the deal. Harvey's bought the film for a million dollars. It couldn't have cost more than a hundred thousand. The problem was, they tacked a new ending onto it. A bogus happy ending, which Chris was not happy about. But that was part of the deal—Harvey Scissorhands."

In the nineties, as the festival explored African, Asian and Indian film, the snow-white complexion of Canadian cinema began to change. In 1991, Srinivas Krishna made a splash with *Masala*, a spirited feature debut set in Toronto's East Indian community, starring *My Beautiful Laundrette's* Saeed Jaffrey. And in 1993, the prize for best Canadian feature went to *Kanehsatake: 270 Years of Resistance*, a small NFB documentary shot on the front lines of the Oka crisis by Quebec native filmmaker Alanis Obomsawin. The jury included Fillipe Sawadogo, former director of the Burkina Faso festival, and Malti Sahai, from the International Film Festival of India. "To them," says Bailey, who chaired their discussions as Perspective Canada's coordinator, "*Kanehsatake* was the most interesting thing about Canadian cinema that year—a film about this real struggle for human rights. That's what they responded to most, I think, because of where they came from. But for a lot of people that was the last straw. How could this little documentary from Oka win a $25,000 prize? A lot of people just felt Perspective Canada had gone to hell in a handbasket—if you're white and male, you don't get a break."

The '93 festival was also a hot year for Asian cinema—with such favourites as *Farewell My Concubine*, *The Scent of Green Papaya*, *The Wedding Banquet* and *The Joy Luck Club*. The following year, Vancouver's Mina Shum scored a sleeper hit with *Double Happiness*, starring Sandra Oh as a Chinese-Canadian daughter at odds with her family over an interracial romance. Then in 1995, the festival presented the first dramatic features ever directed by black Canadians, Clément Virgo's *Rude* and Stephen Williams's *Soul Survivor*, both tales of Toronto Jamaicans cornered in the underworld. "Suddenly Canadian films were something else," says Bailey. "Filmmakers who weren't white or weren't straight were getting attention. And a lot of people felt threatened."

Perspective Canada, once the innocent showcase of local talent, became rife with controversy. There were finally too many Canadian films to choose from. Some producers felt the programme had become a ghetto and angled for galas and special presentations. But with the wrong kind of Canadian film, a gala could be a cold and lonely place, something that Atom Egoyan—the Cairo-born Armenian immigrant who would become the most significant Canadian director of the nineties—came to realize at a vulnerable stage in his career.

PHOTO: PETER BREGG/MACLEAN'S

SANDRA OH AND MINA SHUM

The Adjuster, Jay, Jean-Claud and His Lover

CANNES IS FAMOUS FOR CRUSHING EGOS GREAT AND SMA
AND ONE SIGN THAT TORONTO WAS ON ITS WAY TO BECOMING T
Cannes of North America was that you could be somebody and
mistaken for being nobody, or vice versa. The 1991 opening-night pa

PHOTO: BRIAN WILLER/MACLEAN'S

THE OPENING NIGHT PARTY FOR BLACK ROBE, 1991

ROBERT LANTOS, HELGA STEPHENSON AND BRUCE BERESFORD, 1991

PHOTO: BRIAN WILLER/MACLEAN'S

for *Black Robe*, a majestic epic about Jesuits and Indians, took place under a circus big top down by the waterfront. As several thousand guests milled about, photographers converged on a tattooed man in shorts, knee pads and a black bra, with a golden dollar symbol on a chain around his neck. Introducing himself as Rico Martinez, he was promoting *Desperate*, a $30,000 first feature that he called "a pseudo-autobiographical dramatization of a semi-pathetic life." Back at his day job in Los Angeles, he explained, he wore a suit to work as a studio functionary working on movies of the week. Elsewhere under the big top, veteran publicist Lucius Barre introduced Bruce Beresford, the Australian director of *Black Robe*, to Canadian director Atom Egoyan. "Oh, hi," said Atom. "I know your brother-in-law. I met him at a film festival in Spain."

"Yeah, yeah, when's the car coming?" asked Beresford, assuming that this eager young man in a new suit who looked vaguely Middle Eastern was his limo driver. It was the first time in his life that Egoyan had bought a suit for an opening night, and it was having altogether the wrong effect. The publicist froze. "Lucius, who's unflappable, was just mortified," recalls Egoyan, who decided it was too late to correct the faux pas. "I just muttered, 'Nice meeting you,' and walked away."

A few nights later, there was a gala for Egoyan's own film, *The Adjuster*, and it was another disheartening experience. The director's fourth feature was his strongest work, acclaimed at festivals from Cannes to Moscow. But the Toronto premiere "was the worst screening I've ever had," he says. "It shouldn't have been a gala. People just didn't get it. They didn't laugh. They thought it was way too weird. That scared me off galas for a while." Egoyan's sense of humour is challenging at the best of times, and the corporate crowd at the gala screening may have been unaware they were watching a comedy. Maybe they didn't get the erotic subtext in the scene of the doctor tenderly burning warts off a woman's foot and telling her, "I've had people in here with warts covering their entire sole." Or perhaps they were left cold by the sight of football players servicing a middle-aged cheerleader in an empty stadium to the creamy bump-and-grind of

Rough Trade's "High School Confidential." They might have been puzzled by the professional ethics of a fire-insurance adjuster (Elias Koteas) who has sex with his clients, or those of his wife (Arsinée Khanjian), a film censor who secretly tapes pornography for her sister. Or maybe they wondered why the couple had rented out their house—a model home on the dirt plain of an undeveloped subdivision—to a locations scout (Maury Chaykin) who uses it to stage an erotic fantasy among children at a birthday party.

Full of sexual menace and emotional dissonance, *The Adjuster* put a new kink into Canadian cinema, inaugurating a sexual-Gothic sub-genre that would include *Exotica*, *Kissed* and *Crash*. And although the movie was miscast as a gala, Egoyan was vindicated when he won the Toronto-City Award for best Canadian feature. At the awards brunch, in a spontaneous gesture of magnanimity—or presumption—Egoyan handed over the $25,000 prize to John Pozer, who had received an honourable mention for *The Grocer's Wife*. Wim Wenders had done the same thing for Egoyan with a $5,000 prize at the Festival international du nouveau cinema in Montreal. "I felt guilty for getting this award," Egoyan now explains, "because I'd won it before for *Family Viewing*. It was a very strange time in my life. I remember the moment so clearly. I was looking at my parents, whose lives had been devastated by this fire at their furniture store in Victoria. I'd made the film sort of about that. They were broke because their insurance claim didn't really work. Suddenly I was at the podium and I gave the money away. Arsinée was very pissed—we were broke. But it was one of those snap decisions, and I can't really tell you why. Suddenly I saw everyone on their feet applauding. I used to dream of the standing ovation, and it was the first standing ovation I'd ever received. The only way I've been able to rationalize this is that if I were to set that situation up, if I rented that ballroom and paid that many extras and had them all dressed up and gave them a beautiful brunch, it would cost me $25,000 to generate that moment."

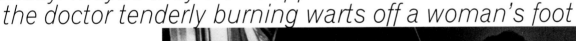

oyan's sense of humour is challenging at the best of times, and th
rporate crowd may have been unaware that they were watching
medy. Maybe they didn't appreciate the erotic innuendo in the scen
the doctor tenderly burning warts off a woman's foot

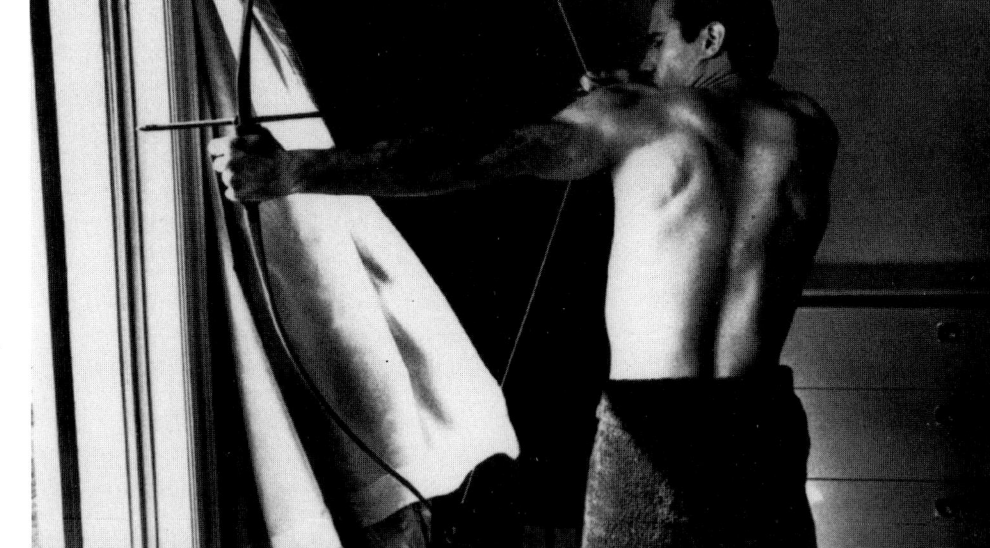

THE ADJUSTER

Bruce McDonald took a more casual approach to his career. To draw attention to *Highway 61*, which opened Perspective Canada, he arrived at the Uptown in a purple hearse escorted by a convoy of twenty-five bikers on Harleys. "It was our way of saying we're this dinky little Canadian film playing at the festival," says McDonald, "so anything we can do for free publicity . . ." The bikers agreed to take part after they were told they could come to the Perspective Canada party afterwards and drink as much free beer as they liked. It was one of the most raucous parties the festival had seen. There was a photo booth promoting Kevin McMahon's *The Falls*, where guests could have their pictures taken in a barrel, and the bikers' girlfriends caused a huge commotion when they started taking off their tops for the photographs.

PHOTO: KEN PICKETT

McDONALD (CENTRE), AND THE HIGHWAY 61 *MOTORCADE, 1991*

In *Highway 61*, the second in McDonald's trilogy of rock-'n'-roll road movies, an aggressive stranger (Valerie Buhagiar) cajoles a shy, trumpet-playing barber (Don McKellar) to drive her from Thunder Bay to New Orleans in his dad's Galaxie 500 with a coffin strapped to the roof. Scripted by McKellar, this comic odyssey into the jaws of America amounted to a wry portrait of the Canadian artist as a fretful naïf literally afraid to blow his own horn. Norman Jewison saw *Highway 61* at the festival and was so impressed he phoned up its director. "Loved your movie," he said. "Maybe you could tighten it up by ten minutes." With a hand from Jewison, McDonald trimmed ten minutes. Later Jewison called him about a script he might want to direct, something about Indians called *Dance Me Outside*. That began a mentor-protegé relationship between two directors that continues to this day.

ruce McDonald arrived at the Uptown in a purple hearse escorted b onvoy of twenty-five bikers on Harleys. They agreed to take part af hey were told they could come to the Perspective Canada party a rink as much free beer as they liked. Their girlfriends caused a co notion when they started taking their tops off for the photographers

---

One of the unique things about the Toronto film community is how tight it has become. As Egoyan, McDonald, McKellar and Rozema encouraged each other's work, they in turn found support from their elders, from Jewison and Cronenberg. Even Robert Lantos, who had built his career around a more old-fashioned style of production, would become a selective patron of Toronto auteurs, but not before launching *Black Robe*, a $14-million period epic starring *Jesus of Montreal*'s Lothaire Bluteau as the dour priest who embarks on a marathon expedition to a Jesuit mission among the Hurons.

Once again, Lantos took the literary high road in his quest to create the Great Canadian Movie. As with *Joshua Then and Now*, he enlisted an eminent author to adapt his own novel, in this case Brian Moore. But to direct the Canada-Australia co-production, he went outside the country to recruit Bruce Beresford, fresh from the Oscar triumph of *Driving Miss Daisy*. Exquisitely shot on Quebec's Saguenay River, *Black Robe* is a film of severe beauty that evolves as a death trip from summer to winter, a drama of conflicting cultures etched against savage shifts in landscape and weather. The novel's psychology loses something in translation, although the film represents aboriginal people with ethnographic accuracy, as did *Dances with Wolves* the previous year. While the Indians speak their own language, the French talk in English, an irony that reflects the colonial imperative of the film business: subtitles would have reduced *Black Robe*'s already limited commercial prospects. It was, after all, a bleak story with a funereal ending, and its hero wasn't a heroic fighter played by Kevin Costner, but a pale cypher of a priest.

Released two weeks after the opening-night gala, the movie grossed $3 million in Canada, then about $12 million in the United States. Lantos admits he "would have liked it to have done a lot better." But for the first time in his career as a movie producer, he could claim a clear critical success. Jay Scott led the charge with a long, rapturous review before the premiere that called *Black Robe* "cause for cinematic celebration." The film's landscapes, wrote Scott, have "a gelid pictorial precision that elicits gasps and raises goosebumps." Lantos had made a deal with Scott to show him *Black Robe* long before anyone else had seen it. "If he liked it, he could review it the day of the festival opening," the producer explains, "and if he didn't he would hold his review. Jay had such authority that if he pronounced himself, the other critics would not go against him. If Jay said something was a masterpiece, no one was going to say it was a piece of shit, and vice versa."

As a critic, you try to avoid other reviews, and I always made a point of not reading Jay's until I'd written mine: he was too persuasive, and he wrote with such a singular combination of flair and erudition that it was impossible to get his voice out of your head when you were trying to listen to your own, even if you thought he was dead wrong. It's hard to overestimate his influence. Although he was not Canadian, he was an ardent champion of Canadian film, and played a major role in putting it on the map.

Like David Overbey, Scott was a gay iconoclast from the American South. As Helga Stephenson notes, "they both grew up in places where it was deeply not interesting to be gay"—David in Arkansas, Jay in Albuquerque. Born in Lincoln, Nebraska, Jay was raised by Seventh Day Adventists who moved to New Mexico when he was young. He was molested by his grandfather, who had also molested Jay's father, who ended up committing suicide. Scott's mother was a schoolteacher who collected native art and artifacts, a passion she passed on to her son, who reviewed movies and paintings with equal alacrity. Jay first came to Canada to dodge the draft and cut his teeth in hard news and investigative reporting, which helps explain why his criticism never seemed to be just about film, but about the world. "He came from a political analysis and applied it to cinema in a way that nobody else did," says French film journalist and

Cannes luminary Henri Béhar, maintaining that "Jay was the best film writer in the English language bar none." That is the sort of superlative that Scott, who wrote with un-Canadian largesse, liked to indulge in. He was unafraid to be a fan, or a star. Waxing lyrical, rhetorical and analytical all at once, he was a rodeo writer on film's wild frontier. "All that western language—slower than a snail crawling down a freezer door—just tickled him pink," says Stephenson, noting that Scott was avidly interested in his own impact. "He loved to discover somebody. He wanted to be the first: it appealed to his ego."

FAR RIGHT, JAY SCOTT AND DAVID OVERBEY; RIGHT: SCOTT WITH THE OFDC'S SHANE KINNEAR AT THE CANNES PARTY

Scott played a crucial role in establishing the reputation of Canadian directors such as Atom Egoyan and Jean-Claude Lauzon. "Jay was a really glamorous figure," Egoyan recalls. "He had to deem that you were of interest, and it took a number of films before he felt I was. When *Speaking Parts* was in Cannes, a meeting was set up for me with him at a Lebanese restaurant. I remember being very nervous, realizing I wasn't saying anything. Then, reading his piece, I saw how he could create a heightened sense of the ordinary, which is what you do as a filmmaker as well. In some ways it was a work of complete fiction."

Unconcerned about keeping his critical distance, Jay enjoyed socializing with directors he admired. Egoyan remembers Jay taking him out on the town during a Canadian film retrospective in, of all places, Indianapolis. "We went to this strange club where there were female impersonators doing drag shows," he recalls, "but the audience was young mid-western lesbians, and they were going nuts. I just couldn't figure out what the sexual connections were, and I got really excited about the idea of this club where you couldn't quite figure out what the energies were about. That evening was the origin of *Exotica*. I started thinking about setting a story in a club like that. Jay was there with the birth of *Exotica*, although he didn't live to see the movie."

Jay took delight in bringing straight people behind the lines of gay nightlife. An official at a government funding agency tells a story of expensing a tab for an exorbitant round of drinks at a gay bar in Cannes that, as it turned out, included the rental of a companion for Jay. And in Montreal once, I was a part of a group that Jay took on a safari deep into East End Ste-Catherine Street, to an underworld saloon of gay strippers and hustlers, assuring us that if we stayed cool our lives would not be in danger. He showed the place off as if it were an obscure film that he'd discovered in Berlin and just had to share. Jay treated art as life and life as art; he was a critic who behaved like a star. One year in Cannes, he created a minor scandal at the annual cocktail party hosted by the Toronto festival and the Ontario Film Development Corporation by showing up in nothing but a Speedo.

Jay Scott died of AIDS in July, 1992. Helga hosted the wake. Two years later, Egoyan premiered *Exotica* in Cannes—Canada's first feature in competition since 1983's *Joshua Then and Now*. The film, which played in Perspective Canada at the Toronto Festival, cemented Egoyan's international reputation. And he found an unlikely ally in Robert Lantos, who—as an executive producer of *The Sweet Hereafter* and co-producer of

y treated art as life and life as art; he was a critic who behaved like a ar. One year in Cannes, he created a minor scandal at a swish cocktai rty hosted by the Toronto festival and the Ontario Film Developmen rporation by showing up in nothing but a Speedo

PHOTO: COURTESY OF DAVIS/DOBSON/MCINTOSH/WEEKS

Felicia's Journey—would use his corporate heft to bring Egoyan to the next level. After *Black Robe*, Lantos had begun to throw his weight behind Canada's most provocative writer-directors, namely Egoyan, Cronenberg—and the uncontainable Jean-Claude Lauzon.

Lauzon had burst onto the scene in 1987 with *Night Zoo*, which was a sensation at the Directors' Fortnight in Cannes and a box-office hit in Quebec. But before its gala screening in Toronto that year, Lauzon suddenly pulled a disappearing act, cancelling a full schedule of interviews. "We had organized the most fantastic press coverage for him," recalls *Night Zoo* producer Roger Frappier. "*The Journal* wanted to follow him all week. But he just disappeared. Nobody knew where he was. Later he said he went to a cheap hotel by the lake and screened porno movies for two days, but I don't believe it." Lauzon resurfaced at the festival press conference for *Night Zoo*. His answer to the first question was: "Michelangelo didn't have to explain the Sistine Chapel. Why do you want me to explain my movie?"

Despite snubbing the press, Lauzon had a field day at festival parties, and ended up winning the prize for best Canadian feature. "He was like a kid in a candy store," recalls Helga Stephenson. "He walked away with the award because he wanted it on his mantelpiece. He had one couch and no furniture. But it wasn't an award that you take home—we had to go out and get one made for him."

Robert Lantos remembers when Lauzon walked into his Toronto office with a script for *Léolo* in English. "You're going to read it while I'm in your office," he told him. "And I did," says Lantos. "He sat there and watched me read it for about two hours. It was pretty hard to say no to Jean-Claude. He was a great salesman. He convinced me it was a masterpiece. But I said, 'You can't make this in English. It's a Quebec story about Québécois characters in the East End of Montreal. If you make this in English it will be ridiculous.' He was very pissed off at me. He took the script back. And he spent the next two years trying to make the movie in English."

Lauzon also pitched Norman Jewison, who had asked him to direct a police thriller in Montreal. After Jewison sent him the script, Lauzon met with him and said, "I'm sure this is an idiot test you sent me, that the little French Canadian will be so impressed he'll say it's a good script. But we both know it's a piece of shit." Lauzon then pulled out his *Léolo* script and said, "Norman, did you read this? This is fucking cinema!" Jewison declined to get involved with *Léolo*, and Lauzon finally agreed to make the movie in French with Lantos.

Ostensibly, *Léolo* is a semi-autobiographical story of a twelve-year-old boy coming of age in East-End Montreal. But that's like saying *Ulysses* is the story of a man who spends a

"Lauzon never made a movie again.... He spent a couple of years in L.A. doing nothing. He wasn't going to make any more Canadian films and certainly no more movies in French. He made commercials and told me how much better it was because nobody judged you"

day wandering around Dublin. Flouting narrative convention, Lauzon pushes back the frontier of personal filmmaking with an assured intensity that recalls Fellini and Truffaut. Comic, tragic, erotic, poetic and operatic, *Léolo* concerns a French-Canadian boy who claims to be an Italian conceived by stray sperm carried to Canada on a Sicilian tomato. He has a grandfather who tries to drown him, parents obsessed with defecation and an older brother devoted to bodybuilding. Mixing dreamlike logic with vivid realism, the drama is propelled by a score that ranges from religious choral music to Tom Waits and the Rolling Stones. This hallucinatory film was Lauzon's distillation of a rough-and-tumble childhood in working-class Montreal. Various members of his family were hospitalized for mental illness, including his father. He dropped out of school at sixteen, lived on the streets, and later worked as a factory labourer, tobacco picker, tree pruner, taxi driver, fishing guide, scuba diver and bush pilot.

Léolo, which opened the Toronto festival in 1992, shocked the gala audience with its graphic scenes, which included one of the boy masturbating with a piece of liver, and another of him torturing a cat. The movie had premiered in competition in Cannes, where Lauzon pulled an outrageous stunt that sabotaged any chance he had of winning. He was lunching with Lantos on the terrace of the ultra-luxurious Hôtel du Cap in

Antibes when some jury members, including Jamie Lee Curtis, walked by their table. Lauzon reached out and grabbed the actress by the belt buckle. Blocking her way, he stood up and pulled her in close to him. "Just remember what I'm going to tell you," he said. "I would much rather fuck you than a piece of liver any time."
Jamie Lee Curtis was horrified.
"What did you just do?" asked Lantos in disbelief as Lauzon returned to the table. "What the fuck was that?"
"She will never forget me," Lauzon replied. "When she sees the film, she will remember this. She's mine."

Lantos tried to persuade him that he'd just committed career suicide, "but I could never be pissed off at him," he says. "The more outrageous he was the more I liked him." Lauzon was sure his strategy would work. He had heard a rumour that Gérard Depardieu, whose childhood was similar to his own, was moved to tears by the film. "Years later," says Lantos, "I got to know Depardieu and asked him. He didn't like the film. He never cried. And Jamie Lee Curtis was completely against it."

Lauzon was shattered by his defeat in Cannes and never recovered, adds Lantos. "He deeply expected to win the Palme d'Or. The Toronto festival screening was very, very silent. Then came the Genie Awards and he didn't win much. That made it even worse. He never made a movie again. I tried. I'd bring him books, stories, scripts. He spent a couple of years in L.A. doing nothing. He wasn't going to make any more Canadian films, and certainly no more movies in French. He made commercials and told me how much better it was because nobody judged you."

Lauzon had a passion for hunting, and for flying his plane. He would spend months at his camp in northern Quebec. Lantos went flying with him once, sitting next to him in the co-pilot's seat. "All of a sudden," recalls the producer, "Jean-Claude took his hands off the controls and said, 'You're flying.' He scared the shit out of me."

Helga Stephenson flew with him more than once. She and Lauzon were both flamboyant personalities with large appetites, and about six months after the '89 festival, they met up in Montreal. "He'd been chasing around after me," says Helga, "but he was chasing around after everyone so I didn't pay it a lot of attention. We were at l'Express having dinner. He had to go to the Miami film festival and I was in the middle of one of my breakups. He kept pushing and pushing me to go to Miami with him. Finally I said, 'Look J.C., I'm in a weakened position. You ask me one more time, I'm going to say yes, and then you're going to have to go buy a ticket and then you're going to have to do all kinds of things, so stop.' But he kept pushing. I said, 'Fine, I'm going.' He ordered the ticket on his cell phone. The next morning we were in Miami. I turned up at work two days later."

It was a makeshift romance. "You'd get a phone call," says Helga, "and three hours later he'd be at your doorstep with a bottle of champagne and Bruce Springsteen blasting.

You'd spend the weekend and just float off. One time we flew for four hours up north to his camp. It was fabulous. We went lake-hopping all over the place. He taught me how to shoot a gun. I'd never fired a gun, and after seeing it in so many movies, I wanted to feel physically in my hand what it felt like. He had millions of guns."

On August 10, 1997, at the age of forty-three, Jean-Claude Lauzon was killed when he flew his plane into a hillside near Kuujjuaq in northern Quebec. Also dying in the crash was his girlfriend, actress Marie-Soleil Tougas. She was twenty-seven. But producer Roger Frappier says Lauzon was not the type to take risks. "I flew in his plane a couple of times, even in bad conditions. I was never scared with him. He was a fantastic pilot. When he went hunting, he would make his own ammunition, because he wanted it to be really precise. He learned to shoot a bow and arrow. There was nothing he didn't do. But when you do a number of dangerous things at the same time, it's dangerous. Something is bound to happen. Strangely enough, it's because he was so cautious that day that it happened—because he wanted to have a second look before landing. He tried to turn and approach it again. But with Jean-Claude, you'd believe that even if he'd crashed in a huge explosion with flames leaping up in the sky, he would just walk out of the debris and come laughing at you. He had such a tremendous vision of life, a tremendous will."

Léolo inaugurated an era in which Canadian cinema, like Canadian weather, would become famous for its inhospitable extremes. That same year, 1992, Perspective Canada opened with *Careful*, a brilliant yet weirdly idiosyncratic feature by Winnipeg director Guy Maddin, who used scratchy soundtracks and special film stock to create dreamlike scenarios that look like motion-picture artifacts. *Careful* is a comic fairy tale about an Oedipal incest scandal in an Alpine hamlet where the villagers talk softly for fear of triggering avalanches. Maddin creates a sublime metaphor for the national character—illicit desire creaking through the pack ice of Canadian caution. But much of the audience was left cold. "We almost cleared the house," recalls Cameron Bailey, then coordinator of Perspective Canada. "Or so it seemed. There were quite a few walkouts."

As filmmakers defied narrative convention and explored dark themes, there was a deepening gulf between Canadian cinema and its audience. In 1993, the festival's Canadian crop was a catalogue of sexual transgression. Cronenberg's *M. Butterfly* confounded the opening-night audience with the tale of a man in love with a woman who is really a man; Gerard Ciccoritti's *Paris, France* unfolded as Canuck *Kama Sutra*; in David Wellington's *I Love a Man in Uniform*, a psychotic actor who makes a fetish of a police costume ends up blowing his brains out; a psychic dominatrix turned out to be one of the saner characters in Denys Arcand's *Love and Human Remains*; and John Greyson's *Zero Patience*, the first AIDS musical, brought us talking butts long before Jim Carrey played Ace Ventura.

HELGA AND JEAN-CLAUDE LAUZON

PHOTO: RAFY

ou'd get a phone call, and three hours later Lauzon'd be at you orstep with champagne and Bruce Springsteen blasting. You'd spend e weekend and just float off"

The '93 festival also included a novel variation on the documentary tradition, François Girard's *Thirty-Two Short Films About Glenn Gould*, which captured the genius of its subject with a deft counterpoint of documentary and drama. Its success marked a breakthrough for producer Niv Fichman and his partners at Rhombus Media, a small Toronto company specializing in music films for international television. Girard and his co-writer, Don McKellar, were pumped when they showed up for the Toronto gala, just two days after premiering *Gould* to raves in Venice. "This was a film I never thought would get beyond PBS," says McKellar, who met Gould's father at the party after the gala. "The family had allowed us to look at a lot of letters and notes that had never been available before, and it was really scary to have his father come out." Gould's father was curious to know how the filmmakers had come up with the film's opening tableau, which shows the pianist walking across the ice of Lake Simcoe, a solitary figure against a white void. McKellar nervously told him they had made it up. "I don't know how you thought of that," Gould's father marvelled. "I always remember Glenn out there walking across the ice when he was a kid. That's the way I always think of Glenny."

In June of 1992, at the age of forty-five, Helga Stephenson, who had given up on having children after trying unsuccessfully for several years, gave birth to a baby girl. "She was a miracle baby," says Helga, who was onstage to introduce *Léolo* on opening night less

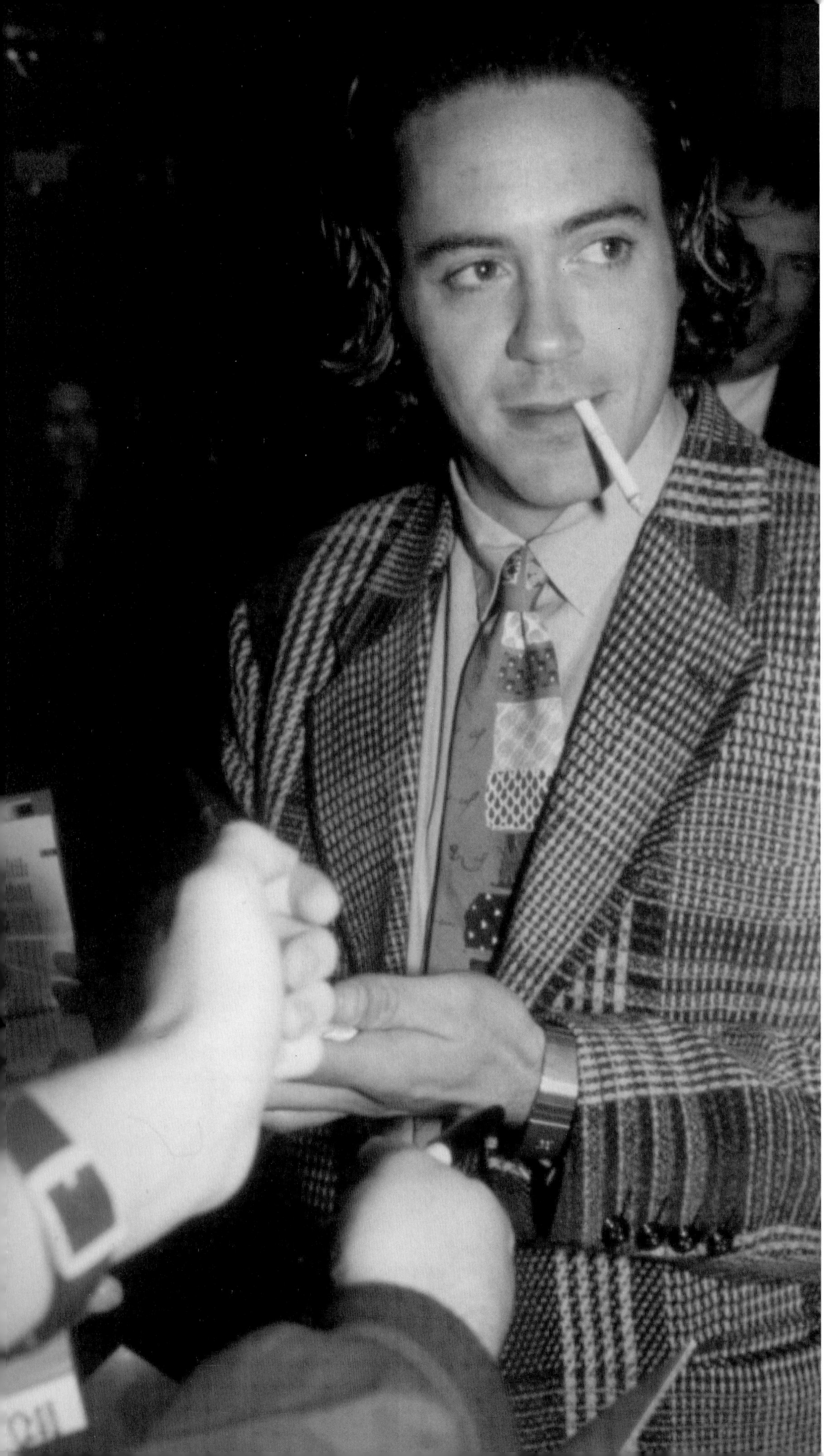

PHOTO: JIM STEELE

LEFT, ROBERT DOWNEY JR., 19
RIGHT, ROBERT DE NIRO, 1993

PHOTO: DEAN GOODWIN

the set, Jewison couldn't keep Downey from tumbling into a romance h Tomei. At the party after the premiere, "I have to chaperone him the tire evening. By now, he's turning on—everyone was on something— d I'm just a tired farmer trying to get home"

PHOTO: SARA MOORE

RAIN PHOENIX, 1993

than three months later. "You wouldn't believe what it's like trying to fit into designer outfits when you have lactating breasts." Setting up house with her nanny in a hotel room, Helga breast-fed her way through the festival. And she stayed on for another year. Then, in 1994, she stepped down to devote herself to being a single mother and Piers Handling took over her job as director.

"It was terrifying," Handling recalls, "because I was following in Helga's footsteps, and she was a larger-than-life, a very extroverted character who had the complete faith of the board. I'm somewhat the opposite of Helga—shyer, more academic, less perceived as the business person. I'd kind of enjoyed being number two, out of the spotlight. I'd always thought the number-one job was more corporate. And I wasn't going to become a Helga clone." But just as Helga had made up for her weak suit by hiring Piers as artistic director, he delegated the business side to a managing director, Suzanne Weiss. "She had everything I didn't have," he explains. "She had the corporate connections and was very presentable."

WHALE MUSIC

As the festival's CEO, however, Handling would come to acquire the skills of a politician, whether navigating the media or negotiating with Hollywood studios. He was tested in his first year as he haggled with Alliance over the opening gala. Because the festival always tries to open with a Canadian movie, and because Alliance distributes the lion's share of Canadian productions, negotiations with Alliance had become an annual ritual. In 1994, the obvious choice was *Exotica*, but after his experience with *The Adjuster*, Egoyan preferred to just slip it into Perspective Canada without fanfare. So the festival settled on another Alliance movie, *Whale Music*, a quirky first feature directed by Richard J. Lewis, adapted by Paul Quarrington from his own novel, and starring Maury Chaykin as a faded West Coast rock star. *Whale Music* was an underwhelming choice to open the festival—"even Robert admits that was a mistake now," says Handling—and it ushered in a festival that was relatively low on Hollywood glamour. But the '94 programme contained some of the decade's brightest international gems: Nanni Moretti's *Caro diario*, Massimo Troisi's *Il Postino*, Abbas Kiarostami's *Through the Olive Trees*, Krzysztof Kieslowski's *Three Colours: Red*, Nikita Mikhalkov's *Burnt by the Sun*, Tomás Gutiérrez Alea's *Strawberry and Chocolate*, Peter Jackson's *Heavenly Creatures*, Lee Tamahori's *Once Were Warriors*, Shekhar Kapur's *Bandit Queen* and Louis Malle's *Vanya on 42nd Street*.

Norman Jewison closed the festival with *Only You*, his romantic love letter to Italy starring Robert Downey Jr. and Marisa Tomei. The premiere went well, so well that Jewison says he thought "it was going to be an enormous hit," but it wasn't. "They turned against Marisa," he said, referring to the media backlash against her post-Oscar hubris. "They thought she was not respectful, too self-important, playing the star." On the set of *Only You* in Italy, Jewison had managed to keep Downey off drugs, but he couldn't keep the actor—who was married with a young child—from tumbling into a romance with Tomei. "As a father, I was sitting with one, then sitting with the other, trying to keep things cool," he recalls. "But you can't control people's emotions. They were extremely attracted to each other, which worked for the film like gangbusters." At the Harbourfront party after the premiere, the two stars were together again for the first time since the shoot. "It was really embarrassing," recalls Jewison. "Bob Downey had gone back with the wife, and he didn't want to come. So not only do I have to talk him into coming, I have to chaperone him for the entire evening. By now, of course, he's turning on, and the whole thing. Everyone was on something. And I'm just a tired farmer trying to get home."

Piers Handling, meanwhile, grew into his new job as if he were born to it. Running the Toronto festival requires a particular combination of cinephile obsession, political diplomacy and sheer physical stamina. Helga Stephenson bounced back after giving birth in her mid-forties; Wayne Clarkson runs marathons in his fifties; Handling goes climbing in the Himalayas each spring before tackling Cannes. And as the director who would guide the festival into the new millennium, Handling came to personify its ever more vertiginous balancing act between corporate muscle and artistic integrity.

32 SHORT FILMS ABOUT GLENN GOULD

uld's father was curious to know how the filmmakers had come u
th their opening tableau, which shows the pianist walking acros
ice of Lake Simcoe. McKellar nervously told him they had made i
. "I don't know how you thought of that," Gould's father marvelled
always remember Glenn out there walking across the ice when h
s a kid. That's the way I always think of Glenny"

To Die Fo

ANYONE VISITING THE '95 FESTIVAL FROM OUTER SPA
MIGHT HAVE ASSUMED THAT LIFE ON THIS PLANET WAS GOVERN
y cycles of alienation and nihilism, masochism and cruelty, mur
nd suicide. This was the year that Pulp Fiction *had faced off agai*
orrest Gump *at the Oscars, and the gulf between amoral indie in*
ence and moralizing Hollywood sentiment had never been wi
ipping the scales of independent cinema, Pulp Fiction *was the pivo*

PHOTO: JIM STEELE

GUS VAN SANT, 1995

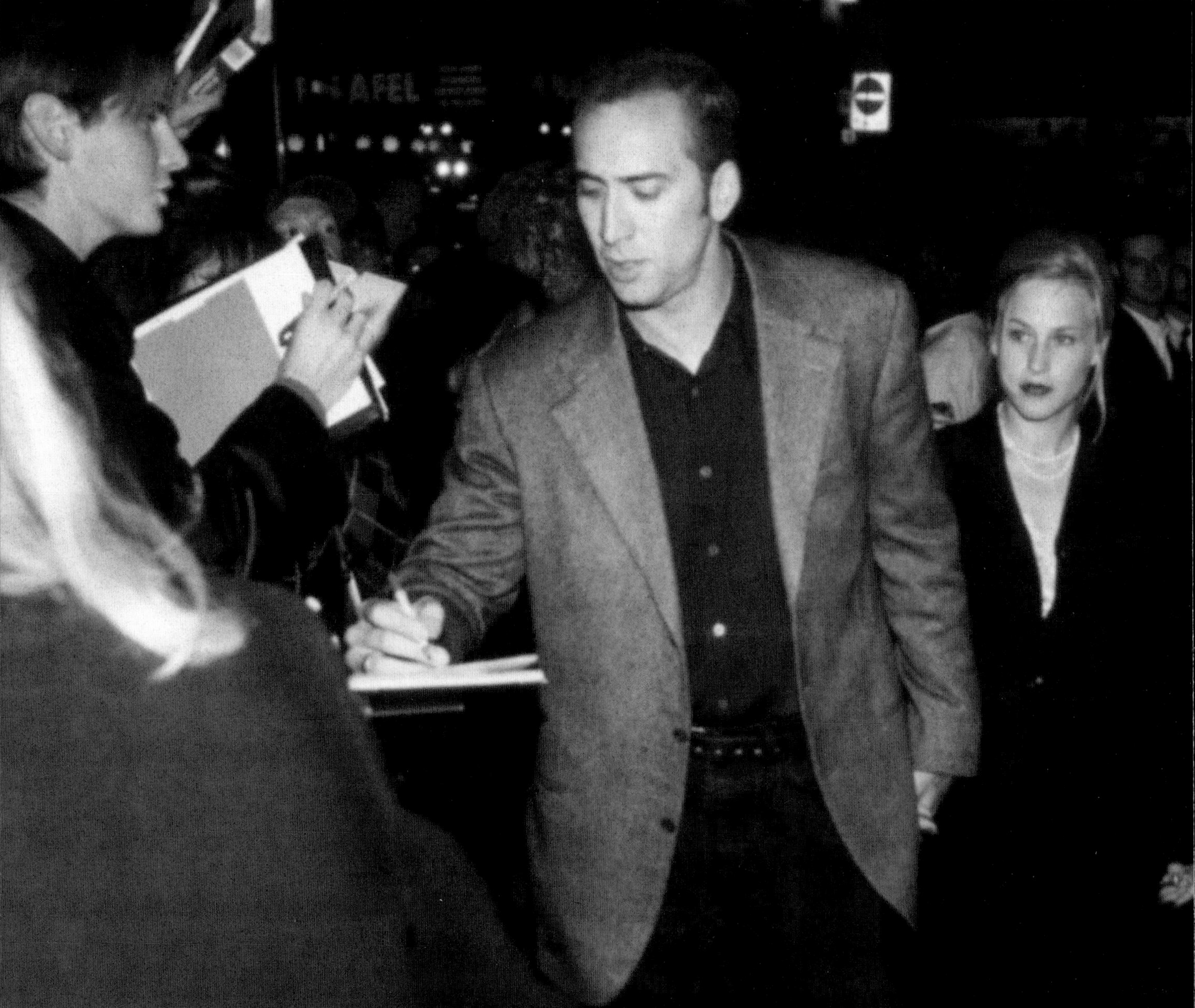

PHOTO: JIM STEELE

movie of the nineties. Tarantino's gonzo extravaganza proved it was possible to subvert linear narrative, shoot scads of tangential dialogue, cast a has-been star in the lead role—and still gross $100 million. It proved that you could joke about a blood-drenched car interior being used for "dead nigger storage" and get away with it. But *Pulp Fiction* was a cheery farce compared to some of the dark adventures that premiered at the twentieth-anniversary Toronto festival in 1995:

A hell-bent Nicolas Cage drinks himself to death, and to an Oscar, in *Leaving Las Vegas*. An unjoking Jack Nicholson strips his emotions to the bone as a father determined to avenge his daughter's death in Sean Penn's *The Crossing Guard*. As a lesbian psychopath with pierced nipples and chain-mail lingerie, Amanda Plummer considers murder the least of her crimes in Michael Winterbottom's *Butterfly Kiss*. The pubescent heroine of *Welcome to the Dollhouse* looks for romance in threats of rape. *Georgia*'s Jennifer Jason Leigh self-destructs onstage as an alcoholic singer. As poet Paul

LEFT, NICOLAS CAGE AND PATRICIA ARQUETTE, 1995; RIGHT, SEAN PENN

PHOTO: JAN BIRD

Cage and Shue, Figgis had two non-bankable stars: "There's a certair idio head I won't mention who said, 'Never ever will I have Nic Cag one of our films.' Well, Nic's done three leading-man roles with tha me studio since then. And Lisa Shue, she was the girl next doo rget it. Lisa Shue as a hooker? Are you kidding?' "

Verlaine in Agnieszka Holland's *Total Eclipse*, David Thewlis kicks a pregnant wife downstairs and sets her hair on fire. In Gregg Araki's *The Doom Generation*, a shotgun blows the head of a Korean convenience-store clerk into a jar of hot-dog relish, where it keeps on screaming. In Nicolas Roeg's *Two Deaths*, Romania's civil war rages around a dinner party of macabre confessions. In *Margaret's Museum*, a Cape Bretonized Helena Bonham Carter goes mad when her man dies in a coal mine. A retired hit man employs a corpse as a punching bag in *Things to Do in Denver When You're Dead*. A woman intent on a TV career seduces a student into killing her husband in *To Die For*. And a nice English lad devises agonizing deaths for family and friends in *The Young Poisoner's Handbook*.

The '95 festival opened with *Le confessionnal*, a coldly disturbing feature debut by Quebec stage sensation Robert Lepage. A mystery set against the backdrop of Alfred Hitchcock filming *I Confess* in Quebec City, it is about identity of every description—a hall of mirrors reflecting past and present, male and female, straight and gay, English

LEFT, LOTHAIRE BLUTEAU AND ROBERT LEPAGE; RIGHT, KRISTIN SCOTT THOMAS, AT CANADIAN FILM CENTRE BARBEQUE, 1995

"Confessionnal *is wonderfully ambitious. It fails in the sense that it doesn't quite work as a thriller. What happens with people as gifted as Atom and Robert is they have an overwhelming desire to break the code. There are certain codes you can't break"*

PHOTO: SAM BARNES

and French, Occident and Orient. Lepage directs the camera with mischievous sleight of hand, cutting from a man shaving with a straight razor to a sink swirling with blood that turns out to be red paint being cleaned from a brush. A mild-mannered Lothaire Bluteau plays the protagonist in a story that is, in the tradition of Quebec cinema, obsessed with fatherhood. But as a claustrophobic puzzle of sexual secrets and repressed guilt, *Le confessionnal* was also reminiscent of Atom Egoyan, suggesting that the two solitudes of Canadian cinema were not so distinct after all.

Landing the North American premiere of Lepage's feature debut was a coup that almost didn't happen. And the politics behind launching the film were as Byzantine as its plot. First of all, Serge Losique, the director of the rival Montreal festival, was desperate to have it for his opening night and told everyone in sight, including the funding agencies, that an important French-Canadian film had no business premiering in Toronto. *Le confessionnal*, meanwhile, had been rejected for the main competition in Cannes. When it opened the Directors' Fortnight instead, co-producer Denise Robert made a public remark about the Cannes competition that could be construed as negative. Losique immediately faxed the comment to Cannes czar Gilles Jacob, who became angry with

ANGELS AND INSECTS

PHOTO: LISI TESHER

LE CONFESSIONNAL

her for criticizing the competition. "As a result," says Handling, "Serge burned a bridge so big with Denise Robert that over her dead body would that film run at the Montreal film festival."

Robert wanted the movie in Toronto. But the distributor, Alliance's Victor Loewy, was resisting for a variety of reasons. After Robert had quietly sold *Le confessionnal*'s international rights to Polygram—a company that was trying to crack Alliance's domination of Canada's domestic distribution—he was in no mood to do her any favours. Also, ever since the grim opening-night gala for *Léolo*, in 1992, Loewy had been leery of exposing challenging films to the Toronto festival's most conservative audience. "I knew *Confessionnal* was not commercial at all," says Loewy, "and wouldn't benefit from the wide exposure to the kind of public they have on opening night. It's a night where the festival has to pay back debts to various politicians and corporations and cultural figures who have nothing to do with culture. This was not the natural clientele for the film. I thought the reception wouldn't be good and it wasn't." Although Loewy is on the Toronto festival board, he's also a close friend of the Montreal festival's Losique. With *Confessionnal*, he says, Toronto was just re-opening its old feud with Montreal. "The only reason Toronto wanted to open *Confessionnal*," he maintains, "was to prevent Montreal from showing it. It was wrong politically and it was wrong for the film. It was a French-Canadian film, financed to a large extent with French-Canadian money. It should have been shown in Montreal."

At the eleventh hour, *Le confessionnal*'s co-producer, David Puttnam, intervened and Loewy finally relented. By then, Handling was in a panic. "I got that film four days before the programme book went to bed," he says. "I had no backup plan. If Victor had said no, I have no idea what I would have opened the festival with."

Looking back on the premiere four years later over breakfast in London, Puttnam concedes that Loewy might have been right. Puttnam remembers that Roy Thomson Hall was not packed. "It was about two-thirds full. It was the wrong venue for the movie. The movie wasn't big and grand enough, and I remember feeling a little awkward. But I was very proud of it," he adds. "*Confessionnal* is wonderfully ambitious. If you imagine it as a movie that sets off to achieve, say, ten things, it achieves seven of them wonderfully well, two of them pretty well, and probably fails at one. It fails in the sense that it doesn't quite work as a thriller. It works as a visual film, as a mystery, but what it hasn't got, ironically, is the Hitchcockian component."

When I met Puttnam that morning, in May of 1999, I had just seen the premiere of *Felicia's Journey* in Cannes, and I told him a number of critics had felt that Egoyan's movie suffered from the same problem. "What happens with people as gifted as Atom and Robert," replied Puttnam, without missing a beat, "is they have an overwhelming desire to, as it were, break the code. There are certain codes you can't break."

WALTER MATTHAU, 1995

PHOTO: JIM STEELE

PHOTO: JIM STEELE

"When I played prostitutes, I had boyfriends and they'd s 'Maybe I should pay you tonight.' No. You can't. There are lir I don't cross. I've never done heroin. What I do is talk to as ma people as I can about their experiences"

Breaking codes, however, is what made movies interesting in the nineties. And while directors such as Lepage and Egoyan subverted the grammar of film, a number of American directors challenged its romantic conventions. Among them, three filmmakers defied expectations with breakthrough hits that premiered at the '95 festival—*Leaving Las Vegas*, *To Die For* and *Welcome to the Dollhouse*—all black-humoured tales of desperation about characters stuck on the wrong side of the American Dream.

A suicide trip scored by Sting, *Leaving Las Vegas* is the ultimate lounge movie. Shooting handheld in Super 16 mm, Mike Figgis swerves his camera through Vegas like a drunken saxophone. The film plays as woozy romance drowning in liquid. Liquid jazz and liquid neon and lots of wet, sexy alcohol. In one delirious scene it all flows together on a poolside patio at the edge of the desert, as Nicolas Cage suckles the Scotch that Elizabeth Shue pours over her breasts—a sunlit slice of ecstasy that shatters as Cage staggers to his feet and falls through a glass table. At the festival, promoters of *Doom Generation* were handing out black-and-red buttons with the slogan EAT FUCK KILL; if *Leaving Las Vegas* had a button, its slogan would be DRINK KISS DIE.

By the time Figgis showed up at the festival, he had no great expectations for the film. In Cage and Shue, he had two non-bankable stars. "Nic wasn't happening then," the director told me, explaining that he hadn't been able to convince studio executives that Cage was worth casting. "He was the man who ate cockroaches, or did other bizarre things in films. They'd say, 'We'd love to do this, but not with Nic Cage.' There's a certain studio head I won't mention who said 'Never *ever* will I have Nic Cage in one of our films.' Well, Nic's done three leading-man roles with that same studio since then. And Lisa Shue, she was the girl next door. 'Lisa Shue as a hooker? Are you kidding?'"

Leaving Las Vegas was rejected by every independent distributor until UA Classics finally agreed to take it. Figgis was proud of the film, and expected to unveil it in Cannes or Berlin. "I thought the French would eat it up," he says. "I was secretly thinking Palme d'Or thoughts, or Golden Bear thoughts." But those thoughts evaporated as the Cannes, Venice and New York film festivals all turned it down. "Nobody wanted it. I remember showing the film to Nic and he said, 'I think it might be a masterpiece, but I wonder if anyone will ever see it.'"

The reaction at the gala premiere in Toronto, however, was "phenomenal," Figgis recalls. Afterwards, he and the stars showed up at a zoo-like party for the film at the Left Bank. I remember seeing Cage make his entrance, his eyes boring a hole through the crowd as bodyguards cleared a path to a roped-off pen at the back of the room. "The party was distressing," says Figgis. "People screaming at each other, a lot of trendy people. A red line between people who were in and people who were out—the VIP area. People gawking. I just wanted to get out and go home. So we went back and had a drink at the hotel."

Now, looking back on the film's unlikely success, the director gives credit to Shue. "She framed a Nic Cage performance to make Nic accessible. Her love for the character was so heartbreaking that you went with it. And Nic's aloofness and coldness became a positive thing. Nic in that context was Jimmy Stewart in a kind of Scott Fitzgerald setting for the nineties. He's a character out of time. In other words he's a quintessential romantic male lead. And she—forget the bustier, the breasts almost popping out—she is the girl next door, the quintessential American woman. A pure-hearted person. These were two absolutely straight-down-the-line American characters who have become flawed by the culture. And alcoholism is a gigantic problem in our culture. Everybody in the audience was either a reformed drunk or related to one. There's not a single person who remained unscathed, and that's why it went all the way to the Oscars."

Cage's Oscar-winning performance was the turning point in his career, and since then he has become a staple of Hollywood action movies. "He's a banker," says Figgis. "In my opinion, he's lost the plot. It's as simple as that. You can do two of those [blockbusters] as long as you balance the emotional books by doing something that has some sacrifice attached to it. If you do five in a row, you may become one of the richest actors in the world—which, at about $20 million a film, I assume Nic has become—but you may start to lose contact with the people in the audience who revered you in the first place because you actually took risks."

In *Leaving Las Vegas*, as a failed screenwriter and terminal drunk, Cage's character seals his commitment to Shue, the gold-hearted hooker, by saying *never ask me to stop drinking*—and he delivers the line with the same dead-eyed, don't-mess-with-me attitude that would become a macho trademark in his action pictures. But behind the fiction of *Leaving Las Vegas* was an autobiographical novel by John O'Brien, who killed himself before the film was released. Only in Hollywood can acting out the failure, and suicide, of the writer who created your role turn into a smart career move.

Bringing a woman's touch to self-destruction, the perennially underrated Jennifer Jason Leigh gave an equally raw performance as an alcoholic singer in Ulu Grosbard's *Georgia.* As her character crashes and burns on a concert stage in front of a big crowd, she sings off-key with such conviction that her vulnerability is almost unbearable. After seeing her portray substance abusers in *Last Exit to Brooklyn, Rush, Dolores Claiborne, Dorothy Parker and the Vicious Circle* and now this, I had to ask Leigh about her method. "I can't drink to save my life," she said, lighting a cigarette. "I'll have a glass of wine occasionally, maybe a margarita. When I played prostitutes, I had boyfriends and they'd say, 'Maybe I should pay you tonight.' No. You can't. There are lines I don't cross. I've never done heroin. What I do is I talk to as many people as I can about their experiences. They talk about this womb-like feeling where everything is so safe and all your muscles and bones melt and your eyelids get heavy and you just feel so good and warm. Heroin must feel fucking great. That's why people get addicted."

It was a good year for uncontainable women in movies, from Amanda Plummer's serial killer in *Butterfly Kiss* to Kristin Scott's proto-feminist in *Angels and Insects*. But the most surprising, and uncharacteristic, performance came from Nicole Kidman in *To Die For.* While *Leaving Las Vegas* staged the demise of the American Dream as tragedy, *To Die For* played it as satire. Director Gus Van Sant had launched all his films at the Toronto festival, and his was the blithely erratic career of an artist unafraid to risk failure. But after the surreal promise of *My Own Private Idaho*, the bohemian savvy of *Drugstore Cowboy*, and the catastrophic muddle of *Even Cowgirls Get the Blues*, with *To Die For* Van Sant placed mainstream America squarely in his sights. Kidman is porcelain-perfect as the small-town TV weather girl who is consumed by the importance of being famous, and who manufactures her own story by coaxing a spaniel-sweet student (Joaquin Phoenix) into murdering her bone-headed husband (Matt Dillon). Van Sant's direction is a dream. Especially the ending: Kidman in a Chanel suit and high heels is led down a snowbank to a frozen lake by a genteel Mafia hit man in the person of David Cronenberg; cut to snow drifting across the ice until—shades of *Orlando*—her pale face and pink suit become faintly visible from below the surface; cut to Illeana Douglas figure-skating

PHOTO: JIM STEELE

victory circles around her grave to Donovan's "Season of the Witch." Based on the Joyce Maynard novel, and scripted by Buck Henry, *To Die For* dissected America's culture of celebrity with a crisp, Warholian wit. But it was less a media satire than a black comedy of suburban manners. And in that sense, it served as an unsentimental precursor to movies such as *The Ice Storm*, *Happiness*, *Very Bad Things*, *Election* and *American Beauty*.

Todd Solondz's feature debut, *Welcome to the Dollhouse*, was the other suburban comedy that struck a chord in '95, and it was a true festival discovery. The film had been rejected by Cannes and Telluride. Like Hal Hartley, Solondz sent a videotape to Toronto unsolicited, and Kay Armatage sent back a fax a few weeks later confirming acceptance. "I was shocked," Solondz told me over coffee one morning in Manhattan. "I'd just bought a fax machine, and I thought it was some prank. Because I was at such a low ebb. My level of confidence in the film was extremely low. I thought the whole endeavour had been such a folly and a mistake and an embarrassment. I suppose success had been very alien to my experience for a long time, so I couldn't imagine it."

As a child of the New Jersey suburbs who grew up as a social outcast, Solondz captured the alienation and horror of adolescence in *Dollhouse* with uncanny veracity, even

PHOTO: HEATHER MCKINNON

"That Sam Mendes! He can say what he wants, but I can in for the kill also. I think his movie is phony and sentimen It's a feel-good movie. People walk out and they just feel gc about themselves in a very false way"

though the protagonist is an eleven-year-old girl. Sitting across from me a few years later, he still looks like a nerd, and speaks with a high, strangled voice, but the thick glasses have cool frames, and there's a suave assurance behind the geek-chic persona. At the festival, recalls Armatage, "he was a huge curiosity. Everybody was completely thrilled by him. He was pretty shy when he came, but when he saw how well the film was being received, he warmed to it."

Dollhouse ignited a bidding war in Toronto. The first offer came from Bingham Ray of October Films. "I wanted it so bad," Ray recalls. "It was this perfect gem. I thought, let's have a go at this. It's raw and dangerous and scary, but this guy is hugely talented and the performances he gets take your breath away. People were chasing it big time. But you gotta be running numbers in your head. How much can we release this for? How much can we afford to spend on it? All these questions you're trying to answer as you're watching the movie." Tom Bernard and Michael Barker eventually snagged *Dollhouse* for Sony Classics, paying $350,000 for a film that cost less that $1 million to make and grossed $5 million. But October and Bingham Ray helped Solondz make his second feature, *Happiness*, which won the Metro Media Award at the '98 Toronto festival after generating major controversy. Set in a New Jersey suburb, *Happiness* intertwines the stories of three sisters with a variety of creepy characters and a number of taboo-shattering scenes. What caused all the fuss was the pedophile father played by Dylan Baker, who drugs and rapes his son's eleven-year-old playmate, then in an excruciating scene tries to explain himself to his son, who asks Dad if he would rape him too. Ron Meyer, president of Universal Studios Inc., which owned October, said he would sooner get hit by a truck before letting his company or its subsidiaries release the picture, which was picked up by Good Machine. Bingham Ray, who has since left October, was furious. "When you buy a company like October," he says, "you have to let it flourish. This isn't Disney and Miramax, where you're branded as the 'family' company so you don't want Harvey to release a film about a gay priest. This is Universal. It's Seagram's for crying out loud—they sell alcohol."

Happiness was adored by many critics but was simply too dark to win over a large audience. A year later, courtesy of DreamWorks, Sam Mendes wowed the festival with his feature debut, *American Beauty*—a far less threatening, and more popular, movie with a strong streak of suburban satire. Solondz says that he was initially asked to direct *American Beauty*. "But I had no interest. Having done *Happiness*, why would I do that? It's not that my work is *about* the suburbs. It's not the focus of what I do, to make some sort of diatribe about what happens in the suburbs."

Mendes expressed a similar fear, of seeing his movie typecast as suburban satire. I asked him about *Happiness*. "I thought it was a really original film in which the writer and filmmaker were cleverer than everybody else onscreen," he said, "and I felt very strongly that I didn't want that to be the case with this movie." When I relayed the comment to Solondz, he was taken aback. "That Sam Mendes! Well, he can say what he wants, but I can go in for the kill also. Rather than defend, I'd rather just attack. I think his movie is phony and I think it's sentimental. When people talk of his transcendent ending, I find it preposterously phony. I find the relationships transparent. It's a feel-good movie. People walk out and they just feel good about themselves in a very false way." They don't call it DreamWorks for nothing.

Somewhere between *Welcome to the Dollhouse* and *American Beauty* something was happening to independent film. The lines were shifting. By the late nineties, a new generation of hotshot directors, following in the wake of *Pulp Fiction*, would lay siege to Hollywood just as Scorsese, Coppola and Altman had done in the seventies. Directors like Sam Mendes, Paul Thomas Anderson, Spike Jonze, Kevin Smith, Mary Harron and Kimberly Peirce. And even more remarkable, they were winning.

'he Shining

'TER A STRING OF OPENING-NIGHT FILMS THAT HAD
:KED OFF FESTIVITIES WITH SUICIDE (DEAD RINGERS, M. BUTTERFLY
confessionnal), *genocide* (Black Robe) *and cat torture* (Léolo), *the
ıck-tie patrons at the '96 festival must have been relieved to see
opening gala that left them with nothing to worry about excep
ıether a flock of Canada geese would find their way back to the farm*
Away Home *was not a Canadian movie. It was a studio film by an*

PHOTO: ROSEMARY GOLDHAR

OPENING NIGHT GALA, 1996

FAR RIGHT, JEFF DANIELS AND ANNA PAQUIN

American, Carroll Ballard, the director of *Never Cry Wolf* and *The Black Stallion*. But the story was shot in Ontario, and inspired by local hero Bill Lishman, who taught geese to fly behind an ultralight aircraft. And with a panoramic shot of the birds winging past Toronto's CN Tower, this featherweight fable ushered in a festival that was decidedly more upbeat than usual. From the piano glissandos of *Shine* to the rock-'n'-roll froth of *That Thing You Do!*—the closing-night offering from Tom Hanks—this was a festival with a song in its heart and a spring in its step.

The gala audience was more than willing to overlook the shortcomings of Hanks's directorial debut, a sixties nostalgia piece about a fictional band of wannabe Beatles. Even if he was not the next Orson Welles, *That Thing You Do!* was a feel-good flick with closing credits you could dance to. Hanks says he wrote the film to get some perspective on the insanity of his own sudden celebrity. But for the festival audience, the main draw *was* his celebrity—the simple fact that he was there.

He was not alone. The '96 festival attracted a bonanza of American stars, from Faye Dunaway to Dustin Hoffman, including a record number of actors making their debuts behind the camera. Al Pacino showed off *Looking For Richard*, in which he performs, directs and deconstructs the royal chaos of *Richard III*. Stanley Tucci and Campbell Scott served up *Big Night*, a tale of two brothers trying to save a dying Italian restaurant with a single meal. Angelica Huston launched *Bastard Out of Carolina*, a harrowing incest drama. Matthew Broderick worked both sides of the camera in *Infinity*. Kevin Spacey tried his hand at a heist movie with *Albino Alligator*. In *Losing Chase*, Kevin Bacon put Helen Mirren through her paces as a woman on the verge of recovering from a nervous breakdown. And in *Trees Lounge*, Steve Buscemi directed himself as a small-town barfly who hits on an underage girl while driving an ice-cream truck. Meanwhile, Cher and Demi Moore sent the media into a tizzy as they premiered *If These Walls Could Talk*, a trio of abortion dramas that Moore co-produced for HBO and Cher helped direct.

The problem with Hollywood stars is that they require high maintenance. They move in their own world, and tend to be uninterested in the life of the festival. At the closing-night soiree for *That Thing You Do!* Tom Hanks and Rita Wilson dutifully did the "entry walk" for the cameras, then promptly left. As for Cher and Demi, according to party organizer Barb Hershenhorn, "all they wanted to know was how long they had to stay at the press conference and how long they had to spend at the party." They were both flown in on private jets. Demi was travelling with her personal trainer, her make-up artist and her hairdresser. Exactly why she needed a hairdresser remains a mystery: she was still wearing her military buzz-cut from *G.I. Jane*.

One visiting icon who did not require much maintenance was Jean-Luc Godard, who was at the festival again with *For Ever Mozart*. All he wanted was access to a tennis court each morning. Director Peter Mettler attended a dinner with Godard and Madeleine Assas, the young star of *For Ever Mozart*. "He was just sitting there staring at his salad," Mettler recalls. "He got up to leave and she said, 'You better follow him, he might not

PHOTO: ROSEMARY GOLDHAR

FLY AWAY HOME

From the piano glissandos of Shine *to the rock-'n'-ro[ll] froth of* That Thing You Do!*, this was a festival with [a] song in its heart and a spring in its step*

come back. He does that. He just disappears sometimes.'" Later that night, Mettler ran into Godard in a hotel sports bar, where he was by himself, nursing a beer. Mettler wondered how to approach him. "Anything you would ask seemed ridiculous," he says, "but we managed to have a conversation. He started talking about youth, and how all the people in the sports bar were young but actually old in spirit. He talked about money, and how, when he was working in America, producers gave him handfuls of cash."

Godard lived up to his image, treating the media to cryptic pronouncements about the death of film and droll one-liners. Before a rapt press conference, he idly suggested that the French New Wave of the fifties marked the end of cinematic history rather than a new beginning. Then, asked about American studios remaking French movies, he said, "Hollywood has no ideas and French filmmakers have no money."

Godard is a contradiction in the flesh, a high priest of cinema who has lost his congregation, who makes films that are rarely seen outside the pressurized confines of a festival. And even festivals are not what they used to be, as he lamented in an interview with Geoff Pevere in *The Globe and Mail*. When Pevere asked him what overlooked films he might programme at a festival, Godard replied: "I wouldn't. Maybe when festivals were like they were before, when there weren't many movies, maybe I might show three or four. . . . Today there are two hundred movies at a festival. Too many. . . . Toronto is interesting for people because they get to see what is being done all around the world. But for me, it's like corpses in a sense . . . like dead people who are resurrected for a few days and then dead again. It looks to me like that, seeing all those people. Haunting the corridors of a big hotel."

The festival produces a bizarre inversion of box-office reality. "One year I spent an afternoon trying to get in to see these quite obscure films in the festival," recalls director

FOR EVER MOZART

Michael Winterbottom, who has come to Toronto with half a dozen features. "I wandered from one queue to another, and I couldn't get into anything. In the end, I just went around the corner and saw *Natural Born Killers* and there were eight people in the cinema. You try to go to some Iranian film at the festival and it's packed." The lineup to see *For Ever Mozart* at the Uptown One stretched all the way around the block. When Godard entered the theatre, he received a standing ovation. As I watched the film that night, I understood how a festival projection can have the thrill of live theatre: what transpires between your eye and the screen that night will never happen again. Even if you see the film a second time, the chemistry will be different.

It was thrilling to watch a fresh Godard projected on a huge screen, like magnified poetry, to have your breath taken away by the surgical rigour of the cuts, the violent beauty of images that do not belong together. The "story" unfolds as four films in search of an *auteur*, as a director abandons a film to produce a play by Musset amid the war in Bosnia, then resumes the film, only to give up in frustration as he tries to direct an actress to say a single word. Along with the war, the story keeps exploding, a fragmen-

ndling, who climbs in the Himalayas each spring before Cannes me to personify the festival's balancing act between corporate muscl d artistic integrity. "Art cinema and commercial cinema," said Godar e more segregated from each other than ever"

PHOTO: TYRONE KERR

ABOVE, HANDLING AND GODARD, 1996

tation bomb lobbed by the old master of deconstruction. Back from the dead like Bob Dylan. It was so strange to feel the Uptown One, home of the Hollywood blockbuster, quake with the mortars of Godard's soundtrack—the revenge of the art house. God knows what the movie was about, or not. Did Godard know? In the Q&A, he deflected interpretation, and adoration, with deadpan calm as aspiring director Jeremy Podeswa nervously moderated. *For Ever Mozart* seemed to be about the impossibility of art and the inevitability of politics. I didn't understand it and don't remember much about it, although I immediately wanted to see it again. But that would not be possible. *For Ever Mozart* was not forever. It was never released in North America, not even on video. Now I'm not even sure what I saw. If a film falls in the forest and no one sees . . .

"Art cinema and commercial cinema," said Godard, "are more segregated from each other than ever before." Film festivals try to straddle the two worlds. On the one hand, they serve as sanctuaries for endangered species of cinema that can't survive in the marketplace; on the other, they provide a showcase for movies on the verge of commercial release. And as the stars descended on Toronto in 1996, Piers Handling was beginning to worry. "The real challenge now," he told me at the time, "is to maintain a balance. There's more and more pressure to act as a showcase."

No one has applied the pressure more strategically than Miramax. "Everyone has learnt

PHOTO: TYRONE KERR

from them," says Handling. "Miramax has used festivals better than anyone else to get their agenda across, to create a profile for themselves, and to work films." In 1996, Miramax used Toronto to launch *Kolya*, a heart-warming Czech movie about a cellist who gets stuck taking care of a five-year-old boy. "It's a great place to launch," Miramax executive Cynthia Schwartz told *The Washington Post* the following year. "You don't get this kind of U.S. press contingent anywhere else in the world. The audience was incredibly enthusiastic and *Kolya* goes from being another foreign film to one the press has to pay attention to."

Of all the films showcased in '96, none got more attention than *Shine*, an uplifting drama based on the true story of an eccentric pianist driven mad by the pressure of playing Rachmaninov. *Shine* had already created a sensation at Sundance. And its Australian director, Scott Hicks, flew to Toronto directly from the Venice festival with the roar of a nine-minute standing ovation still ringing in his ears, his triumph dampened only by the fact that his wife had to be lifted onto the plane in a wheelchair after tripping on the red carpet going into the theatre. Toronto would give *Shine* its first real test with a North American audience. But when Hicks walked into the vast Roy Thomson Hall for the gala premiere, he says, "my heart sank. I thought, my little film is just going to get lost in here. How is it going to hold its own? It can't possibly speak to two thousand people at once. But the presentation was phenomenal. Not only did it not get lost, but the sound was the best I've heard with *Shine* anywhere. The sound was *gigantic*, and I'm not just talking about volume, but its spread. It was on a colossal symphonic scale."

Shine won both the Air Canada People's Choice Award and the journalists' Metro Media

LEFT, ANGELICA HUSTON, 1996; ABOVE, HANDLING, ELIZABETH HURLEY AND HUGH GRANT

Award, then went on to score seven Oscar nominations, including a Best Actor victory for Geoffrey Rush. This was the year that the tide of independent film clearly turned, with only one of the Best Picture nominees, *Jerry Maguire*, being produced by a Hollywood studio. The festival was developing a knack for helping to propel small films to the Oscars, including gems such as *Il Postino* and *Breaking the Waves*.

But the studios remain leery of launching their products at the festival. They offer up the weird ones that they don't know what to do with. And, taking advantage of a captive press corps, they piggyback media junkets onto the festival for movies that are scheduled for release in the following weeks, even if they aren't in the festival programme. "The studios are more careful about the films they give to Toronto, as opposed to Cannes," explains Piers Handling, "because it's a domestic festival. There's much more at stake. If there's damage control needed in Toronto, they can't fix it. If a film doesn't do well in Cannes, they can fix it, because there are just a few key North American critics. And they can fix those critics." Fix them? Yes, and Miramax does it better than anyone, he adds. "Harvey has people who will work diligently on critics. I've seen them in action. When they know a critic doesn't like their film, they'll go after him until they make him doubt his opinion."

SHINE

Filmmakers sometimes have to push studios to get their work into the festival. In 1996, Warner Bros. was reluctant to give Toronto the world premiere of *Michael Collins*, Neil Jordan's breathless epic about the struggle for Irish independence. "Warners didn't want to show it, but eventually they caved in," says its producer, Steve Woolley. "It created a bit of bad will between us." As it turned out, Warners' worries about the movie were well founded: the festival could not save *Michael Collins*, which tanked at the North American box office. Woolley blames that partly on a resistance to Irish politics. "*The Crying Game* had enough politics for American audiences. With *Michael Collins*, it was too much. Are the IRA good or bad? Whose side are we on? In the end that hurt us.

"But in the final analysis," he adds, "something that hurt us really badly on that film was casting Julia Roberts. We had the film set up, it was ready to go. Liam Neeson, Aidan

Quinn, Stephen Rea, they were happy with. The budget was set. Then we got a call from an agent saying could you meet Julia. I was like, 'Jeez, Julia Roberts. We've only got this much in our budget.' 'That's okay.' 'We can only fly her over club class.' 'That's okay.' 'She won't get any special trailer treatment.' 'That's okay.' Nothing I said would shock them. So we met with Julia and she was so great. We thought her Irish accent was fine. And she was great in the film. She was a dream. Then we released it in North America, and there was this carping. What I realized, watching the film in Toronto, was when Julia Roberts came onto the screen, looking as dowdy as she could look, I felt an unease in the audience. Once she came on, they suddenly questioned the film. 'Am I watching a Hollywood film, or am I watching a real story?' It wasn't her performance. It was, 'What's she doing in this kind of movie?'"

In Canadian cinema, there was no room for that kind of confusion. Our only movie with Hollywood stars that year was Cronenberg's *Crash*, and no one could mistake it for a Hollywood movie. *Crash* was never considered for opening night. After dropping it on Cannes like a Molotov cocktail, its producers felt that putting it in the Toronto festival would be redundant. But *Crash* set the tone for Canadian cinema in 1996, as a variety of young directors unveiled films that enhanced our reputation for breaking sexual taboos onscreen.

Vancouver's Lynne Stopkewich created a sensation with her debut feature, *Kissed*, adapted from Barbara Gowdy's short story about a necrophiliac embalmer. The movie picked up worldwide distribution at the festival and launched the career of Molly Parker, a remarkable actress who managed to make a sympathetic heroine of a woman who enjoys sex with dead white males. Toronto's John Greyson followed *Zero Patience*, his AIDS musical, with *Lilies*, a sexual-Gothic intrigue involving young boys and a Catholic priest in rural Quebec at the turn of the century. In *Hustler White*, porn provocateur Bruce La Bruce led a guided tour of the gay sex trade in Los Angeles, featuring such pastimes as amputee fetishism. And Deepa Mehta returned from her homeland with *Fire*, a feminist fable of lesbian romance that ignited some heated controversy in India. However, the Toronto-City Award for best Canadian feature went to a scandal-free labour of theatrical love, David Wellington's definitive adaptation of *Long Day's Journey into Night*, with William Hutt and Martha Henry reprising their stage roles. Toronto filmmakers have an affinity for dark, interior dramas that offer no escape, but it would be hard to find material any darker or more interior than this play. Instead of taking the play outdoors, Wellington did the opposite, intensifying the claustrophobia.

KISSED

Although none of those pictures were deemed sufficiently mainstream for opening night, the following year the festival opened with what would be the most highly acclaimed movie in the history of Canadian cinema. In 1997, fifteen years after projecting his student film on the sidewalk, Atom Egoyan celebrated a breakthrough with *The Sweet Hereafter*, which won three prizes in Cannes and went on to receive Oscar nomi-

WEET HEREAFTER; THE HANGING GARDEN

nations for best director and adapted screenplay. Egoyan's layered rendering of the Russell Banks novel, about the aftermath of a school bus crash, was a quiet revelation. And Sarah Polley's performance as a crash survivor waking from an incestuous spell would make her a star. But the movie arrived at the festival with eerie timing. I'd written a cover profile of Polley for *Maclean's*; at the last minute, as it was going to press, it was pulled from the cover. Princess Diana had just died in a car crash.

The '97 festival opened with a movie about mourning at a time when mourning was all anyone could talk about. Instead of the usual loop of movie clips, Diana's funeral played on the TVs at the media junkets, and at an event fuelled by celebrity, the subject insinuated itself at every turn. In a state-of-the-festival essay on opening night, *Globe and Mail* critic Rick Groen wrote: "A pop culture that is driven so single-mindedly by rough commerce and peopled so abundantly by empty celebrities appears to be speeding through a dark tunnel on a drunken collision course. At its best, in those endangered yet not-quite-extinct moments when art and glamour and wide-eyed innocence converge, the Toronto film festival seems like a temporary U-turn in that destructive course." The zeitgeist works in strange ways. A year after Cronenberg's *Crash* had been attacked as pornographic for making a fetish of the car wreck, everywhere the mainstream media were doing what amounted to the same thing. As Salman Rushdie pointed out in *The New Yorker*, in a culture that "routinely sexualizes" both the automobile and the celebrity, the ideas and themes of Cronenberg's film—a collision between the camera and the car—were "lethally acted out in the car accident that killed Diana."

The Sweet Hereafter, about a crash that kills eleven children, offered a sombre fable about the death of innocence. And it ushered in a festival saturated with films about lost children: the Birmingham children killed by a bomb in Spike Lee's *4 Little Girls*, the refugee children in Michael Winterbottom's *Welcome to Sarajevo* and Ademir Kenovic's *The Perfect Circle*, the little boy who thinks he's a girl in Alain Berliner's *Ma vie en rose*, the young daughter who discovers her father's dark secret in Kasi Lemmons's *Eve's*

PHOTO: SANDY MIDDLETON

PHOTO: JOELLE MEDINA

OPPOSITE, PARKER POSEY; ABOVE, CHER AND DEMI MOORE, 1996

Hollywood stars require high maintenance. Demi Moore was travelling with her personal trainer, her make-up artist and her hairdresser. Exactly why she needed a hairdresser remains a mystery: she was still wearing her military buzz-cut from G.I. Jane

Bayou, the young Dalai Lama of Jean-Jacques Annaud's *Seven Years in Tibet*—and the obese teenager who hangs himself from a tree in *The Hanging Garden*.

A magic realist tale of a gay son trying to reconcile with his dysfunctional family, *The Hanging Garden* was the surprise hit of the festival. This $1-million first feature provoked a bidding war in which MGM snapped up the U.S. rights for $500,000. And no one was more surprised than the movie's Halifax director, Thom Fitzgerald, when it won the Air Canada People's Choice Award. This is the only time in the festival's history that the prize has gone to an English-Canadian film—and the only French-Canadian film to win it was Denys Arcand's *The Decline of the American Empire* (1986). Fitzgerald's movie also shared the $25,000 Toronto-City Award for best Canadian feature with Egoyan's *The Sweet Hereafter*. Egoyan, who by this point was behaving like the de facto ambassador for Canadian cinema, declared that the festival's success "is a testament that we can have a showcase of culture without having to have a showcase of celebrity."

As if.

American

IN 1997, THE FESTIVAL SEEMED TO ENTER A NEW STRATOSPHEF

IT WAS THE YEAR THAT A ROADIE FROM THE ROLLING STONES STOPP

by the office to pick up a couple of programme books for the bai and the year Mick Jagger strolled into a Miramax party at Pre unannounced and chatted up Helena Bonham Carter. It was the y the new Rosewater Supper Club stockpiled a small fortune in Hava cigars, Iranian caviar, and Belvedere vodka, giving the Bistro 990 cro another nightspot where they could drink until four in the morning the days of stars slumming after hours at festival booze cans w a distant memory. It was a year thick with celebrity. Bombshell K

PHOTO: TYRONE KERR

BEN STILLER, 1998

Boogie

21

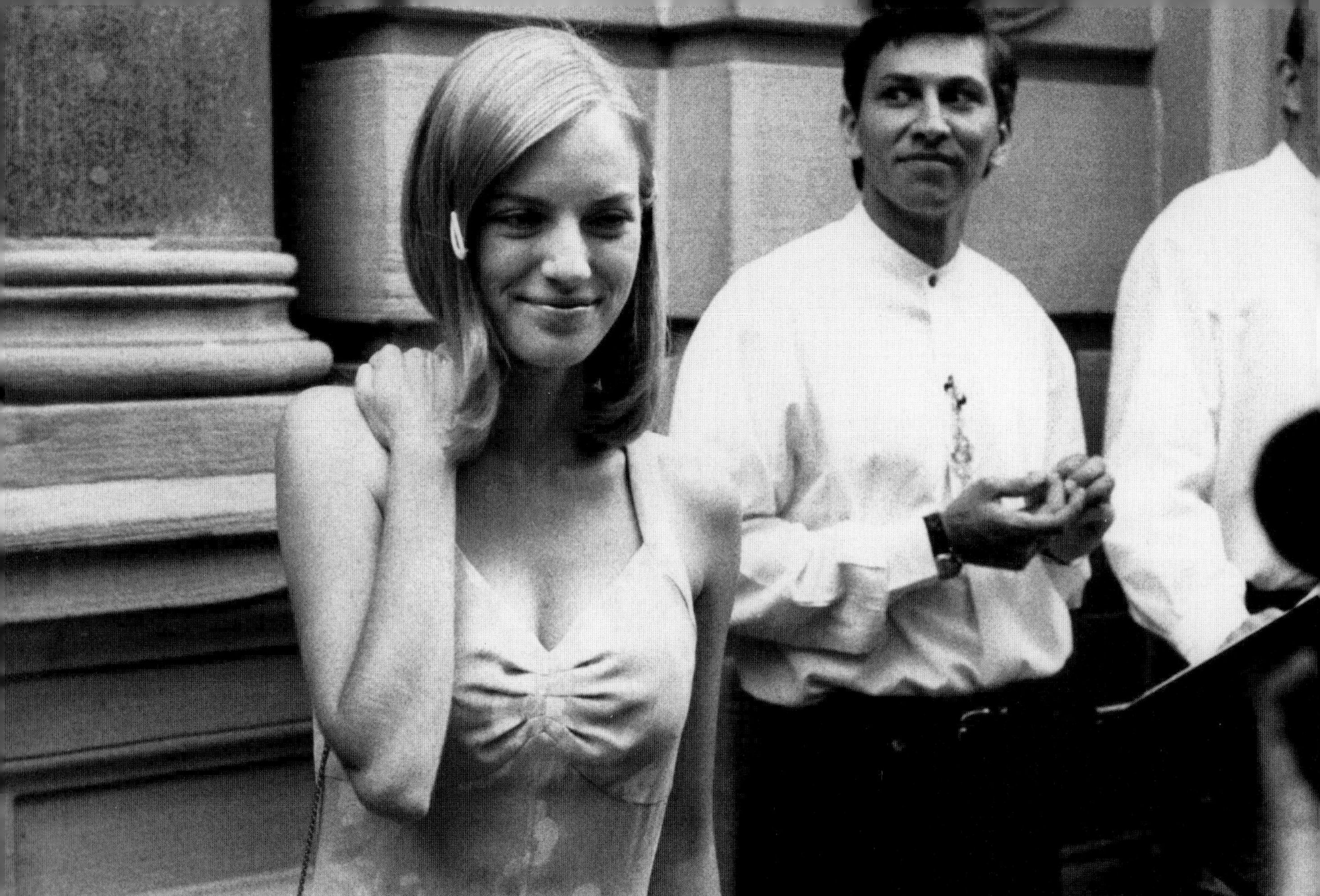

PHOTO: DOUG MACLELLAN

Basinger christened the launch of *L.A. Confidential*. Brad Pitt glowed like a gold Buddha at the closing-night premiere of *Seven Years in Tibet*. And in this week of Princess Di hysteria, celebrity was a loaded word. Michèle Maheux, then festival communications director, fielded anxious calls from the studios, who wanted to know what would be done to control the paparazzi. "This is Toronto," she told them, "and frankly, we've never had a problem." The festival even accredited a couple of paparazzi so they would play by the rules.

Still, everyone was nervous about Pitt's red-carpet appearance on closing night. "We had tons of security," recalls Nuria Bronfman, then the festival's gala coordinator. "The studio was really concerned. It was the first time we'd hired security for the red carpet. And it was the first really long red carpet we'd ever had. It was Brad Pitt so we got an extra long one." But Pitt threw his handlers for a loop when, instead of stepping out of the limo onto the carpet, he got out on the other side—then strolled across the street to sign autographs for a mob of two hundred screaming fans behind a barricade. "It was a sea of women basically," says Bronfman. "When we realized what was happening, we went over and finally got him onto the red carpet. It was incredibly exciting."

Celebrities were so ubiquitous at the '97 festival they were even harassing each other. At the premiere of *The Edge*, Anthony Hopkins and Alec Baldwin waited patiently while

LEFT, SARAH POLLEY, 1997; RIGHT, KEVIN SPACEY

PHOTO: ALEX NEUMANN

L.A. CONFIDENTIAL

BRAD PITT, 1997

SEVEN YEARS IN TIBET

"We had tons of security. The studio was really concerned. It was t first really long red carpet we'd ever had. It was Brad Pitt, so we got extra long one . . . there was a sea of women"

PHOTO: HAIDEE MALKIN

director Lee Tamahori introduced the film with a speech that dragged on for twenty minutes, until finally the lights went down and the unmistakable voice of Danny DeVito could be heard shouting from the audience: "Geez, this film better be good."

That year, the festival also witnessed the wildest bidding war in its history. Robert Duvall had spent $4 million of his own money to make *The Apostle*, in which he directs himself as a charismatic Southern preacher trying to escape his past. Until the Toronto premiere, no one had seen the movie except Duvall, his editor and his co-producer, Robert Carliner. "Once we were accepted into the festival," says Carliner, "it became this full-court press to build the frenzy leading up to it. We did everything we could to maximize the heat. The card that we held was that no one had seen the film and everyone was desperate to see it before the festival. We became paranoid that someone was going to pay off someone at the lab to get a copy."

Tensions were running high at the premiere, where the rival distributors sat together in a reserved section. Half an hour into the movie, they began to slip out of the theatre one by one. "Bobby was oblivious to it," Carliner recalls. "But I was very conscious of these key people leaving the theatre. I didn't know what was going on. We went into the lobby afterwards and saw all these distributors huddled around our sales agent, people on cell phones." By midnight Miramax and October were slugging it out. Harvey Weinstein was in New York, bargaining by phone—he had watched *The Apostle* at a simultaneous private screening that night. Bingham Ray, October's buyer, had left the Toronto premiere after forty-five minutes to make his bid. He was desperate to get the film. October had just been bought by Universal that summer and was itching to take on Miramax. "We were dealing with the studio's money, the house money," Ray explains, "and we wanted to stir it up, to send a signal. There are all kinds of reasons to buy movies. The right reasons are because you love them and there's an audience for them and you can build long-lasting relationships with the people who made them. Then there's just trying to get on the map in a big, sexy way. October wasn't bought by Universal to be a nice high-end art-house company. They wanted a vehicle to really compete with Miramax. I think that's folly. Harvey had become a serious mogul. At October, we were just getting our feet wet."

Bingham Ray pulled Duvall's agent, Cassian Elwes, into October's office at the Sheraton. "It's the old thing—you never let the guy get out of the room," he says. "But Cassian had to check with Duvall. Then he fielded offers from Miramax, back and forth and back and forth. At one point we felt we were being really jerked around. I didn't like the smell of it. And we pulled out. This was two or three in the morning. The price was up to $7.5 million. Then Cassian split. He ran down the hallway. He escaped. I came back, despairing that we couldn't keep him in the room. This pressurized deal-making was clouding our judgment. I'd never operated like that before. I don't believe you can see forty-five minutes of a movie and make a decision."

October finally bought *The Apostle* for $5 million. Harvey Weinstein later claimed he didn't even want the movie, that he was only jacking up the price. "He said he was just jerking our chain," says Ray, "and it could have been that we were being played, because we were susceptible to being played. But the movie did $25 million, Duvall was nominated for best actor, and in North America it was a huge success for us, even if we paid an outrageous amount of money to get it."

Carliner looks back on the *Apostle* premiere like a wild night in Vegas. "It's spinning the wheel, putting $4 million on black seven and hoping you land it," he says. "Had we not closed the deal that night in Toronto, the next morning the bottom feeders would have closed in, offering bargain-basement prices." Duvall, on the phone from his house in Los Angeles, tells his side of the story. "We were told that the Toronto film festival was maybe the most important in the world in terms of distribution and making deals. It was kind of an exciting process. I'd never been in on that before. We went from the screening to a private dinner party, and after about the first course all the bartering started. Finally I said, 'Let's cut it off. Let's don't get greedy. Let's go for what they've offered.' We didn't want to blow it. It wasn't the greatest offer. It could have been twice what it was. But at least I got my money back plus change."

ALEC BALDWIN AND KIM BASINGER, 1997

PHOTO: ALEX NEUMANN

MONICA POTTER AND DONALD SUTHERLAND, 1998

While Robert Duvall flogged a tale of old-time religion, an American filmmaker forty years his junior created a sensation around an ode to old-time pornography. Paul Thomas Anderson's *Boogie Nights* was the most anticipated and talked-about movie at the '97 festival. This sprawling epic about a "family" of porn stars and sleaze merchants in late-seventies Los Angeles tore up the screen with the kinetic virtuosity of a junior *Goodfellas*. Like Scorsese's film, it was a seventies nostalgia piece, the crash-and burn saga of a young man who is adopted by a local patriarch, embarks on a cocaine-fuelled ride to the top, then falls from grace when the soulless entrepreneurs of the eighties move into the business. Novice actor "Marky" Mark Wahlberg carried the film on his shoulders, and in his Calvins, with the swagger of a young John Travolta. And Anderson, at the age of twenty-seven, let go with the kind of whiz-bang, bravura filmmaking that had people calling him the new Quentin Tarantino—from the unbearably tense scene of a drug dealer setting off firecrackers in his living room as we wait for the shootout to the denouement in which Marky Mark unzips his pants to reveal the year's most astonishing special effect.

Three years later, when Anderson was in town to accept the Toronto film critics' award for *Magnolia*, he told me he wished that movie had also premiered at the festival. "But it was not ready in time. I look at what did premiere here—*American Beauty*—and the festival gave it an unbeatable launch. I remember when *Boogie Nights* was here and what that did. It was insane." Anderson, however, had resisted the idea of bringing *Boogie Nights* to the festival. "I had to be talked into Toronto by the studio because I wasn't done with the film and I didn't want to show an unfinished print. There was still work to be done on the colour timing and the sound mix in the last two or three reels." Arriving

"I remember when Boogie Nights *was here. It was insane. T laughs in all the right places, the shocks in all the right plac Just the perfect audience reaction. It was slightly misleadir It led me to believe I had a movie that was going to make $1 million and get standing ovations around the country"*

PHOTO: HAIDEE MALKIN

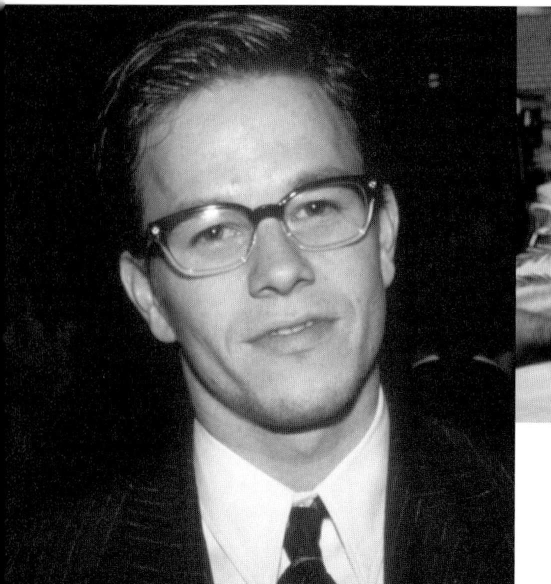

BOOGIE NIGHTS

FAR LEFT, MARK WAHLBERG

PHOTO: ROSEMARY GOLDHAR

in Toronto, he was told the press screenings had gone through the roof, but he did not believe it until the premiere. "I sat next to Marky and when we got the reaction that we got, I was fuckin' blown away. The laughs in all the right places, the shocks in all the right places. The dick at the end. Just the perfect audience reaction. It was slightly misleading. It led me to believe I had a movie that was going to make $100 million and get standing ovations around the country."

Anderson is in the forefront of a generation of young filmmakers who are laying siege to Hollywood in a way that hasn't been seen since the heyday of Scorsese, Coppola and Kubrick. And he seems to be taking his cues from that generation as much as from his own. In casting Tom Cruise for *Magnolia*, Anderson met Stanley Kubrick on the set of *Eyes Wide Shut*. Kubrick told him he'd watched *Boogie Nights* by himself in his private screening room, changing the reels. "He'd watch one reel," says Anderson, "then he'd go back to the booth, watch reel two, reel three, four and on. It's a two-and-a-half-hour movie. It must have taken him five hours to go through it." Anderson has also struck up a close friendship with Warren Beatty. Initially, Beatty had considered playing Jack Horner, the porn king in *Boogie Nights* portrayed by Burt Reynolds. "But he wanted a moral moment at the end of the film where someone could explain that porno was wrong," says Anderson. "After he saw it, he called me up and said, 'I was wrong, it's there, I didn't see it in the script.' I just wasn't good enough in articulating it. I would say to him, 'The good thing here is that I'm confused about porno. You've got to see that. I love it; it disgusts me. I can't tell you that porno is bad. I like watching it too much.' And he'd say, 'How would you feel if your daughter did it?' 'Terrible! But I'm still going to rent another porno movie if I'm feeling frisky enough.'"

Beatty has become a mentor of sorts. "He's someone to really learn from and listen to," says Anderson. "I think he's a genius. And he keeps his eye on everything. There's a nice feeling that I get—that I'm self-conscious of Warren over my shoulder." Anderson looks around his suite. "I think he's in this room right now. He just has that thing, that sixth sense. The phone will ring at just the right time, and he'll be on the other end going, 'What are you doing? What are you saying?'"

CATE BLANCHETT AND DIRECTOR SHEKHAR KAPUR ON THE SET OF ELIZABETH

Anderson is also close to Quentin Tarantino. They got to know each other after *Boogie Nights* came out and critics began to hail its director as Tarantino II. "There was a lot of pressure on me to say something bad about him," says Anderson, so he asked his publicist, who also represented Quentin, to put them in touch. "I called him up and we talked. We just started drinking and became friends." Anderson insists that he's not influenced by Tarantino's work so much as by the films that influenced them both. "Quentin and I have the exact same movie library. We've both seen Stanley Kubrick's movies, and we know how to use music ironically in violent or funny situations. The influence that Quentin has is the fact that I can get a movie made."

Only Canadia around with a is when he pr

Although they are both gonzo directors keen on defying narrative convention, what distinguishes Anderson from his pal is a streak of old-fashioned sentiment. As a child of the post–*Pulp Fiction* generation, he allows that *Pulp Fiction* "completely changed movies—it's one of the most important films ever made, and God knows I love it. But there's an emotional distance in that movie that people are now responding to. They want to take all there is to gain from *Pulp Fiction*—the ability to get a movie made, how to structure it, who to cast, what budget to make it on—and now they're applying real heart and soul to it. Quentin didn't put heart and soul into that movie. And I get mad at him for not making me more emotionally connected to his movies. Because that's what I love. I love *Terms of Endearment* or *Ordinary People* as much as *Pulp Fiction*."

Tarantino's influence seemed ubiquitous in the late nineties. At times it was exhilarating, as in *Run Lola Run*, German director Tom Tykwer's amphetamine thriller about a red-haired heroine who sprints through Berlin with a twenty-minute deadline to save her lover—a real-time sequence that is played in three versions, with butterfly-wing beats of fate changing the consequences in each one. (At the jammed festival press screening of *Run Lola Run*, distributors seemed as frantic to see it as Lola was to get across town; Sony Classics snapped up the rights on the eve of the first public screening.) Elsewhere, the Tarantino Effect was more alarming. Perhaps Q.T. should not be held responsible for his imitators, but at the '98 festival, the new cinema of cruelty took a dire turn. *Boogie Nights*, with its mom-and-pop porn trade in the Valley, offered an almost reassuring vision of family values compared to much of the American fare. There was Larry Clark's

PHOTO: MARTIN MORDECAI

SAMUEL L. JACKSON, 1997

Another Day in Paradise, a blood-and-drugs road movie with James Woods and Melanie Griffith scarily well-cast as junkie thieves who take a teenage couple on a Bonnie-and-Clyde family outing. And if you didn't like the scene of Melanie jamming the syringe in her neck, there was one just like it in *Permanent Midnight*, starring Ben Stiller as a screenwriter who leaves his infant daughter alone in the car while he scores some smack and shoots up in the vicinity of his jugular vein.

There was also a spate of black comedies, from *Happiness*, Todd Solondz's acidic vision of suburban purgatory, to *Clay Pigeons*, David Dobkin's smart-ass film noir about murder in a dead-end town. But *Very Bad Things* took black comedy about as far as it could go. This was a suburban satire in Grand Guignol overdrive, a morality tale about men who will never, ever be able to clean up their mess, physically or morally. The mess is a drug-crazed bachelor party in a Vegas hotel room and cleaning it up means burying an Asian hooker in the desert, and that's just the beginning. There are priceless moments—when the bride (Cameron Diaz) hears her fiancé confess to multiple murders that began with *killing* a hooker, her reaction is: "You *slept* with a hooker?" But this

ould cast Pulp Fiction*'s Samuel L. Jackson as a heavy who walks n case that actually contains a violin—the only time he gets tough s room service and asks not to be disturbed*

VERY BAD THINGS

LEFT, CAMERON DIAZ, CHRISTIA SLATER AND JOHN FAVREAU, 19

The Very Bad Things *party was emblematic of all the very bad things about the festival. Polygram's Judy Holm was blocked from taking a guest up to the VIP section, even though she was the host—"it took me twenty minutes to realize it was my party"*

PHOTO: ROSEMARY GOLDHAR

is a cake-and-eat-it movie. Let the camera linger on the hooker's naked bleeding body, but tack on a moral epilogue showing all the bad men getting their comeuppance, flailing about as paraplegics on a suburban lawn. I saw *Very Bad Things* at an early-morning press screening the same day that *The Ken Starr Report* first hit the media. Between reading Monica Lewinsky's moist diary and weathering the movie, you felt the world was a more dismal place than the day before.

At the festival, the boys from *Very Bad Things* did their best to live up to the title. Director Peter Berg and his cast tore up the party circuit with a posse that included Vince Vaughn and Janeane Garofalo of *Clay Pigeons*, and Ben Stiller of *Permanent Midnight*. Egos were a little fragile. Diaz had just split up with Matt Dillon. And Stiller had just split up with Garofalo—at parties they worked hard to show each other they could have fun with new people. Stiller worked so hard one night, past 4 a.m., that he blew off several interviews the next day complaining of "a stomach thing." Later he apologized to *The Toronto Star*'s Peter Howell that he'd been on "a self-destructive tear." A devastated Peter Berg, meanwhile, conducted interviews from his bed the morning after drinking all night with some of the Medieval Babes, a choral group that serenaded the *Elizabeth* bash at the Courthouse. "It was all a bit of a throwback to the old days of the festival," recalls former Polygram executive Judy Holm, who was minding the *Very Bad Things*

ANOTHER DAY IN PARADISE

RIGHT, MELANIE GRIFFITH

PHOTO: TRACEY SAVEIN

cast. At the dinner for the premiere, she recalls, they were like kids at a summer-camp reunion, but kids with extravagant tastes: "They said, 'It's a festival. Let's drink champagne!' And they ordered bottle after bottle of it."

Ironically, the best behaved of the bunch was Christian Slater, clean and sober after a stint in jail for playing with guns and drugs. Then there was his co-star Jeanne Tripplehorn, whose idea of making trouble was to insist on a bottle of Limoncello during the *Very Bad Things* party at the Phoenix nightclub. There was no Limoncello at the Phoenix, so Barb Hershenhorn placed a call to the Rosewater. "We got some high maintenance happening here," she said. "Could you bring up a bottle of Limoncello?" A driver in a suit arrived with the bottle, looking like he didn't belong at the party; security wouldn't let him into the VIP area upstairs to deliver it.

For the local media, the Polygram party at the Phoenix became emblematic of all the very bad things about the festival. Festival press veterans wearily making their rounds would find themselves shut out by the American publicity machine. At the Polygram party for *Very Bad Things*, as Rob Salem followed Rita Zekas up to the VIP area, a security guard grabbed him and pulled him down the stairs—a moment captured by a *Star* photographer. Things got so absurd at the party that Judy Holm was blocked from taking a producer up to the VIP section, even though—as Polygram's Canadian vice-president in charge of film distribution—she was the host. "It was crazy," she says. "It took me twenty minutes to remember that it was *my* party."

HAPPINESS

Such incidents only enhanced the growing perception in the industry and the media that the Toronto festival had been hijacked by the major studios. For Hollywood, September in Toronto has become just another date on the press junket calendar. The

PHOTO: HAIDEE MALKIN

LEFT, JANEANE GAROFALO, 1998; RIGHT, ROBERTO BENIGNI

FAR RIGHT, LIFE IS BEAUTIFUL

PHOTO: TYRONE KERR

festival accredits about eight hundred journalists, but the junkets attract a whole other tier of media who remain unaccredited. Travelling at the studios' expense, the frequent-flyer horde of junketeers descend on the city from across the continent, log a dozen interviews at the celebrity buffet, then skip town. To appease their editors, local journalists feel obliged to get in on the action, but to get an audience with one star they have to sit through half a day of interviews with the film's lesser talents. Junkets play havoc with the life of the festival. How do you persuade journalists to interview a director from France or Japan when their day is spent punching in and out of the studio assembly line? And with so many stars in attendance, they have come to monopolize the media. The '98 guests included Tom Cruise, Meryl Streep, Holly Hunter, Drew Barrymore, Neve Campbell, Gene Hackman, Jennifer Lopez and Billy Bob Thornton.

LAST NIGHT

Piers Handling now concedes that the American presence at the festival has become a problem, but he's not sure what to do about it. The star-studded Hollywood gala "is the engine of the festival," he says. "It drives the financial side enormously and it drives the press. My attitude is still that it allows us to do Iran and Spain and Portugal, and people like Kiyoshi Kurosawa and Nanni Moretti as Spotlight directors, and keep a programming team of ten people out there covering the globe, doing Latin America and Planet Africa. The European festivals are totally state-supported and we're not. If I were a European festival director, I'd be running a very different kind of event. We have to go a

:h Miramax running his campaign, Italy's clown prince charmec ; media. Life is Beautiful *conjured sentiment with a conviction tha. ›llywood could never manufacture in its wildest dreams*

certain route that purists don't like."

Also, the stature of the galas has risen to the point that the festival's reputation is closely tied to them. The '98 crop included *Elizabeth*, *A Simple Plan*, *Hilary and Jackie*, *Pleasantville*, *Antz*, *Little Voice*, *Central Station* and *Life is Beautiful*—which all went on to receive Academy Award nominations. But by 1998, with a slate of 310 films from 53 countries, the festival had become a juggernaut. And with so many significant releases crowding the programme, discovering smaller films became much harder, like trying to pick out a faint constellation from the night sky while looking up from a brightly lit city. *Rushmore*, Wes Anderson's cool little high-school comedy, premiered as a special presentation but generated almost no buzz—perhaps because its distributor, Paramount, had no idea how to market it.

However, Italy's clown prince, Roberto Benigni, managed to create a sensation around *Life is Beautiful*. In Toronto, he charmed the North American press with his manic shtick, and his film—which won the festival's audience award and three Oscars—became the top-grossing foreign-language picture in North American history. With Miramax running his campaign, that was not just a triumph for international cinema but also for American marketing savvy. But the breakout pattern of *Life is Beautiful*—from Cannes to Toronto to the Oscars—was a model of festival strategy. The film itself was not universally admired. With some critics arguing that the very notion of a sentimental comedy set against the Holocaust was sacrilege, Benigni pleaded that it was a fable, not a representation of the Holocaust. Even for a fable, the premise begs disbelief, that a boy could be kept so innocent in a death camp. But there is an inspired brilliance in the anti-fascist satire, and in how the farce chills into tragedy, turning on

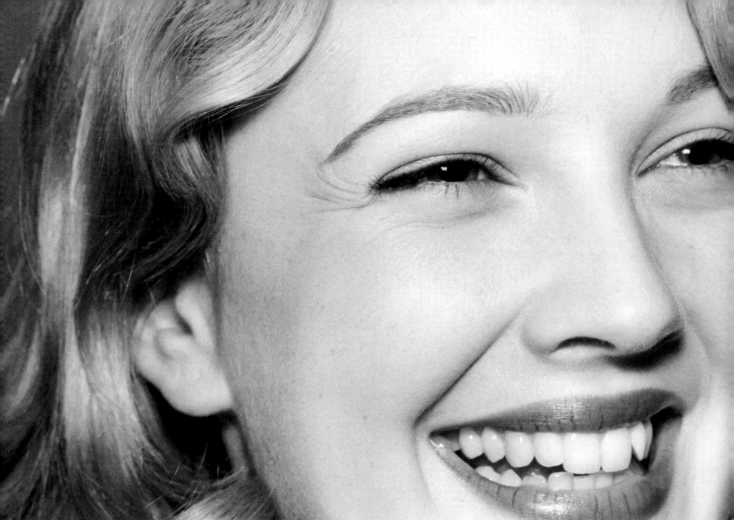

Piers Handling now concedes that the American presence at the fes
t: "The Hollywood gala is the engine of the festival. It drives the fin
ran and Spain and Portugal, and people like Kiyoshi Kurosawa and

PHOTO: HEATHER MCKINNON

LEFT, DREW BARRYMORE
RIGHT, BILLY BOB THORNTON

that surreal image of a horse painted green with racist graffiti. *Life is Beautiful* is sentimental, but bravely sentimental if that's possible.

By the late nineties, independent cinema had become polarized. There were films that were dark or subversive, openly hostile to Hollywood values. Then there were films, like *Life is Beautiful*, that conjured sentiment with a conviction that Hollywood could never manufacture in its wildest dreams. And in this year of *Happiness* and *Very Bad Things* and syringes in the neck, the year American indie cinema imploded with fear, cynicism and self-loathing, at the '98 festival you had to look further afield to find a little human warmth—to Brazil's *Central Station* or Italy's *Besieged*, France's *Autumn Tale* or Greece's *Eternity and a Day*, Lebanon's *West Beirut* or Ireland's *Waking Ned Devine*. Even some of the bleakest dramas from Europe still had a redeeming emotional reality—notably *The Dreamlife of Angels*, Erick Zonca's blunt tragedy of two young women falling through the frayed edge of working-class France; *Celebration*, Thomas Vinterberg's Hamlet-like psychodrama of a family reunion at a Danish manor; and *My Name Is Joe*,

has become a problem, but he's not sure what to do about side enormously and it drives the press. It allows us to do Moretti"

PHOTO: TRACEY SAVEIN

Ken Loach's grim romance about a reformed alcoholic in Glasgow.

Meanwhile Canadian film, land of the cold, dark and misanthropic, showed signs of warming. The '98 festival opened with the unashamed romance of *The Red Violin*, a sweeping epic shot in five countries and five languages with a story spanning three centuries. Directed by Quebec's François Girard as a follow-up to *Thirty-Two Short Films about Glenn Gould*, it's the most international movie ever made in this country, a cinematic equivalent to Canadian peacekeeping. Only Canadians could cast *Pulp Fiction*'s Samuel L. Jackson as a heavy who walks around with a violin case that actually contains a violin—the only time he gets tough is when he phones room service and asks not to be disturbed.

BESIEGED

The Red Violin was a coup for the underdogs of the Canadian industry. It was created by Rhombus Media, the tiny filmmaker-owned production house that made *Gould*. By putting together a $14 million movie, showcasing it as an opening-night gala, scoring a

TOM CRUISE, 1998

PHOTO: TYRONE KERR

LEFT, ROBIN WRIGHT PENN, 19
RIGHT, FRANÇOIS GIRARD, SYLV
CHANG AND MCKELLAR, 1998

PHOTO PREVIOUS PAGES: BARRY SHAINBAUM

PHOTO: HAIDEE MALKIN

modest triumph at the box office—then going on to win an Oscar for best score—Rhombus was moving into terrain traditionally owned by Lantos and Alliance. And for Don McKellar, the former festival theatre manager, the year was especially rewarding. As well as co-writing and acting in *The Red Violin*, McKellar wrote, produced and starred in his own feature debut, *Last Night*, which opened Perspective Canada. A $2 million movie about the end of the world, *Last Night* offered a nifty antidote to the summer blockbusters about meteors *almost* annihilating the planet. For a fraction of the price, McKellar actually delivered the end of the world, not with a fireball but with a white-out, while resolving questions of love and death with a Mexican standoff between a gun and a kiss.

For the festival, 1998 marked the end of an era. It was the last festival that David Overbey would attend. On December 16, he died suddenly from a stroke at the age of sixty-two. In his final years, the festival had overtaken him. As its *enfant terrible*, he was loved and tolerated, and still permitted to programme his favourite Asian directors. But his role had been diminished by the ascension of younger programmers, and by the festival's embrace of corporate respect and Hollywood glamour. With his death there was a sense that a way of life at the festival was gone forever.

Beauty and

22

the Hurricane

PHOTO: MARC ALFIERI

DAVID OVERBEY'S WAKE WAS A STRANGELY JOYFUL AFFA

A LONG NIGHT OF DRINKING AND LAUGHTER AND RIOTO anecdote, the kind of night Overbey would have relished. Although never reached a ripe old age, there was a sense that he had lived uller life than the rest of us. Everyone seemed to agree that his dea was as timely and natural as a death can be

"David and Jay Scott used to get drunk together once every Cannes film festival," recalls Helga Stephenson. "Jay would plead with me to tell David not to kill himself. David would explain at great, boozy, Gauloise length how he was not going to get old and that if that horrible fate befell him, he was going to take himself out. Thank God he did not have to do that."

Overbey would not have extended God that courtesy. His will decreed that "there is to be no religious service of any kind. No mention of the afterlife, of God, or of any other religious matter is to be uttered. No public prayers are to be uttered. Those who believe can

PHOTO PREVIOUS PAGES: TRACEY SAVEIN

do what they do privately, for all the good they believe it might do." David left no possessions to bequeath. But he requested that his ashes be scattered on a Philippine beach where beautiful boys might make love on them.

At the wake, eulogies poured forth like stand-up routines. Programmer David McIntosh regaled the mourners with stories of how Overbey once spent an afternoon drinking vodka with Tuesday Weld in her bed instead of interviewing her; of how he offered his myopic eyes to his friend Fritz Lang when the filmmaker was losing his sight; of how, when accosted at a Gay Pride parade by a supercilious man wearing only balloons, he started jabbing them with his unfiltered Gitane to clear a path through the crowd. In a hilariously blunt requiem, Helga Stephenson remembered first meeting Overbey. "I was not a guy, I was not gay, I did not know much in his terms about cinema, and so I was dirt to be ignored, which he did in grand style. I started to work at the festival in charge of publicity. At that point, I became more attractive. When he realized that I could drink and that I laughed a lot, my stock moved up. . . . He was always difficult. I spent time in Hollywood—the death of film as far as he was concerned—so I was part stupid, part smart, part useful, part of The Problem, which was whatever he defined it to be at the moment.

PREVIOUS PAGES, KEVIN SPACEY, 1999; LEFT, OVERBEY AND STEPHENSON IN CANNES

"One of his great uses for me was the Gay Flambé," recalled Helga, referring to an annual party at her house for gay festival guests—named by her live-in boyfriend at the time, drummer/contractor Nigel Dean, who manned the barbecue. "I was told I was not allowed to attend," she said. "After people were found doing interesting biological experiments in my Korean neighbour's goldfish pond, and the police were called, the party moved on to newer and better quarters." (The Gay Flambé went on to become another large, sponsored festival function.) "I could have lived without the young boys," Helga added. "I could have lived without some of them in my house, one in particular who had come from Manila who was shocked to hear that Marilyn Monroe had died. I rolled my eyes, David rolled his eyes, we both shrugged our shoulders and gently broke the dreadful news to the young man who was devastated." Helga then went on to toast Overbey as "a man of extreme contradictions who taught me so much about life, movies and remaining true to yourself. . . . That outrageous personality kept us on the edge no matter how respectable and responsible we were trying to get."

At the '99 festival, Hollywood was out in force. The guest list included Denzel Washington, Robin Williams, Bruce Willis, Matt Damon, Susan Sarandon, Sigourney Weaver, Kevin Spacey, Holly Hunter, Sean Penn, Tim Roth, Elton John, Ralph Fiennes, Alec Baldwin, Nick Nolte and Catherine Deneuve. The programme was strong on feature debuts. Tim Roth proved to be as powerful a director as he is an actor with *The War Zone,* an excoriating portrayal of father-daughter incest on the Devon coast. And with *Human Traffic*, an exhilarating ride through rave culture in Cardiff, Justin Kerrigan did for ecstasy what *Trainspotting* did for heroin, without the nasty bits. Kerrigan had given

-le spoke of Denzel with the cadence of a gospel preacher: "I liked liked his tenacity. And I loved his attitude. I loved him more and mc vhoa, maybe you have spent too much time in prison . . ."

PHOTO: TRACEY SAVEIN

up on getting North American distribution for his film when he received the festival's invitation. "It all happened for me in Toronto," says the twenty-five-year-old director. "I came in and I saw all these great filmmakers and all these wicked films and I was depressed, man. I just wanted to go home." But *Human Traffic* was a hit, and Kerrigan celebrated by dropping ecstasy at a rave staged to promote the premiere. "Everyone was flying," he says. "The next morning I'd had about an hour's kip, I'm on a come-down, I get a phone call. 'Harvey Weinstein's watching the film as we speak. Can you get your ass over to the Four Seasons Hotel?' So I splash water on my face, go over there, they're all raving about the film. I'm on a come-down, talking to Harvey Weinstein. He said the film really reminded him of when he was young." Weinstein bought *Human Traffic* and gave Kerrigan a three-picture deal.

Of course, the '99 festival's most buzzed directing debut was Sam Mendes's *American Beauty,* which would turn out to be the movie of the year. With a barometric accuracy that has become almost predictable, the Toronto audience anticipated its success by voting it the prize for most popular film—the first in a cascade of awards leading up to eight Academy Award nominations and five Oscars.

Like an inversion of *The Graduate* thirty-two years down the road, *American Beauty* spoke to two generations at once, to parents who don't want to act their age and to children

FAR LEFT,
DENZEL WASHINGTON,
1999

mature beyond their years. It dealt with sex and dope and death, and the issue of older men craving young girls. It was a movie about growing up that seemed to grow up as we watched it, morphing from suburban satire to zen drama, from mid-life crisis to afterlife calm. *American Beauty* belonged to a new breed of movies in 1999 that brought the ideas and attitudes of independent film into the mainstream more prolifically than ever—pictures such as *Magnolia*, *Boys Don't Cry*, *Being John Malkovich*, *The Insider* and *Mansfield Park*. *Beauty* wasn't an independent film; it was produced by Steven Spielberg's DreamWorks. But it cost just $15 million and, as director Sam Mendes told me, "the material was so edgy and dark, there was widespread concern in the studio that we were going to make that back." On the other hand—as Todd Solondz was quick to point out when Mendes accused him of patronizing his characters in *Happiness*—the material is not *that* dark. *American Beauty* presents "an Everyman figure, a universal hero you root for against his callous boss," says Mendes, who prepared for the shoot by taking "a very close look" at Billy Wilder's *The Apartment*. "Kevin Spacey is a huge Jack Lemmon fan. I remember the moment I said to him, 'It's a kind of Jack Lemmon part, like in *The Apartment*,' and his eyes lit up." Spacey acknowledged the homage by thanking Lemmon in his Oscar acceptance speech.

THE HURRICANE

·ay he talked.
·en I thought,

While *American Beauty* was the festival favourite, the year's breakout performance belonged to Hilary Swank of *Boys Don't Cry*. Based on the true story of Nebraska's Brandon Teena, who was murdered for acting as a man in a woman's body, Kimberly Peirce's debut feature dramatized the dilemma of transsexuality with breathtaking tenderness and brutality, as a *Romeo and Juliet* of star-crossed genders. An actress playing an actor in an Oscar-winning performance, Hilary Swank transformed herself into an androgynous James Dean, a brave and gentle outlaw who bursts into the saloon, dying to be one of the boys, only to get shot in a showdown over sexual identity. And long after the horror of her fate wears off, we're left with the beatific spirit of the original Brandon Teena, this sweetly ingenuous version of the American cowboy.

Boys Don't Cry was a low-budget labour of love that took Peirce five years to make. After its Venice premiere, in Toronto she watched her film for the first time with an audience that had some familiarity with the story. "It was a very tense screening, in the best sense," she recalls. "They were feeling for Brandon in a very personal way because they already identified with him." After the screening, the Q&A was like an emotional decompression. "Then there was an exodus of people that gathered around us," says Peirce. "There was a back door to the theatre and we were all just flowing out into the alleyway. We had all these limos, but none of us got in the cars. It was a nice cool night. We wanted to just walk with the audience. We walked to the party, and everybody was there. I was shell-shocked. It was so much stimulus, to screen it and then receive so much emotion from these people."

AMERICAN BEAUTY

While Americans learned to appreciate the un-American beauty of a Toronto premiere, the festival's role as a showcase for local filmmakers had also come fully into its own by 1999. At the final festival of the millennium, Canadian cinema was firing on all cylinders, with its directors making movies produced both inside and outside the country. Patricia Rozema showed off *Mansfield Park*, the spirited Jane Austen adaptation that she had written and directed for Miramax. Jeremy Podeswa, an emerging talent—and former festival employee—opened Perspective Canada with *The Five Senses*, which won the Toronto-City Award for best Canadian feature. Ex-Montrealer Alan Moyle (*Pump up the Volume*) captured Cape Breton in a quirky teenage comedy, *The New Waterford Girl*. Ron Mann fired up *Grass*, his cool documentary on the pot wars. Producer Robert Lantos premiered his Hungarian roots epic, *Sunshine*, directed by István Szabó. And Norman Jewison weighed in with *The Hurricane*, his first truly Canadian story, and arguably his most powerful movie since *In the Heat of the Night*. Atom Egoyan, meanwhile, provided a memorable opening-night gala with *Felicia's Journey*.

The party for *Felicia's Journey* took place amid carnival rides and a Ferris wheel at the SkyDome. It was the first opening-night party where the room was too big for the crowd, although there were three thousand people in attendance. One of them was Elaine Cassidy, the nineteen-year-old Irish actress who played opposite Bob Hoskins as Felicia, the psychopath's innocent prey. Cassidy was standing in the VIP area, a little cluster of people absurdly roped off in the middle of the SkyDome, when she was informed that Alec Baldwin wanted to meet her. "At first I was completely taken aback," she recalled later at the Genie Awards. "Why does he want to meet me? Then I remembered I'd already met him." They'd crossed paths two years earlier, when she was working in a coffee shop back home in Ireland. "Two people came in and they were wearing sunglasses," she explained. "It was the middle of winter, and I was like, 'Who are these two people? Only famous people wear sunglasses in the winter.' I looked up and saw Kim Basinger and Alec Baldwin. I said, 'Gosh.' Then I made their sandwiches and off they went. Now all of a sudden he wants to meet me. So I go up to him and he says, 'I like the film,' or whatever, and I say I've already met him and tell him the story."

Robert Lantos had initially wanted *Sunshine* to open the festival. He was used to getting his way. After *In Praise of Older Women*, *Joshua Then and Now*, *Black Robe*, *Léolo*, *Whale Music* and *The Sweet Hereafter*, Lantos had produced or executive-produced six of the festival's opening-night films. And he wanted a momentous world premiere for *Sunshine*, which had been rejected by Cannes and which was still looking for an American distributor. But Handling persuaded the producer that the three-hour epic was too hefty to serve as an appetizer before the opening-night party. Instead it premiered as a regular gala, where Lantos watched it with an audience for the first time. "We didn't know if people would sit still for three hours," he said. To his relief, they did.

Sunshine is the most valiant project of Lantos's career. Hungarian director István Szabó, an old friend, had originally planned to make it as a mini-series for German television. But after reading Szabó's four-hundred-page script—a semi-autobiographical saga that traces a Budapest Jewish family through the cataclysms of the Austro-Hungarian Empire, the Holocaust and Stalinism—Lantos persuaded him to make it as a feature film. With Fiennes playing three characters from successive generations, history bleeds

BOYS DON'T CRY

CHLOË SEVIGNY, 1999

"We were all just flowing out into the alleyway. We had these limos, but none of us got in the cars. It was a nice cool night. We wanted to just walk with the audience"

PHOTO: TYRONE KERR

through every frame of *Sunshine*—its scene of an icy crucifixion in a Nazi death camp is unforgettable. But bouts of soap opera undermine the drama's veracity, and the momentum flags badly by the third act. *Sunshine* is, in the end, the noblest of failures. In his magnanimity as an auteur's producer, unwilling to reign in the script, Lantos allowed Szabó to make a movie that was almost crushed by the weight of its own ambition.

For Lantos and Fiennes, however, *Sunshine* was not just a movie. It was an act of devotion to Szabó's singular vision. I'd been on the set with them in Budapest, where the cast treated Szabó like the venerated father of an intimate family. "István is very rigorous," Fiennes told me. "He sees everything in your eyes and your face. Initially it's daunting, because you know that every fluid, muscley bit of your face—every spirit, thought, idea—he can see it all. But afterwards I realized it's wonderful. I can just send the stuff out and trust that he'll see it."

After the premiere, Lantos took Szabó and Fiennes to his cottage on Lake Joseph in

PHOTO: HAIDEE MALKIN

"Like an inversion of The Graduate *thirty-two years down the ro*
American Beauty *spoke to two generations at once, to parents w*
don't want to act their age and to children mature beyond their year

Muskoka. It was unseasonably warm for September. "We swam and ate and drank," says Lantos. "We ate very well."

Just as *Sunshine* was a landmark for Lantos, so was *The Hurricane* for Norman Jewison. At the age of seventy-three, he was on the ropes, without a hit since *Moonstruck* (1987). After twenty-three movies, this was his first non-studio picture, and throughout the shoot he had battled over the script with his producers from Beacon Communications. It was also his first solidly Canadian story, the remarkable saga of a Toronto household that helped spring a black American boxer from a New Jersey prison. Its hero, Rubin "Hurricane" Carter, was now living in Toronto after serving nineteen years for a triple murder he did not commit. And *Hurricane* was the kind of movie that Jewison does best, an unsubtle, unhip, grandly old-fashioned civil rights drama in the tradition of *A Soldier's Story* and *In the Heat of the Night*.

Jewison was reluctant to show *The Hurricane* at the festival. The movie was not quite finished. He was also worried about generating a buzz that might fade in the months before its Christmas release. And he had been burned in the past by a premature review of a movie premiered at the festival. At first Jewison requested an exclusive screening for industry insiders that would not be open to the public or the press, but Piers Handling flatly refused. This was, above all, a public festival, not an industry convention. Finally, Jewison agreed to show *The Hurricane* at the Elgin theatre as a special presentation of "a work in progress."

On the night of the screening, there were more than a dozen men in suits lined up onstage by the time Jewison had introduced his collaborators, his co-producers and the studio executives who were distributing the film. Then he introduced the star, Denzel Washington, who ambled onstage in a baseball cap and sweats. "The reason I'm here," said the actor, "I love him like a brother, like a father, like a son—Rubin 'Hurricane' Carter." The audience erupted as Carter stepped onstage and moved to the microphone. Jewison was worried. Carter was now making his living as a motivational speaker. Once he got started there was no telling when he might stop. And for an audience that was about to sit through a three-hour movie, a long speech could be lethal.

But this was Carter's moment. After two decades in jail, he knew a thing or two about waiting, and he was going to take his sweet time. He spoke with the luxurious cadence of a gospel preacher. He spoke of Denzel Washington, and how he caught the actor staring at himself in the mirror in the lobby of a restaurant where they met for lunch, and how they talked, and how the more they talked, the more he liked him. "I liked the way he talked. I liked his tenacity and I *loved* his attitude. I loved him more and more. And then I thought, whoa, maybe you *have* spent too much time in prison. . . . But when I saw him in the lobby, he was clearing his canvas in preparation to portray me. And from the time that he sat down at that table, he was giving me *back* to me. And I was *loving* it! I think everybody should have that experience—to see oneself mirrored in the art of a consummate professional."

Carter thanked his saviours, beginning with John Artis, who was convicted with him but refused to sell him out. "The reason I am standing here right now is John Artis," said Rubin. "He suffered for fifteen years in prison for something that he never even *thought* about doing. John Artis is my hero." Carter went on to thank Lesra Martin and the dozen Canadians who devoted their lives to setting him free, including his estranged wife Lisa. "Is Lisa here?" he asked. No one replied. Artis and Martin were at the premiere. But Lisa, along with Terry Swinton and Sam Chaiton—the characters played by Deborah Unger, John Hannah and Leiv Schreiber in the film—boycotted the premiere. Beneath the glowing show of solidarity onstage, there was a bitter rift between Carter and the insular commune of Canadians who had helped free him.

That night, however, we knew nothing of that. We were in the presence of a legend, the man in the Bob Dylan song, and he was making the fable real. Rubin Carter spoke for twenty minutes, and by the end of it, the audience wasn't exhausted; it was enthralled. As the movie began, I was hooked from that first wail of Scarlet Rivera's gypsy violin as Dylan sings, "This is the story of the Hurricane . . ." The movie played like a house on fire. The crowd loved the local references. A huge laugh went up at the sight of an Eaton's

PHOTO: TYRONE KERR

TIM ROTH, 1999

box visible through the torn wrapping paper of a Christmas present being delivered to Rubin's cell—causing one of the movie's American screenwriters to panic, wondering what on earth the audience found so funny.

When the final credits rolled, the audience stood up as one and applauded the movie, its star and its hero for a full ten minutes. It was a thrilling moment, a cathartic celebration of a hometown triumph and a victory against racial injustice. Months later I saw the movie again. It was not the same. By then, I'd come to know the facts behind the story. And under the cold scrutiny of a press screening, although Washington's performance was as brilliant as ever, Jewison's melodramatic feints seemed more transparent, the script more heavy-handed. The magic was gone.

But you can't see the same movie twice. The second time, for better or worse, it's different. And in that sense, at least, film is just like live theatre. A motion picture doesn't really exist outside that ephemeral moment of projection, an event that passes between the eye and the screen as light plays tricks on the retina. At the premiere of *The Hurricane*, I forgot I was a critic. I joined in the wholesale suspension of disbelief that occurs when an audience wills its whole weight behind a movie. That doesn't happen very often. When it does, you go with it.

A film festival is, in the end, a celebration of live cinema. An event. The Toronto festival has become much more than that. It has spawned one of Canada's largest and most successful non-profit corporations in the cultural sector, Toronto International Film Festival (TIFF) Group, which has an annual budget of $10 million—$7 million for the festival proper. Other divisions include Cinematheque Ontario, which conducts year-round screenings, and the Film Reference Library, which has amassed a major collection of books, periodicals, photographs, videos and film production files. The TIFF also governs The Film Circuit, which takes films on the road to thirty-six communities around Ontario, and Sprockets, an annual film festival for children. Then there are dozens of small; independent film festivals that have popped up in the wake of the TIFF, from Hot Docs to Rendezvous with Madness.

The Toronto festival itself seems to grow in size and stature with each year. Its staff of thirty-six swells to about four hundred during the event itself, not to mention some one thousand volunteers. It has projected 5,680 titles since its inception. In 1999, it showed 319 films from 52 countries, including 64 world premieres and 107 North American premieres. It attracted more than eight hundred journalists. And in the thick of a Toronto newspaper war, it generated unprecedented coverage, with the newly launched *National Post* accrediting twenty-four staff and publishing a separate festival section each day.

THE LIMEY

The coverage, however, has become increasingly fixated on Hollywood stars. And that is distressing to brokers of foreign films, such as Jacques Strauss, a French sales agent who has been coming to the festival for a decade with movies like *Cyrano de Bergerac* and *The Hairdresser's Husband*. "The drift of the festival is now much more American than European," he told me in his Paris office. "In the past two or three years there's been a huge change. The festival has been taken over by the American studios. It's not the festival's fault. The studios stage these big junkets, and it monopolizes the press. I tell Piers there's no point bringing directors and actors here if there is no press interest, if there are no interviews. For the Americans, cinema is not a cultural product but a commercial product. For us it's both commercial and cultural. It's another form of cinema, and it's a pity that a festival like Toronto gives our cinema less and less importance."

But it is not just Toronto that has changed. The movie industry has become globalized to the point that, with some celebrated exceptions, non-English-language films are being squeezed out of the market. And in the festival's defence, Handling argues that the world is a different place from the one in which Jay Scott filled newspaper pages with festival stories on challenging foreign films. "Editorial policies have changed significantly in the past five years," he says. "There's much more attention being paid to the weekly grosses, and to film as commerce rather than art. It's the industrialization of culture, not just the festival. Whether Jay would have been allowed the same freedom now as he had then I don't know. Generally there's been a drop-off in that kind of coverage all around the world. Just try to sell a story on Kiarostami to a newspaper."

The festival began as an anomaly, a brave blast of culture in a city that was not fully awake. Now it is part of Toronto's fabric, greater than any of the larger-than-life characters who have left their mark on it. There is no longer anything the festival can do to scandalize Toronto, with the possible exception of scaling back instead of expanding. The parties are organized with military precision. There's no hospitality suite where the festival can shrink back into a small club at the end of the night. "In the old days, you could go out after a movie and run into someone you knew," recalled Margot Kidder when I spoke to her at the '99 festival. "Now it's like the Democratic National Convention." Even the censorship battles seem a quaint memory. In 1999, Catherine Breillat's *Romance* showed extended scenes of hard-core sex without causing a ripple of controversy. Suddenly, we are all adults.

Not much can be done about growing up. But at the twenty-fourth festival, the founders were still on hand to provide a link to the past. Henk van der Kolk dropped in on parties with his wife, Yanka, who was still snapping Polaroids as if she had never left the Carlton terrace. Dusty Cohl, still wearing a grin and a cowboy hat, was ubiquitous—and every second winter, he hosts the Floating Film Festival on a cruise ship in the Caribbean, with cronies such as Roger Ebert and Richard Corliss among the regular guests.

And Bill Marshall? When he showed up at lunch for the first of several interviews, though impeccably dressed, he looked unrecognizably gray and gaunt, and made his way to the table in slow motion. He dismissed his condition as "a liver scare." Over a year later, I ran into him at a party. He was still frail, but looking much better. Nursing a glass of Coke, he told me he was responding well to a new liver treatment involving a shunt. In fact, he was hoping to attend the Cannes film festival for the first time in five years. But Marshall never made it to Cannes. And just as this book was going to press, it came to light that—while trying to fund the trip—he had already filed for personal bankruptcy with unsecured debts of almost $1 million, including credit-card bills of more than $200,000. In Cannes, Marshall had planned to announce the creation of an Internet film festival devoted to launching movies in cyberspace. Twenty-five years down the road, he was still chasing the dream.

For less quixotic veterans of the festival, however, the thrill of the early years is gone for good. "In those days," recalls David Gilmour, "you had the feeling you were somewhere

LIV TYLER, 1999;
BELOW, RALPH FIENNES

PHOTO: MARTIN MORDECAI

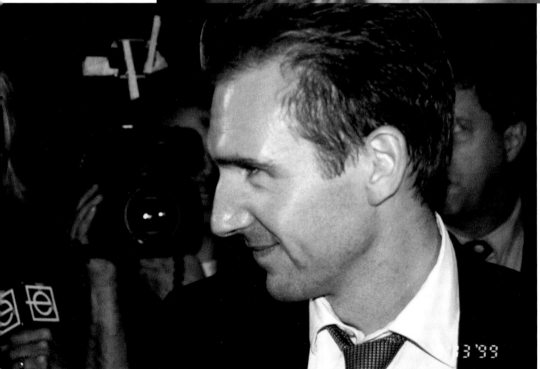

PHOTO: CRAIG COWAN

ı can't see the same movie twice. The second time, for better o
rse, it's different. In that sense, a film is like live theatre—it doesn'
st outside that moment of projection. And a film festival is, in the end,
elebration of live cinema

very special. There were no people more restless than film festival people at parties. They were constantly moving, from floor to floor, party to party, conversation to conversation, convinced that it wasn't quite here. It was just a little bit ahead of them. So you kept moving like a shark all night for ten days." Gilmour doesn't go to the festival any more. "I've had enough," he says. "But even though I never need to go to another party, or another screening, whenever I go by a movie theatre during the festival and people are lined up outside and the limos are there and the searchlights are swinging around, there's some physical reaction in my body, some sickening pull that drags me toward it. I'm sure junkies feel the same way when they go by places where they used to get high."

For those of us who still go to the festival to get high, the rush may be more elusive. Chances are it won't be found at a party, but in a darkened theatre, seeing something unforgettable for the first time, and maybe the last. As a critic I spend too much of the festival each year watching movies that *have* to be seen for one reason or another. But there is always the lure of discovery, the hope of finding some brilliant obscurity that will never see the light of commercial release.

On the final day of the '99 festival, I walk to the Varsity Cinemas with B. Ruby Rich, one of the sharpest American critics I know. After having spent a good part of the festival ploughing through twenty Canadian features as a member of the Toronto-City Award jury, she's craving something exotic. And on an urgent tip from Piers Handling, both of us are off to see *Beau travail*, a film by Claire Denis about the French foreign legion in East Africa. We rush to get there early, worried about finding a seat. The theatre is half empty. We end up sitting with Atom Egoyan and Arsinée Khanjian, who received the same tip.

At first *Beau travail* seems like some kind of strange and exquisite documentary. A literal tracking shot skims across the African desert from the window of a moving train. The train's shadow flows over the sand, a shadow that includes the outline of passengers sitting on the roofs of the carriages. We end up at a military base. There are tableaus of young French legionnaires performing drills and manoeuvres. It all looks very authentic. But then we see half a dozen soldiers, stripped to the waist, at ironing boards outside their barracks, pressing their khaki shirts in the sun. And in the symmetry of their move-

ments, you begin to detect a discreet choreography. Ironing with irony. The legionnaires—played by modern dancers, we learn later—pick-axe meaningless holes in a black lava bed by the sea to the sound of trumpets and operatic choirs. As they quick-march along a desert road, a Neil Young ballad drops into the soundtrack like a UFO. At one point, out of nowhere, the screen explodes with an underwater blossom of red in a turquoise sea. Blood from a helicopter crash, it turns out. A story of sorts insinuates itself into the images. There is a bitter feud between two soldiers. One man leaves the other to bake to death on a white salt flat. But the real suspense lies in not knowing what amazing image lies just over the horizon of the next cut.

After the final credits, the four of us—two critics, a director and an actor—turn to one another in stunned disbelief, anxious to confirm our exhilaration, as if we've just witnessed a supernatural phenomenon and have to corroborate the experience. The film we've seen was not difficult or pretentious, just astonishing. And even if it's so weird that no distributor would dream of releasing it, we can't imagine anyone not loving it. Like surfers who have spent ten days on a quest for the perfect wave, at the eleventh hour of the festival we've found what we were looking for. An oasis of pure cinema.

UNIVERSITY THEATRE, 1983

Acknowledgements

When Piers Handling and Michèle Maheux first asked me to write a book about the Toronto International Film Festival for its twenty-fifth anniversary, I told them I'd be interested only if the festival had no control over it, and if I were independently hired by a publisher. To my surprise, they found that arrangement not only acceptable but desirable. They liked the idea of an independent book that would tell the story of independent film—and the culture surrounding it—through the festival lens. From its inception, part of what has made the festival so popular is its openness. It has a tradition of granting its programmers creative autonomy. And in posing for this documentary portrait in print, the festival has taken the same hands-off attitude. So my gratitude goes out to Piers and Michèle for unconditionally trusting me with their story, opening up their archives, and helping me to track down dozens of filmmakers around the world. At the festival, Pauline Mizzi helped guide me through Piers's Rolodex. Everyone at the Film Reference Library was immensely helpful, in particular Robin MacDonald, who took a special interest in the book and cheerfully responded to requests for the most arcane information. Nuria Bronfman, Steve Gravestock, Gabrielle Free and their staff consistently made the festival press office an enjoyable place to do business. The Cinemathèque's James Quandt offered his experience. And I'm grateful to all the festival employees, past and present, who spoke to me so candidly—especially former executives Bill Marshall, Dusty Cohl, Henk van der Kolk, Wayne Clarkson, Anne Mackenzie and Helga Stephenson, as well as Bill House and John Allen. Yanka van der Kolk was kind to donate her personal photo archive, and thanks to both her and her daughter, Yolanda, for volunteering the services of their photo studio. Thanks also to the film-makers who provided their stories, and my apologies to those who have searched in vain for their names in the index. Although I ended up conducting well over a hundred interviews, I soon realized that a readable history of the festival can be kaleidoscopic, but not encyclopedic.

On the publishing side, Sarah MacLachlan played a crucial role in developing the initial proposal for the book. My agent, Suzanne DePoe, navigated some challenging contractual waters with her customary insight. And I am indebted to Anne Collins, my editor at Random House Canada, who took on this project with vision and enthusiasm. She has been a treat to work with at every turn, an editor who worked to open up the writing rather than contain it, while saving me from my worst excesses. Thanks also to Pamela Robertson for her editorial assistance and her patient and dogged tracking of photo permissions; to Cheryl Cohen, who surpassed her mandate as copy editor to serve as a dedicated checker of cinematic fact; and to Alan Terakawa for his production expertise. Meanwhile Jenny Armour, the book's photo editor and art director, made sure that a book about film was true to its subject. She has done a remarkable job of capturing the festival's energy and spirit with her kinetic design.

At *Maclean's*, I am grateful to Bob Lewis and Geoff Stevens for allowing me the time off to work on this project; to Entertainment Editor Patricia Hluchy for covering for me at the magazine; to Shanda Deziel for assisting in my absence as well as contributing research to the book; and to photographer Peter Bregg for donating his talent. Thanks also to the friendly staff at Revue Video for fueling my own private film festival during the past year. Finally, in putting up with the grueling pace of this project, my family deserves more than the usual nod of recognition. My wife, Marni, found it in her heart to be generously supportive even while she was on deadline writing her own book for the same editor, a test of love that seems to be above and beyond anything mentioned in the marriage vows. I can't begin to say how much I owe to her discerning eye as a reader, and to her enviable example as a writer. Our son, Casey, who had a few of his own projects in the works, was invaluable for his encouragement, his sense of humour—and his willingness to spend entire meals riffing on ideas for the title.

Illustration credits

Every effort has been made to contact copyright holders; in the event of an inadvertent omission or error, please notify the publisher.

CANDID PHOTOGRAPHS

Photographs by Nancy Ackerman reprinted with permission courtesy of the TIFF Archive, The Film Reference Library. pp. 55, 126, 145, 149, 167, 168.

Photographs © Marc Alfieri reprinted with permission courtesy of the TIFF Archive, The Film Reference Library. pp. 255, 312.

Photograph by Robert Baillargeon reprinted with permission courtesy of the TIFF Archive, The Film Reference Library. p. 177.

Photographs by Sam Barnes reprinted with permission courtesy of the TIFF Archive, The Film Reference Library. pp. 172, 182, 213, 268.

Photograph by Fitzroy Barrett reprinted with permission courtesy of the TIFF Archive, The Film Reference Library. p. 210.

Photograph by Keith Beaty. reprinted with permission by Toronto Star Syndicate. pp. 44–45.

Photograph by Jan Bird reprinted with permission courtesy of the TIFF Archive, The Film Reference Library. p. 267.

Photographs by Peter Bregg reprinted courtesy of *Maclean's*. pp. 8, 230, 247.

Photograph by David Chan reprinted with permission courtesy of the TIFF Archive, The Film Reference Library. p. 154.

Photograph by Esmond Choueke reprinted courtesy of *Maclean's*. p. 49.

Photographs courtesy of the Cinema Canada Collection, The Film Reference Library. pp. 50, 71.

Photograph by Y. Coatsaliou courtesy of Davis/Dobson/McIntosh/Weeks. p. 73.

Photograph by Shelley Cohl courtesy of the TIFF Archive, The Film Reference Library. p. 41.

Photograph courtesy of Shelly Cohl/Angel Wells. p. 28.

Photograph by Craig Cowan reprinted with permission courtesy of the TIFF Archive, The Film Reference Library. p. 323.

Photograph by Barrie Davis. reprinted with permission by The Globe and Mail. pp. 38–39.

Photograph courtesy Davis/Dobson/McIntosh/Weeks. p. 255.

Photographs © Eva Everything reprinted courtesy of Eva Everything. pp. 61, 90–91, 92, 94, 100–101, 105, 106, 109, 111, 112, 325.

Photographs by Rosemary Goldhar reprinted with permission courtesy of the TIFF Archive, The Film Reference Library. pp. 278, 281, 285, 297, 300.

Photographs by Dean Goodwin reprinted with permission courtesy of the TIFF Archive, The Film Reference Library. pp. 200, 260.

Photograph by Barry Gray. reprinted with permission by Toronto Sun Syndicated Services. p. 69.

Photograph courtesy of Piers Handling. p. 159.

Photographs by Gail Harvey reprinted with permission courtesy of the TIFF Archive, The Film Reference Library. pp. 42, 59, 78, 85, 86–87, 99, 102, 104, 110, 113, 115, 116–117, 118, 120, 122, 129, 133, 229.

Photographs by Chris Holland courtesy of the Cinema Canada Collection, The Film Reference Library. pp. 26–27, 52.

Photograph by Ben Mark Holzberg reprinted with permission courtesy of the TIFF Archive, The Film Reference Library. p. 245.

Photographs by Cathy Johnson–Campbell reprinted with permission courtesy of the TIFF Archive, The Film Reference Library. pp. 179, 223.

Photographs by Tyrone Kerr reprinted with permission courtesy of the TIFF Archive, The Film Reference Library. pp. 217, 283, 284, 291, 303, 308, 317, 320.

Photograph by Frank Lennon. reprinted with permission by the Toronto Star Syndicate. p. 36.

Photograph by Motty Levy reprinted with permission courtesy of the TIFF Archive, The Film Reference Library. p. 191.

Photograph by James Lewcun. reprinted with permission by *The Globe and Mail*. p. 62.

Photograph by Michael Libby reprinted with permission courtesy of the TIFF Archive, The Film Reference Library. p. 76.

Photographs by Doug MacLellan reprinted with permission courtesy of the TIFF Archive, The Film Reference Library. pp. 130, 163, 181, 218, 239, 292.

Photographs by Haidee Malkin reprinted with permission courtesy of the TIFF Archive, The Film Reference Library. pp. 294, 296, 302, 309, 318.

Photographs by David Maltby reprinted with permission courtesy of the TIFF Archive, The Film Reference Library. pp. 203, 240.

Photographs by Heather McKinnon reprinted with permission courtesy of the TIFF Archive, The Film Reference Library. pp. 276, 304.

Photograph by David McLeod reprinted with permission courtesy of the TIFF Archive, The Film Reference Library. p. 206.

Photograph by Joèlle Medina reprinted with permission courtesy of the TIFF Archive, The Film Reference Library. p. 289.

Photographs by John Medland reprinted with permission courtesy of the TIFF Archive, The Film Reference Library. pp. 204, 224.

Photograph by Sandy Middleton reprinted with permission courtesy of the TIFF Archive, The Film Reference Library. p. 288.

Photographs © L. Mirkine, Studio Mirkine courtesy of the TIFF Archive, The Film Reference Library. pp. 20, 156.

Photograph by Sara Moore reprinted with permission courtesy of the TIFF Archive, The Film Reference Library. p. 261.

Photographs by Martin Mordecai reprinted with permission courtesy of the TIFF Archive, The Film Reference Library. pp. 299, 323.

Photograph by Susan Morrow reprinted with permission courtesy of the TIFF Archive, The Film Reference Library. p. 185.

Photographs by Alex Neumann reprinted with permission courtesy of the TIFF Archive, The Film Reference Library. pp. 293, 295.

Photograph by Ken Pickett reprinted with permission courtesy of the TIFF Archive, The Film Reference Library. p. 252.

Photograph by Rafy reprinted with permission courtesy of the TIFF Archive, The Film Reference Library. p. 259.

Photograph by Steven Robinson reprinted with permission courtesy of the TIFF Archive, The Film Reference Library. p. 226.

Photographs by Tracey Savein reprinted with permission courtesy of the TIFF Archive, The Film Reference Library. pp. 301, 305, 310–311, 314.

Photograph by Barry Shainbaum reprinted with permission courtesy of the TIFF Archive, The Film Reference Library. pp. 306–307.

Photographs by Susan Shaw reprinted with permission courtesy of the TIFF Archive, The Film Reference Library. pp. 141, 153, 173, 195.

Photographs by Jim Steele reprinted with permission courtesy of the TIFF Archive, The Film Reference Library. pp. 260, 265, 266, 271, 272, 275.

Photograph by Lisi Tesher reprinted with permission courtesy of the TIFF Archive, The Film Reference Library. p. 269.

Photograph by Rob Teteruk reprinted with permission courtesy of the TIFF Archive, The Film Reference Library. p. 244.

Photographs courtesy of the TIFF Archive, The Film Reference Library. pp. 14–15, 65, 97, 142, 163.

Photograph by Angel Wells reprinted courtesy of Dusty Cohl. p. 31.

Photograph by Sylvia Train reprinted with permission by Toronto Sun Syndicated Services. p. 66.

Photographs reprinted with permission courtesy of Yanka van der Kolk. pp. 16, 23, 32.

Photograph by Bob Villard reprinted with permission courtesy of the David Cronenberg Collection, The Film Reference Library. p. 171.

Photograph by Angel Wells courtesy of the TIFF Archive, The Film Reference Library. p. 31.

Photographs by Brian Willer reprinted courtesy of *Maclean's*. pp. 70, 249, 250.

Photograph by Ken Woroner reprinted with permission courtesy of the TIFF Archive, The Film Reference Library. p. 262.

FILM STILLS

Photographs by Johnnie Eisen for the motion picture *The Adjuster* reprinted with permission by Johnnie Eisen. Photograph © 2000 Johnnie Eisen, all rights reserved. Image courtesy of The Film Reference Library. p. 251 and cover.

Photograph by Lorey Sebastian for the motion picture *American Beauty*™ © 1999 DreamWorks L.L.C., reprinted with permission by DreamWorks L.L.C. Image courtesy of The Film Reference Library. p. 315.

Photograph for the motion picture *Angels and Insects* reprinted with permission by MGM Clip + Still. Copyright © 1996 Orion Pictures Corporation. All rights reserved. Image courtesy of The Film Reference Library. p. 268.

Photograph for the motion picture *Another Day in Paradise* reprinted with permission by TVA International. Image courtesy of The Film Reference Library. p. 301.

Photograph by Gillian Lefkowitz for the motion picture *Boogie Nights* reprinted with permission. Copyright © 1997, New Line Productions, Inc. All rights reserved. Photo appears courtesy of New Line Productions, Inc. Image courtesy of The Film Reference Library. p. 296.

Photograph by Rick Porter for the motion picture *The Brood* reprinted with permission by Laurem Productions Inc. Image courtesy of The Film Reference Library. cover.

Photograph for the motion picture *Choose Me* reprinted with permission by Alive Films. Image courtesy of The Film Reference Library. p. 178.

Photograph by Claudel Huot for the motion picture *Le confessionnal* reprinted with permission by Cinémaginaire Inc. Image courtesy of The Film Reference Library. p. 270.

Photograph for the motion picture *Crumb* reprinted with permission courtesy of Terry Zwigoff. Image courtesy of The Film Reference Library. p. 196.

Photograph for the motion picture *The Crying Game* reprinted with permission courtesy of Miramax Films. All rights reserved. Image courtesy of The Film Reference Library. p. 214.

Photograph by Ana Muller for the motion picture *Dark Habits* reprinted with permission by El Deseo S.A. Copyright © El Deseo S.A. Image courtesy of The Film Reference Library. pp. 160–161.

Photograph for the motion picture *Dead Ringers* reprinted with permission by TVA International Distribution Inc. Image courtesy of The Film Reference Library. cover.

Photograph for the motion picture *Divine Madness* reprinted with permission by Warner Bros. Entertainment Inc. Copyright © 2000 Warner Bros. Entertainment Inc. Image courtesy of The Film Reference Library. p. 67.

Photograph for the motion picture *Fallen Angels* reprinted with permission by Aska Film Distribution. Image courtesy of The Film Reference Library. p. 209.

Photograph by Johnnie Eisen for the motion picture *Family Viewing* reprinted with permission by Johnnie Eisen. Photograph © 2000 Johnnie Eisen, all rights reserved. Image courtesy of The Film Reference Library. p. 175.

Photograph by Johnnie Eisen for the motion picture *The Five Senses* reprinted with permission by Five Senses Productions. Image courtesy of The Film Reference Library. p. 324.

Photograph for the motion picture *Goin' Down the Road* reprinted with permission courtesy of Don Shebib and Edvon Films Ltd. Image courtesy of The Film Reference Library. p. 134.

Photograph for the motion picture *The Grifters* reprinted with permission by Allliance Atlantis Motion Picture Group. Image courtesy of The Film Reference Library. p. 204.

Photograph by Chris Reardon for the motion picture *The Hanging Garden* reprinted with permission courtesy of Louise Garfield, Triptych Media. Image courtesy of The Film Reference Library. p. 287.

Photograph for the motion picture *Hav Plenty* reprinted with permission courtesy of Miramax Films. All rights reserved. Image courtesy of The Film Reference Library. p. 246.

Photograph by Michael Vendruscolo for the motion picture *Highway 61* reprinted with permission by Shadow Shows. Image courtesy of The Film Reference Library. p. 182 and cover.

Photograph for the motion picture *The Hurricane* © 2000 by Universal Studios, Inc. Reprinted courtesy of Universal Studios Publishing Rights, a Division of Universal Studios Licensing, Inc. All rights reserved. Image courtesy of The Film Reference Library. p. 314.

Photograph for the motion picture *Il Postino* reprinted with permission courtesy of Miramax Films. All rights reserved. Image courtesy of The Film Reference Library. p. 234.

Photograph for the motion picture *In Praise of Older Women* reprinted with permission by Serendipity Point Films. Image courtesy of The Film Reference Library. p. 46.

Photograph for the motion picture *I've Heard the Mermaids Singing* reprinted with permission by Some Films Inc. Image courtesy of The Film Reference Library. p. 174.

Photograph by Bénédicte Delessalle for the motion picture *Je, tu, il, elle* reprinted with permission by Paradise Films. Image courtesy of The Film Reference Library. p. 35.

Photograph for the motion picture *Killer of Sheep* reprinted with permission courtesy of Charles Burnett. Image courtesy of The Film Reference Library. p. 81.

Photograph for the motion picture *Kiss of the Spider Woman* reprinted with permission by HB Filmes. Image courtesy of The Film Reference Library. p. 83.

Photograph for the motion picture *L.A. Confidential* reprinted with permission by Warner Bros. Entertainment Inc. Copyright © 2000 Warner Bros. Entertainment Inc. Image courtesy of The Film Reference Library. p. 293.

Photograph by Cylla von Tiedemann for the motion picture *Last Night* reprinted with permission courtesy of Rhombus Media. Image courtesy of The Film Reference Library. p. 302 and cover.

Photograph for the motion picture *The Last Waltz* reprinted with permission by MGM Clip + Still. Copyright © 1978 The Last Waltz Productions, Inc. All rights reserved. Image courtesy of The Film Reference Library. p. 56.

Photograph by Jorge Aparicio for the motion picture *Law of Desire* reprinted with permission by El Deseo S.A. Copyright © El Deseo S.A. Image courtesy of The Film Reference Library. p. 246.

Photograph by Sergio Strizzi for the motion picture *Life is Beautiful* reprinted with permission courtesy of Miramax Films. All rights reserved. Image courtesy of The Film Reference Library. p. 303.

Photograph for the motion picture *The Limey* reprinted with permission by Artisan Pictures Inc. Copyright © 1999 Artisan Pictures Inc. All rights reserved. Image courtesy of The Film Reference Library. p. 321.

Photograph for the motion picture *The Little Girl who Lives Down the Lane* reprinted with permission by TVA International and courtesy of Astral Films and Nicholas Gessner. Image courtesy of The Film Reference Library. p. 34.

Photograph for the motion picture *Little Man Tate* reprinted with permission by MGM Clip + Still. Copyright © 1991 Orion Pictures Corporation. All rights reserved. Image courtesy of The Film Reference Library. p. 231.

Photograph by Ricardo Aronovich, Director of Photography, for the motion picture *Lumière* reprinted with permission by Jeanne Moreau. Image courtesy of The Film Reference Library. p. 28.

Photograph for the motion picture *M. Butterfly* reprinted with permission by Warner Bros. Entertainment Inc. Copyright © 2000 Warner Bros. Entertainment Inc. Image courtesy of The Film Reference Library. p. 181.

Photograph for the motion picture *Mad Love* © Touchstone Pictures Company. All rights reserved. Image courtesy of The Film Reference Library. p. 232.

Photographs for the motion picture *Mon oncle Antoine* reprinted with permission by the National Film Board of Canada. Images courtesy of The Film Reference Library. pp. 136, 137.

Photograph for the motion picture *Next of Kin* reprinted with permission courtesy of Ego Film Arts. Image courtesy of The Film Reference Library. p. 130.

Photograph for the motion picture *Outrageous!* reprinted with permission by the Film Consortium of Canada Inc. Image courtesy of The Film Reference Library. p. 32.

Photograph for the motion picture *P4W: Prison for Women* reprinted with permission courtesy of Janis Cole. Image courtesy of The Film Reference Library. p. 192.

Photograph by Bob Marshak for the motion picture *Passion Fish* reprinted with permission courtesy of Miramax Films. All rights reserved. Image courtesy of The Film Reference Library. p. 216.

Photograph for the motion picture *Pixote* reprinted with permission by HB Filmes. Image courtesy of The Film Reference Library. p. 151.

Photograph for the motion picture *Priest* reprinted with permission courtesy of Miramax Films. All rights reserved. Image courtesy of The Film Reference Library. p. 232.

Photograph for the motion picture *Reservoir Dogs* reprinted with permission courtesy of Miramax Films. All rights reserved. Image courtesy of The Film Reference Library. p. 198–199.

Photograph for the motion picture *Roger and Me* reprinted with permission by Warner Bros. Entertainment Inc. Copyright © 2000 Warner Bros. Entertainment Inc. Image courtesy of The Film Reference Library. p. 187.

Photograph by Peter Mettler for the motion picture *Scissere* reprinted with permission by Grimthorpe Film Inc. Image courtesy of The Film Reference Library. p. 173.

Photograph for the motion picture *Seven Years in Tibet* reprinted with permission courtesy of TriStar Pictures. Copyright © 1997 Mandalay Entertainment. All rights reserved. Image courtesy of The Film Reference Library p. 294.

Photograph for the motion picture *sex, lies and videotape* reprinted with permission courtesy of Miramax Films. All rights reserved. Image courtesy of The Film Reference Library. p. 201.

Photographs for the motion picture *A Soldier's Story* reprinted with permission courtesy of Columbia Pictures. Copyright © 1984 Columbia Pictures Industries, Inc. All rights reserved. Image courtesy of The Film Reference Library. p. 131 and cover.

Photograph by Hugh Brown for the motion picture *Stop Making Sense* reprinted with permission by David Byrne, Overland Productions. Image courtesy of The Film Reference Library. p. 129.

Photograph for the motion picture *Stranger Than Paradise* © Jim Jarmusch 1984, reprinted with permission by Cinesthesia Productions. Image courtesy of The Film Reference Library. p. 121.

Photographs by Johnnie Eisen for the motion picture *The Sweet Hereafter* reprinted with permission by Johnnie Eisen. Photograph © 2000 Johnnie Eisen, all rights reserved. Image courtesy of The Film Reference Library. p. 287 and cover.

Photograph by Mark Lipson for the motion picture *Thin Blue Line* reprinted with permission courtesy of Miramax Films. All rights reserved. Image courtesy of The Film Reference Library. p. 188.

Photograph by Cylla von Tiedemann for the motion picture *32 Short Films About Glenn Gould* reprinted with permission courtesy of Rhombus Media. Image courtesy of The Film Reference Library. p. 263.

Photograph for the motion picture *Tokyo Decadence* reprinted with permission by Filmes sans Frontieres. Image courtesy of The Film Reference Library. p. 210.

Photograph by Chris Buck for the motion picture *Trust* reprinted with permission by True Fiction Pictures/The Sales Company/Zenith Productions. Image courtesy of The Film Reference Library. p. 205.

Photograph for the motion picture *Twist* reprinted with permission courtesy of Sphinx Productions. Image courtesy of The Film Reference Library. p. 197.

Photograph for the motion picture *Whale Music* reprinted with permission by Alliance Atlantis Motion Picture Group. Image courtesy of The Film Reference Library. p. 262.

Index of Films, Related Organization and Locations

Page numbers in **boldface** refer to **photographs**.

Name Index

Page numbers in **boldface** refer to **photographs**.